P.F.M. FONTAINE

THE LIGHT
AND
THE DARK

A CULTURAL HISTORY OF DUALISM

VOLUME VII

J.C. GIEBEN, PUBLISHER
AMSTERDAM

THE LIGHT AND THE DARK

P.F.M. FONTAINE

THE LIGHT AND THE DARK
A CULTURAL HISTORY OF DUALISM

VOLUME VII

DUALISM IN THE PALESTINIAN-SYRIAN REGION
DURING THE FIRST CENTURY A.D.
UNTIL CA. 140

J.C. GIEBEN, PUBLISHER
AMSTERDAM 1992

To our beloved friends
and 'adoptive children'
Peter and Martine Berns-van Dinter

No part of this book may be translated or reproduced in any form, by print, photoprint, microfilm, or any other means, without written permission from the publisher.

© by P.F.M. Fontaine / ISBN 90 5063 085 5 / Printed in The Netherlands

"For all things are called
light and darkness"

Parmenides

CONTENTS

Preface		xiii
I	THE ROAD TO THE GNOSIS	1
1.	On terminology	1
2.	A short survey of the history of research on the Gnosis	3
	a. The beginnings in the eighteenth century	3
	b. The Gnosis seen as a heresy of Christianity	4
	c. Widening of the prospect	4
	d. Relations of the Gnosis with Judaism	5
	e. Back to the Greeks	5
	f. Concepts of fusion	5
	g. The vision of Hans Jonas	6
	h. Conclusions	6
3.	The Gnosis unique and syncretistic	7
4.	On constitutive elements in the Gnosis	7
5.	'Gnosticizing' elements in the Hellenic stream	8
	a. Knowledge	8
	b. Dualism	9
	c. Élitism	10
	d. Esotericism and dogmatism	12
	e. The attack on reality	13
	f. Two worlds	15
	g. The demise of the gods	16
	h. The origin of evil	18
	j. Conclusion	19
6.	'Gnosticizing' elements in the oriental stream	19
	a. The Iranian connection	19
	b. A Babylonian connection?	20
	c. The Jewish connection	20
7.	Two prototypes of the Gnosis	22
	a. Orphism	22
	b. Mahayana Buddhism	24
	c. A possible explanation	27
8.	The Syrian cradle	27
Notes to chapter I		28

II	'GNOSIS': ITS SEMANTICS AND ETYMOLOGY	33
1.	The words 'gnosis' and 'gignooskein'	33
2.	Other words for knowing in Greek	34
3.	Words for 'knowing' in Homer	36
	a. Homer's use of eidenai	37
	b. Homer's use of epistasthai	41
	c. Homer's use of phronein	42
	d. Homer's use of noein	43
	e. Homer's use of gignooskein	45
	f. Distinction	46
	g. Discernment	47
	h. Recognition	48
	j. Conclusions	53
4.	Homer and the Greek mind	55
5.	Words for 'knowing' in Hesiod	56
6.	'Know yourself'	57
7.	Words for 'knowing' in some lyric poets	58
	a. Archilochus	58
	b. Solon	58
	c. Pindar	59
8.	Words for 'knowledge' in the Tragedians	60
	a. Aeschylus	60
	b. Sophocles	61
	c. Euripides	62
9.	Knowledge and the Hellenistic poets	64
10.	Words for 'knowledge' in historians and doctors	64
11.	A tentative conclusion	68
12.	A meagre harvest in the early Presocratics	69
13.	Occurences in later Presocratics	69
	a. First occurence of 'gnosis' in Heraclitus	69
	b. Parmenides and knowledge	70
	c. Knowledge in other philosophical texts	71
	d. Gnosis and the practical tribe of the Sophists	71
	e. The Pythagoreans	72
14.	The 'gnosticizing' of Plato	72
15.	Knowledge in Aristotle	74
16.	Among the successors of Plato	75
17.	Conclusion	77
	Notes to Chapter II	77

III DUALISM IN GNOSTIC SYSTEMS IN SAMARIA, SYRIA, AND ASIA MINOR (until A.D. 130)   86

1. Simon Magus   86
   a. The man   86
   b. His spiritual background   88
   c. The divinization of Simon   89
   d. The role of Helena   90
   e. The Simonian Book of Revelation   92
   f. The Boundless Power   93
   g. The two roots   95
   h. The Father   95
   i. Inclusiveness   96
   j. The seeds of dualism   97
   k. The function of Epinoia   97
   l. The cosmos and mankind   98
   m. A recapitulation   98
   n. The Redeemer   99
   o. Simonian antinomianism   99
2. Menander   101
3. Saturnilos   102
4. Cerinthus   104
5. The Gnosis of the Pseudo-Clementina   106
   a. On the text   106
   b. On the Spirit of Truth   107
   c. The spiritual Christ   107
   d. Two opposed worlds   108
   e. The problem of evil   109
   f. The male-female duality   113
6. The Carpocratians   114
   a. The name of the sect   114
   b. Who was the founder?   114
   c. Carpocrates   115
   d. The supreme godhead   115
   e. The negative powers   115
   f. The hopeless situation of mankind and Jesus the Redeemer   116
   g. The return to heaven   117
   h. The 'gnoosis monadikê'   118
   j. Epiphanes' 'On Justice'   119
   k. The adherents   120
Notes to Chapter III   121

IV	ANTAGONISTIC, DUALISTIC, AND GNOSTICIZING ELEMENTS IN THE NEW TESTAMENT	129
1.	On the New Testament in general and its authors	129
2.	The New Testament as history	131
3.	The homogeneity of the New Testament	132
	a. Its historicity as an expression of its homogeneity	132
	b. Its homogeneity expressed as pleroma	133
	c. Its homogeneity expressed by the terms 'Son of God' and 'Son of Man'	134
4.	Dualistic tendencies that are not be found in the New Testament	134
	a. The failing ethical distinction	134
	b. 'Two powers in Heaven'?	135
	c. Jesus and the Samaritans	136
	d. No hard feelings towards the Romans	137
	e. No antagonism towards the Gentiles	139
	f. No two sets of human beings in Jesus' preaching	141
	g. No negative attitude to women and sexuality in the New Testament	142
5.	Antagonistic or dualistic attitudes in the New Testament	145
	a. Two sets of people in John	145
	b. John as an author with a penchant to dualism	148
	c. Two sets of people in Revelation	150
	d. A pointe against politics	150
	e. Enmity towards the Romans in Revelation	152
	f. An eschatological element in the idea of the Kingdom	153
	g. Jesus and the Pharisees	155
	h. Paul and the Law	162
	j. Tension in the early Church	165
	k. The Jews in the judgment of Paul and the Gospels	167
	l. Jewish enmity towards the Christians	171
	m. A curse on the 'minim'	175
	n. The Christians seen as sectarians	176
6.	Gnosticizing tendencies in the New Testament	177
	a. The word 'gnosis' in the New Testament	178
	b. Paul and the mysteries	180
	c. The Messiah motif	181
	d. The Law given by angels	182
	e. The contrast between flesh and spirit	182
	f. The use of the term 'aeon'	183
	g. The use of the term 'archoon'	184
7.	The anti-Gnostic stance of the New Testament	185

		a. The attitude of Peter and Paul with regard to the Gnosis	185
		b. John and the Gnosis	186
		c. Conclusion	189
	Notes to Chapter IV		189
V	THE DUALISM OF THE ESSENES		201
1.	On the road to Qumran		201
2.	The site of Qumran		202
3.	The discovery		202
4.	The scrolls on sale		203
5.	The scrolls inspected		204
6.	The site inspected		206
7.	The deposits		207
8.	The Essenes and the Qumran Community		208
	a. The Essenes mentioned by ancient authors		208
	b. The discovery of the Qumran settlement		209
	c. The history of the Qumran community		209
	d. Who were the Essenes and how to become one		210
	e. The Essenian way of life		212
	f. Essenian misogyny		213
	g. The Essenes and the Temple cult		213
	h. Purity and impurity		214
9.	Essenian dualism		216
	a. The dualism of the Community Rule		217
	b. The doctrine of the Two Spirits		219
	c. The Sons of Zadok		221
	d. The Rule's dualism summarized		222
	e. The provenance of the Damascus Rule		223
	f. The New Covenant		223
	g. A new beginning		224
	h. The Essenes and political power		225
	j. The Kittim		226
	k. The self-expression of the Teacher of Righteousness		227
	l. What others say of the Teacher		229
	m. What we know of the Teacher		230
	n. The Prophet of Lies		231
	o. The eschatological war against the Kittim		235
	p. The Essenes' notion of God		239
	q. The personal dualism of the Essenes		241
	r. Types of dualism		242
	Notes to Chapter V		244

VI ON THE TALMUD AND EARLY JEWISH MYSTICISM

1.	On the Talmud as such	256
	a. The composition of the Talmud	256
	b. The origin of the Talmud	257
2.	The Talmud not a dualistic work	258
3.	The Jewish-Christian relationship	259
	a. Why Jesus does not occur in the Talmud	259
	b. Once again, who are the minim?	260
	c. The Jewish reproach	261
	d. No intercourse between Jews and Christians	262
4.	The Talmud and the Gnosis	262
5.	Shades of ethical dualism	264
6.	The formalism of the Halahkah	266
7.	Jewish apocalypses	267
8.	Jewish mysticism	268
	a. Asceticism	268
	b. What is Jewish mysticism?	269
	c. The mystic notion of God	270
	d. Angelic mediation	271
	e. Merkabah mysticism	271
	f. The Book of Enoch	273
Notes to Chapter VI		278
Bibliography		283
General index		299

PREFACE

1. Two worlds in Mozart's opera 'The Magic Flute'

In Mozart's 'The Magic Flute' (KV 620, 1791) two mentalities, two attitudes to life, perhaps even two worlds, are opposed. There is the world of Sarastro, the high priest of the Temple of Wisdom, with his chorus of priests. Tamino, a prince, and Pamina, the daughter of the mysterious Queen of the Night, desire to be accepted as adepts by Sarastro. There is also the world of Papageno, the birdman, and Papagena, a beautiful girl who is precisely eighteen years and two minutes old and who happens to be in love with him.

The world of the Temple of Wisdom is one of ideals, of aspiring to a higher form of living, even of initiation into mysteries. The road to superior wisdom is long and dangerous. Tamino and Pamina, who are in love with one another, have, by order of Sarastro, to subject themselves to terrifying water- and fire-ordeals. But once having stood these tests they are declared fit to enter the Temple of Wisdom.

How different from these two noble persons are Papageno and Papagena. True enough, in the beginning Tamino does not seem to differ greatly from the simple birdman. His very first words are a cry for help; he faints when he sees a monstrous snake. But little by little, spurred on by his love and guided by Sarastro, he becomes ever more courageous and steadfast.

Papageno, however, is no dare-devil. Quite the contrary! We may in all honesty accuse him of cowardice. Chattering fool as he is, he is incapable of remaining silent, although silence is the fundamental precondition for initiation. He has no taste for mysteries and is too afraid of the ordeals to take part in them. He only wants one thing, a wife, not so much out of brute lust, but to marry her and to have children with her, whereas Tamino and Pamina do not seem to think of offspring.

There is every reason to detect in this opera two 'côtés', to borrow a term from Proust, the côté-Sarastro and the côté-Papageno. For the really unbridgeable opposition is not that between Sarastro and the Queen of the Night but that between the High Priest and the birdman. It is for this reason that Papageno and his bride are no longer present in the final scene, the solemn introduction into the Temple, and do not sing in the final chorus. Before the last curtain, the two côtés are once and for all separated from each other.

2. A masonic opera?

It is repeated with depressing monotony that this is a 'masonic' opera. True enough, both Emanuel Schikaneder, the librettist, and Mozart, the composer, were members of the Masonic Lodge 'Zur Wohltätigkeit' in Vienna. But indications of freemasonry, in the libretto as well as in the music, are hard to find. The three tutti chords with which the overture begins are often explained as the three knocks on the door that form the opening of masonic sessions. But the number 'three' is the esoteric symbol par excellence, and certainly not the monopoly of freemasons.

It is highly important to free ourselves from such popular misunderstandings, since they obscure the real nature of the work. The first publisher of 'The Magic Flute' adorned the booklet with a picture of a pyramid and of hieroglyphs. In those days these were utterly mysterious signs since nobody was able to read them as yet. True enough, pyramids and 'old-Egyptian doors' are mentioned in the text as scenic elements. The main reference to Pharaonic Egypt, however, is the repeated invocation of Isis and Osiris who are presented as gods of wisdom. This is wrong, of course, for the Egyptian god of wisdom was Toth; Isis and Osiris are divinities of fertility and life, of death and resurrection.

Perhaps the first publisher had an idea that the explanation of the work as an 'Egyptian opera' was not really satisfying, for he added a five-pointed star, although this venerably ancient symbol does not occur in the opera. This well-known magical sign was in use with many esoteric societies, with Pythagoreans, Neopythagoreans, and Neoplatonists, and also in Gnostic circles [*]. This publisher understood at least that The Magic Flute's esotericism contained more than masonic and Egyptian lore.

3. Names and numbers

The difference between the two 'côtés" is exemplified by the fact that the inhabitants of the first one carry names consisting of three syllables (Sarastro, Tamino, Pamina), those of the second having names with four syllables (Papageno, Papagena). The number three refers to the three phases of the moon, that is to the heavens, the number four to the four quarters of the earth, that is to this world. Germans would speak of 'jenseitig' and 'diesseitig'. This is a typical Gnostic element because Gnostics aspire to the beyond and consider earthly life with disdain and abhorrence.

The name of Sarastro might remind us of that of Zoroaster, or Zarathustra, the Iranian prophet, and one of the great dualists. However, the Temple of Wisdom is not Iranian (Zoroastrians had no temples), but brings to mind the sanctuary of Apollo at Delphi. This indeed was a place from where wisdom was distributed to Hellenes and non-Hellenes alike. Probably Schikaneder unconsciously related Sarastro to Apollo, the sun god, since the High Priest wore a sevenfold solar jewel on his breast. It is a revealing element that in the closing scene the Temple of Wisdom has become the Temple of the Sun.

---

[*] See Vol. I, Ch. I.6.

4. Greek mythology and mysteriosophy

Let me mention in passing yet another element of Greek mythology, viz. Tamino in the role of Orpheus : when he is playing his flute, all kinds of wild animals appear in order to listen to him. (We must forgive Schikaneder for forgetting that Orpheus did not play the flute but the lyre).

Yet, the most important 'mysteriosophic' element has still to be mentioned. The basic reference is not to the ceremonies of a masonic lodge but to the Eleusinian mysteries *. Just as in Eleusis, the crowning ceremony takes place in the night ('Verwandlung, Nacht'). The scene is the court of the great temple; in Eleusis it was the 'telesterion', the enormous mystery hall. Sarastro is playing exactly the same role as the 'hierophant' in Eleusis, that of presiding over the initiation ceremony. In both cases silence is imposed (but Papageno is unable to hold his tongue).

In the telesterion the terrified initiates, standing in the pitchdark hall, must have felt forlorn and shut out from the outer world. Tamino and Papageno too are duly shocked by a violent thunderstorm. Tamino is far from his country and utterly alone; even his condition as prince counts for nothing here. Just as the new life did not come as a free gift to the Eleusinian initiates, Tamino and Pamina have to go pass through water and fire. Only after this proof may they enter the main hall of the temple. The last thunderclap resounds, the last flashes of lightning blind the eye, but then the sun radiantly rises, and the chorus welcomes the initiates : "Heil sei euch, Geweihten!".

In order to allay any bewilderment, I do not contend that Schikaneder and/or Mozart made a penetrating study of the history of religions in classical Antiquity. Mozart never went to school, and his librettist either very shortly or not all. But far more than in our own days, classical lore was omnipresent and was, so to speak, in the air.

---

* See Vol. I, Ch. IV.9.

5. A hotchpotch of antique elements

So we have before us a curious hotchpotch of Egyptian, Iranian, and Greek ingredients, mainly Greek; the Hellenic part in its turn is composed of Orphic, Delphic, and Eleusinian ingredients, mainly Eleusinian. In turn, these elements are modified by such themes of the Enlightenment as virtue, humanity, and friendship. And it is, indeed, the ideology of the Enlightenment that dictates the central theme, that of wisdom, in contrast to the victory over death that was basic to the Eleusinian mysteries.

6. The role of wisdom

The dominating role of wisdom in this opera is also the main theme of this volume on the Gnosis. The wisdom that is the final reward of the new initiates has a distinctly Gnostic flavour. No pedestrian wisdom, no practical knowledge is meant. It is not given to everybody; Papageno will not be a recipient. It is connected with the sphere of the divine; Sarastro promises Tamino that he will "enter the realm of eternal light"; he implores Isis and Osiris to "grant the spirit of wisdom to the new pair (Tamino and Pamina)". That the initiated will be transformed appears from these lines sung by the three boys : "Then earth will be a heavenly kingdom and mortals will be like the gods". And still more telling is what the 'two men in armour' have to add to this : "He (the initiated) will soar away from this earth toward Heaven". Here 'Heaven' (the new life of the initiated) and 'earth' (normal life) are dualistically contrasted.

7. Papageno as the opponent of wisdom

The 'earth' is conspicuously present too; it is represented by Papageno and Papagena. This work has a Gnostic side but equally a non-Gnostic one. In the libretto the last word is given to the Gnostic side; our earthly couple has left the stage before the final triumphal scene begins.

But it is not hard to see where Mozart's sympathies lie : he obviously sided with Papageno. The first great aria is for the birdman : "Der Vogelfänger bin ich ja, stets lustig heisza hopsasa!". The composer, who also was 'stets lustig', ever merry, must have applied the birdcatcher's words to his own person : "I know how to handle decoys and how to whistle". He too might say that, even to this day, "all the birds are his". The composer, who once said of himself that he was 'only a Papageno', had this aria sung to him on his death-bed.

The Papageno of the opera is no great friend of the initiation ceremonies, to put it mildly; he abhors the 'Zauberspuk'. When the priests warn him that he never will savour 'the divine pleasure of the initiate', he answers laconically : there are more so. His is the other 'côté', that of simple people who are content with simple things. For them no esotericism, no mysteriosophy. They need not be initiated since they have no spiritual problems and understand life such as it is.

For Papageno the real fulfilment of life is a woman. "Oh, such a gentle dove would be a blessing for me!" (O, so ein sanftes Täubchen wär Seligkeit für mich!"). He does not, however, desire with brute sensuality like the vicious Moor Monostatos; on the contrary, his wish is to contract a virtuous matrimonial alliance with Papagena. Here the scene has a biblical tinge : "It is not well that man should remain alone" (Gen. 2:18); "if one (i.e. a girl) does not save me in my need, I'll surely be grieved to death" ("helf eine mir nur aus der Not, sonst gräm ich mich wahrlich zu Tod!"). It even comes so far that Papageno tries to commit suicide after the sudden disappearance of Papagena.

"And the man said : 'Here, at last, is bone that comes from mine; she shall be called woman' " (Gen.2:23). In just the same way Papageno recognizes Papagena as 'a mate of his own kind" (Gen.2:18) in the famous scene in which they, stammering, pronounce each other's names : man - wo-man, Papageno - Papagena, a still greater degree of similarity than Tamino - Pamina. "Increase and multiply" (Gen.1:28); "so liebe kleine Kinderlein! Erst einen kleinen Papageno, dann eine kleine Papagena, dann ...".

The simple history of Papageno and Papageno runs from beginning to end through the whole libretto, as a contrast to the mystery play. The 'côtés' never come together. If the Sarastro-part ends in the celebration of beauty and wisdom, then the Papageno-part concludes with a song of praise on the family that is richly blessed with children. And at the end their ways part.

8. The Gnosis not very well known

Although the Gnosis was a widespread and lasting phenomenon in the history of religions, it does not seem to me that it is widely known nowadays. Of course there are many eminent specialists on the Gnosis; congresses are held and there is a large library of publications. Some of these, like one by Hans Jonas[*], are intended for the general public. But when I once asked a group of fifty history students, all of them in their last year, if they knew what the Gnosis is, none of them had the slightest idea; most of these historians had never even heard of it.

Some years ago I attended a Plotinus-day at the Free University of Amsterdam; of course the speakers mentioned every now and then this philosopher's relation to the Gnostic movement. At lunch a student girl sat down next to me and asked : "This Gnosis they are talking about all the time, whatever is that?". Apparently my answer seemed perfectly satisfying to her, for when I had finished explaining, she abruptly went on with her next question : "What is your opinion on nuclear armament?". So I did not have much of a lunch. I fear that knowledge of the Gnosis does not spread very far beyond the circle of historians of religion.

9. Introducing the Gnosis

Although this volume does not pretend to offer yet another history of the Gnostic movement, principally written as it is to bring out its dualistic aspects, enough will be said about it to present an ample

---

[*] Hans Jonas, The Gnostic Religion. Boston, 1963 3 (1958 1).

picture of the Gnosis. I feel that readers who perhaps do not know much more about it than that student I mentioned will be helped by a short summary of this ideology.

I prefer to speak of the Gnosis and to avoid the term 'Gnosticism' which is a neologism on the analogy of all those other -isms of our modern era; it does less than justice to this movement. 'Gnosis' is a common Greek word signifying knowledge. But in the history of religions the noun 'gnosis' is used in a specific and religiously relevant sense. For there exists a 'Gnostic religion'. This must not be seen as a split off from or a variety of either Judaism or Christianity, although both these religions were not without influence on it. Its roots, as Chapter I will show, reach deep into the ancient Hellenic and more recent Hellenistic worlds, and also into the eastern world of Iran and India, far before the advent of Christianity.

10. A special sort of knowledge

The 'gnosis' of the Gnosis represents a special and very peculiar sort of 'knowledge' that has nothing to do with common knowledge acquired by study or training or practice. It is a religious kind of knowledge indispensable for 'redemption', that is for eternal salvation. Often the Gnosis is redemption itself; whoever possesses it is saved. This is the main point : redemption results from knowledge, it is gnosis that redeems. This is the first and most principal point of difference with Christian orthodoxy, since, according to Christian doctrine, it is God, and God alone, who redeems through the merits acquired by the death on the cross of Jesus Christ.

The special knowledge that is called 'gnosis' is not given to everyone. It has a secret, an esoteric character. It is only available to the chosen, to the happy few; he who possesses it is proud of it. This is a second essential difference with Christianity which does not know of secret knowledge; the whole doctrine is open and public. Needless to say that the Gnostic tenets are not to be found in the Bible.

11. Gnostic sects

It is not entirely correct to speak of 'the Gnostic religion' or 'the religion of knowledge'. This movement by no standard was a unity; there existed many Gnostic groups and sects, many schools and writings, many kinds of ritual, that certainly are not similar in every respect. On the contrary! They differed widely among themselves. The Gnosis does not, like orthodox Christianity, know an officially approved body of doctrine. Gnostic groups concur only on this main issue : knowledge is redemptive. This knowledge is not of the intellectual kind; it is not expressed in dogmatic tenets or in a theology.

12. The Gnosis as theosophy

Far more than a theology, the Gnosis is a form of mysticism, or, if one wants to use a modern term, a 'theosophy'. In some branches of the Gnostic movement it seems as though the distiction between the divine and the human sphere has been abolished so that man finally incorporates the divine into himself. This too is a difference with Christianity, since in Christianity the distinction between God and man is never ultimately cancelled.

13. The acquirement of knowledge

How is this indispensable knowledge to be acquired? The Gnostic believer answers : by revelation. And revelation in his view means intuition, visions, fortune-telling, prophetism, and so on. By revelation is always meant something subjective : a personal communication, an 'illumination' received by a privileged person. The Gnostic, therefore, understands by 'revelation' something else than the orthodox Christian to whom it means the speaking of God to all men, to humanity as such, in the Bible. Gnostic revelations have a subjective and personal character; they seem to have their source in the individual person himself. The consequence is that there cannot exist a uniform and generally accepted doctrine; hence it does not seem surprising, but rather a matter of course that the opinions of the Gnostics do not tally with each other.

This brings us to an essential feature of the Gnosis, viz. the doctrine of the 'sovereign spirit', that is of the independent human mind that in perfect freedom decides on matters of truth - with the consequence that everybody possesses his own truth. The place, the 'locus', where truth is found is man himself. This forms a contrast with Christianity that holds that the sole source of Truth is God himself - a Truth objectively valid for all people, although the Christian must personally accept this Truth and live according to it.

14. The unknowable God

It will be evident that the Gnosis is not atheistic. But its God is unknowable; human beings are incapable of saying something meaningful about him. He is utterly alien to man and creation; he dwells somewhere in the inacessible. Natural man has no means for knowing God in any way; there is no 'natural theology', no natural religion. Nothing in creation or in human intelligence can bring us any closer to God; reason is absolutely powerless. This again is an overt contrast to Christian theology which says that human reason can at least know God as the Creator. At the utmost the Gnostic God may reveal himself, along the way of inner illumination, to a few elect. God and man stand far apart from one another, at an endless distance that for most people remains unbridgeable.

15. The Gnostic myth

Nevertheless, the object of Gnostic knowledge is God, and his relation to the world. This is one of the rare points of concordance between Gnostics and Christians. As I stated previously, this doctrine is not expressed in a doctrinal way or in a theological system; instead, it is made known in the form of a 'myth'. The Gnosis renders what is known of God, of the origin of the cosmos, of man, and of evil, in a 'mythological' form, as literature, as a story. This is a heritage of the entire ancient world that presented what is known of the gods and the relation between them and humanity as mythology, or as philosophy that, in so far as it was a theology, used the myths as source of knowledge. According to Christian orthodoxy, the Bible does not contain mythology but history, albeit not history in the modern and profane form.

The climactic part of Gnostic mythology is its cosmology. The question is how creation - as seen from a religious point of view - is constructed. The principal component of this cosmology is its cosmogony, viz. the question how the cosmos came into being.

The details may diverge widely but all systems share some general traits. God did not create the world. He is utterly foreign to creation because the cosmos, mankind included, is darkness. This is the typical and basic Gnostic dualism on which the whole idea is based : God and creation have nothing to do with each other. But if God did not create the world, who then did?

Creation is the work of inferior powers, usually called 'archonts' (=rulers). With regard to the number and nature of these archonts there is a wide diversity of opinions. Some Gnostic sects hold that they have a supreme commander who is called the 'demiurge' (the maker of the world); he is considered the true creator. Fairly often the God of the Old Testament has to pose as demiurge, called 'Jehova' (faulty Hebrew for 'Jahve'), and also 'Jao'. Jao is a horrible, vindictive, and bloodthirsty being, truly a god of the empire of darkness.

16. The imprisonment of man

The universe is represented by the Gnostics as a prison; in its deepest dungeon man lies jailed. The interstice between God and man, consisting of a number of 'spheres', is filled with archonts who maliciously try to prevent the ascent of human souls to God. Their government of the world is tyrannical; they rule with the help of inexorable Fate. A human being is nothing more than a slave, helplessly lost in a pitiless universe. Creation in all its aspects is profoundly evil; it came into being as a result of a malevolent will or an initial error; from its very first beginning everything went wrong. Man is not involved; it is not his fault (there is no doctrine of the Fall), but nevertheless, he is the main victim. This 'a-cosmism' runs not only counter to Christian doctrine but also to the classical Greek idea of the cosmos.

According to the Gnosis, man consists of flesh, soul, and spirit (not, therefore, of body and soul). The archonts who created man performed this not as an original creation but as an imitation. The model was the First Man, the 'archetype', created (or thought) by God. Sometimes Adam and sometimes Jesus is seen as this First Man. If Jesus is the First Man, then Adam, as he is described in the Book of Genesis, may not claim this title. The human 'soul' ('psyche') is only a bunch of passions; man is utterly and entirely bad, because the archonts have wilfully and intentionally spoiled the imitation.

However, the 'spirit' ('pneuma', also 'spark') has not been created by the archonts but by God. He has dropped some part of his own divine substance (that is 'light') into the world; a little spark of light is present in every human being, even in the darkest pit of the cosmic prison. The archonts hate this divine light; they created mankind in order to hermetically lock up this parcel of light in every human being so that they remain unaware of it. Unredeemed man knows nothing of this light; he is 'unknowing' about it, he never will see it, he will forever remain a slave as long as he is not redeemed.

17. The liberation of the chosen

The true aim of the Gnosis is to liberate 'spiritual man', to free him from himself and from the world, and bring him to God. 'Redemption' consists in the fact that man receives 'knowledge' - 'gnosis' - about himself and the Light that is in him and about God. This knowledge has been revealed by a luminous being (for instance 'Jesus'); it is knowledge of the road one has to take to reach God. It is contained in the 'myth' (myths, mythology) of the Gnosis'; this comprised the Gnostic sacraments and the magic ritual (the role of magic is important), and also the secret names and maxims one has to know in order to participate in the redemption. Who possesses this knowledge can after death pass fearlessly past the archonts and through the spheres and return to God. Often more than one life is needed for achieving this end; the doctrine of the transmigration of souls is not rare in the Gnosis.

The great mass of people will never be saved; they will remain unknowing. It is only a few elect that receive knowledge; they are called 'pneumatici', people of the spirit. The gnosis comes to them as a personal and immediate revelation. Pneumatici, therefore, form an élite with secret meetings; they look down on the 'massa damnata' since all other people are bad. The pneumaticus is free of the law and of the coercion of Fate. He no longer has obligations, neither to himself nor to his fellow-men; he may do what he likes. Nothing can damage him since he is above or beyond Evil.

It will be clear that this may lead to libertinism. In some libertine Gnostic groups evil was done expressly in order to show that one is no longer subject to it; sinning then is the proof of redemption. Some Gnostic groups indulged in gross, even devilish excesses. But on the whole the Gnostic doctrine of redemption led to a severely ascetic way of life. One shuns as far as possible everything that is 'worldly'; the diet is vegetarian, alcohol is prohibited, frequent washings are the rule, luxuries are avoided.

If feasible, it is thought better not to have a professional occupation, in order not to contribute to the upkeep of this bad world. Often there is firm opposition to sexuality, in particular to the physical part of it. If need be, it is permitted to have children, but ideally one should remain childless, since in every child a spark of the divine light will become imprisoned. Nobody can tell whether this child will receive knowledge. For these reasons it is preferable not to marry. If humanity will in consequence cease to exist, so much the better!

17. The ambience of the Gnosis

A wide-spread movement like the Gnosis that came near to triumphing over all other ancient doctrines and mythologies must have had its roots in the past. Elements of it were very long in the making. But it should never be forgotten that the Gnosis was an autonomous movement existing in its own right. This signifies that it is not a derivation of some older ideology. Consequently, it may not be considered, as it was considered by many Fathers of the Church, as a Christian heresy. On the other hand, it was a typically syncretistic movement that adopted elements of the most diverse origins. We find in it Hellenic, Hellenistic, Jewish, Iranian, and perhaps even Indian elements; the Christian ones should not be forgotten either. The Gnosis, therefore, has occidental as well as oriental connections, pagan as well as Judaeo-Christian relations.

Usually a pre-Christian Jewish and a Hellenistic-pagan Gnosis are distinguished. Then there is Mandaeism which has an eastern origin and is equally Gnostic. Perhaps also Manichaeism should be mentioned, although this religion stresses dualistic anticosmism rather than 'knowledge'[*]. Jonas characterizes the spiritual climate of the eastern Mediterranean world where the Gnosis first originated as definitely religious.

This means that solutions to human problems were not sought in science or philosophy but in religion. Secondly, the idea of redemption was dominant; it was the main element of the religions of that time. Thirdly, all these religions had a strong bias towards the transcendent or the transmundane; they situated God far beyond this world. And fourthly, they posited a radical dualism of the ontological spheres : God and world, spirit and matter, soul and body, light and darkness, good and evil, life and death[**]. This dualism appears at its most radical in the Gnostic movement; this is the reason why it is made the main subject of this volume.

---

[*] Jonas, Het gnosticisme 47.
[**] Jonas, Het Gnosticisme 45/46.

18. Mozart and the Neognosis

It was not for nothing that I began this preface, this whole book in fact, with a discourse on Mozart's 'The Magic Flute', to be followed only at some remove by an exposition of the essentials of the Gnosis. If one were to ask any number of cultivated, even erudite persons what the opposite of Christianity is, almost everyone would answer, perhaps with a look of amazement, that its opposite is paganism. And paganism for them would be more or less synonymous with atheism. But more correctly, we can talk of pagan religions, and many of these religions are based on a purely natural religion that is also to be found at the heart of Judaism and Christianity, the religion, I mean, of water and fire, of bread and wine, of temple and priest, of altar and sacrifice, of incantation and prayer, of human supplication and divine response.

The common trait that binds together Judaism and Christianity on the one side, and much of paganism on the other, is the 'analogia entis', the analogy of being, or the similarity (not the identity) of the divine and the terrestrial or human worlds. Although these worlds are, of course, very different from each other, they are, nevertheless, related and, on principle, open to each other.

It is exactly this analogy that is vehemently and consequently denied by all Gnostic and gnosticizing movements. Instead, they proclaim the radical separation of both worlds, to such a degree that they are not only kept apart but, still more, are opposed, alien and inimical to each other. It is by no means easy, quite the contrary!, to proceed from the nether to the upper world.

In the history of dualism, as well as in that of religions, the Gnostic period, the first centuries of our era, constitutes an ideological platform, as it were, on which many trends and tendencies and ideas meet and mingle. Chapter IV of Volume VI sketched the general climate of Hellenistic society in which the Gnostic tenets could be conceived. Chapter I of the present volume resumes this theme, starting this time from the Gnostic movement itself and showing how many constitutive elements of the Gnosis had a long gestation period in the Hellenic, Hellenistic, and Indo-Iranian worlds.

But even more than a platform where many older trends met, the Gnostic movement was a power-house from which heavy ideological charges were transmitted to future centuries. If we use the analogy-concept as a dowsing-rod for detecting dualistic tendencies, I think we may be fairly safe in separating dualistic from non-dualistic religious ideologies. If this is correct, then natural religion (I am not referring here of what David Hume understood by natural religion), Judaism, and the Roman-Catholic religion belong to the last category.

The Indian religions that include Hinduism, Buddhism, and Jainism are decidedly dualistic, and the same may be said of Chinese Taoism. Manichaeism, Bogumilism, and Catharism are equally dualistic, while German mysticism shows Gnostic traits. Protestantism hovers somewhere between both categories but slants into the direction of non-analogy.

Our modern era is, in my view, characterized by a resurgence of Gnostic elements, so that we are entitled to speak of a 'Neognosis'. I believe that modern science, with its élitist and esoteric nature, is a fine example of this. It made Raymond Ruyer speak of the 'Gnosis of Princeton'. For all these reasons some scholars speak of the Gnosis as 'the third component of western cultural tradition', the two others being that of belief and that of reason. And it was one of the greatest experts on the Gnosis, my compatriot Gilles Quispel, who felt justified in thinking of it as a 'world religion'. Since dualism is so deeply engrained in the Gnosis that a Gnostic system without dualism is unthinkable, I feel we should equally speak of dualism as a world-wide phenomenon. I must, however, add this caution that, although there is no Gnosis without dualism, there is dualism galore outside it.

I do not believe that it is accidental that, at the beginning of our modern era, Mozart and Schikaneder produced their opera. It marvellously exemplifies the ideological trend of the time, away from Christianity and towards a Neognosis. By the same token it demonstrates the age-old opposition, dualistic in itself, of Gnosis and Christianity. Between these no compromise proved possible. This controversy has by no means run itself out; the battle is still raging, with, as the result of the irresistible vogue of modern science, Christianity apparently on the losing side.

When all is said and done, it must be categorically stated that the subject of this volume is not the Gnosis 'an sich' but, as in all previous ones, dualism. By no means all dualistic systems and ideologies are Gnostic, but the Gnosis is invariably and basically dualistic. So there is every reason to give the Gnosis pride of place in this and the next volume(s).

With regard to the phenomenon of dualism, I still see no reason for altering the definition of it which I proposed in the preface of Volume I. The term 'dualism', as used by me, refers to two utterly opposed conceptions, principles, systems, groups of people, or even worlds, without any intermediate term between them. The two opposites cannot be reduced to one another; in some cases they are not even dependent on each other. They are considered to be of different quality - so much so that one of them is always regarded as distinctly inferior, and hence must be neglected, repudiated, or, if need be, destroyed. This same definition will serve as a premise for the discussions in the present volume.

I must caution my readers, and in particular reviewers, against one or two misunderstandings which seem almost ineradicable. The first is the contention, brought forward with disheartening frequency, that dualism has an Iranian origin. There is no denying that the inbuilt dualism of Zoroastrianism and still more of Zervanism is an intriguing and important phenomenon in the history of religions but it is totally unfounded - and also beyond any possibility of proof - to make it into the source and fountain-head of all dualistic phenomena in all civilizations and in all periods of world-history. Iranian dualism is just one of the manifestations of dualism in general.

The second misunderstanding is that dualism does indeed occur often but then only in the realms of religion and philosophy. But as the subtitle of my work, 'A cultural history of dualism', indicates, I give this term a far wider sense since I see absolutely no reason why unbridgeable oppositions should occur only in philosophy and religion. In my opinion dualism is an anthropological phenomenon manifesting itself in every field and walk of life, in politics, in social life, in the arts, in science and scholarship, and, indeed, in religion and philosophy.

The impulse for dualism is not to be found in Iran or in any other country or culture or in the fields of religion and philosophy but in human nature itself, in the human identity. Peter Sloterdijk hits the mark when he says that Gnosis arises from self-ignition [*], and just the same applies to dualism. But just as a haystack spontaneously bursts into flames only in certain circumstances, so Gnosis and dualism only originate under special conditions. The reader will find these specified in the account of how the Gnostic-dualistic climate of the first century A.D. came about in Chapter I.

Perhaps I should ask the reader to beware of yet another misunderstanding, namely that I, to vary a famous dictum of Karl Marx, am converting the history of dualism into the history of the world. This is far from being the case. One has only to consider how many persons, events, periods, historical constellations, ideas, etcetera, are not mentioned in my work, to see that this charge is unfounded.

Lest I should make this introduction too long, I must refer the benevolent and inquisitive reader to the long prefaces of the Volumes V and VI in which the basic idea of dualism is given an extensive and fundamental treatment. In particular I ask reviewers not to judge this volume on the basis of the one or two chapters in which they are especially interested, taking the rest in their stride, but to consult these two prefaces first.

I dare not ask anybody to read all the volumes I have published so far. May it be a consolation that this book can be read independently of

---

[*] Sloterdijk, Die Wahre Irrlehre. Über die Weltreligion der Weltlosigkeit. In 'Weltrevolution der Seele. Eine Lese- und Arbeitsbuch der Gnosis von der Spätantike bis zur Gegenwart. Herausgeber Peter Sloterdijk und Thomas H. Macho. Erster Band, p. 25. Artemis & Winkler Verlag, 1991.

the others. But, notwithstanding this, I must quote the British novelist Susan Howatch in the Author's note to her intriguing book 'Scandalous risks' (New York, 1990), the fourth in a series of six novels about the Church of England in the twentieth century, where she writes as follows : "Each book is designed to be read independently of the others, but the more books are read the wider will be the view of the multi-sided reality that is presented". Deo volente, Volume VIII will continue the discussion of Gnostic and other dualistic systems and trends but will shift the scene to Egypt.

There is nobody responsible in the last resort for this work with its contents, wording, and typography but myself. But not a few people helped me to bring it about. I feel indebted to the librarians of the Classical Institute, the Theological Institute, and the Bibliotheca Rosenthaliana, all of them departments of the University of Amsterdam, not omitting that admirable institution, the University Library itself.

Chapter II was read and commented upon by Dr. J.-M. Bremer, professor of Greek literature at the University of Amsterdam, Chapter III by Dr. R. van den Broek, professor of the history of Christianity and of Christian dogmatics at the State University of Utrecht, Chapter V by Dr. J. van der Ploeg, emeritus-professor of the Old Testament and of Hebrew and Syriac at the Catholic University of Nijmegen, and Chapter VI by Dr. N.A. van Uchelen, professor of Hebrew and Aramaic from the first century of the Christian era at the University of Amsterdam. For Chapters I and IV I trusted to my own devices. Professors Bremer and Van der Ploeg went out of their way to have long discussions with me on the chapters I submitted to them. To all those commentators I feel extremely grateful for spending so much of their valuable time on my work and for saving me from errors and omissions.

As always, my faithful 'team' was with me throughout this volume too. Dr. J.R. Dove, a retired associate professor of English and American literature living in Amsterdam, for the seventh time in succession corrected my chapters with much prudence and tact. My two 'general readers', Dr. A. Budé, a classical scholar, and my daughter, Dr. Th.A.M.

Smidt van Gelder-Fontaine, a philosopher, went carefully through the whole text, jotting down many useful notes while doing so. Finally my loving wife Anneke (with whom - together with all the family - I celebrated the fortieth anniversay of our marriage in April last) patiently corrected the almost camera ready pages, sometimes sighing deeply and sometimes skipping along happily. My relation with my publisher, J.C. Gieben, was as pleasant as ever. I could not be more grateful.

P.F.M. Fontaine
Amsterdam NL

CORRIGENDA

1. In Volume II, on page 136, I mentioned a Greek geographer, called 'Euphorus of Cnidus'. A Greek geographer of this name did not exist. It is a contamination of Eudoxus of Cnidus (4th century B.C.) and Ephorus (3d century B.C.); both of them drew rectangular maps.

2. In Volume III, on page 86, I wrote that the first sentence of Margaret Mitchell's great novel 'Gone with the wind' (1936) runs like this : "Scarlett O'Hara had green eyes". I read this book half a century ago with the inevitable consequence that my memory deceived me (for I was quoting from memory). Shortly after I had written this I reread the novel, and lo! its first sentence is : "Scarlett O'Hara was not beautiful", which is fine enough, but not what I thought it was. True enough, only a few words further on it is said that Scarlett had green eyes indeed.

3. In Volume IV, on page 288, in the last paragraph of this page, it is stated that Spenta Mainyu (the Good Spirit) and Angra Mainyu (the Evil Spirit) have a common origin. This is a deplorable slip, if not of the pen, then of the mind. The point is that, although they are called 'twins' (meaning only that they are co-eval), they have no common father. This is correctly stated on page 288 as well as on pages 19 and 20 of Volume V.

1

CHAPTER I

THE ROAD TO THE GNOSIS

1. On terminology

In April 1966 a congress on the origins of Gnosticism was held at Messina where almost every scholar who had a reputation to lose in this field was present. In order to reach a consensus regarding the terms Gnosis and Gnosticism that would be as broad as possible, a commission was formed out of the participants. Bianchi, Bleeker, Daniélou, Jonas and Widengren served on this commission. It produced a document entitled : 'Proposals regarding the scientific use of the terms gnosis (and) Gnosticism' [1]. In the closing session of the congress the final statement of the commission was presented for discussion and accepted as such by the great majority. Yet already on this occasion, and later when it was published in English, French, German, and Italian, objections were raised against it, as might be expected [2].

The Messina statement proposed to make a distinction between 'gnosis' and 'Gnosticism'. 'Gnosis' was to refer to knowledge of the divine mysteries in general; 'Gnosticism' was to be used for the well-known Gnostic systems of the second and third centuries A.D. In this way 'gnosis' was meant to be a far wider concept than Gnosticism; there are after all so many groups, religions, and sects that pride themselves on knowledge of divine mysteria. Even Buddhism and Taoism might be included. The unavoidable result is that the term becomes meaningless.

The idea did not really strike root in the scholarly world. Kurt Rudolph, who does not find the proposal very felicitous, thinks that we should not draw a distinction between the gnosis phenomenon in itself and Gnosticism (as a religion). The term gnosis should only be used, he says, for 'knowledge of an élitist character about special mysteries and that is characteristically at home in late Antiquity' [3]. As historical phenomena Gnosis and Gnosticism remain, therefore, restricted to the centuries around the beginning of our era and to the Roman-Hellenistic world.

This restriction would also render a term like 'Pregnostic' senseless. The term contains, moreover, a contradiction because 'gnostic' says that we have to do with Gnosticism, whereas 'pre' assures us that this is not the case [4]. One might, however, show some leniency towards the term 'Protognostics'. Some ancient ystems, in particular Orphism, came so close to what at a much later stage Gnosticism proper would be, that the term 'Protognostics' seems justified. I intend to come back to this point in a later section. To quote Robert Grant, "we have to admit that something to be called 'proto-Gnostic' or 'incipiently Gnostic' or 'Gnosticising' was in existence at an earlier date" [5].

It is true that not all the sects that we dub 'Gnostic' would have thought of themselves as such. The common denominator that, according to the Fathers of the Church, bound these sects together was not so much the name 'Gnostic' but rather their general conviction that this is an utterly bad world and that 'knowledge' (of a very special type) can free the divine spark in man.

Quite another question is whether we are entitled to use the term 'Gnosticism'. To begin with, it is simply ugly. Secondly, it is a neologism, probably coined in the eighteenth century, on the analogy of the equally ugly 'Orphicism'. Like all other -isms, it was entirely unknown to the ancients themselves. This brings us to a third and, in my opinion, convincing argument for avoiding as much as possible the term 'Gnosticism'. This is that Antiquity itself called the phenomenon 'Gnosis'. And it was quite right to do so, for the whole Gnostic religion is based on the idea that there exists a knowledge that brings about redemption [6].

Very probably the first text to refer by the word 'gnosis' to a certain (new) religion was the first Letter to Timothy in the New Testament : the author exhorts its addressee to beware of the falsely so-called gnosis [7]. If this letter really was written by the apostle Paul himself, then this text dates from a year between 60 and 70 A.D. But many scholars doubt that Paul was the author and think of a later author, perhaps around 100 A.D. Next, around 180, it was Irenaeus of Lyons who refers to this religion as 'gnosis' [8]. For these reasons I prefer to refer to it with the term 'Gnosis' [9].

2. A short survey of the history of research on the Gnosis

a. The beginnings in the eighteenth century

A short survey of the history of research on the Gnosis would be useful since it might be enlightening on a few important issues. 'Gnosticism' as a separate religious phenomenon was 'discovered' in the eighteenth century. This rediscovery occurred in the wake of the rise of neo-Gnosticism that is connected with the name of the German mystic Jakob Boehme (1575-1624). Quispel states that it was in his school that "scholarly study of gnosticism has it roots; the first scholar to pay attention to it was probably Gottfried Arnold in his two-volumed book 'Unpartheyische Kirchen- und Ketzergeschichte' the first part of which appeared in 1699 [10]. In this work "all heretics, including the Gnostics, are represented as the true Christians" [11].

Arnold was followed in 1739 by another German scholar, Johann Lorenz von Mosheim. This man displayed some memorable insights about the Gnosis. To begin with, he obviously saw the Gnosis as a kind of theosophy. Furthermore, for its origins he looked not so much to the Greeks but rather eastward. Thirdly, he said he was sure that the philosophers gave the name of Gnosis to this doctrine before Christianity originated [12]. It would have been a good thing if research had continued along this line. But this was not to be.

b. The Gnosis seen as a heresy of Christianity

During the nineteenth century great German theologians and church historians, famous scholars like Baur and Harnack, paid ample attention to the Gnosis. Their decisive point of view was that the Gnosis was a Christian heresy, a deviation, therefore, from orthodoxy. The cause of this aberration was said to be that some Christians allowed themselves to be tainted by pagan philosophies. For this aberration Harnack coined the well-known phrase 'the acute secularization, respectively Hellenization of Christianity' [13].

It must be admitted that early Christian authors were finally responsible for this point of view. Irenaeus called his voluminous work 'against all heresies' with which, of course, Christian heresies were meant, mainly, although not exclusively, the Gnosis. Irenaeus' disciple Hippolytus of Rome equally wrote a 'Refutation of all heresies' dating from some time after 222, which in its second part listed thirty-three Gnostic systems. In his preface he put this question : "Let us ask, at this beginning, which people among the Greeks were the first to teach natural philosophy. For it is so that the founders of the sects (the Gnostics are meant) have initially stolen their doctrines from these" [14].

c. Widening of the prospect

The first one to widen this prospect considerably was W. Anz in 1897. He removed the subject from ecclesiastical history and made it part of a more general history of religions. Looking eastward, he believed to have discovered the origin of the Gnosis in Babylonia [15]. Anz's book is completely disregarded nowadays but the widening of the prospect remains his lasting merit.

Ten years later Wilhelm Bousset put the study of the Gnosis on an entirely new footing. In his still valuable book 'Hauptprobleme der Gnosis' (Göttingen, 1907) he directed the attention of the scholarly world to the Iranian origins of the Gnosis. He described this religion as a mixture of Greek, Babylonian, and Iranian components. The radical

Iranian dualism of Good and Evil allied itself in this doctrine with the Platonic dualism of celestial and material, of body and spirit. With regard to the general line of research we must state that it was Bousset who definitely disconnected the Gnostic myth from Christianity.

Later Richard Reitzenstein emphasized the Iranian connection very strongly, for instance in his work 'Das iranische Erlösungsmysterium' (Bonn, 1921) [16]. His approach was indubitably one-sided but to all intents and purposes the Iranian connection was there to stay.

d. Relations of the Gnosis with Judaism

During our century the relations of the Gnosis not so much with Samaritanism but rather with Judaism and the community of Qumran became the subject of much discussion and research and led to many publications. In his turn Rudolph Bultmann concentrated his efforts on the relations between the New testament, in particular the Gospel of John, and the Gnosis [17]. Many of his students took the same approach.

e. Back to the Greeks

Perhaps Carl Schneider found that the discussion on the sources of the Gnosis was slanted too much into an oriental direction since, according to him when writing in 1954, the spirit of the Gnosis is Greek, mainly Platonic; it is a derivation, he contends, of late Platonism, although he does not exclude some Iranian influence [18]. Equally, Simone Pétrement defined Gnosticism as 'un Platonisme romanesque' [19], while Nock spoke of 'a Platonism run wild' [20].

f. Concepts of fusion

Fusion of modes of thought is a regular occurrence in the study of the sources. For Leisegang it was the intermingling of mystical and mythical thought on the one hand, and rational and conscious thinking on the other that produced 'the disagreeable outgrowths of Gnostic speculation'

[21]. For R. McWilson the Gnosis is a product of the fusion of Christianity and Hellenistic thought [22], or 'the accomodation of Christianity and Hellenistic culture' [23].

g. The vision of Hans Jonas

The most authoritative work on the Gnosis at present is still Hans Jonas' 'Gnosis and spätantiker Geist', the first part of which appeared in 1934; then there came a long interruption because the author, as an opponent of Nazism, had to leave Germany. The publication was continued only in 1958. Jonas stressed the following two points. 1. Gnosticism is a predominantly pre-Christian and non-Christian phenomenon that, however, involved Christianity too. 2. Gnosticism is in general an oriental religion inspired by the Iranian religion [24].

h. Conclusions

I fear that this survey, that has not the slightest pretension of being exhaustive, will make the guileless reader confused. Where, he or she will ask, do we then find the origins of the Gnosis? He or she should keep in mind what Rudolph, himself a great expert, said, namely that "the colloquy of Messina (on the origins of the Gnosis) did not bring a solution or a unanimous answer to this question" [25]. This is not due to the fact that scholars love disagreeing with one another (although there is much difference of opinion among them on this subject). Rather, the attitude of the experts regarding the Gnosis (and its origins) is to a certain extent determined by their attitudes to this religion; they vary from Quispel who is a neo-Gnostic himself to Leisegang for whom the Gnosis is a degenerate doctrine. I myself am not a (neo-)Gnostic, although I find the Gnosis deeply fascinating; here as elswehere I shall try to be as objective as possible.

3. The Gnosis unique and syncretistic

The Messina gathering was unanimous on one point : that the Gnosis is sui generis, unique and entirely original. It was based on an attitude to existence and an idea of the world that is wholly its own [26]. It seems to me, therefore, that the term 'origins' is somewhat of a misnomer; the Gnosis had no direct ancestors.

At the same time, however, the Gnosis was a syncretistic religion, if there ever was one; its prophets and teachers borrowed freely without any scruples from all the religions and systems of thought before them and around them. The Gnosis drew from a great variety of sources, assimilated the most diverse elements, and managed to synthesize the most highly disparate components, often transforming them out of all recognition.

There were two great inflows, the one Hellenic-Hellenistic, the other oriental. To the oriental main stream several rivers contributed, the Iranian, perhaps the Indian (Buddhist) one, and certainly the Judaistic, including Qumran [27]. I must emphasize, however, that in almost all these cases it is impossible to establish a direct lineage of some Gnostic tenet to some older or contemporaneous element or component.

4. On constitutive elements in the Gnosis

There is also a fair amount of disagreement among scholars on the question what was the constitutive element in the Gnostic make-up, the really determining factor, the axis around which all systems turned. Some say it was the idea of the Unknown God, others the Divine Man, or the ascent to heaven, or dualism; some even mention the superior knowledge, the gnosis. In my opinion this gnosis stands a fair chance; the whole movement is called after it, and rightly so since without this gnosis there would simply be no Gnosis.

For our main subject the question is not really important since all experts agree that the Gnosis is dualistic to the core. Whether or not it was the all-determining factor, what Widengren wrote is true : "Dualism is the mark of recognition of the Gnosis"[28]. This is not yet the place to expatiate on this point; a few preliminary remarks may suffice. Gnostic dualism is closely bound up with the idea of superior knowledge. A person to whom this knowledge is revealed knows at once how utterly bad this world is, and how at the same time he can turn his back on it.

In Gnostic dualism the decisive opposition is that between a good godhead with his luminary beings, the aeons, who is not a part of the cosmos himself and did not create it , and, utterly opposed to them, the demiurge, the real creator of the cosmos (together with matter and the human world), and his archonts [29]. Here two dualistic streams converge. The first is Platonic, with the opposition of spirit and matter; this is a philosophical dualism. The other is Iranian, with the opposition of Good and Evil; this is an ethical dualism.

In late Hellenism the two streams began to merge into each other thus becoming an inalienable element of the Gnosis. Under Iranian influence matter became a spiritual power : matter as intrinsically bad and spirit as absolutely good from now on were located at the opposing ends of the mental spectrum [30].

"From the viewpoint of the history of ideas the Gnosis was initiated by the campaign of Alexander. The merging of the Hellenic spirit with Iranian and Babylonian thought signifies the mark of the beginning", says Ulrich Mann [31]. Hans Jonas begins his great book at this juncture. However, this merger of Greek and oriental would not have made possible the birth of the Gnosis if both streams had not contained 'gnosticizing' elements of a much earlier date.

5. 'Gnosticizing' elements in the Hellenic stream

a. Knowledge

In several of the previous volumes I have argued how from the first beginnings of Greek thought there has existed a specific idea of knowledge that was almost invariably denoted by the verb gignooskein and the noun gnosis. This was knowledge of a superior and uncommon kind, intuitive, spontaneous, revealing, esoteric, even divine, and not given to every one. Often we may call it 'gnosticizing'. The interested reader will find a full treatment of the development and use of the words gignooskein and gnosis in Chapter II.

b. Dualism

With regard to dualism, we must not forget that the pre-Alexandrian Hellenic world was one of the two most divided societies of Antiquity (the other one being India). Greek poleis endlessly waged bloody internecine wars with each other; it was only the Romans who, after 146 B.C., succeeded in making an end to this senseless strife. Within the cities political and social factions fought each other relentlessly, if need be - and this need obviously often arose - putting their vanquished opponents to the sword [32]. The Greeks never knew the meaning of national unity; quite the reverse in fact!

Furthermore, there was a sharp division between men and women that reached down into the households. Athenian democracy was an all male affair; women did not possess the vote [33]. The free Hellenes controlled, moreover, an enormous mass of slaves to whom they did not pay much respect [34]. Outward bound, there was that common feeling of Greek superiority which made the Hellenes, no matter how humble their status, look down in haughty disdain on all other peoples whom they stigmatized as 'barbarians'.

In these respects the campaign of Alexander did not usher in an wholly new age; it only transferred the old divisions to a much larger field. After Alexander's sudden demise his generals were at one another's throats for decades. When finally the Hellenistic kingdoms had been established, mutual relations between their Graeco-Macedonian rulers never were friendly, to put it mildly. Their wars lasted for centuries; I need only point to the five wars between Syria and Egypt. The existence of the largest of these kingdoms, the Seleucid Empire, was always threatened. At one time stretching beyond the Indus it was gradually forced back, in particular by the Parthians, to the Euphrates. And none of these kingdoms was able to withstand the Romans [35].

We must also reckon with the, at least partial, failure of Hellenization. The Greeks always remained an often isolated minority in a largely 'barbarian' world. Every trace of Greekdom between the Euphrates and the Indus disappeared in the end. And if many 'barbarians' indeed became 'hellenized', the Greeks in their turn often were 'barbarized', or rather 'nationalized'. To many people this Hellenistic world must have seemed a dangerous and uncomfortable place to live in!

Feelings of insecurity and pessimism were the result, most marked in those regions such as Syria, Samaria, and Palestine that had suffered most from the interminable wars [36]. There God and the world seemed farthest apart; doubts arose whether existence had any sense [37]. This prompted Hans Jonas, in the Epilogue of his book, to suggest a comparison with modern existentialism.

c. Élitism

So much for the general condition of Hellenic-Hellenistic society. Of the more specific elements I must mention first of all the élitism that is so obvious in Greek culture; the Gnostics too saw themselves as different from and superior to all others. Such élitism, with the ensuing attempt to keep apart from 'common' people, was already an important feature of the Pythagorean fraternity; as I argued before, Pythagoreans showed a certain contempt for their fellow human beings and an unmistakable self-exaltation [38]. Later those having been initiated in the mysteries of Eleusis became 'epoptai' those who have 'seen'; this made them fundamentally different from from all others, the 'witless' [39]. Orphics too stood apart from the common run, since they had tasted of immortality [40].

If anything, Greek philosophers were élitist. I know of hardly one who did not consider himself far above the rank and file; none of them saw his hard-working and perhaps less gifted fellow-men as his equals. If we leave apart the earliest Presocratics of whom we know relatively little, we first of all meet around 500 B.C. the élitism of Heraclitus who, expressing himself in obscure terms, obviously did not want to be understood by his compatriots. As I wrote earlier, the élitist tradition begins with this philosopher. And I added that there is a strong element of dualism in it [41].

We also find indications of élitism in Plato, perhaps not so much in his Academy, although this was a school for the (intellectually) privileged, and although he declared that "his doctrines should not be divulged to uneducated people" [42]. Rather I am thinking of his three-dimensional ideal state, thoroughly undemocratic and anti-democratic as it is. The top layer of his republic is formed by the rulers; respecting our present subject it is a very important thing that they, and they alone, possess the special form of knowledge that may be called wisdom [43]. The great mass of people must try to manage without this wisdom. Commoners are not initiated and are no lovers of wisdom. The philosopher even compared the actual populace of Athens, such as he knew it, to a great wild beast [44]. In contrast to this, he had a very lofty idea of philosophers, the real lovers of wisdom; they are endowed with every conceivable fine quality.

The second head of the Academy after Plato, Xenocrates (who died in 314 B.C.), did not even allow his works to leave the Academy, lest they should come under the eyes of the 'uneducated'. The Stoa distinguished two sets of people, the wise and the dull, the free and the slaves, the good and the bad. "A man must be either just or unjust" [45]; for the unjust there is no possibility of moral improvement. Here we are coming very close to the Gnostic position that the great mass of mankind will be doomed and only a few elect saved [46].

The school of Epicurus, the 'School of the Garden' in Athens, was staunchly and unashamedly élitist; it sealed itself hermetically off against the uneducated vulgus. Those who were initiated into Epicurean wisdom were the 'gnoorimoi', 'those in the know'; the great mass outside was composed of the ignorant and uninterested [47].

d. Esotericism and dogmatism

Closely connected with this élitism is the tradition of esotericism and dogmatism. This began already in the sixth century B.C. in the Pythagorean fraternity with its special signs and numbers that pointed to another, mystical world, such as the five-pointed star and the Theory of Numbers, to say nothing of its secluded way of life with its obligation to remain silent about the mysteries, its vegetarianism, and its abhorrence of the profane [48].

Mystical and esoteric to a degree was, of course, the ritual of Eleusis; the initiates stepped out of their normal life never to return, after having witnessed the secret mystery. The same applies to those who took part in the rituals of Dionysus; they were beside themselves to such an extent that they were considered to be mad. Plato called this mania 'a divine release from the customary habits' [49].

Traces of mysticism are also to be found in the Presocratics. The teachings of Pherecydes in the sixth century B.C. showed marked affinities with conceptions alive in that age in Phoenicia and Babylonia, and possibly also with the doctrine of Zoroaster. According to Saint Clemens, this early philosopher had made use of the 'revelation of Ham' and of 'secret Phoenician books' [50]. Heraclitus, who not for nothing was called 'the obscure', compared what he had to say with the pronouncements of the mysterious Sybil or those of the oracle in Delphi [51]. Self-conscious as he was, he was also very dogmatic. Real insight he found only in himself. Earlier I characterized him as a man with a mystical temperament and wrote that persons endowed with such a temperament easily resort to esoteric associations. I described Heraclitus there as one of the forefathers of the Gnosis, of that very special way of knowing higher things that its adherents denied to established religion and science alike [52].

The great philosopher Parmenides, the founder of what we now use to refer to as 'ontology', spoke as a mystic of the 'heavenly voyage of the soul' (which also reminds one of the Gnostics' 'ascent to heaven'); only a privileged person can make this voyage from the dark to the light. He viewed himself as a prophet who had received a private revelation [53]. A considerable step further was taken by Empedocles who dubbed himself 'an immortal god, no longer a mortal' [54].

In Plato's line of thought one must be a lover of wisdom, a philosopher, to come into contact with the gods; a philosopher is an exceptional person, his soul has wings, he is able to ascend to heavenly things. It is as if the philosopher has been initiated into a mystery cult. It is not every day experience or study that can inform us about heavenly things, it is only contemplation. Through contemplation 'the heavenly model' is revealed to the philosopher; he identifies with the divine order of things and in doing so becomes divine and 'cosmic' himself, in so far as this is possible for mortals [55].

We should not be surprised to find a strain of mysticism in Plato's nephew and successor in the Academy, Speusippus. He replaced his uncle's Theory of Forms by a Pythagoras-like Theory of Numbers. According to Zeller, he and other followers of Plato introduced an element of 'arithmetical and theological mystics' into their physics and turned philosophy into 'an absolute dogmatism' [56]. An esoteric Theory of Numbers is also to be found in Xenocrates and in the pseudo-Platonic treatise 'Epinomis'. Knowledge of numbers, in the esoteric sense, is a gift from above; it is the basis of all intelligence and understanding. Nobody without it may be called wise; without it there is neither goodness nor happiness [57].

No school was more dogmatic than that of Epicurus. His word was infallible; he acted and was venerated as a prophet. He was the object of a cult; this brings us into the sphere of mysticism. As Von Arnim said, "the members of the school were bound together by their unconditional belief in the redemptive power of the doctrine of their master"; to them he was 'a founder of religion' [58].

e. The attack on reality

For the Gnostics our actual, phenomenal, historical world was an object of deep contempt, even of hatred. They saw it as utterly evil and tried to escape from it. They fostered 'a sense of alienation and recoil from man's environment'[59]. Such escapism had its forerunners in the secluded Hellenic schools of philosophy, not the least in Plato's Academy. To quote Gilbert Murray : "the general trend of religion from ... the Peripatetics to the Gnostics" was that people "instead of appealing to objective experiment ... appealed to some subjective sense of fitness". The great exception was, of course, Aristotle. But "there was a strong tendency to follow Plato in supposing that people could solve questions by an appeal to their inner consciousness"[60].

This growing tendency to subjectivism was strongly invigorated by the attack on reality mounted by the philosophers. From the beginning Greek philosophical thought had its problems with reality. Or should we say that many a philosopher had an idea of reality differing radically from that of non-philosophers? Already in Anaximenes, in the sixth century B.C., the ontological status of all things is weak; in themselves they do not possess existence or reality since they are dependent on this philosopher's prime matter which is 'air'. Even man is hardly more than a 'qualification' or 'manifestation' of air [61].

But it all really began with Parmenides who posited Being - the most abstract of all concepts - as the ultimate reality. Our present world, together with mankind and its history, is no more than 'seeming', than appearance, and cannot be the object of philosophical thinking. It is a common understanding among people that they are busying themselves with reality, with real things, but nothing could be more wrong [62].

Although Plato did not share Parmenides' dogmatism about the phenomenal world, it is clear that he felt somewhat unhappy with it. When all is said and done, in his system concrete objects do not possess reality in themselves but owe it to the Forms; Plato, however, was never quite capable of proving the exact relation between the Forms and concrete objects. In the last resort the ontological status of things in his system remains undefined. Another proof of his uneasiness is his attempt, undertaken in his 'Republic', to reshape the socio-political world from top to bottom.

The line followed by the Hellenistic philosophers was not the realistic one of Aristotle but that of Plato. Xenocrates, for one, took a low view of the physical world; in his opinion there is no truth to be found in it but only error and false judgments, governed as it is by sensory perception [63]. Stoic materialism may be seen as a protest against all those abstract conceptions indeed; in this system it is the other way round, for what we miss here is the upper half, the world of ideas. The Stoic world is governed by Fate or Necessity which is not a very consoling idea [64]. This hopeless materialism is still more present in Greek Atomism. Everything is material, soul and thought not excluded. The phenomenal world consists of random combinations of atoms. We find some Atomism in Epicureanism; there are no other causes than mechanical ones [65].

Needless to say, Scepticism takes a bewildering view of reality! There is no reason why reality should not exist but nothing definite can be said about it; the most radical Sceptics did not even trust their own sceptical pronouncements. The beginning of wisdom is to realize that things in themselves are nothing; they are uncertain and (intellectually) indiscernible. Therefore, we should have no opinions at all. There is no truth, there is not even probability [66].

Other schools too, like the Middle Academy, faithfully adhered to this scepticism. We must not trust our observations of reality, we have no means for deciding which can be trusted. The individual mind and objective reality were growing apart ever more. Thus there originated a general climate of doubt and uncertainty.

f. Two worlds

The foregoing sections lead us to the idea of two different and opposed worlds. This was, of course, a main tenet of the Gnostics but it has its prehistory in Hellenic thought. The idea of two worlds is first to be found in the philosophy of Anaximander. One world is that of the apeiron, the boundless, which is immortal and eternal; it never grows old. The other world - our world, the universe - is movable, changeable, and doomed to perdition. Consequently, it is of a lesser quality. We are in the presence here of two fundamentally different realities [67].

But the best-known prophet of the two-world system is Parmenides. The higher world is that of Being; it is perfect, unique, uniform, imperishable, complete, and unhistorical. The second world, our world, is that of Seeming; it is far inferior to that of being because it is full of changeable and perishable things, including human beings. This world does not possess an ontological status of any kind [68].

Plato never said in as many words that there are two worlds. Nevertheless, in the cosmos, as he describes it, there is a higher and a lower creation. On the one hand the universe is governed by reason, on the other primordial matter is chaotic and unspecified. These two elements, one rational, one irrational, contract an uneasy alliance. Although the cosmos is fundamentally one, it contains all the same two opposed principles which try to steer it into two contrary directions [69].

In Xenocrates we come very near to a dualistic bipartition of the cosmos. There obviously is an upper world and a nether world. These are separated by the moon; there is, therefore, a sublunar world that is peopled with demons (the philosopher does not mean the Hades). The upper world is that of the gods (who are not the Olympians); human beings are incapable of conversing directly with the gods [70].

Although the thorough materialism of the Stoa, of Atomism, and of the Epicureans would exclude the possibility of another world besides the physical one, Epicurus nonetheless acknowledged a world of gods, of divine beings entirely free of sorrow who do not care for the sublunar world [71].

g. The demise of the gods

Although Greek philosophers sometimes postulate the existence of gods, they hardly ever mean the Olympian divinities. It is already significant that many of them, and not the least, never mention the twelve Olympians at all. For instance, Fränkel is of the opinion that in Anaximander who remained silent on the traditional gods, the apeiron took their place

[72]. Xenophanes was full of scorn for people who believed in anthropomorphic gods; in his view, an authentic godhead should not resemble mortals in any way [73]. Parmenides' Being leaves little room for divinities. But right in the centre of his cosmos there is a female daimoon who governs everything; she also brought forth the gods who, however, do not control the world. This runs counter to traditional Greek mythology [74].

So much for the Presocratics who do not give the impression of having been deeply devout believers. But also among the poets we find much doubt. Nestle coined the term 'Götterburleske' which is the habit of ridiculing the gods; this became very popular. Even the pious Homer was not always reverent about the gods. Later, in Greek comedy, gods are openly made a laughing-stock [75]. Greek tragedy amply showed how difficult it is to live with the gods. The Olympians are portrayed as spiteful, vindictive, untrustworthy, and immoral; they do not care a straw for mankind [76]. No wonder that they seem constantly on the retreat; in Thucydides the gods simply have left history [77].

Not one of the Hellenistic philosophers gives us the impression of having been an orthodox believer. Since every creed rests on unconditionally accepted tenets, Sceptics, by definition, could not be believers. Greek Atomism which was profoundly materialistic had no use for gods. Although the Stoa was materialistic too, it nevertheless admitted the existence of a godhead. The Stoic idea of this divinity was pantheistic, the godhead suffusing the whole cosmos [78]. Epicurus was more of a believer but surely not an orthodox one; he was strongly critical of popular belief. His gods are super-Olympian, abstract, and impersonal beings [79].

The second successor of Plato as the head of the Academy, Xenocrates, did not profess belief in the traditional gods either. He acknowledged eight astral gods the lowest of whom is the moon [80]. In the Middle and the New Academy the old creed is simply dead; arguing against the existence of gods, Carneades did nothing but kick against a corpse [81].

We find the old popular idea that the gods can be vicious and instigators of evil in the Gnostic dogma of the bad Demiurge. The philosophical idea of abstract divinities we rediscover in the unknown and unknowable prime godhead of the Gnosis.

h. The origin of evil

This leads us to the problem of the origin of evil that has always haunted mankind, the Hellenes no less than others. With them it became really acute and painful in the Hellenistic period, perhaps because of the often unsatisfying and contradictory general situation.

The old idea of the Greeks was that the gods were the cause of evil. Although the Stoics believed in a godhead that has ordered everything for the best, they could not deny that there is evil and wickedness in the world. One of the leading spirits of the Stoa, Chrysippus, could devise no other solution than admitting the possibility of the existence of malevolent spirits. With the opposition of an all-ordering cosmic divinity and base spirits who are responsible for evil we are nearing Gnostic ideology. In Stoic philosophy the problem of evil became more acute than it had been ever before [82]. Epicureans too wrestled with this problem. Their founder did not want to impute the origin of evil to the gods; his divinities were pure; perhaps his solution was that, because of the existence of evil, the world could not have been made by divine powers [83].

The consequence is world-alienation. "For the Epicureans ... there is no reason to feel any admiration for this random, meaningless, transitory, and very badly arranged cosmos ... The blessed gods of Epicurus are more complete strangers to the cosmos than the true God of the Gnostics : for they cannot and do not disturb their divine peace by doing anything to help their true worshippers to escape from this world to a better one". It is true, of course, what Armstrong whom I am quoting here says, that world-alienation is "not in itself an infallible indication of Gnosticism" but all the same the resemblance is striking [84].

j. Conclusion

If the question is asked whether elements of Greek thought went into the making of the Gnosis, I think I must side with my compatriot Mansfeld when he poses this question : "Is it possible, in Greek philosophy before the Christian era, to indicate elements or features which even a slight familiarity with the main tenets of Gnosticism may help us to understand it somewhat better (M.'s underlining)? ... Could such ideas possibly have appealed to a Gnostic, i.e., have lent themselves to an interpretatio Gnostica?". And this is his answer to his question. "The original Gnostic dualistic impulse cannot fully be derived from Greek antecedents ... Enough resemblances of a partial nature, however, can be indicated to make the fact that the Gnostic religion was capable of flourishing in a Graeco-Roman environment somewhat more understandable" [85].

6. 'Gnosticizing' elements in the oriental stream

a. The Iranian connection

It cannot be doubted that Iranian dualism was highly influential in the shaping of Gnostic dualism. And it was a dualism of Good and Evil, an ethical dualism. Zoroaster posited 'initial spirits', divinities that existed from the beginning. One, Ahura Mazda, is essentially good, the other, Angra Mainyu, intrinsically evil. These two spirits will fight one another as long as the world lasts. The whole universe is split up into two halves and involved in constant warfare. By the same token mankind is partitioned into a good and a bad half which are inimically and fundamentally opposed [86].

Zervanism was an heretical version of orthodox Zoroastrianism; it had a strong position in Iran during the first centuries of our era, more or less contemporaneously with the Gnosis, that is. In this doctrine everything started with a primeval being called Zervan (which means Time). He was a dual entity with a good and a bad side. He procreated two sons, Ormuzd (Ormizd) who was good (the fruit of his begetter's sacrifices), and Ahriman (the fruit of his doubts). "And everything that Ormizd created was good, but that Ahriman created was evil and corrupt"[87]. This is dualism with a vengeance.

We must not overlook the fact that the source of evil is Zervan, and that Ahriman represents the bad side of his father. The split dates in fact from before the universe since Zervan was already there before it existed. But Zervan is not really important to Zervanites; their ideology is wholly dominated by the inexorable enmity of Ormuzd and Ahriman. Zervanism is even more dualistic than orthodox Zoroastrianism[88].

Widengren and Jonas point to the essential relationship between (Iranian) dualism and the Gnosis. "The more consequent dualism is, the more original and pure Gnosticism will be, for then the polarity of God and world be at its greatest, and this, as Jonas, points out, is a characteristic of Gnosticism." This consequent dualism can be found precisely in the Iranian model. "The Iranian model incorporates the pure Gnosis and displays its most essential motives"[89].

b. A Babylonian connection?

Did the Gnosis assimilate Babylonian elements too? Why not? This is in itself quite possible since this syncretistic religion was not fastidious in its choice of constitutive elements. Nevertheless, it is difficult to speak of relations between the Gnosis and Mesopotamia. By playing the Babylonian card so one-sidedly W. Anz has discredited this possible link and seems to have discouraged other scholars from exploring this issue [90]

c. The Jewish connection

In my chapter on Jewish religion and life in Volume IV of this series I argued that Jewish society in Antiquity was the least dualistic imaginable. At the same time, however, even this homogeneous religion was not wholly free of tendencies to dualism. For this reason it is at least thinkable that late Judaism contained some 'gnosticizing' elements which could be gratefully picked up by the Gnostics.

First of all, there is the idea, or rather the person, of Wisdom. Several late books of the Old Testament are devoted to it : Proverbs, Jesus Sirach, Ecclesiastes, the Wisdom of Solomon. This proves that the Wisdom concept occupied an important place in Jewish religious thought in the centuries after the Babylonian Captivity. 'Wisdom' is a female being; she is not God but very close to him and with him from the beginning. One sometimes gets the impression that God leaves the guidance of the world to her [91]. She herself has been initiated into the divine wisdom [92]. And she communicates herself to human beings but not to everyone indiscriminately. "Age after age she enters into holy souls, and makes them God's friends and prophets, for nothing is acceptable to God but the man who makes his home with wisdom" [93].

Many persons, however, will be silly enough not to listen to her but will rather turn to her rival, the foolish woman. "She sits at the door of her house, she takes a seat on the high places of the town, calling to those who pass by, who are going straight on their way. 'Whosoever is simple, let him turn in here'. And to him without sense she says, 'stolen water is sweet, and bread eaten in secret is pleasant'. But he does not know that the dead are there, that her guests are in the depth of sheol" [94]. Here are several 'gnosticizing' elements : the female entities, the opposition of the wise and the foolish, the redeeming power of wisdom.

Special mention must be made of the Books of Job and Ecclesiastes. They display what Rudolph calls 'Jewish scepticism' [95]. At his wit's end Job desperately asks for the meaning of existence; he no longer can understand God, it has become all senseless to him. The tone of Ecclesiastes, the Preacher, is one of doubt, even of cynicism. All is vain and in vain. God seems to have withdrawn into a far distance; here the idea of the Unknown God is announcing itself.

Despair of the present world becomes apparent in Jewish apocalypses of which the Book of Daniel is the only specimen in the Old Testament. The main idea is that this world is utterly lost and will go to wrack and ruin. Only the elect will be saved. Knowledge of what will come is not vouchsafed to everyone. In the Book of Daniel the secrets of the future are revealed to Daniel by angels; it is, therefore, esoteric knowledge. "None of the wicked shall understand, but those who are wise shall understand" [96]. This is the dualistic opposition between the pious (who know) and the bad.

7. Two prototypes of the Gnosis

a. Orphism

The similarities between Orphism and the Gnosis are so striking that we would not be wholly wrong in calling it a Proto-Gnosis. Orphism is a Hellenic religious movement with a history of twelve centuries. Its inception was in the sixth century B.C.; traces of it are still to be found in the sixth century of the Christian era. So its course ran partly parallel with that of the Gnosis.

The first point of resemblance is that Orphism, just like the Gnosis, stood apart from established religion. Orphism was something quite different from the official polis-religion. Although Orphics were a minority among the Greek population, and although there is discussion on the question whether something like an 'Orphic society' ever existed, its ideas, in partiular that of the possibility of attaining immortality, were found attractive by many who were not really Orphics. Burkert has suggested the possibility that in the 'Orphic' ideology one can distinguish two directions : an Attic-Eleusinian one to be found in the cult of Demeter and in the mysteries of Eleusis, and a South-Italian one which took shape in the Pythagorean fraternities with their doctrine of the migration of souls and their ascetic-vegetarian mode of life [97].

A second point is that Orphism, like the Gnosis, was based on writings, on prophetic and sacred books, just as is the case in Judaism and Christianity. This made it different from the Olympian religion. It is true that the Homeric epics often are called the 'Bible of the Greeks', but this is not correct since it is usually claimed that the Bible rests on divine revelation, while the epics make no pretense to this. The Olympian religion in fact functioned without books; its foundation was found in a great many ancient myths many of which are not even recorded in Homer. In the polis-religion the really important element was the ritual; this expressed the myth in such a perfect way that it may be said that the rite was the myth itself. For the Orphics this was not so; for them the ideology, that is to say the cognitive, speculative, and intellectual contents of the poems played an important role. Let us remember that the Gnosis can be characterized as a theosophy.

Burkert points out that the existence of fundamental religious texts may make religion into a more personal and individual affair; he who is able to read does not need the communal lessons of the cult any more. He can consult the books independently and interpret them in his own way [98]. This individualizing tendency, this urge to self-willed interpretation, became extremely powerful in the Gnosis.

Orphic poems related the origin of the world, the cosmogony, in a mythological way. There is a long succession of cosmic rulers of whom Dionysus is the last. Of extreme importance is the dominating position of Night; this is stressed in the different versions of the 'Orphic poem' whether or not she is thought of as an 'archè'. She is the supreme ruler, she is the councillor of Zeus during the foundation of the cosmos. This means that a black, dark, negative principle is in control; somewhere along the cosmogonic line something has gone wrong. There is an initial error, a fundamental and fatal flaw in the universe. The Orphics had a profoundly pessimistic view of cosmogony, a view that we find still more clearly stated in the Gnosis.

Orphic anthropology was essentially dualistic. Zeus, ruler of the universe, gave his overlordship to young Dionysus. The jealous Titans refused to recognize the young man as their king. Instead, they killed and devoured him. Angrily Zeus unleashed his lightning against them so that they were reduced to ashes.

Now Orphic myth has it that mankind has its origins in the ashes of the Titans. This explains why man has a lower nature, for the Titanic component is the negative pole of his being. But there is also a higher side to him, the Dionysian pole; the Titanic ashes contained a Dionysiac element since the Titans had eaten the flesh of the young god. The result is that man has a double nature, a lower Titanic and a higher Dionysian one. This idea of a twofold nature is also present in the Gnosis, alhough the Gnostics explained its origin in a different way.

It is evident that the Orphics - and in this the Gnostics did not differ from them - took a gloomy view of human life. Having been composed of the ashes of the Titans, we mainly consist of an antidivine and anticosmic substance. It is true that we also possess a parcel of higher, Dionysian life, but this in itself is not sufficient to save us. One's only possibility of freeing oneself from the 'wheel of rebirth' - the Orphics believed in the migration of souls - is to live like the Orphics; only on this condition will Dionysus (who has been revived by Zeus) deliver his follower. This is a typically gnosticizing element : man needs a special knowledge (with the mode of life consequent on it) to find his way to beatitude. The final aim of the Orphic was unification with the godhead and the return of the divine component in man to its celestial origin.

In order to liberate oneself from the effects of the original error on human life - this original error being the slaying of Dionysus by the Titans -, the Orphic needed to live an ascetic life. To quote Detienne, they were 'renunciants'. "They strive for saintliness. They devote themselves to techniques of purification in order to separate themselves from others" [99]. For this reason they subjected themselves to all kinds of taboos and lived as vegetarians. All this made them into an élistist and esoteric group, just like the Gnostics.

b. Mahayana Buddhism

There exists a curious resemblance between the Gnosis and the Buddhist religious system that goes by the name of 'Mahayana', the 'Great Vehicle' [100]. The Great Vehicle, which still exists, originated in the first century B.C. and flourished in the first centuries A.D., that is contemporaneously with the Gnosis. The other main stream in Buddhism was the 'Hinayana', the 'Lesser Vehicle'. As the older form Hinayana was accused of having been overgrown with accretions, additions, and reworkings of the original doctrine. Mahayana, as a reformist movement, claimed to be the superior interpretation of original Buddhism, more strict and more orthodox.

Now in all Budhhism there is present a sharp dualistic distinction between the holy or 'noble' and the foolish common people. These two groups inhabit 'two distinct planes of existence', the 'worldy' and the 'supramundane'. Those who are 'spiritually awakened' and have seen the light "have attained a positively superhuman stature and no common bond of humanity unites them with the rest of us. They have conquered death and have become immortal; they have become divine, equal to God" [101]. The Mahayanists improved on this ancient scheme by introducing - some say under Gnostic influence - three classes of people, "those destined for salvation, those destined for perdition, and those whose destiny is not fixed either way' [102].

The most striking element of resemblance is that salvation is only possible through knowledge, through 'jnana' that is, etymologically the same word as 'gnosis'. Although the two concepts are not wholly identical, "in both cases the mere insight into the origination and nature of the world liberates us from it, and effects some kind of re-union with the transcendental One, which is identical with our true Self" [103]. The source of this jnana is revelation; its experience is subjective and personal.

'Wisdom' plays the climactic role, as Sophia in the Gnosis and as Prajna in Mahayana. Conze says that it is primarily archetypical because it is the ideal fundament of all existence, even of the cosmos. Prajna is cosmogenetic; the Hevajra Tantra says that "Prajna is called Mother, because she gives birth to the world" [104]. Acccording to Conze this is not vintage Buddhism; "it must have come from outside, and the Gnostics seem the most likely source" [105].

It should be noted that the divine Prajna is feminine, like Sophia. Mahayana introduced female deities. "If it makes sense to distinguish between 'matriarchal' and 'patriarchal' religions, then surely the Mahayana and Gnosticism are more 'matriarchal' than, say, the 'Hinayana' and Protestant Christianity"[106].

Mahayana, like the Gnosis, is totally uninterested in historical reality, and, instead, displays a marked predilection for myth. And again like the Gnostics, the adherents of Mahayana feel that they are above the prescriptions of moral law - which does not necessarily entail that they, in consequence, live profligate lives. But one can observe what Conze calls 'antinomianism', "a certain disdain for the puny demands of conventional morality"[107]. Mahayana is not a theistic religion; it does not acknowledge a personal god. The true godhead lives somewhere in the unknown; he is the Absolute. He has nothing to do with the world that is ruled by Mara the Evil One.

Like the Gnostics, the Mahayanists despise the multitude and do not want to enlighten it. "In consequence there is everywhere a predilection for the mysterious, the secret, the enigmatic, the hidden, the esoteric"[108]. Finally, although Mahayana, just as the Gnosis, is dualistic to the core, the ultimate ideal is monistic. The dualistic 'revulsion from multiple things' must in the end lead to a reunion with the One 'which transcends the multiple world'[109].

According to Isaac Jacob Schmidt, the German scholar who was the first to direct the attention of European scholars to the affinities between Gnosis and Mahayana[110], "the (Gnostic) tenets sound almost exactly as if they had been verbally transcribed from the Buddhist writings". Schmidt himself cautiously wrote 'as if', and indeed, no scholar believes that there existed a direct relationship. However, there is such a degree of congeniality that the similarity cannot have been entirely accidental.

There is, of course, no saying how the channels of transmittance ran between Gnosis and Mahayana. But we know that there lived Buddhist Greeks in India[111], and that the whole area between the Indus region and Greece was studded with Hellenic cities. Buddhist or Gnostic ideas would not have had to cross large empty spaces. There may have been mutual borrowing, says Conze; the development may have been either joint or parallel.

c. A possible explanation

Is there perhaps an explanation for this remarkable correspondence between Mahayana and Gnosis? Perhaps there is. In the sixth century B.C. a revolutionary change in the mental climate occurred. The main focus of intellectual interest shifted from mythology to rationality, from myth to reason, from mythos to logos. This change took place on a worldwide scale since it involved countries as far apart as Greece, Israel, India, and China. For this reason Karl Jaspers called this period the 'Achsenzeit', because world history then took a turn around its axis [112].

Now it seems to me that a similar revolutionary change took place in the first century A.D. Once again the focus of attention was shifted, once again the world began to revolve around another axis in a different direction. Rationality was substituted by subjectivity, reason by intuition, logos by sophia. Wasn't this period a second 'Achsenzeit'?

8. The Syrian cradle

We have now traced the origin and course of a great number of constitutive elements that went into the making of the Gnosis. These elements can be arranged along two lines of transmission, a western and an eastern one. At two points the gnosticizing tendencies came so near to each other that it is permissible to speak of a Proto-Gnosis : in Orphism and in Mahayana Buddhism. In the Hellenistic world, after the campaign of Alexander, when east and west became politically intertwined, the lines began to converge.

The question now is where these electric currents, so to speak, would spark off enough energy to give birth to the Gnosis. Very probably this happened in the Syrian region comprising Phoenicia, the hinterland east of Phoenicia called Coelesyria, Samaria, and Palestine. It was there that for centuries the great religions had met and competed with each other : Judaism, Samaritanism, the Qumran sect of the Essenes, early Christianity, and pagan religions, comprising the official Olympian creed, the Hellenistic ruler cult, elements of Egyptian and Mesopotamian religions, and mystery religions. If anywhere, the situation was rife with syncretism here.

Of old, the relatively narrow corridor between the Mediterranean and the Arabian desert had been a transit area for marching armies. Great battles had been fought there; rulers from different empires had laid their greedy hands on this region, only to lose them to their enemies. Cities and populations had changed hands endlessly. The feeling of destabilization that is so characteristic of the late Hellenistic world must have been especially acute here. Jewish apocalyptic literature, with its images of impending doom and its promise of an eternal paradise, sure and uniform, testifies of this. It should not surprise us that the two religions that promise redemption, Christianity and the Gnosis, sprang up in this area. For this was the neuralgic spot of the ancient world.

NOTES TO CHAPTER I

1. This document is printed in Origini XX-XXXII. See also my Vol. I, Afterword : On Definitions, 260-264.
2. Bianchi, A propos 419-429. This passage is repeated verbatim from my Vol. I, 260/261.
3. Rudolph, Randerscheinungen 75.
4. Van Baaren, Towards 177.
5. Gnosticism, ed. Grant 14.
6. See for the use of the terms 'gnoosis' and 'gnoostikos' the Patr. Greek Lex.
7. 1Tim.6:20.
8. Ir., Adv.haer. 1.11.1.
9. For further study of this complex subject I recommend Ugo Bianchi, Le Gnosticisme : Concept, Terminologie, Origines, Délimitations, in Gnosis 33-64.
10. Gottfried Arnold, Unpartheyische Kirchen- und Ketzergeschichte; vom Anfang des Neuen Testaments bis auf das Jahr Christi 1688. Frankfurt am Manin, 1699-1715.
11. Quispel, s.v. 'Gnosticism', Enc.Hist.Rel. 5, 573.

12. J. von Mosheim used the word 'gnosis' in 1739 in his 'Institutiones Historiae Christianae Maiores', Helmstedt, 1739, 136. Mosheim has the following intriguing text here. "In notioribus Asiae & Africae provinciis singulare quoddam philosophiae genus de Deo ... quod gnoosin (in Greek) seu cognitionem appellare solebant amatores eius : alii philosophiam seu doctrinam orientalem. ideo haud dubie, ut a Graecorum philosophia distinguere vocabant."

13. Harnack, Lehrbuch I, 154. Harnack himself said that the first one to have expressed this opinion was Franz Overbeck in his 'Studien zur Geschichte der alten Kirche'. 1875, 184.

14. Hipp., Ref. 4:6-7.

15. W. Anz, Zur Frage nach dem Ursprung des Gnostizismus. Texte und Untersuchungen zur Geschichte der altchristlichen Literatur XV.4. Leipzig, 1897. Already F.C. Baur in 1835 and other German scholars in the early nineteenth century had pointed to oriental influences, see Rudolph, Gnosis 36.

16. Many scholars now believe that Reitzenstein was wholly wrong and that there never existed anything like an Iranian mystery of salvation but this is not at issue here.

17. Rudolph Bultmann, Das Evangelium des Johannes. Göttingen, 1941 1.

18. Schneider, Geistesgesch. 1, 254.

19. Pétrement, Dualisme 129.

20. Nock, Essays II, 949.

21. Hans Leisegang, Die Gnosis. Stuttgart, 1955 4 (1924 1).

22. R. McL.Wilson, The Gnostic Problem. London, 1958, VIII, cit. Haardt, Methoden 163.

23. R. McL.Wilson, Gnostic origins, in Vigiliae Christianae IX, 1955, 199, cit. by Haardt, Methoden 163.

24. Widengren, Origins, in Origini 37. For this section I am much indebted to essays by Geo Widengren, Les origines du Gnosticisme et l'histoire des religions, in Origini 28-60; Robert Haardt, Die Gnosis. Wesen und Zeugnisse. Salzburg (1967), 16-27 Einführung; Kurt Rudolph, Die Gnosis. Wesen und Geschichte einer spätantiken Religion. Göttingen, 1977, 35-39; Gilles Quispel s.v. Gnosticism, Enc.Hist.Rel. 5, 573/574.

25. Rudolph, Randerscheinungen 773, in Gnosis und Gnostiz. 773.

26. Rudolph, Randerscheinungen, in Gnosis und Gnostiz. 774.

27. It seems safer to me to remain silent here on connections between Babylonia and Mesopotamia. The reader will find a few words more on p. 20. See further Rudolph, Zum Problem : Mesopotamien (Babylonien) and Gnostizismus, in Origini 302-306.

28. Widengren, Origines, in Origini.

29. See Haardt, Gnosis 12.
30. Mann, Vorspiel 325/326.
31. Mann, Vorspiel 324.
32. I decribed this bloody history in Vol. II, Ch II and IV.2.
33. Vol. II, Ch. IV.4a-h.
34. Vol. II, Ch. IV.4i-k.
35. Vol. VI, Ch. I.
36. Rudolph, Randerscheinungen 775. See my Vol. VI, Ch II.
37. Rudolph, Gnosis 302.
38. Vol. I, Ch. I, p. 14.
39. Vol. I, Ch. IV, p. 215.
40. Vol. I, Ch. IV.9 and 10.
41. Vol. I, p. 65/66.
42. Plato, Ep.II, 314A-B.
43. Plato, Rep. 429A.
44. Plato, Rep. 439A-C.
45. DL 7.127.
46. Vol. VI, Ch. II.2h.
47. Vol. VI, Ch. III.4a and c.
48. Vol. I, Ch. I, 5.6, and 10.
49. Plato, Phaedrus 265A.
50. Vol. I, Ch. II.1.
51. DK 22B92 and 93.
52. Vol. I, Ch. II.6.
53. Vol. I, Ch. II.8.
54. DK 31B112; Vol. I, Ch. II.9.
55. Vol. III, Ch. III.8 and 14c.
56. Zeller, Phil.d.Gr. II.1. 995.
57. Vol. VI, Ch. III.1d.
58. H. von Arnim s.v. 'Epikuros' in PW VI (1909), 135.
59. Nock, Essays II, 946.
60. Murray, Five Stages 160/161.
61. Vol. I, Ch. II.5.
62. Vol. I, Ch. II.8.
63. Vol. VI, Ch. III.1c.
64. Vol. VI, Ch. III.2g.
65. Vol. II, Ch. III.4h and g.

66. Vol. VI, Ch. III.5.
67. Vol. I, p. 180.
68. Vol. I, pp. 81-84.
69. Vol. III. Ch. III.19.
70. Vol. VI, p. 129.
71. Vol. VI, Ch. III.4k.
72. Fränkel, Dicht.u.Phil. 301.
73. Vol. I, p. 75.
74. Vol. I, p. 85.
75. Vol. I, Ch. IV.5.
76. Vol. III. Ch. I.5.
77. Vol. II, Ch. III.1j.
78. Vol. VI, Ch. III.2e.
79. Vol. VI, Ch. III.4h.
80. Vol. VI, Ch. III.1c.
81. Vol. VI, Ch. III.7b.
82. Vol. VI, Ch. III.2l.
83. Vol. VI, p. 172.
84. Armstrong, Gnosis and Gr.Phil. 91, in Festschrift Jonas.
85. Mansfeld, Bad World 262/263 and 314, in Studies in Gnost. Contrary to Jonas, Armstrong, Gnosis and Gr.Phil., does not believe that Greek philosophy influenced Gnosticism strongly; this influence was "not genuine but extraneous and for the most part superficial". Nevertheless, he admits the possibility of a more than superficial influence emanating from 'the Pythagorean-Platonic type of Greek philosophy' (p. 101). I myself would not speak of influences, direct or indirect, but rather of morphological resemblances and of elements of Gnosticizing. Eclectic and syncretistic as they were, "Gnostics did certainly refer to Greek philosophy and mythology and interpreted them in their own way to give authority to their views among people of Hellenic tradition" (Armstrong p. 99). But was this only for reasons of propaganda? Couldn't it have been that such elements suited them?
86. Vol. IV, Ch. IV.8b-d, and Vol.V, Ch. I.4.
87. Eznik II, Irrlehren, Buch 1, 83/84.
88. Vol. V, Ch. I.5b.
89. Widengren, Origini 681.
90. See Rudolph, Mes. und Gnost., in Origini 302-306.
91. Wisd. 7:22-24.
92. Wisd. 8:4.
93. Wisd. 7:27-28.

94. Prov. 9:14-18.
95. Rudolph, Gnosis 298.
96. Dan. 12:10.
97. Burkert, Hist.Gr.Rel. 445. For this section see also Vol. I, Ch. IV, 10 and 11.
98. Burkert, Hist.Gr.Rel. 442.
99. Marcel Detienne s.v. 'Orpheus' in Enc.Hist.Rel. 11, 112.
100. See my Vol. V, Ch. II.23f and g. This section is based on Conze's essay, Buddhism and Gnosis, in Origini 653-667.
101. Conze, Buddh. 654.
102. Conze, Buddh. 654.
103. Conze, Buddh. 653/654.
104. Cit. Conze, Buddh. 656.
105. Conze, Buddh. 656/657.
106. Conze, Buddh. 657.
107. Conze, Buddh. 659.
108. Conze, Buddh. 660.
109. Conze, Buddh. 661. Throughout this section I have been faithfully following Conze but I have an uneasy feeling that was he is saying applies to the Hinayana rather to the Mahayana. However this may be, the two streams are in many respects very similar and we should not stress the differences too much.
110. Isaac Jacob Schmidt, Über die Verwandtschaft der gnostischen theosophischen Lehren mit den Religionssystemen des Orients, vorzüglich dem Buddhaismus. Leipzig, 1828. Cit. Conze, Buddh. 653.
111. Vol. VI, Ch. II.7a.
112. Karl Jaspers, Vom Ursprung und Ziel der Geschichte. 1949, 19sqq. See Vol. I, Ch. I.7.

CHAPTER II

'GNOSIS': ITS SEMANTICS AND ETYMOLOGY

1. The words 'gnosis' and 'gignooskein'

Since 'gnosis' will be a key-word in this volume and the next, let us first examine what this word means etymologically and semantically. The Greek word 'gnosis' [1] is a very common word meaning 'knowledge'. It possesses several shades of meaning which are listed by the Liddell-Jones Greek-English Lexicon (ed. 1968) as follows : 1. seeking to know, inquiry, investigation; 2. result of investigation, decision; 3. knowing, knowledge; 4. higher, esoteric knowledge; 5. acquaintance with a person; 6. recognizing; 7. means of knowing; 8. being known; 9. fame, credit; 10. statement in writing (produced by a means of knowing). One notices that among these is also 'higher, esoteric knowledge'. But at the same time it is astonishing that this authoritative dictionary only quotes in support of the last two texts of the apostle Paul [2] - as though the notion of esoteric knowledge does not occur in classical Greek writings.

The verb from which the noun 'gnosis' is derived is 'gignooskein'; this is used far more frequently than the noun; "'gnosis'", says Chantraine, "is rather rare" [3]. The already quoted lexicon gives as its meanings 'to know by observation, to perceive, to be aware of, to feel that, to understand, to judge, to decree or determine'. Finally, there are texts in which it signifies 'to know carnally'.

'Gignooskein' belongs to a group of verbs ending in -skoo, which is a form often expressing redoubling or reiteration; such forms seem to indicate an action that one has to repeat in order to succeed [4]. The suffix -ske/o occurs in several Indo-Iranian languages, for instance in Armenian and in Hittite; "it underlines the duration of an action and at the same time envisions its achievement" [5]. One could say that the suffix suggests achievement after an effort. With regard to the verb 'gignooskein' this is well exemplified by the way Idomeus uses it in the Iliad. He is watching the horse-racing that forms part of the funerary games for Patroclus but "cannot well make out" who is leading [6]. Here the effort is stressed rather than the achievement.

The root 'gn' (cn, kn) is very common in Indo-European languages. The oldest form is to be found in Sanskrit where we encounter the verb 'janati' = to know, its past participle 'jnataj' = known (to which the Greek 'gnootos' is very similar), and the two nouns 'jnanam' = knowledge, and 'jnata' = connoisseur [7]. Already in Sanskrit these words have a connotation of special or specified knowledge. In particular this is the case with the noun 'jnanam'; often this means higher knowledge or insight with regard to the highest principle or highest godhead as the result of meditation [8]. Apart from jnanam there exists yet another word for knowledge, namely 'vijnanam'; this noun denotes knowledge of a profane character. The Sanskrit root 'jn' recurs in a great number of Indo-European languages as 'gn' or 'cn, kn'. To cite just a few instances, 'ignarus, cognotus' in Latin, 'connaître' in French, 'to know' in English, 'kennen' in Dutch and German. In international scholarly discourse several Greek words with specific meanings have been preserved, like diagnostic and agnostic.

2. Other words for 'knowing' in Greek

'Gignooskein' is not the only word for 'to know'; there are several others, 'gnoorizein, daênai, eidenai (oida), epistasthai, sunienai, phronein'. To indicate the differences in meaning between these verbs and the way they are used, I can do no better than follow the learned disquisition by Heinrich Schmidt on Greek synonyms for knowledge [9]. According to this scholar, the different Greek verbs express shades of meaning determined by the intensity of a person's involvement. Words derived from the roots 'gno and 'gnoo' (gignooskein, gnoorizein, gnoomê, gnoosis, gnoosimos, gnootos) indicate the engagement of the whole person, subjectively and objectively.

There is an intellectual aspect to these words, that of knowing by means of the intellect and being able to express this in words. But at the same time this manner of knowing is something of a personal experience, a kind of intuition, not without consequences in the moral sphere. This is very well exemplified by negative words like 'agnoia' which not only means 'ignorance' but also 'mistaken conduct', and 'agnoomoon' which means 'senseless, inconsiderate'. Positive words like 'gignooskein' can be found in expressions like these : "he knows what poverty is" = he has experienced to his own cost what it means to be without money. Or one (I myself, for instance) could say : "A person who never suffered from migraine does not know what it is" - migraine being an extremely painful and lonely experience. This degree of engagement is also expressed by the fact that 'gignooskein' may also mean 'having carnal knowledge' [10].

The original significance of 'gignooskein', says Schmidt, has an inchoative character, namely 'to realize, to get to know'. From there it can come to mean 'to realize (inwardly, personally), to recognize (somebody or something for what he/she/it is), as different from 'to know' (factually or intellectually). The next stage is 'to have a judgment or a conviction'.

Following Schmidt further, we discover a second group of verbs, like 'eidenai' or 'epistasthai (epistamai), with the connotation that the knowing subject becomes active. 'Eidenai' denotes knowledge of a clear, purely spiritual or intellectual sort, like Descartes' 'cogito'. Somebody sees a person or an object for himself and then comes to a mental conclusion. 'Epistasthai' stands for knowledge that has been won from practice or learning. It is more or less equivalent to 'understand'

'Noein' means mainly 'to perceive', by the eyes (observe) as well as by the mind (apprehend), and then 'to think, consider, presume', and 'to have a purpose, to intend'. Schmidt says that its principal significance is 'observation by the mind', whereas as observation by the senses is rendered by 'aistanesthai' ('aisthèsis'). 'Phronein' means 'to have understanding, to be prudent or wise, to be consciously aware, to know full well'[11].

The clearest opposition is that between, on the one hand, 'gignooskein' = to feel, to experience, and, on the other, 'eidenai' = to know for certain - intuition opposed to intellectual or mental certainty. 'Eidenai' is contrasted with 'epistasthai' = to have practical knowledge. Schmidt unfortunately has little more to say on the substantive 'gnosis' than that it means 'spiritual discernment' as opposed to pure contemplation [12], as expressed by the verb 'theoorein'.

3. Words for 'knowing' in Homer

As I attempted to demonstrate in my Volume III, Ch. III.12, Plato is not only a mine of dualistic tendencies but every now and then he seems to me to come very close to fundamental meanings of the Gnosis. He surely handles his terms for 'knowledge' in a peculiar way; his notion of 'gnosis' bears a strong resemblance to that of the Gnostics. When I discovered this - only one or two scholars have written about it -, I thought it very remarkable that this morphological likeness appears so many centuries before the full development of the Gnosis itself. Could not the special meaning of the word have a still older history?, I kept asking myself. I therefore went straight back to the first literary products of the Hellenic language, the Homeric epics.

When Homer uses words for 'knowing', 'understanding', and 'knowledge', does he make a distinction then between plain meanings and special meanings? Given the fact that he indeed uses different nouns and verbs, would he perhaps utilize one term for commonplace knowledge and another for specified knowledge? And if he uses some word(s) in a particular way, would he give them meanings which are pointing in the direction of 'gnosis' in its esoteric significance? Naturally this must not be taken to mean that I hoped to detect a kind of early Gnostic in

Homer. But it might be conceivable that his words for knowledge share some characteristics with the Gnostic meanings of the term.

First of all, it must be pointed out that Homer does not use the noun 'gnosis'; it never occurs in his works. Neither does one find 'phronêsis' and 'phronêma'; the same applies to 'epistêmê'. The noun 'noêma' is found a few times meaning 'thought, idea, way of thinking'. It seems therefore that Homer had not much use for such abstract nouns. His epics are tales of action, the scene is constantly occupied by fighting warriors or by the adventures of the seafaring Odysseus. This leaves no room for philosophical considerations or a theory of knowledge. So it need not surprise us that even in this field Homer preferably makes use of verbs, that is to say of words indicating some sort of action. There are five of them : 1. eidenai; 2. epistasthai; 3. noein; 4. phronein; 5. gignooskein, all of them covering sections of the vast semantic field of 'knowing, understanding, thinking' (and partially overlapping each other). Gehring's invaluable Homeric lexicon [13] contains nearly eight hundred entries with words denoting 'knowing' and 'understanding'. I checked all of them with the purpose of discovering how in Homer 'gignooskein' compares with the four other verbs [14].

a. Homer's use of eidenai

Let us begin with eidenai and its numerous irregular forms (for, like love, this verb is a many-splendoured thing). It is Homer's most common word for 'knowing'; there are in all 355 entries with it, that is nearly half the total number of knowledge verbs. In the epics this verb normally signifies 'to know'. Most of the time it means common knowledge, open to everyone, without even a shade of special or secret or esoteric knowledge. This should cause no surprise since eidenai is used as the perfect of the verb 'horan' = to see. The original meaning of 'eidenai', therefore, is 'to have seen' [15]. This is born out by the poet's invocation of the Muses : "You are present and you have seen (= you know) everything" [16]. The main idea in Homer, says Snell, is that perfect knowledge means the recollection of having seen much. Because of this visual element this scholar could argue that 'eidenai' denotes theoretical skill rather than practical [17]. If we stick to the double meaning of 'vision', it is quite plausible, as Von Fritz does, that the term 'idein' "covers all the cases in which something comes to our knowledge by the sense of vision" [18].

"That truly all of us know", says Idaeus, the herald, speaking to Greeks and Trojans [19]. "All this the Achaeans, both young and old, know" [20]; "we (the Greeks) know how far you (Agamemnon) are excelling all" [21]. In cases such as these, commonplace knowledge is meant. A very good instance is Od. II.211 : "Now the gods know it and all the Achaeans", because here no difference is made between the knowledge of gods and men. Sometimes 'eidenai' signifies 'to know a person' but the instances I found are in the negative : "I know no one of the people who possess this land" [22]. Sometimes unspecified knowledge is meant : "Well he (Zeus) knows all things" [23].

Very often, however, eidenai denotes specified (but not technical or specialistic) knowledge, that is to say factual knowledge of events and things; then again very often only the most commonplace knowledge is meant. If I may be forgiven for making not too much of shades and gradations of meaning, I reckon that eidenai about a hundred and ten times means 'to know for a fact, to be informed about something, to be in the know', in most cases by virtue of sense perception, because one has seen with his own eyes and heard with his own ears. A good example is : "This further thing I know, for I saw it with my own eyes" [24].

Normally this knowledge is about facts that are not to be kept secret. "Tell me this truly", says Antinous, and what he wants to know is : when did Telemachus go, which young men went with him, and other plain facts of this kind [25]. And about harbouring no secrets : "Speak out, hide it not in your mind that we both may know", this is what Thetis says to Achilles [26].

In a number of verses a negative word goes along with eidenai : not to know, not to be sure. "Nor I know anything of the others, who of the Achaeans were saved, and who were lost". This is what Nestor answered him when Telemachus asked him whether his father Odysseus would return home [27]. The negation is used about forty-five times.

A somewhat different significance of eidenai, but still very much akin to that of 'factual knowledge', is 'to be able to', in a purely technical sense, that is knowing how to handle instruments and implements, understanding a craft. In such cases Homer's use of eidenai seems indistinguishable from epistasthai. "I know well how to wield right and left my shield of seasoned hide", Hector boasts [28]; "Polydamas, you know you are able to devise better words than these" [29]. We hear of 'understanding remedies' [30], even of somebody 'well skilled in soothsaying' [31]. Sometimes this verb can mean 'to be crafty' : "she (Penelope) is crafty above all women" [32].

About 260 times in all (out of 355) eidenai means 'to know a person, to know for a fact, to come to know, to be in the know, to be able to'; therefore I am justified in saying that having factual knowledge of persons, events, and crafts, is the basic and general meaning of this verb. This means that there is nothing special or exceptional about it.

We begin to deviate somewhat from this fundamental meaning when we discover that eidenai may also signify 'to be minded, to ponder, to brood on something'. In these cases its meaning comes very near to or is even identical with that of 'phronein'. The difference with eidenai's basic meaning is that disposition rather than meaning is meant; here we approach man's inner world. Sometimes the two meanings are juxtaposed. "I know for a fact that the heart in your breast knows friendly and kindly thoughts" = that you are of a kind disposition towards me; even the verb phronein is not very far here : "you are minded (phroneis) even as I am" [33]. And "he was of a kindly mind towards him" [34]. The pejorative side of 'to be minded' can be found too : "her heart is set (iduia) upon utter wickedness" [35].

We denote a slight tendency to a more special or specialized kind of knowing when we see that eidenai may also mean 'bearing witness'. The knowledge one has then serves to affirm something solemnly; here we are getting out of the reach of purely factual and commonplace knowledge. This knowledge is still there, of course, but a dimension is added to it. "Hereto be Earth my witness and the broad Heaven above", says Hera, "with winged words" [36]. In a small number of cases it is said expressly that this knowledge is private and does not need to be communicated; one then knows something 'in his heart'. Here eidenai comes near to noein. "Of myself I know in my heart (thumooi noeoo) and understand (oida) each thing, the good and the evil" [37]. A remarkable case is Od. II, 211/212 where the basic meaning and this more special meaning are juxtaposed : "that you may yourself know in your heart (= personal knowledge) and that the Achaeans may know (= common knowledge)".

Sometimes eidenai can come to mean a knowledge that is more interior and spiritual than the purely factual and technical; it then signifies to have insight, a deeper awareness. A very fine instance is that of the ships of the Phaeacians which "of themselves understand the thoughts and minds of men" [38]. Another good indication that eidenai may also refer to higher things is Od. XIV, 365/366 where Eumaeus states about the return of Odysseus : "I know well regarding the return of my master that he is utterly hated by all gods". In a negative sense it is used in Od. II, 385/386 to refer to the wooers of Penelope, who are "in no wise prudent and just, nor do they know anything of death and black fate which really is near at hand for them".

In a small number of cases eidenai means information that is not normally accessible to man. "I know that when you go hence from the house of Hades you will touch at Aeaen island with your well-built ship'" this is what Elpenor, the first spirit he meets in the underworld, tells Odysseus [39]. And Achilles sighs : "Well I know even of myself that it is my fate to perish here" [40]; here the hero possesses knowledge about the future that is passed on to him by his divine mother. In cases such as these the meaning of eidenai approaches that of gignooskein.

I conclude this section with the one or two cases in which the meaning of eidenai is more or less equal to that of gignooskein. First a proverb that is cited more than once : "When it is done even a fool gets understanding" = to be wise after the event. And a still stronger example : "We (Odysseus and Penelope) have knowledge which we two alone know, signs hidden from others" [41]; here secret knowledge is meant. We shall see later that the same sentence is repeated, but then with a form of gignooskein. Even in this passage this verb is not far away, for Penelope says in vs. 109 that she and her husband "shall surely know (ghnoosometh') one another more certainly". In one verse eidenai and gignooskein are clearly equivalents; here perhaps something like esoteric knowledge is meant. It is Il. VIII, 17/18 where Zeus is speaking to the gathering of the gods : "Then you shall know (gnooset') how far the mightiest I am of all the gods. Nay, come, make trial, you gods, that you all may know (eidete)".

Summing up the result of this first and longest part of our investigation, we may safely conclude that the most frequent and general, and therefore the most basic, meaning of eidenai is 'to have knowledge of a factual or technical kind'. However, in a restricted number of cases there is a divergence from this basic significance : 1. to be minded, to be of a mind, to brood; 2. to bear witness; 3. to have inner knowledge; 4. to have insight or understanding; 5. sometimes generalized into 'to be wise'; 6. to have a foreboding or foreknowledge; 7. to possess secret knowledge. We shall now see that Homer also uses other verbs for all those special meanings of eidenai.

b. Homer's use of epistasthai

Let us start with the least complicated of these, epistasthai. This verb recurs thirty times in all. To it we must add the adverb 'epistamenoos' which we find fourteen times; in each of these cases it means 'able, skilful, capable', especially 'skilled, workmanlike, professional'. "Cunningly he smoothed all the planks, and made them straight to the line"; here one sees Odysseus working as a carpenter [42]. In Il. V, 60/61 Pherecles is mentioned "who was skilled (epistato) in all manner of handicraft". Il. V, 222/223 even shows a horse "well skilled to course fleetly over the plain".

A very interesting case is Il. XIII, 222/223 where the difference between epistasthai and gignooskein becomes evident. "There is no man now at fault so far as I know (gignooskoo); for we are all skilled (epistametha) in war". Still clearer evidence yet of the difference between these verbs we find in Od. XIII, 312/313 where Odysseus says to Athena : "Hard it is, goddess, for a mortal man to know (gnoonai) you when he meets you, however wise (epistamenooi) he may be". For to recognize a god at sight is a thing beyond the competence of mortals.

c. Homer's use of 'phronein'

We may now turn to 'phronein' which, with its one hundred and nine instances, is more frequent than epistasthai. The basic meaning of this verb in Homer is 'to think or to have an opinion'. "I must necessarily speak my word outright, just as I am minded (= as I think)", says Achilles in Il. IX, 309/310. And Menelaus speaks likewise in Il. III,98 : "My mind (= my opinion) is that Argives and Trojans now be parted".

A few times phronein is identical with gignooskein, while noein is not far away too : "I see (gignooskoo), I give heed (phroneoo), this you ask of somebody with understanding (noeonti)" [43]. A similar connection exists in Il. XXIII, 305 : "A wise man (phroneoon) gave counsel to one who himself has knowledge (noeonti)". The verb can sometimes mean 'to be wily'. A remarkable verse is Il. XXII, 59 where we seem to find Descartes' 'cogito, ergo sum' : "Have compassion on me who still can think (phroneonta)", that is 'me who am still living' [44]. Thus Priamus implores his son Hector.

Very often the basic meaning of phronein deviates somewhat towards 'to be minded, to dispose, to brood on'. "He it was who with good intention (euphroneoon) addressed their assembly" [45]; we see "Odysseus pondering in his heart evil for the wooers" [46], and Apollo "thinking thoughts of bane for him (Patroclus)" [47]. A variation on this theme is 'to have a high idea of yourself' or 'to be in high spirits' : "with high heart (mega phroneoon) Hector strode among the foremost" [48].

In conclusion it seems to me that phronein is a 'compact' verb; it has a basic meaning with only slight variations from it. Therefore it does not rub shoulders with other verbs for knowing and thinking; rather it stands alone.

d. Homer's use of noein

Can the same be said of noein? This verb in its different forms occurs 141 times in Homer's work, considerably more often than phronein. This time there is also a noun, 'noŭs', used by Homer 107 times. This means 'mind, thought, thinking-capacity, intellect, plan, intention, way of thinking, disposition'. The meaning of the verb noein is often very much akin to that of phronein, but it has a tendency to go into the direction of thinking with a practical effect, whereas phronein denotes more often an 'inward' manner of thought (in so far as the word 'inward' may be applied to the musings of Homeric heroes). Von Fritz describes the meaning of noein as 'becoming aware of a situation'; "the realization, for instance, that this brown patch is not only a human being but an enemy lying in ambush" [49].

In one or two cases noein signifies simply 'to think', just like phronein. "I have such thoughts in my mind and will give such counsel, as I would devise for myself" [50]. Hera says to Poseidon : "Shaker of the Earth, of your own self take counsel in your heart" [51]. From here it can easily come to mean 'to understand'. Diomedes says regarding Odysseus : "Wise above all he is in understanding (noĕsai)" [52] in which line 'wise above all' is the translation of 'peri oide'. Odysseus has the knack of understanding. In a few instances the difference with eidein is barely perceptible. "Of myself I know (noeoo) in my heart and understand (oida) ech thing" [53].

However, such abstract meanings are the exception. Frequently it means, in a practical sense, 'to think out, to devise, to invent'; this indicates a line of thought that ends in a tangible effect. "No man beside me shall devise a better thought than I have in my mind", the speaker is, of course, Nestor [54]. "I am not able to plan all things wisely", says young Telemachus [55]. The practical side of noein is brought out in Od. V, 170 where Calypso tells Odysseus : "They (the gods) are mightier than I, both to purpose (noêsai) and to fulfil (krênai)", and perhaps still more in Il. XXIII, 415 where we hear Antilochus speaking to his horses : "Run after them with all speed, and this will I myself contrive (technêsomai) and plan (noêsoo)".

Nevertheless, I do not see these several meanings as the basic significance of noein. In 85 out of 141 entries noein means 'to perceive, to be aware of'; since this adds up to 65 % of the cases I take this to be the basic meaning in Homer. It seems a far cry from 'think' to 'see', but I believe the connection is this. In all those cases noein means 'to know for a fact', as in many uses of oida, that is to arrive at a mental conclusion. "Neither did she (Andromache) know otherwise than that ... Athena had laid him low by the hand of Achilles" [56].

But whereas the use of oida stresses the mental or inner side of the process, noein puts the accent on the outer side : to arrive at a (mental) conclusion by means of the senses, mainly by seeing. The word 'to see' must therefore be taken as a kind of shorthand or as a circumlocution of what the whole process means.

The far more frequent employment of the verb runs like this. "She made a sign with her brows, and goodly Odysseus perceived it" [57]. Even the gods see (with their eyes). "Whomsoever I (says Zeus) shall mark (noêsoo) having different plans from those of the gods to go and bear aid to either Trojans or Danaäns (Greeks) ..." [58]. This differs in no way from Agamemnon's threat : "Whomsoever I shall see (noêsoo) having an idea to tarry apart from the fight beside the beaked ships ..." [59].

Sometimes the identification with the irregular aorist of the verb 'horan', 'eidon', is complete. "Telemachus did not see (iden) her (Athena), or notice (enoêsen) her" [60]. However, a slight difference is perhaps indicated in Il. X, 550, where Murray's translation runs as follows : "Never yet I saw (idon) such horses neither thought (enoêsa) of such". One cannot be quite sure, of course, whether Nestor, who is speaking here, means that he was comparing these horses to an ideal or had actually never perceived them in reality (in the Budé translation 'ni vu ni entrevu').

The range of meanings of noein is extensive. It stretches from 'to think' (as a mental operation) to 'to see' (sensory perception). It sometimes comes very near to some meanings of eidenai or of phronein, but generally speaking, it has few connections with similar verbs and is leading a life of its own.

e. Homer's use of 'gignooskein'

Finally, we have the verb 'gignooskein'. Homer uses it 126 times in all (out of eight hundred entries with words for knowing). This frequency lies in the middle between epistasthai and phronein with their lesser frequencies (respectively thirty and one hundred and nine), and noein and eidenai with their higher frequencies (respectively one hundred and forty-one and three hundred and fifty-five). If we set eidenai apart as the verb with the most general meaning, then gignooskein is the most frequently used verb except one (noein). But noein too is a verb with a rather broad meaning; if we take this into account, we may conclude that gignooskein is the most frequently used of the three more 'specialized' verbs. It was worth the trouble to write out, as I did in the course of my research, all the Homeric citations with forms of gignooskein one after another. This labour has proved rewarding since, by considering each usage, one perceives that Homer uses gignooskein in a sense different from all other verbs. The basic meaning surely is 'to know', but not really 'to know for a fact' or 'to detect with the eyes'.

Snell states that in Homer gignooskein does not yet indicate a sort of knowledge that is connected with effort or reflexion [61]. Von Fritz sees gignooskein as opposed to noein; according to him, gignooskein designates a simpler and noein a more complex form of awareness [62]. But Lesher writes that "noein can on occasion designate simple objects of recognition, and gignooskein a more complicated realization of what one has seen and recognized" [63]. We shall see that, if not effort, then anyhow some retardation in the process of recognition is apparent.

Mader [64] gives as the verb's basic meanings : to acknowledge, either the identity of persons or objects, mainly to recognize either a hitherto unkown person or a not immediately recognized state of affairs (purposes, intentions, characters, properties, situations, spiritual contents). It always denotes "a mental effort but ... closely connected with sense perception". But "when an object is hard to identify, it is mostly seen as a spontaneous act".

Mader then specifies as follows. 1. Recognition of a (person's) identity, of somebody one knows already, but also recognition from a great distance, after prolonged observation. It can occasionally mean drawing a conclusion, in particular when a person or object is yet unknown or hard to identify. In both cases the conclusion has a spontaneous character. 2. To acknowledge that somebody or something belongs to a certain group or kind, but to a different one than seemed apparent at first sight (for instance, not a man but a god, not just a bird but an omen). This too happens mostly spontaneously. 3. To recognize momentaneous intentions, etc. or the nature of persons. This hardly is a result of sense perception. 4. To recognize spiritual, mental, or similar contents, to distinguish truth from lies, for instance in prophecies and declarations.

We must keep in mind that, pace Snell, gignooskein involves mental (but not intellectual) effort, spontaneity, sudden insight, recognition of identities and inward states, discernment. In order to handle the ample material more easily, I shall group the relevant and most revealing texts under three headings : 1. distinction; 2. discernment; 3. recognition.

f. Distinction

A great many times gignooskein may indicate a distinction between several persons or phenomena or events. When Odysseus has entered his own palace in the guise of a beggar, "Athena roused him to go among the wooers and gather bits of bread, and learn which of them were righteous and which lawless" [65]. In the Iliad (II.348/349) Nestor implores Agamemnon to go on fighting for the Greek cause, although there may be a few comrades who secretly plan "to depart for Argos before we have learned (gnoomenai) whether the promise of Zeus who bears the aegis is a lie or no".

There are one or two 'neutral' cases of such distinctions, for instance when nobody could discern "with which of the two hosts (Diomedes) was joined, whether it was with the Trojans that he had fellowship or with the Achaeans, for he stormed across the plain like a winter torrent" [66]. But in nearly all other cases the difference is one in quality, and mostly in moral quality; there are two sets of people then or two phenomena, one of which is seen as superior to the other. The most telling example of this is Od. XXII,373 where Odysseus says to Medon of his son Telemachus : "He has delivered you and saved you, that you may know in your heart and tell also to others how far better it is to do good deeds instead of evil ones". Wily Odysseus becomes downright moralistic here! I call this a telling example, because here we have the opposition of good and evil.

g. Discernment

More often than not the meaning of gignooskein has something to do with insight, discernment, deeper understanding. In Il. I,411-413 Achilles wishes that Agamemnon 'may know' his blindness ('atên'), "because he in no way honoured the best of the Achaeans" (e.g. himself, Achilles does not fail in self-respect); to know your atê certainly is a mark of insight. In Il. VI,230/231 Diomedes wishes "that these men too may know (gnoosin) that we declare them to be friends from our fathers' days"; here we have a connection with a solemn declaration. In another verse Achilles proposes a way "that we may yet further know what purpose the Trojans have in mind" [67]; here the reference is to something the Trojans may be secretly planning. To Poseidon, Zeus says : "You know ... the purpose in my heart", even if he has not yet spoken about it [68]. In these instances the knowledge meant is an insight into the minds of other people, or even into the purposes of gods.

A very fine example of discernment is to be found in the first book of the Odyssey. Telemachus, Odysseus' son, who thinks his father lost and dead, very courteously welcomes a stranger, a certain Mentes, king of the Taphians, to the palace in Ithaca. This royal visitor tells the prince in private that his father lives and will return home soon. After this communication the man disappears as mysteriously and suddenly as he has arrived. Having returned among the wooers, Telemachus is asked by one of them, Eurymachus, who this stranger really was; "he seemed no base man to look upon". Telemachus answers that the visitor was a friend of his father's, King Mentes of the Taphians. "But in his heart he knew the immortal goddess". She was indeed Athena sent to Ithaca by Zeus himself to prepare the young man for the home-coming of his father [69]. The Greek words used are 'phresi ... egnoo', inwardly he knew.

A still more remarkable thing is said by Athena to Diomedes. The goddess exhorts the hero not to fight any disguised god on the battlefield, with the exception of Aphrodite (whom she hates heartily). In order to make this possible for him, "I have taken", she says, "the mist from your eyes that afore was upon them, to the end that you may well discern (eu gignooskeis) both god and man" [70]. This shows that such discernment is not the result of normal eyesight. As a consequence of this suprahuman faculty, he immediately recognizes (gignooskoo) Athena holding the yoke of his horses during a fight, and also somewhat later Ares who has come to the help of the Trojans [71]. This verse brings us to the element of recognition in gignooskein.

h. Recognition

Aristotle wisely said that "the Odyssey is full of 'discoveries'", by which he meant (sudden) recognitions [72]. This work, indeed, relates several fascinating stories of such recognitions; we think, of course, of those moments when the hero, disguised as a beggar, has returned to Ithaca and there not only meets his former servants but also his son and his faithful wife Penelope. However, the only one to recognize him at first sight is his old dog Argos. The poor neglected animal "wagged his tail and dropped both his ears" on seeing his master but lacks the strength to move nearer to him [73]. It should attract our attention that here, for the dog's recognition noein (enoêsen) rather than gignooskein is used. Animals obviously are not capable of this sudden illumination. But neither the old swineherd Eumaeus (who continuously addresses Odysseus as 'stranger' and 'old man') nor the king's aged nurse Eurycleia nor even Penelope and her son Telemachus recognize him straightway; for each of them it is a long process.

The first to discover the beggar's real identity is Telemachus. The prince meets him in Eumaeus' hut; he too addresses him as 'stranger'. When the swineherd has gone to the city, Athena appears, touches the beggar with her golden wand, and changes him into the imposing figure of King Odysseus. But even then the son refuses to admit that this man is his father. It is only when Odysseus has affirmed over and over again that he really is Odysseus, that the boy throws himself into his father's arms. "And they wailed aloud ...". Nowhere in this long passage [74] is the verb gignooskein employed, in all probability because there is no sudden illumination or an inward vision. Telemachus has to be persuaded with difficulty that this man is really his father the king.

We read one of the most moving scenes in all literature in Book XIX in the Odyssey where Homer describes how Odysseus' former nurse Eurycleia discovers her master's identity. Penelope who still has no idea of this orders her to wash the feet of her poor guest. The nurse, looking attentively at the beggar, observes that she has never seen anyone more alike Odysseus than him. Recognition obviously is at hand but does not yet materialize. As soon as she has begun to wash his legs, she discovers a scar just above the knee. Here the word 'egnoo' is used because she immediately knows how this scar was caused and, in consequence, who this man is in reality.

But now something happens that will astonish the modern reader. Homer has used forty lines to bring up his tale to this point, and now we expect the climax, Eurycleia full of joy recognizing the king. But there is nothing of the kind. Instead of depicting the reaction of the old woman, the poet, in a flash-back of seventy-five lines, relates how young Odysseus long ago has sustained this scar. It was caused by a boar wounding him with his tusk during a hunt.

In his masterpiece 'Mimesis' [75], Auerbach wrote that for Homer it must have been an intolerable thought that this scar would light up suddenly against the dark background of an unexplained past. The reader (or rather hearer) would ask 'whence this scar?' Therefore, its origin must be explained broadly and at the poet's ease and discretion.

Valuable though this is, there could be yet another reason. The long digression into the past also serves to mark what happens in that moment of recognition by the nurse in which she recovers the whole person of her master with all his past. And her own too, for the flashback tells not only the story of that infelicitous hunting-party but also how he was born and given a name. Here Eurycleia, the nurse, is mentioned. This convincingly exemplifies what is meant by gignooskein (for this word is used here).

It is only after we have been informed in detail about that hunt and its consequences, that we are transported back to the old woman who, with the leg between her hands, suddenly 'knew' (egnoo) by the touch. She is so surprised that she lets the foot fall into the basin which overturns and spills the water on the floor. Weeping and with choking voice she touches Odysseus' chin saying : "Really you are Odysseus, dear child, and I knew (egnoo) you not till I had handled the body of my lord" [76].

In comparison, the scene in which Eumaeus recognizes his lord is extremely short. Only shortly before the slaughter in the great hall is about to begin, and at the moment that the swineherd utters a prayer 'to all the gods' that his master may once return, Odysseus reveals himself saying : "Here I am, yes I myself". And as a proof he throws off his rags and shows his scar, "so that you know me for certain (gnooton)" [77].

The series of recognitions at the end of the Odyssey reaches its climax when Penelope at last discovers the true identity of her humble visitor. Always looking forward to her husband's return, she confidently says to her son that she will doubtless recognize Odysseus on his homecoming. "We two shall surely know (gnoosometh') one another more certainly, for we have signs hidden from others" [78]. Here the difference between gignooskein and eidenai becomes clear. Husband and wife have knowledge (eidenai) of special signs that, although hidden from others, is factual knowledge for them; with the help of this knowledge they will recognize (gignooskein) each other 'in the mind'.

Nevertheless, for a long time her eyes remain blinded. When she has a long conversation with Odysseus in the hall of her palace concerning the fate of her husband, she does not see through his beggarly guise, although she treats him with respect. At the end he assures her that Odysseus is safe and will be back soon, but she finds it hard to believe this. Later, during the scene of the foot-washing, Penelope does not understand what is happening, for "Athena had turned her thoughts away" [79].

During the night that follows Odysseus has a foreboding of the coming event. From the place where he is lying he hears Penelope weeping, and of course he knows why she cries. "And it seemed to his heart that she knew him (kata thumon gignooskousa) and was standing by his head" [80].

After the terrific scene of the bloody slaughter in the great hall among the suitors of Penelope, Eurycleia goes to the upper chamber where her mistress is asleep and tells her that her husband is back. The woman's answer is : "Dear nurse, the gods have made you mad" [81]. Having descended to the hall, she sits down opposite Odysseus "in the light of the fire, ... she sat long in silence ... and again she failed to know him (agnoosaske)", because he had again draped himself in his beggar's rags [82].

Even when Odysseus has taken a bath and has put on a fine cloak and a tunic, his wife keeps aloof and gives orders to spread a bed for the stranger "outside the bridal chamber which he made himself" [83]. This mention of the bedstead gives Odysseus the opportunity to speak of 'the things which we two alone know', namely that long ago, when he was building the bedroom with his own hands, he had constructed the bed on the trunk of an olive tree. This becomes the moment of great recognition. "Her heart melted, and she knew (anagnousêi) the sure tokens which Odysseus had told her. Then with a burst of tears she ran straight to him, and flung her arms about the neck of Odysseus and kissed him"[84]. After much effort and hesitation her eyes are opened at last. And now they enter their bedchamber and have 'their fill of the joy of love'[85].

It is remarkable that, whereas this kind of recognition always points to a very special knowledge, in Homer it never gets the meaning it can have in Hebrew, that of 'carnal knowledge', or sexual intercourse. The kind of knowledge that is indicated by gignooskein in Homer is exemplified in the friendship between Odysseus and Iphitus. Long ago the two had exchanged presents; on that occasion Iphitus had given to Odysseus the famous bow with which he later plays havoc with his enemies. But although they were great friends, "they never knew one another at the table", because Iphitus met an untimely death [86]. Perhaps this constitutes a kind of equivalent to the biblical meaning : real human friendship should be consolidated in a 'sacramental' way, in Homer by sharing a meal together [87]. Only then does one know one's friend. Concerning carnal knowledge the difference in meaning is probably caused by the fact that in the Old Testament the relationship between husband and wife is much more important than that between comrades in arms as in the Iliad.

The kind of knowledge I am speaking of becomes still more special if it is a god or goddess who is recognized. To Athena the bewildered Odysseus says : "Hard it is, goddess, for a mortal man to know you when he meets you, however wise he may be"[88]. Here the difference between gignooskein and epistasthai is spelled out; however competent (mal' epistamenos) a man may be, that does not enable him to recognize a divine person (gnoonai) at first sight. Somewhere else Diomedes is only able to 'know' Athena after she has spoken to him [89]. Sometimes there is no recognition. "Yet you did not know (egnoos) Pallas Athena, daughter of Zeus, even me who ever stand by your side and guard you in all your toils", says Athena reprovingly to Odysseus [90].

During Odysseus' descent into Hades he meets his old comrades, but they are all shades and ghosts. There, in the underworld, the power of recognition is blurred to such an extent that magical means are necessary to open the eyes of the deceased. They recognize him indeed, but only after they have drunk the sacrificial blood. Even Odysseus' own mother Anticleia can only recognize her son after having tasted "the dark blood, and at once she knew me" [91].

j. Conclusions

The result of this investigation is that in Homer gignooskein is a verb that stands clearly apart from the other four. In epistasthai, the least used of the five verbs, we find the most simple form of knowledge; it means 'to possess a skill, to be able to'. Eidenai, the most frequently used, is the basic and universal verb for 'to know'. If often denotes 'common knowledge' but also factual knowledge of specified things and events. It may occasionally denote an inner disposition of the mind or heart; along this road it can even come to mean an interior or spiritual knowledge.

Phronein, too, can signify 'to be minded, to be disposed', but its usual meaning is 'to think, to have an opinion'. It seems that phronein is more abstract : to arrive at a mental conclusion, but not by means of the senses. In this verb it is a more intellectual activity that is indicated. Noein has more practical meanings. At the edges the meanings of these two verbs are (nearly) identical, so that the one may be used for the other. But it is no tombola. I have, for instance, found no instances in which phronein has the same meaning as epistasthai.

The same applies to gignooskein; there are some (only a few) instances in which its meaning is nearly the same as that of phronein or eidenai. But most often, nearly always, a kind of special knowledge is meant. In the way it is used one can always detect a mental operation, but not of an intellectual or logical kind. The knowledge that is attained is not the product of sensory perception nor of reasoning or abstract thinking; it springs from sudden insight, sometimes even from a sort of revelation. It is a reading of the future, of other people's minds, of signs and tokens, of the intentions of the gods; it is also an understanding of what fate has in store for one. It is the art of making (intuitive) distinctions, often between one person and another (recognition); in the realm of moral categories we must call it discernment, with discernment of the difference between good and evil as the climactic one.

Let us now stake out whether Homer is using the verb gignooskein in a way that resembles that of the later Gnostics or the uses to which Plato puts the word gnosis. As I said already, we must content ourselves with gignooskein because the poet has no noun gnosis. Now first of all, one thing must be stated very clearly. The significance which is the kernel of the Gnostic word 'gnosis' is completely lacking in Homer. There is not the slightest indication in his work that knowledge may bring salvation to man, that it has a redemptive function. It would have been very remarkable indeed if this had been the case. For then we would have discovered an authentic Gnostic eight hundred years before the Gnosis began to develop!

However, the Homeric gignooskein does denote a special kind of knowledge, called 'mysteriosophic' knowledge by me at the beginning of this section; it then has a meaning different from other, more down-to-earth kinds of knowledge. Even in Homer this verb is often the key to penetrating into a mystery. There is such a mystery about Odysseus when he has returned to his native island. Nobody recognizes him, but slowly he becomes discernible for his relatives and his loyal servants alone. Early in the Odyssey, this mysterious element is very striking during his descent into Hades, when the spirits are only able to recognize him after partaking in the blood ritual. It is also present in the meetings of humans with gods or goddesses; these sometimes acquire the character of a sudden enlightenment.

This last instance is already pointing in the direction of that 'élitist' tendency of Gnostic knowledge : it puts a person apart from others because of his special insights. It is rarely an insight that makes one happy. On the contrary, the knowledge some people have of what fate has in store for them, makes them afraid. This is a kind of knowledge common mortals normally do not possess. Sometimes it takes a god or goddess to assist somebody in acquiring such an insight. Most of the time those who know are much better qualified than others to make distinctions in quality and especially in moral quality. This makes them different from the common run who have less discernment in this respect. Here we remember that the ability to separate good from evil was the great asset of the Gnostics.

Of secret, esoteric knowledge, only to be gained by means of (divine) revelation, we do not find much in Homer. But there is one notable exception : Odysseus' descent into Hades to which is dedicated the whole Book XI, the Nekyia. There, in the underworld, Odysseus hears and sees things no living mortal can experience before his death.

There is another, more pragmatic secret in the Odyssey, one that plays a great, even decisive role, the secret of Odysseus' and Penelope's bedstead. Several servants and Telemachus have already recognized their master and father but Penelope's eyes remain veiled, although she has spoken face to face with her husband in the palace. As long as he does not mention the secret between them, she is not able to recognize him. Odysseus mentions it only after he has slaughtered the suitors, and then it leads to immediate recognition. We saw that the fact of being informed about the secret was indicated with the word eidenai (for to them both it was no secret, of course). But their real knowledge of each other crowned by recognition and reunification is indicated by the word gignooskein. In this jubilant episode it is the possession and sharing of secret knowledge that leads to happiness and solves all problems. And this is the nearest as one can get in Homer to the redemptive knowledge of the Gnosis.

4. Homer and the Greek mind

I have been very detailed in my treatment of the Homeric epics because, according to a word of Plato, the Greeks were of the opinion that Homer "has educated the Hellenes" [92]. "Right from the beginning all have learned according to Homer", said Xenophanes [93]. Every Greek knew his works and the stories he had told, not a few of them by heart, either from reading or far more often from hearing them recited.

Mothers told them to their infants standing at their knees. Not only his mythology and his tales but no less his way of expressing himself, his images and Homeric comparisons, his proverbial sayings and his choice of words, made a deep and lasting impression on the mind and mentality of the Hellenes. By the same token his peculiar use of gignooskein will, at least unconsciously, have influenced the idea the Greeks had of knowledge. His was the basic and initial influence and therefore the lasting one. We may deal with other authors and thinkers more briefly.

5. Words for 'knowing' in Hesiod

In the poems of Hesiod the harvest is less rich. In his works, including the fragments, words for 'knowing' occur ninety-six times in all [94]. This poet's favourite word is 'eidenai', in its various forms occurring in three-quarters of the entries with knowledge-verbs (73 times). Next comes noein with a bare fourteen, gignooskein and phronein with four each, and finally epistasthai that occurs only once.

Forms of eidenai occur twenty-one times in the Theogony, fourteen in the Works, eight in the Shield of Heracles, and twenty-eight in the fragments. According to the Lexicon Hesiodeum it means 'to see, to regard' (voir, regarder) and in the perfect tense 'to know, to be acquainted with" (savoir, connnaître). With this verb we are on the practical side of knowledge, as the following line proves : "The fool does not know (oid') that there are a hundred timbers to a waggon" [95]. This refers to the concretely practical. The mental aspect is stressed in this verse : "Men call him (Nereus) the Old Man because he is trusty and gentle and does not forget the laws of righteousness, but thinks (oiden) just and kindly thoughts" [96].

Phronein, which occurs only rarely, means transitively 'to understand, to intend, to project' (comprendre, projeter), and intransitively 'to have thoughts or intentions, to be sensible or wise'. "Though they (Heracles and Iphicles) were (twin) brothers, these were not of one spirit (ou kath' homa phroneonte)" [97].

Noein is used somewhat more frequently; it means 'to perceive' (percevoir), to have an idea of, to have a right idea, to understand (comprendre)'. "The father of the gods (Zeus) was quick to perceive it", namely that he was dangerously threatened by the monster Typhoeus [98].

We must remain content with only one mention of epistasthai : "...so that all may be able (epistoont') to do what is fashionable" [99].

Gignooskein is sparsely used, once in the Theogony and in the fragments respectively, and twice in the Works. "Whoever knows the right and is ready to speak it, far-seeing Zeus gives him prosperity" [100]. It is a feat of great discernment to know what is right; it brings near to the divine sphere. This element, which in the following entry is the discernment of a god, is worded in this way : "(Zeus) saw (gnoo) and failed not to perceive (egnoiese) the trick of Prometheus" [101]. Awareness after an effort is shown by this line : "Only when he has suffered, does the fool (Hesiod's brother Perses) learn (that Justice is stronger than Hubris)" [102]. The kind of knowledge referred to is not of the practical kind but belongs to the moral order. That gignooskein denotes a higher plane of knowing, in the form of deep insight, is proved by this line from a fragment of the Catalogue of Women : "He (Sisyphus) knew (egnoo) nothing at all of the mind of shield-bearing Zeus" [103].

The few times that Hesiod employs gignooskein do not admit hard and fast conclusions, except, perhaps, that he seems not to deviate from the line of Homer since his instances of gignooskein indicate discernment, not of a practical kind but of a higher, or moral, order in which we are either on the verge of the divine sphere or even within it. The Lexicon Hesiodeum gives, theferore, as its first meaning 'to discern' (discerner), and further 'to know, to understand' (comprendre).

6. 'Know yourself'

Remaining in this ambience, I feel perfectly entitled to cite the famous Delphic maxim 'gnoothi sauton', know yourself, that, according to Snell, is of considerable antiquity [104]. It does not refer, as a modern would be quick to think, to self-knowledge of the practical psychological kind. Its significance, to use the words of Snell, is : "Open your eyes, then you will see what you are : a human being and not a god". Once again discernment of a higher order, relating to the sphere of the divine, is meant.

7. Words for 'knowing' in some lyric poets

a. Archilochus

Forms of the verb occur in the lyric poet Archilochus who lived in the seventh century B.V. and who was the forefather of all 'angry young men' [105]. There are only two entries with gignooskein. The first time it means 'to understand well'. "Let them understand well (gnoothi) what I care to tell them" [106]. The second time there is a broader meaning. The poet is speaking to himself, to his 'thumos' or 'heart' advising himself to follow a moderate course. And he concludes : "Learn (ginooske) the rhythm that determines the life of men" [107]. Snell remarks here that whereas in Homer the organ is discernment is the noüs, the brain, in Archilochus it is the 'thumos', the 'heart', feeling [108]. The poet gives his thumos a command which implies some effort.

Archilochus' use of other verbs for knowing does not differ from that in Homer and Hesiod, 'phronein' meaning 'to think', 'eidenai' 'to know for a fact', and 'epistasthai 'to be able to'. Noein does not appear [109].

b. Solon

The incomparable Snell draws our attention to a two-line fragment of an elegy by Solon. "It is very difficult to discern that hidden measure of wisdom that alone contains the end of all things" [110]. For 'knowing' two verbs are used here; they are even contrasted. In 'to discern the hidden measure', discern is the translation of noêsai; we know that the verb noein indicates normal mental activity often if not always based on sensory perception which in this case proves insufficient. Here there can be no sense perception since the object (the 'measure of wisdom') is unseen, concealed, secret (aphanes). Beyond the reach of the brain there is, therefore, an area of wisdom. This wisdom is decribed by the noun 'gnoomosunê', knowledge or wisdom, a word that is derived from gignooskein.

As far as I know this is the first time that this word is employed. This is an important step since not only it is etymologically akin to 'gnosis' but has almost the same meaning here it had for the Gnostics. This qualification is given in the subordinate clause : "(Wisdom) which alone contains the ends (peirata) of all things". The fragment being so pitifully short, it is not at all clear what is meant exactly. But one thing is certain : this wisdom reaches to the limits of everything, of the universe that is. It is at once esoteric, all-comprising, and determinant [111]. In another fragment the word gignooskein itself appears : "I am aware (ginooskoo) - and pain lies deep in my heart - that I behold the oldest land of Ionia tottering" [112]. We do not know to what situation these lines refer but obviously something visionary is meant.

c. Pindar

The verses of other lyric poets yield very little for our subject, mainly because they are all extant only in a fragmentary state. But the four books of odes by Pindar, the last and greatest of them, who lived during the first half of the fifth century B.C., are nearly complete; furthermore, there is a growing body of fragments [113]. In his poems epistasthai, occurring three times, means 'to know to', phronein 'to be minded, to think' (six times), and noein (four times) 'to observe, to be aware of, to intend'. With its twenty-six occurrences eidenai is far more conspicuously present, mainly meaning 'to know for a fact, to be certain of' [114].

Pindar has no noun 'gnosis' but forms of gi(g)nooskein appear fifteen times. In his texts too this verb stands somewhat apart from the others. We are still close to the more pedestrian meanings when the indignant poet, who came from Boeotia, known among the Greeks for a boorish country, exclaims : "Let us see whether we will be able (gnoonai) to expel that vile old notion of the 'Boeotian swine'" [115]. But soon enough recognition comes into play.

When Jason, after a twenty-year absence, returns to his native country, all admire him but nobody knows (ginooskon) him. Could he be a god? But then Pellas arrives, the usurper of the crown, and perceives the conspicuous (arignooton) sole sandal on Jason's right foot, the sure sign that this young man is the legitimate pretender to the throne. As soon as his old father Aeson has come he recognizes (egnon) his son [116].

More than once gignooskein in Pindar signifies recognition with the connotation of acknowledging the value of somebody or something. "Threefold Olympic is the house I am praising, for I recognize (gnoosomai) it for the prosperous Corinth ..., the portico of Isthmian Poseidon, mother of young heroes. There resides Eunomia (= good laws), with her sister steadfast Justice, the support of cities, and her other sister, Peace, dispenser of riches, all three golden daughters of wise Themis" [117]. Once again we are close to the sphere of the divine. Some sort of identification is suggested by this line : "Now show (know, gnoothi) the wisdom of an Oedipus" [118].

There is no need to go into the meaning of other knowledge-verbs in Pindar; they do not differ from what we have seen already.

8. Words for 'knowledge' in the Tragedians

Turning now to the Tragic poets, we must first of all state that not one of the three has the word 'gnosis'.

a. Aeschylus

In Aeschylus the verb gignooskein, in its different forms, occurs seventeen times [119]. We find a slight variant of the Delphic maxim when Oceanus prompts Prometheus 'to know himself' (gignooske sauton), that is, who he is compared with Zeus [120]. Discernment is meant when the leader of the chorus tells Agamemnon that "he (the king) will learn (gnoosei) who behaved loyally and who in a troublesome way (during his absence)" [121]. And Clytemnestra addresses the chorus in this way : "If the godhead decides differently, you will be taught wisdom and know (gnooei) it later" [122]. Here the divine sphere and knowledge or wisdom are connected.

In the 'Choephoroi' the nurse says that Orestes is dead, but the leader of the chorus rebukes her : "Not yet; it would be a bad prophet who would form that judgment (gnoie)" [123]. Prophetic insight is meant in this line; deep insight is also expressed in these words : : "Know the hubris of human beings" [124], just as in Prometheus' dejected saying : "My allotted doom I needs must bear as lightly as I may, knowing (gignooskoon) that the might of Necessity brooks no resistance" [125].

b. Sophocles

In the body of Sophoclean plays gignooskein occurs ninety-one times. In Sophocles the verbs for knowing carry their usual meanings with, once again, gignooskein standing apart. It always denotes a more than practical knowledge or one that cannot be put into practice immediately. The difference with common knowledge is well brought out by a line in 'Oedipus in Colonus' (852) : "For hereafter, I know (for a fact, oid'), you shall come to know (gnoosei, understand) all this".

The element of recognition is still present. The blinded Oedipus says to the chorus : "I clearly recognize your voice although I am wrapped in darkness" [126]. Sharp discernment is meant when Philoctetes says to Neoptolemus : "I know you (=I see right through you), you will destroy me with your counsels" [127]. This discernment often comes after an effort or a lapse of time : (Creon is speaking) "In due time you will surely learn (gnoosei) this : time will only show a man as just but to recognize somebody as bad one day suffices" [128].

Gignooskein often refers to a situation that is beyond the reach of our perception. "Don't you see you are in great danger?", says the old paedagogue to Electra and Orestes [129]. Or it is used in expressions that resemble proverbs. In Antigone 188, Creon speaks of "remembering (gignooskoon') that our country is the ship that bears us safe". Addressing her sister Chrysothemis, Electra says : "Be mindful (gignooskous') of this that an ignoble life brings shame upon the noble (=noblesse oblige)" 130.

Still higher, even esoteric forms of knowledge are also found. The seer Tiresias prophesies to King Creon : "You shall learn (gnooseis) (your fate), when you hear the warnings of my art" [131]. The finest example of how remote in Sophocles the significance of gignooskein is from practical knowledge and sensory perception is a complaint of King Oedipus. A messenger appears relating how the king has blinded himself. He pulled the golden clasps from Queen Jocaste's dress and thrust them into his eyes, crying that he would never again see the horrors that he suffered nor those that he wrought himself. "Let my eyes see in darkness what they should never have seen, failed in knowledge of what I should have known (gnoosoiaoto)" [132]. Here knowledge attainable by keeping one's eyes open is indicated by forms of opsomai (irregular form of horan = to see) and contrasted with the deeper insight Oedipus should have had but did not possess; for this a form of gignooskein is used.

c. Euripides

It need not surprise us that the meanings of gignooskein in Euripides are on the whole somewhat flatter and less 'esoteric' than in Aeschylus and Sophocles. Isn't he the most rationalistic of the Tragedians, the most susceptible to Greek Enlightenment ideas? Connotations of this verb concerning the sphere of the divine and the mysterious are rare, although not wholly absent [133]. Usually it remains somewhat closer to the functions of the other verbs for knowing while, nevertheless, remaining slightly or sometimes even far apart from them. No really deep insight is meant when Phaedra says : "Well I know what it is to be a woman" [134], nor anything particularly profound when Creusa asks Ion which of Delphi's daughters has sucked him and he answers : "I knew never the breast" [135].

A marked difference with idein (to see with one's eyes) is indicated when Ion remarks : "In a man one may often discern (gnoiê), marking (idoon) his bearing, a strain of gentle blood" [136]. Here a mental conclusion is inferred from a visual observation. That there are more meanings than one of knowing is stated in the following manner. Agamemnon is relating that it was his intention to marry his daughter Iphigeneia to Achilles. "Not one of the Achaeans knew thereof (ismen), except Menelaus, Calchas, and Odysseus. What I did not know (egnoon, understand), I shall write in this letter (namely that the marriage should not take place)" [137]. What he means to say is that he is rescinding a decision taken on (ethically) unjust grounds. Eidenai means to know for a fact here, whereas gignooskein stands for a moral decision.

That epistasthai and gignooskein have different meanings appears from this quotation. "That which is good we learn (epistamestha) and recognize (gignooskomen)" [138]. First we experience the good as such and then we jump to a definite conclusion about it. The difference between common learning and intuitive insights is exemplified by these words of Jocaste : "My son, divining (gnous) or of someone told (mathoon), set out to find his parents" [139].

Such superior or uncommon understanding is also expressed when Dionysus says to Agave : "Had you but learnt wisdom" [140], and in this line : "Know your strength and the evils that threaten you" [141]. Knowledge is sometimes generalized and gets a proverbial character. Theseus complains : "O fools, learn the real ills of men, our life is conflict all" [142]. Or the chorus addressing Admetus : "Be sure (gignooske), from us, from all, this debt is due - to die" [143].

The sphere of the divine is sometimes approached. Dionysus says of King Pentheus : "He shall know (understand who is) Zeus' son Dionysus" [144]. When Helena meets Menelaus in Egypt, she remarks : "It is something (literally : it is a god, theos) to recognize one's friends" [145]. Iris speaking of the mad Heracles says : "Then he may learn how dreadful is Hera's wrath" [146]. Euripides is coming closest to 'mysteriosophic' meanings in this verse : "That which is dark and that which we cannot discern (gignooskomen) clearly, that will be revealed by the seer" [147].

This is also an indication that, even for Euripides, there exists a kind of knowledge that is only available to the elect.

9. Knowledge and the Hellenistic poets

In the works of the great Hellenistic poet of the third century, Callimachus, we do not find the noun gnosis, but forms of gignooskein occur eight times [148]. In this poet the verb can mean 'to know for a fact' but can also indicate higher knowledge. "Tiresias shall know the birds (i.e. the omens)" [149]; "(Eumedes) knew that the people were planning and plotting death for him" [150]. It can also refer to supreme knowledge - "Stupid olive (the laurel tree is speaking), I know no sorrow nor the path trodden by the carriers of the dead, and men do not tread on me (i.e. as they do when pressing olives), for I am holy" [151].

In Callimachus' contemporary Theocritus, gignooskein usually denotes somewhat more than practical knowledge. "Oh, I know what Love is" [152]. A fine example is the following. "Say who had known aught of them (the heroes of the past), had not the poets hymned the battle-cries of an older day" [153]. Here the poets are portrayed as the guardians of mythological lore which, of course, is knowledge of a higher kind.

10. Words for knowledge in historians and doctors

In Herodotus' 'Historiai' forms of gignooskein occur sixty-one times, which is far less than the use of eidenai with its 152 times. According to Benadete, Book IV has the most entries with gignooskein, seventeen in all, but, says this scholar, none in the Libyan section [154]. The second place is occupied by epistasthai (118 times). Phronein and noein are not frequently used, respectively thirty-three and nineteen times. The noun gnosis is not found in Herodotus [155]. The five verbs total a number of 322 occurrences of which gignooskein takes up a bare 19 %. It is remarkable that the two verbs phronein and noein, have only 12 1/2 % between them.

These relations are somewhat different in Thucydides. In his 'Historiai' gignooskein is present 130 times, followed by eidenai (107), epistasthai (31) and phronein (10); noein does not occur. This means that gignooskein has 46 % of the entries, a considerable difference from its frequency in Herodotus [156]. Although in Thucydides gignooskein forms a semantic couple with gnoomē (occurring 170 times), gnosis is to be found too, but only once, and, indeed, this is the first time in literary and historical texts. The passage is worth quoting since gnosis stands here for recognition under difficult circumstances. The issue is a night battle during the Athenian siege of Syracuse in 415/413 B.C. The Athenian hoplites are groping about in the darkness hindered by low visibility. "Though there was a bright moon, they could only see one another, as is natural to do in moonlight - seeing before them the vision (opsin) of a person mistrusting their recognition (gnoosin) of their own friends" [157].

But it is true, as Huart says, that it is not the number of references that is decisive; "the essential is the value that is ascribed by every author to the different terms" [158]. If we take this as our guide-line, we shall arrive at some unexpected conclusions. In Herodotus more than 84 % of the entries with knowledge-words are taken up by those verbs that express know-how and factual knowledge, viz. epistasthai and eidenai. Herodotus was essentially a reporter and a story-teller; I suppose this is why. It is in accordance with this that in his Histories the meaning of gignooskein is not really different from that of the other verbs. "Thus the first knowledge of Libya was gained (egnoosthē)" [159]; "now the Ister (Danube) is known (gignoosketai) to many because it flows through inhabited country" [160]. There is nothing special about this.

It is only rarely that gignooskein has a meaning in Herodotus that has a somewhat more general character without becoming really specific. Croesus says to King Cyrus I : "If you but knew (realized, egnookas) that you are human yourself ...". And Darius I says to Histiaeus, the tyrant of Milete : "I had learned (egnookoos) that of all possessions the most precious is a prudent and generous friend" [161]. But references to really deep insight, to mystery, or to something esoteric are utterly lacking.

Taking the profound and detailed study of Huart [162] as my guide, I come to the conclusion that the situation is somewhat different in Thucydides. This historian approaches his subject-matter as an analyzing psychologist; this explains why gignooskein has pride of place in his work. Only a few times does this verb signify 'to recognize'. More often it means 'to remark, to become informed', that is to acquire factual knowledge. It differs, however, from the verb 'aisthanesthai' in so far that there is a connotation of reflection in gignooskein, of coming to a (practical) conclusion. From there we arrive at 'to understand', for instance in 2.4.1 where the Thebans understand (egnoosan) that they have been deceived by the Plataeans.

In such instances, says Huart, we have to do with reflections or inferences based on observation of reality. In other cases, however, gignooskein can refer to a state of mind about possibilities that have not been realized yet. Then conclusions of a more general character may be drawn. A case in point is the speech in which Nicias warns the Athenians against the Syracusan expedition. "We know that few successes are won by greed, but very many by foresight" [163].

There is also a connotation that Huart charcterizes as 'the strong value of gignooskein'; it denotes the activity of the mind, in particular judgment and discernment. Thucydides lodged this faculty in intelligence; it will not surprise us that he applies it to the man he admired most of all, Pericles. But nowhere do we leave the field of politics. There is not the slightest reference to the divine sphere.

We should not expect much more of Xenophon. He was an eminently practical man, an able general interested in politics, an agrarian expert, a gentleman fond of hunting, an historiographer, but no philosopher, although he knew and admired Socrates. According to Sturz's lexicon [164], in Xenophon gignooskein 'simply' means 'to recognize, to understand, to learn'; 'simply' signifies that there are no overtones. The basic meaning is 'to know', for a fact, that is; in such cases its use does not differ from that of eidenai, it may even be synonymous with epistasthai. A somewhat higher level of knowledge is reached by understanding based on exploration, investigation, and reasoning, but also on experience. This may lead to intelligent insight, judgment, and sound conclusions. Once again we remain far from the kind of meanings found in Homer and other poets.

There is in all Xenophon's works only one allusion to really superior knowledge; it is no wonder that we find it in connection with Socrates. It is the only time that Xenophon uses the word 'gnosis'. This occurs in the concluding passage of his Memorabilia where he writes that "he (Socrates) was so wise that he was unerring in his judgment of the better and the worse, and needed no counsellor, but relied on himself for his knowledge (gnoosin) of them" [165]. Here gnosis means a kind of knowledge that, in its intuitive character, is unique and highly personal, and, at the same time, unerring. Suddenly we are at an immense distance from know-how and factual knowledge.

In the Corpus Hippocraticum the doctors take the floor. In their texts, of which some date from the late Hellenistic period, the word 'gnosis' occurs several times [166]. In these medical treatises there is nothing special about the term. 'Gnosis' can stand for what we would call 'diagnosis', of a disease of the womb for instance [167]. Elsewhere it means nothing more than practical medical knowledge; the study of medicine is called 'mathèsis' [168].

Twice gnosis refers to the kind of knowledge one can acquire by means of one's senses and physical functions [169]. What Hippocrates understands by 'knowledge' is unambiguously expressed in this statement. "There are in fact two things, science (epistèmè) and opinion (doxa); the former begets knowledge (epistasthai), the second ignorance" [170]. This great doctor's down-to-earth, wholly 'secularized' approach is plainly illustrated by the way he speaks of the so-called 'Sacred Disease', of epilepsy, that is. "It is not any more divine or more sacred than other diseases but has a natural cause" [171].

11. A tentative conclusion

It is time now for a tentative conclusion. Two lines of thought are clearly discernible. Along the first line the poets are grouped, from Homer through the lyric poets to the Tragedians; they hold that, apart, from practical knowledge and experience, a kind of higher, special knowledge exists that has an intuitive character and is often connected with the divine. The noun gnosis itself is hardly ever used by them but, instead, they employ the verb gignooskein to indicate this kind of knowing.

Along the other line we find the historians, the reporters, the political analysts, the generals, and the doctors - all of them people with practical occupations and with a corresponding matter-of-fact attitude to life. Although they sometimes use the word gnosis, they hardly ever mean anything else by it than just 'knowledege'.

To these practitioners we must add the two great comic poets Aristophanes and Menander. That they indeed do fit into the line of the other poets is not astonishing since they find their subject-matter in the lower echelons of life; we should not look for 'higher knowledge' here. In Aristophanes, gnosis itself does not appear, and gignooskein never means anything else than 'to know for a fact' [172]. In Menander it means 'carnal knowledge' [173].

These two lines roughly represent the poets on the one hand and the scholars and scientists on the other. I suppose that the first group was, in many respects, an isolated minority, while the second group that, as we have seen, was not interested in special knowledge, in 'Gnosis' with a capital, would have had a far larger following. This bipartitioning of the Hellenes foreshadows that of later days between the Gnostics and 'the others'.

There seems to have been little correspondence between the two groups. We should, however, not overlook that one glaring example of the noun 'gnosis' used in the poetic sense, viz. when Xenophon applies it to Socrates. This brings us to the question of how the philosophers looked at the matter. Would they have sided with the first group or with the second? Putting the question is perhaps tantamount to answering it. But let us nevertheless take a sharp look at it.

12. A meagre harvest in the Presocratics

We are greatly hindered in our quest by the fragmentary state in which the Presocratic writings have been handed down to us. That, for instance, we do not find gnosis or gignooskein in Anaximander (ca. 611-547 B.C.) or in Anaximenes (ca. 590-ca.527 B.C.) does not mean that they never used these words [174]. However, we are lucky enough to discover, not gnosis, but gignooskein in the father of all philosophy, Thales, who lived about 585 B.C.. In response to the famous Delphic injunction 'to know oneself' he repeatedly stated that it is difficult to know oneself [175]. The verb here already implies a measure of insight.

In Xenophanes, who was born about 570 B.C., there is only one instance (of gignooskein) but that is a very telling one [176]. It occurs in the well-known passage in which this philosopher ridicules the Pythagorean belief in metempsychosis. Pythagoras heard a dog wailing and said : "Stop beating for I recognized (egnoon) the soul of a friend (in the voice of the dog)" [177]. Although Xenophanes was mocking, this did not prevent him from using a word that conveyed the idea of deep insight.

13. Occurrences in later Presocratics

a. First occurence of 'gnosis' in Heraclitus

Our harvest becomes somewhat richer in Heraclitus [178] whose 'floruit' fell about 500 B.C. This Presocratic philosopher uses the word 'gnosis' once. This represents, as far as I know, an historic moment since this must be the very first time the word 'gnosis' itself was used.

In this single instance of the use of this noun by Heraclitus he says that "men are self-deceived (or mistaken) in their knowledge (gnoosin) of manifest things" [179]. This at least suggests that what men take to be knowledge, i.e. of manifest things, is not the real knowledge; they have a wrong idea of gnosis. For the rest we must content ourselves with gignooskein. "Of all whose teachings I have heard", says the sage, "no one reaches the point of recognizing (gignooskein) that the wise (sophon) is diferent from any other thing" [180].

This is a splendid example of the élitist use of this verb. The haughty sage did not hold a very high conception of the knowledge and insight of other people; he even ridiculed Hesiod because this poet "did not recognize day and night (i.e. for what they really are). For they are one" [181]. The poet obviously was stupid enough to believe (together with the rest of us) that day and night are different; their unity was meant by the philosopher "as something self-evident ..., probably because they succeed each other every day" [182].

In other quotations (seven in all) it becomes clear how much this sage despised his fellow-men. "What the most esteemed man (among the Greeks) knows (gignooskei) and maintains are but fancies (or false opinions) [183]. "The majority of men do not notice (or apprehend) the things they meet with (or comprehend, gignooskousin) them when they have learned (mathontes) about them" [184]. But the crowning phrase is this one : "It is because of want of (human) confidence that it escapes men's knowledge" [185]. By 'it' very probably the Logos is meant [186], or, according to Plutarch who quotes this text, 'the greater part of the divine sphere' [187]. It is always the same : there exists a knowledge that is more than just knowledge, but learning is not the way to it. Heraclitus obviously is confident that he can attain to it.

b. Parmenides and knowledge

Parmenides of Elea who 'flourished' about 475 B.C., uses the noun 'gnosis' once, connecting it with being : "In general everything that is has some understanding (gnoosin)" [188]. The only time that Parmenides employs gignooskein it also refers to Being. "You can neither know what is not (for it is impossible) nor tell of it" [189].

c. Knowledge in other philosophical texts [190]

Melissus, a pupil of Parmenides, employed the word gnosis in a negative sense but nevertheless refers with it to the world of the gods. For, according to him, "it was impossible to have knowledge (gnoosin) of them" [191].

Anaxagoras, who lived from ca. 500 to ca. 428 B.C., and to whom Mind (Nous) is everything, said that "Mind knew (egnoo) all" [192]. Even in an Atomist like Democritus (born ca. 460 B.C.) the idea of higher knowledge is not wholly absent; not gnosis but gignooskein occurs several times in his fragments. "Man must understand according to this rule that he is far distant from reality (or truth)" [193]; and "it is evident that it is impossible to know how everything is in reality" [194]. In this last quotation the philosopher is hinting at an ultimate knowledge of reality.

d. Gnosis and the practical tribe of the Sophists

Since Sophists, when all is said and done, are practical people, it may come as a surprise that even in their texts we find that special kind of knowledge. True enough, they do not use the noun gnosis but, instead, the verb gignooskein occurs a great number of times in the writings of Antiphon who lived in the fifth century B.C. [195]. One of his texts is very revealing because in this fragment, as Diels says, he "opposes sensory perception to intellectual comprehension". "If you know this, you will comprehend that for it (the mind?) nothing is single (apart?), neither that what he sees nor what he understands whose insight reaches as far as possible" [196]. Here seeing with the eye and understanding with the mind are clearly distinguished; for the first horan is used, for the second, and this three times, gignooskein. This is similar to what the Sophist Critias (who met his end in 404/403 B.C.) said : "Neither what one perceives with the rest of the body nor what one understands with the help of one's intelligence ..." [197] (the rest of the phrase is missing).

e. The Pythagoreans

Let us conclude the Presocratic part of this section with a short look on the Pythagoreans. They really do not yield very much, but one quotation is a gem - one of the sort we might expect from a follower of Pythagoras, the great Sage! It is a phrase by Philolaus, around 500 B.C., or perhaps by a later Pythagorean around 400 B.C.; the word gnosis itself appears in it. "The essence of things, and Nature herself, requires divine knowledge (gnoosin), not of the human sort" [198].

14. The 'gnosticizing' of Plato

Turning now to Plato, I must sollicit the kind indulgence of the reader for repeating more or less verbatim what I wrote in my Volume III, Ch. III, Sections 4 and 12; there already I gave Plato's handling of the knowledge-concept an extensive treatment. It is of course true what some scholars say, that Plato did not always differentiate between his several terms for 'knowledge', in particular not between epistêmê and gnosis. Epistêmê had his predilection; he uses it dozens and dozens of times [199]. Gnosis occurs only thirty-six times.

Nevertheless, as we shall see, Plato sometimes makes a distinction between gignooskein and epistasthai. This does not really matter since the all-determining opposition is that between (true) knowledge and opinion (doxa). Everyone has opinion(s) but not everyone possesses knowledge. Opinions are not necessarily erroneous but right or wrong; they do not form the royal road that leads to wisdom [200]. Knowledge is about essential things, opinion about the rest. "It is the nature of the true lover of knowledge (philomathês) to strive emulously after true being and that he does not linger over the many particulars that are opined (doxazomenois) to be real". Holding on to this way, "he ... may attain to knowledge (gnoiê) and truly live" [201]. One should realize that for this highest and life-giving form of knowledge the verb gignooskein is used.

The several kinds of knowledge differ in this respect that they are directed to different objects; it is even implied that the various sorts of knowledge are related to different faculties, since Socrates says that he knows 'with his soul' [202]. There is even a field of action that lies below the level of knowledge : politicians do not act on the strength of what they know but of 'eudoxia', that is on the ground of an opinion that may be correct in itself but for which there is no (intellectual, logical) foundation. In other words, they are guided by suppositions, and this places them on the same level as soothsayers [203].

Here we see one of the greatest oppositions in Plato's theory of knowledge coming to light : the opposition between knowledge and doxa. The philosopher always speaks denigratingly of doxa. But after all an opinion may be correct, as I said already, and then it is useful and a good guide for acting in the right way [204], but philosophically it is not on the same level with knowledge. Knowledge rests on a much firmer basis than right opinion.

Among the scholars who think that Plato makes some distinctions between his terms for knowledge, nobody wishes to assert that he used the word gnosis as the 'terminus technicus' it was to become some centuries later - nor do I. But there is a first step in that direction. If this is correct, then epistēmē would mean knowledge, and gnosis comprehension or insight. Again and again Plato emphasizes the dualistic bipartition of mankind into those who have seen and know and those who remain blind.

This appears extremely clearly in the renowned myth of the cave [205]. This parable presents to us, on the one hand, a blind humanity that is satisfied to take appearances for being itself, and, on the other, the lonely philosopher who has viewed the Good but can find no hearers. The real world is to be found outside and above the cave (our phenomenal world); it is the world of the Forms. This abstract and absolute world represents the highest field of knowledge. No matter how Plato explains his theory, it invariably becomes a dualistic scheme.

Two typical Gnostic elements are already plainly discernible. The one is that true knowledge transports us out of the visible, historical world into the realm of true reality which can only be perceived as a vision of the spirit. It has nothing to do with the body or with sensory perception. "Pure knowledge (gnoonai) is impossible while the body is with us" [206]. Once again a form of gignooskein is used here. The other element is the purely dualistic dinstinction between the few who strive towards that noble vision, and the great mass that prefers to stay down, in the dark that is.

15. Knowledge in Aristotle

We are justified in thinking of Aristotle as a scholar, a naturalist, a researcher, who made occasional but rather frequent forays into the fields of philosophy, politics, poetics, and a great many other subjects [207]; his interest was catholic and his scope almost unlimited. Being preëminently a research-worker and a teacher of science, the turn of his mind was practical. The tendency to mysticism that is so obvious in Plato was wholly alien to him. This is also reflected in his usage of terms for knowledge. He has not a few words for it but his favourite term is epistēmē which we may safely translate by 'science'.

The Platonic distinction between opinion (doxa) and science also occurs in Aristotle. Opinion is either right or wrong; epistēmē is necessarily true [208]. But we do find in him the dualistic distinction between those who have only opinions and those who possess (scientific) knowledge. As a result of teaching, resarch and study, epistēmē is on principle open to all.

The word 'gnosis' also occurs but not very often [209]. In his review of the forms of knowledge Granger does not even mention it [210]. This is small wonder since the philosopher never uses it in any special sense; there are no overtones to it. In the top gear it can refer to universals. "That which is prior to knowledge (gnoosei) is treated as asbolute prior", for instance, "universals are prior in formula (kata ton logon)" [211]. Another time it signifies abstract reasoning. "The Infinite does not exist potentially in the sense that it will ever exist separately in actuality; it is separable only in knowledge (gnoosei)" [212]; this means that the Infinite as such is a concept of thought.

At a lower level gnosis is not even about essentials but about particulars. "(The senses) are our chief sources of knowledge (gnooseis, in the plural!), but they do not tell us the reason for anything, as for example why fire is hot, but only that it is hot" [213]. Parmenides and Plato would have turned in their graves to hear that the senses are sources of knowledge!

Somewhere else, Aristotle equals experience and knowledge (gnosis) [214]. Yet another revealing passage is this : "Limit (peras) means ... the reality of each thing, for this is the limit of our knowledge, and if it is the limit of the knowledge it is the limit of the thing" [215]. Is a more level-headed idea of knowledge imaginable? This sounds very much like Gertrude Stein's 'a rose is a rose is a rose'. However, we can descend yet another two steps : "familiarity (gnoosis) increases mutual confidence" [216], and finally the lowest grade : "All animals (living beings) have .. some measure of knowledge (gnoosis tis)" [217].

In conclusion we may state that Aristotle, with his conception of knowledge, forms quite an exception among philosophers. We should, however, not forget that most of the time he is not speaking as a philosopher but as a naturalist. He finds himself, therefore, in the company of the doctors and the historians.

16. Among the successors of Plato

As far as I know, the terms gnosis and gignooskein do not occur in Eudoxus and in Speusippus, the first successor of Plato as head of the Academy. This does not say very much in view of the fragmentary state of their writings. But both of them rejected Plato's Theory of Forms because they would have nothing to do with its most important element, the 'chorismos', the distinction between the objects and their Forms. This makes it improbable that they would have believed in higher forms of knowledge. This is also born out by the fact that, for Speusippus at least, the bridge from man to the cosmos was not philosophy but music.

With Xenocrates we are once again moving into the general direction of philosophy on this point because he, not wanting to write for the public at large, turned to esoterism. This would imply that there are two kinds of knowledge, one of which is for the lovers of wisdom only. We can only have true knowledge of that which is beyond the heavens. Perception by the senses leads to error and false judgments. All the same, in the Xenocratic fragments the word gnosis does not appear.

The same is the case in the pseudo-Platonic treatise the 'Epinomis' [218]. The term its author prefers above all others is 'sophia'. He opposes this sophia or higher wisdom to the sciences (technai) and to knowledge of a scientific kind (epistêmê). These do not make man wise. The true source of wisdom is to be found in the Heavens; the regular movements of the celestial bodies prove that their intelligence is supreme.

In this anonymous work true knowledge is something highly specialized, and if it is true that the author does not employ the word gnosis, his 'wisdom' is coming very close to what the Gnostics understood by it. But gignooskein is there : a human being who does not know (gignooskei) about numbers (Pythagorean numbers being the key to higher understanding) is an irrational person [219]. In every passage where this verb is used, the meaning of 'to know' is enhanced and lifted to a higher plane, that of more than human, of divine insight.

In the Stoa we find a radically dualistic distinction between those who 'know' and those who do not. This means, of course, the postulating of two kinds of knowledge that have nothing to do with each other. The only real knowledge worthy of that name is that concerning good and bad things. Such knowledge is to be found only in the wise; it is the highest form of knowing. It has a liberating effect; the wise are permitted to do whatsoever they wish [220]. Once again it must be stated that the noun gnosis is not used; the usual term is epistêmê. However, the ignorance of the unwise is called agnoia. Anyhow, the Stoics acknowledged a very special brand of knowledge.

If ever a Greek philosopher despised scientific knowledge and scholarship, it was Epicurus. The true scientific spirit was not his. In his eyes knowledge of this kind was not conducive to salvation. When speaking of salvation, the philosopher invariably uses the word gnosis, seven times in all : without gnosis no salvation. This is Gnostic ideology avant la lettre.

17. Conclusion

To vary a dictum of Eusebius of Caesarea, the 'father of ecclesiastical historiography', there is in Greek philosophy discernible a 'praeparatio gnostica'. The movement is not general : scholars with a practical turn of mind remain alien to it. Neither is the line straight. It is interrupted in Aristotle and still more in Hellenistic Scepticism with its fundamental tenet that true judgments are impossible. But all the same there is a continuous build-up, a slow but certain laying of foundations. We must now see what kind of building was raised upon them.

NOTES TO CHAPTER II

1. Exactly five minutes after I had completed the manuscript of this chapter in the Classical Seminary of the University of Amsterdam, I met Dr. J.-M. Bremer, professor of Greek literature, in the canteen. He drew my attention to the Pandora search system, developed by Harvard University, to explore the Thesaurus Linguae Graecae, CD Rom, composed by the University of California, Irvine, 1987. This Thesaurus contains all Greek texts from Homer onward into late Antiquity. A few moments later a friendly assistant was demonstrating this marvellous electronic device for me on the computer screen. I did not check the verb gignooskein because there are far too many entries with it. But I checked the noun gnoosis. The program did not come too late to be of use, for first of all I wanted to see whether I had not inadvertently omitted some author of importance. But it appeared I had not. Another question was who was the first to use the word gnosis. I thought it was Heraclitus but I saw that Thales has some sort of a claim too, at least this was what Pandora told me. She cited a Proclus text concerning Thales and containing the word 'gnoosis' (Procl. in Eucl. 65.3 = DK I 11.11.3). If this were correct, it would mean that Thales had used this word almost a century before Heraclitus did so. On closer inspection, however, it appeared that it was not Thales who had employed this word but Proclus himself.
2. Cor.8:7,10; Eph. 3:19.
3. Chantraine, Dictionnaire 224.

4. Chantraine, Morphologie par. 258. -ske does not always imply duplication but can also have an inchoative meaning, for instance in didaskein = to learn.
5. Chantraine, Morphologie par. 257.
6. Il.XXIII.469/470 : "ou gar egoo ge eu diagnoskoo". The prefix dia- stresses the idea of effort still more; we have kep it in 'diagnostic'.
7. Boisacq, Dictionnaire s.v.
8. Friendly communication by Dr. H.W. Bodewitz, professor of Sanskrit in Utrecht State University NL, whose words in a letter to me of August 15, 1991, I am repeating here more or less verbatim.
9. Schmidt, Synonimik 282-309.
10. This meaning is rendered more precisely in older Dutch Bible translations by the verb 'bekennen'.
11. Greek-English Lexicon, and Schmidt, Synonimik III, 634'635.
12. Schmidt, Synonimik I, 299. Plamböck's Erfasssen, has very little to add to this.
13. Index Homericus, see bibliography.
14. Another valuable source is Snell, see Bibliography.
15. The present tense would have been 'eidein' but is not extant.
16. Il.II.484. See Snell, Der Weg 26/27.
17. Snell, Der Weg 40.
18. Von Fritz, Noos and noein 88.
19. Il.VII.281. In this section the translations are based on those of Murray in the Loeb Classical Library, but some of them are really too archaic.
20. Il.IX.36.
21. Il.XXIII.890.
22. Od.VII.25/26; the same in Od.VIII.28.
23. Od.XX.75.
24. Od.XVI.470.
25. Od.IV.645.
26. Il.I.362/363.
27. Od.III.185/185.
28. Il.VII.238/239.
29. Il.XII.232.
30. Il.IV.218.
31. Il.VI.438.

32. Od.II.88.
33. Il.IV.360/361.
34. "Philea phresi mêdea eidoos".
35. Od.XI.432.
36. Il.XV.36.
37. Od.XVIII.228.
38. Od.VIII.559.
39. Od. XI.69/70.
40. Il.XIX.421.
41. Od.XXIII.109/110.
42. Od.V.245.
43. Od.XVI.136, XVII.193 and 281.
44. Murray's translation has 'to feel'.
45. Od.XVI.399.
46. Od.XX.5.
47. Il.XVI.701.
48. Il.XI.296.
49. Von Fritz, Noös and noein 88.
50. Od.V.188/189.
51. Il.XX.310.
52. Il.X.32.
53. Od.XVIII.228.
54. Il.IX.104/105.
55. Od.XVIII.230.
56. Il.XXII.445/446.
57. Od.XVI.164.
58. Il.VIII.10.
59. Il.II.391/392.
60. Od.XVI.160.
61. Snell, Der Weg 22.
62. Von Fritz, Noös and noein 88.
63. Lesher, Perceiving 9.
64. Lex.fr.gr.Ep. s.v. 'gignooskein'. Manu Leumann, Homerische Wörter, Schweizerische Beiträge zur Altertumswissenschaft 3, Basel 1950, has no entry 'gignooskein'. Perusal of David W. Packard and Tania

Meyers, A Bibliography of Homeric Scholarship. Preliminary Edition 1930-1970, Malibu (Cal.), 1974, showed me that interest for the term 'gignooskein' is minimal among scholars.

65. Od.XVII.362/363.
66. Il.V.85-87.
67. Il.XXII.382.
68. Il.XX.20.
69. Od.I.63-420; the decisive recognition occurs in vs. 420.
70. Il.VI.121-132.
71. Il.V.815 and 824.
72. Ar., Poet. 1459b.24.3; the Greek word employed by Ar. is 'anagnoorisis".
73. Od.XVII.291-303.
74. Od.XVI.172-216.
75. P. 8, see Bibliography.
76. Od.XIX.349-475; the two instances of egnoo are 392 and 468.
77. Od.XXI.204-220.
78. Od.XXIII.108-110.
79. Od.XIX.479.
80. Od.XX.91-94.
81. Od.XX.11.
82. Od.XXIII.89-95.
83. Od.XXIII.177/178.
84. Od.XXIII.205-208.
85. Od.XXIII.300.
86. Od.XXI.35/36.
87. Compare this passage in the Gospel of Luke : "They recognized (epegnoosai) him (Jesus) when he broke bread". Lc.24:31 and 35.
88. Od.XIII.312/313.
89. Il.V.815.
90. Od.XIII.299/300.
91. Od.XI.153.
92. Plato, Rep.606E.
93. DK I, Xen.B10.

94. Hesiod, Loeb Classical; Fragmenta Hesiodea; Minton, Concordance; Tebben, Hesiod-Konkordanz; Lexicon Hesiodeum; for all these works see Bibliography.
95. Hes., Erga 450.
96. Hes., Theog. 234-236.
97. Hes., Shield 49/50.
98. Hes., Theog. 838.
99. Hes., fr. 302.32.
100. Hes., Erga 280/281. The Greek words 'ta dikaia gignooskoon' reminds one of those in the Roman-Catholic prayer to the Holy Spirit : 'quae recta sunt sapere'.
101. Hes., Theog. 551.
102. Hes., Erga 218.
103. Hes., fr. 43a76/77.
104. Snell, Der Weg 24.
105. Vol. I, Ch. III.10.
106. LB fr. 118.8.
107. LB fr. 118.8.
108. Snell, Der Weg 24/25.
109. See the Index Verborum in Fragmenta, ed. Tarditi 241-256.
110. Solon, El. 16. Solonian texts in Anth.Lyr.Gr. I, ed. Diehl. Diehl concludes his Latin preface of this second edition with the triumphant communication that he wrote this on March 9, 1936, the day on which, 'by order of the Führer' (iussu Ducis), German troops reoccupied the demilitarized Rhineland, "among the declamations of its inhabitants". Some Dutch reader put a large exclamation mark in the margin. Translation of Solonian texts by Freeman, Work and Life 212, nr. 5. Snell's commentary Der Weg 26.
111. Snell, Der Weg 26 thinks that Solon is speaking about 'dikè', justice, here. I don't deny the possibility, but would this lawgiver have stamped knowledge about the law as extremely difficult to discern?
112. Anth.Lyr.Gr. I Solon, El. 4:103, translation Freeman.
113. See Vol. I, Ch. III.15.
114. Lex. to Pind., see Bibliography.
115. Pind., Ol.89/90.
116. Pind., Pyth. 4.86-123.
117. Pind., Ol.13.4-8.
118. Pind., Pyth.4.263.
119. Ind.Aesch., see Bibliography.

120. Aesch., Prom. 309.
121. Aesch., Ag. 807-809.
122. Aesch., Ag. 1424/1425.
123. Aesch., Choeph. 777.
124. Aesch., Suppl. 426.
125. Aesch., Prom. 104.
126. Soph, OR 1325/1326.
127. Soph., Phil. 1388.
128. Soph., OR 613-615.
129. Soph., El. 1130.
130. Soph., El. 988/989.
131. Soph., Ant. 998.
132. Soph., OR 1271-1275.
133. Concordance to Eur., see Bibliography.
134. Eur., Hipp. 406/407.
135. Eur., Io 319.
136. Eur., Io 239/240.
137. Eur., Iph.Aul. 1067-108.
138. Eur., Hipp. 380.
139. Eur., Phoin. 33.
140. Eur., Bacch. 1341/1342.
141. Eur., Hek. 227/228.
142. Eur., Suppl. 549/550.
143. Eur., Alk. 418/419.
144. Eur., Bacch. 859/860.
145. Eur., Hel. 560.
146. Eur., Her.main. 840.
147. Eur., Suppl. 211.
148. Lexico, ed. Fernandez-Galliano, see Bibliography.
149. Call., Hymn V.123.
150. Call., Hymn V.38.
151. Call., fr. 194.37-40.
152. Theocr. III.15.
153. Theocr. XVI.48-50.

154. Benadette, Her.Inq. 106.
155. Lex.Her.; Powell, Lex. to Her.; a help is also Index II in Herodotus, ed. Macan II. See Bibliography.
156. Ind.Thuc.; Lex.Thuc. See Bibliography.
157. Thuc. 7.44.2.
158. Huart., Voc. 290-302.
159. Her. 4.43.1.
160. Her. 2.34.1.
161. Her. 5.24.3.
162. Huart, Voc. 290-302.
163. Thuc. 6.13.1.
164. Sturz, Lex.Xenoph. I, see Bibliography.
165. Xen., Mem. 4.8.11.
166. Index Hipp., see Bibliography.
167. De victu acutorum 522.6.
168. Law 640.
169. De victu acutorum I.494.4 and 496.4.
170. Law 640.
171. The Sacred Disease 352.2.3.
172. Index Aristophaneus; see also the Complete Concordance, ed. Dunbar. See Bibliography
173. Blythe, Voc. of Men. 51.
174. With regard to the Presocratics we would be nowhere without the 'Wortindex' in DK III.
175. DK I.10 (64.6) and 11 (71.19). For a supposed use of the noun gnosis by Thales I refer the reader to the end of note 1.
176. Less. di Sen., see Bibliography.
177. DK. I.21(Xen.), B7.4..5.
178. The Index verborum Heracliti (p. 623) is very useful, see bibliography.
179. Marcovich 21.1 = DK I 22B56.
180. Marcovich 83 (p.440) = DK I 22B108.
181. Marcovich 43 (p. 222) = DK I 22B57.
182. Marcovich 223.
183. Marcovich 20 (p.87) = DK I 22B118.
184. Marcovich 3 (p.14) = DK I 22B5.

185. Marcovich 12 (p.42) = DK I 22B86.
186. Marcovich 43.
187. Plut., Coriolan 38.7.
188. DK I 28A46. In the glossary of Gallop, Parmenides, there is no entry 'gnosis'.
189. DK I 28B2. translation Gallop, Parm. 55. In his glossary he says that this verb "guarantees the existence of the objects or the truth of the propositions that it governs".
190. Theophr., De sens. 15 and 17. See Stratton, Theophr. and the Gr. phys. psych. (see Bibliography).
191. DL 9.24.
192. DK II 59B12.
193. DK II 68B6.
194. DK II 68B8.
195. Index Antiphonteus, ed. Van Cleef, see Bibliography.
196. DK II 87B1.
197. DK II 88B39.
198. DK I 44B6.
199. Brandwood, Word Index to Plato. Also Perls, Lexicon. Stockhammer's useful dictionary does not contain the Greek words.
200. It is not very easy to state what 'doxa' signifies; its meanings vary. Lafrance, Théorie plat. 23-33 gives an exhaustive list of its meanings.
201. Plato, Rep. 490A-B.
202. Plato, Euthyd. 295E.
203. Plato, Meno 99A-C.
204. Plato, Meno 99A
205. Plato, Rep. 514A-517A.
206. Plato, Phaidoon 66E.
207. Wartelle, Lex. 10.
208. Geyer, Erk.theorie 181/182.
209. Index Aristotelicus; Delatte, Arist. Metaph., Index Verborum, Listes de fréquences; Wartelle, Lex. See Bibliography.
210. Granger, Théorie ar., 11-29; it does not figure in his 'Index des mots grecs'.
211. Arist., Met. 1018b30.
212. Arist., Met. 1048b15.

213. Arist., Met. 981b13.
214. Arist., Met. 981a16.
215. Arist., Met. 1022a9,10.
216. Arist., Pol. 1313b5. This is the opposite of the popular saying that 'familiarity breeds contempt'.
217. Arist., Gen.An. 713a31.
218. See Vol. VI, Ch. III.1d.
219. Epin. 997C.
220. Dio Crys. 14,17,18, ed. Cohoon.

CHAPTER III

DUALISM IN GNOSTIC SYSTEMS IN SAMARIA, SYRIA, AND ASIA MINOR
(until ca. A.D. 130)

1. Simon Magus

a. The man

There is really no need, as is done sometimes, to make Simon Magus, Simon the Magician, into the true ancestor of the Gnosis, but he is the first Gnostic of whom we are historically certain [1]. We find him in the Palestinian-Syrian region which I described as the cradle of the Gnosis. The first mention of him occurs in the Acts of the Apostles. When the Apostle Philip comes to Samaria, he meets a man there, a certain Simon, who is called 'the Great Power', because he is the very power of God himself. "He had swept the Samaritans off their feet with his magical arts"; hence his nickname the 'Magician' [2].

Nevertheless, Philip succeeded in converting and baptizing him. But then he desired to buy for money the apostles' gift of bestowing the Holy Spirit. This Peter, who had also gone to Samaria, sternly refused and told Simon to repent [3]. Here we have the origin of the term 'simony', which means the buying and selling of spiritual offices and objects. We can only guess why there is not the slightest allusion in this passage to Simon's Gnostic ideas.

Saint Justin the Martyr knew more about him. Simon, he writes, was a Samaritan who was born in the village of Gitta and was in Rome during the reign of the Emperor Claudius (41-54). This author too calls him a Magician who was considered divine. Obviously he had followers, in particular Samaritans. Justinus adds that Simon lived with Helena, a former prostitute [4]. Irenaeus of Lyons supplies the additional information that Simon had ransomed her in the city of Tyre [5]. He travelled around with this woman and, according to the apocryphal Pseudo-Clementine books, displayed her in the windows of a tower to a great multitude and told the onlookers that this was the Helena on whose behalf Troy was besieged for ten years [6].

Details from a later date are probably pseudo-historical. The same source relates that Simon's parents were Antonius and Rahel, and that the young man received a Greek education in Alexandria where he also learned the magic craft [7]. He is said to have made the acquaintance of the right religion as the most estimated pupil of John the Baptist. He did not succeed his master because at the time of the Baptist's death he was in Egypt studying magic. It was only later that he got the leadership of the Baptist's school by supplanting a rival [8].

He obviously was a pastmaster of magic since he could make himself invisible, fly through the air, change himself into any animal whatsoever, make gold, and perform a great many other tricks; he could even order household utensils to do their work for him automatically [9] (he could have taught Goethe's and Dukas' Sorcerer's Apprentice a lesson!). The Pseudoclementina further relate that there once was a discussion in Caesarea between the Apostle Peter and Simon. As was to be expected, Peter triumphed over the magician who was chased away by the public [10].

Many years later the Christian community in Rome heard that Simon was in Italy. And there he was, all of a sudden appearing in their midst. Nearly all Christians succumbed to his teachings and his magic tricks. But God himself notified Peter in Jerusalem of what was going on in far-away Rome. The apostle succeeded in boarding a ship in Caesarea in the nick of time and sailed to Italy. Shortly afterwards he arrived in Rome.

Preaching on the first Sabbath after that he first of all hauled his Christians over the coals admonishing them that they had only one Redeemer, Jesus Christ. It was obviously quite clear to Peter that his rival posed as a redeemer. Because the apostle showed that he could work miracles just as well, most Christians returned to the flock. The man in whose house Simon was dwelling showed him the door and purified his home with holy water. The next day Peter and Simon met on the Roman Forum and had an acrid dispute there in the presence of a large public. Peter triumphed, mainly because he was able to raise a dead boy [11].

There are two versions of how Simon died. The first is that he told his believers to bury him alive; he then would rise on the third day. But he stayed where he was, under the ground. On the surface it has the appearance that he wished to emulate Jesus Christ, but in fact he was acting as a shaman [12]. The other version is that he tried to fly over Rome by magic means but that Peter made him fall down by invoking the name of Jesus against him. Simon broke this thigh-bone, was transported to Aricia, and died there [13]. In both versions he became the victim of his own magic lore.

b. His spiritual background

Much of this, or even all of it, may be legendary stuff. But there are some conspicuous elements in it. Two religious systems are dualistically opposed here. Peter is acting as the representative of Jesus Christ; Simon only represents himself. If Jesus Christ is a Redeemer, Simon claims to be a Redeemer in his own right. Another point is that those early Christians were so extremely volatile; they were quick to apostatize and equally quick to repent. The final victory was for Peter and orthodox Christianity. We are entitled to assume that under the legendary narrative there is hard-core history.

This recalls to mind a remark made by Daniélou that with Simon "we are for the first time in the presence of specifically Gnostic speculations" [14]. As has been related, Simon was not only a Samaritan but belonged to the 'school of John the Baptist'. This gives him at once Samaritan and Essenian affinities. Furthermore, his predecessor in this school was a certain Dositheus; we have a tractate called 'The Three Steles of Seth' that forms part of the Gnostic library found in Nag Hammadi in Egypt; in its opening phrase it is referred to as 'the revelation of Dositheus' [15]. We must also pay attention, says Daniélou, to his surname of 'Magus' which points in the direction of Iran.

His dualistic speculations "indicate influences foreign to Judaism". Perhaps Simon borrowed this dualism from his Essenian connections but Iranian influence gave it 'a more radical aspect'. Finally, as the quoted passage from the Acts of the Apostles proves, he had some acquaintance with Christianity [16]. It is evident that Simon stood at the crossroads of the principal spiritual and religious currents of his day.

Whereas it really would be too much to see in Simon the well on whom all later Gnostics drew, nonetheless, as Quispel writes, the ancient view that he was the instigator of all heresy may be right 'in an ideal sense' [17], that is if we do not take this ancestorship too literally. It was not only Irenaeus who said that Simon started it all - 'from whom all sects proceed' [18] - but also some Gnostics themselves. Quispel adds to this that it will not be possible to prove that Simon was an 'all-round Gnostic', but all the same, "the Gnosis that was professed in his school might be the most original form of the Gnosis". For this reason, we might justifiably speak of Simon as 'the archetype of the heretic' [19].

c. The divinization of Simon

As a Samaritan, Simon can never have been an orthodox Jew nor did he ever become a faithful Christian [20]. Instead, his adherents saw in him "that power of God which is called Great". This means that he was supposed to be replete with a superhuman, even a divine force; he was so entirely possessed by this force that he identified himself with it, becoming 'the Great Power' himself. One should, of course, think of this 'power' as something irrational welling forth from the deepest unconscious springs of the human psyche and connecting the subject with the occult physical forces of the cosmos which he then can bend to his own will. It is for this reason that Simon was called 'the Magician' [21].

Hence it should not surprise us that Simon was divinized [22]. But Quispel draws our attention to yet another element, namely "the curious trinitarian speculations ... that attached themselves to his person, and that have made Simonianism into a complete contra-Christianity" [23]. In this context he cites Cyrillus of Jerusalem who also called Simon 'the initiator of all heresy'. This Father of the Church wrote that Simon claimed being God the Father who had revealed himself on Mount Sinai; he (Simon) later appeared as Jesus Christ (but only apparently, not corporally), and finally as the Holy Spirit, promised by Christ to the Christians as the Paraclete [24]. Quispel sees no reason to doubt the authenticity of this report. Trinitarian speculations always remained a constitutive element of Gnosticizing doctrines. Quispel mentions Hegel here but he could also have referred to Joachim da Fiore with his Ages of the Father, the Son, and the Holy Ghost.

I believe that this is sufficient to show that, from the onset, the Gnosis was diametrically opposed to both orthodox Judaism and Christianity [25]. For the rest, identification with the godhead himself is a very rare occurrence in the history of the Gnosis; until the prophet Mani appeared in the third century no Gnostic claimed identity with God except Simon and Menander, his principal adherent [26].

d. The role of Helena

Another utterly un-Jewish and un-Christian element in Simonianism is the function of Simon's companion Helena. Her namesake, Helena of Troy, was the most famous 'femme fatale' in all ancient literature; legends accumulated around her that do not occur in the Iliad. There is, for instance, Euripides' play 'Helen' that is based on the assumption that Helen of Troy was only a phantom whereas the real Helena, the wife of

King Menelaus of Sparta, all the while lived in Egypt, totally innocent of the havoc created by her abduction [27].

She certainly stimulated the imaginations of Hellenistic commentators on Homer. Stoic philosophy interpreted Helen as 'anima', as the physical image of the soul. Since the Stoics located souls in the sphere of the moon, Helen was seen as the 'selēnai anthropos'; this tradition was to be preserved as late as the second half of the twelfth century by Eusthatius, a bishop of Saloniki. Either she had fallen down or she had been abducted from the moon and now she had to return to it. This exemplified the fall of the spiritual and divine element into matter. Myth illustrated this by the story of Helen's elopment with Paris. Her adultery with this Trojan prince meant that it was carnal desire that had brought down the soul from heaven. The siege of Troy by the Greeks for the restoration of Helen signified that the soul is destined to return to the celestial sphere [28].

This certainly is an allegorical explanation fit to please the Gnostics. In view of this I ask myself whether 'Helena' was the proper name of Simon's companion, or whether he had rebaptized her. Anyhow, it will be clear why she had to be an ex-prostitute : as a representative of 'anima' she had to be freed from the shackles of sensuality and brought back to the divine orbit.

Yet another curious fact is reported by Irenaeus, namely that the Simonians adored a statue of Simon portrayed as Zeus, and another of Helena as Minerva (Athena) [29]. Now we know that, according to Greek mythology, Athena sprang forth from the head of her father Zeus in full armour and as an adult. Naturally enough, this tale excited allegorical explanations : Athena, it was maintained, was the thought of Zeus, his 'pronoia'. This viewpoint was exceptionally welcome to Platonists, since the old myth enabled them to see in Athena the supreme Idea comprising all other ideas [30]. Later the Simonians identified Helena with Athena which meant that she too was deified. Simon called her 'Ennoia', or 'Epinoia', that is the spirit in or of everything [31]. In modern terms 'ennoia' may be rendered as 'an emanation of the godhead'. Quispel says that she was the 'mundus archetypus', the archetypical world [32].

Jonas argued that Simonianism belongs to the 'female group' of the Gnosis (there was also a 'male group'). With this term he designated those Gnostic systems in which a female person had pride of place. This scholar thinks that the female group is the most specifically Gnostic; it is, he says, mentally independent, autonomous, and totally free of Iranian influence. A female divinity like Helena-Ennoia has a background in the goddesses of Syria, Phoenicia, and Egypt, those of the moon, fertility, and sexuality [33]. Bousset writes that the figures of the Syrian Aphrodite, of the Egyptian Isis, and of the moon-goddess Selene-Helena have merged into each other [34]. It goes without saying that this idea is totally un-Jewish.

Whatever the mythological lineage may have been, the Simonians and other groups of this kind fitted what they found at hand into their own doctrine and charged the divine figures with the roles they wanted them to play. That possibly there is no Iranian influence (but some scholars say there is) does not mean that there is no dualism. On the contrary! Jonas stresses that the blatant dualism of these groups is entirely original [35]. Even at this early stage dualism was a hallmark of the budding Gnosis.

e. The Simonian Book of Revelation

"This is the book of revelation of the voice and the name out of the design (epinoia) of the great Boundless Power". This short statement, cited by Hippolytus as a literal quotation from Simon [36], gives rise to some initial questions and remarks. To begin with, to what is Hippolytus referring here? In all probability it is the so-called 'Apophasis megale'. or 'Great Declaration', of which Hippolytus gives excerpts [37] and that for the rest is lost; its authorship is usually ascribed to Simon himself. If this is correct, then the Apophasis was the first Gnostic writing [38]. Simon by 'apophasis' clearly means a revelation since he is speaking of 'the voice and the name'. In doing this he is pitting himself against Scripture as revealed truth [39].

It is noteworthy, moreover, that he characterizes the Power as 'boundless' ('aperantai') since in consequence the old bogey of Greek thought, the 'apeiron', the 'boundless' or 'infinite', appears on the scene again, this time as something fundamental and constitutive. That the boundless in itself, being indeterminate and formless, could be seen as constitutive, is an idea alien to Greek thinking; instead of giving it pride of place, the Greeks were rather afraid of it. So right from the start Simon takes issue with Judaism as well as with classical Hellenic philosophy.

f. The nature of the Boundless Power

The literal Simonian text continues as follows. "Therefore, it (the Power) must be sealed, hidden, veiled, laid down in the dwelling-place where the root of the All is established." In Simon's view the (Boundless) Power (dynamis) is the beginning of everything. It should be noted that knowledge about the Power is something secret ('sealed'), obviously not generally available. The dualistic bipartition of mankind into those who know and those who do not is already becoming discernible. This becomes also apparent from a prescript of the Simonian sect that any person in their midst who, seeing the statues of Simon and Helena, should refer to them by name, would be expelled, as somebody who did not understand the mysteries [40].

In this Simonian text the word 'archê' (beginning) surfaces again, as though Simon was a late successor to the Presocratics with their several 'archai'. Simon comes very close to Heraclitus indeed when he states that his 'archê', that is the Power, is Fire [41]. Hippolytus emphatically declares that Simon's Power = Fire is not Jahve, the Mosaic God.

Now Fire is one of Empedocles' four elements, and as an element it has to be simple and indivisible. But no, Simon says, Fire is not simple and uniform but twofold. In his Fire there are two parts, one hidden, the other apparent, namely the flames. This last part contains all visible things, that is the whole phenomenal and concrete world. But within the observable part of the Fire there is also the hidden, invisible part, containing all that is spirit and thought and that cannot be observed by the senses [42]. According to Simon, reality has a double, a dual nature; this is not yet downright dualism but we are not far from it.

Simon goes on to say that this supercelestial Fire is like a burning tree. All parts of the tree will be consumed by the flames - trunk, branches, leaves, bark, everything, with the exception of the fruit that will be saved and preserved. The wood of the tree is man but the fruit is his soul [43]. Even if we have not yet entered the realm of dualism, with this analogy we stand on the threshold since we are in the presence of a inferior part that is destined for destruction and a superior one that is to be saved.

Simon describes the Power in the following terms. "It is one, it makes a division upwards and downwards, it increases itself, it seeks itself, it finds itself, it is its own mother, its own father, its own sister, its own wife, its own daughter, its own son, mother, father, it is one being the root of all that is" [44]. Please note that in all these family relations the female ones come first! This is a remarkable example of an comprehensive text; as such it is typically Gnostic. Therefore, confusing as it is, the reader who is not conversant in matters Gnostic must try to get used to this kind of language. Quispel once wrote that the western mind is trained to function like an automatic telephone-exchange. A person who dials a number gets one specific subscriber; this is what he expects. But the Gnostic mind is able of responding to many calls at once without getting disturbed [45].

It is typical that beginning and end are one; Gnostic systems often start from a monistic point of view and are striving backwards to it. Furthermore, it should not be overlooked that the One, although really one, is at the same time divisive since it creates two spheres, the celestial (anoo) one and the sublunary (katoo). This is incipient dualism since we know that the world 'katoo' is doomed to perdition.

Once again, with Hippolytus quoting him textually, Simon defines the Power. "The Power is silence, it is unspeakable, it is not to be grasped" [46]. Here, for the first time in a Gnostic text, we encounter the idea of the deus absconditus, the hidden God, on whom no pronouncement of whatever kind is possible.

g. The two roots

"From this one root two offshoots go out running through all ages; they have neither beginning nor end" [47]. For 'ages' the Greek has 'aioon', aeon, one of the constitutive concepts of the Gnosis. "Of these (roots) one appears in the upper sphere, it is the great force, the mind of all that is; it governs everything, and is of the male sex" [48]. The word used for mind (or spirit) is 'nous'. "The other (root) dwells in the nether sphere; it is the great Thought (epinoia); it is of the female sex and generates everything". Nous and epinoia are related to each other as the brain and its product, thought. Since the Boundless Power is wholly passive and negative - nothing can be stated about it -, active and positive principles, one governing, one generating, are needed to explain why there is a world at all.

These principles, nous and epinoia, are clearly modelled on the traditional sex roles : the male one is the ruler, the woman bears the offspring. There is nascent man-woman dualism here. And indeed, nous and epinoia have intercourse, "and corresponding with each other bring forth the intermediate sphere" [49] which refers to the space between heaven and earth. Their offspring, therefore, is air which, without beginning or end, is once again a concept that transcends the intellect. In this air-space the Father lives.

h. The Father

We must now address ourselves to a very difficult question. Who is this Father? He is not identical with the intermediate space of the air; he only settles himself in it. Nor is he identical with the Boundless Power, for it is emphatically stated that "he is not the first one" [50]. Nevertheless, he closely resembles the Power since he too is alone and pre-existing. The Apophasis characterizes him as a male-female power, "just as the pre-existing Boundless Power" [51]. The Father bore the Epinoia in himself and produced her by doubling himself. We may, indeed, think of the Father as of somebody who is reflecting on himself and thus, by distancing himself from himself somewhat, creates a sort of double. Simon represents this process by means of his usual sexual imagery.

Epinoia grew up and began to call the Father by this name, i.e. to recognize him as her father [52]. The text now goes on to suggest that Epinoia could have doubled herself too but that she did not do this. Instead, she hid the Father in herself and thus also became male-female. And this is the conclusion. "In that what is in the upper sphere the Power is found, in that what is in the nether sphere, Epinoia".

I have pondered for days on end on this baffling text. The problem is that first it is stated that Nous and Epinoia both are roots sprouting from the Boundless Power; and then we hear that Epinoia is the daughter of another Power, the Father, whose origin remains unclear. It is possible that Hippolytus who is constantly polemizing against Simon the heretic - "the stupid think he is a god" [53] - has distorted or misunderstood the original text. But let us argue on the premise that he rendered it in a correct way. My solution in that case is that there is no solution, at least not according to the rules of classical logic. We have before us a fine sample of a-logical, inclusive Gnostic reasoning.

i. Inclusiveness

Although the Boundless Power, Nous, the Father, and Epinoia all are different entities, they are also all and sundry called 'power' (dynamis). The Father is introduced as a new and separate concept but in the concluding phrase he appears to be identical with Nous. "Nous is in Epinoia" [54], whereas a few sentences earlier it was said that the Father was in Epinoia. Other inclusive elements are that there is very little difference between the Father and the Boundless Power, that the Father and Epinoaia both are male-female, and that Epinoia first is in the Father and then the Father in Epinoia.

That all this is really meant to be inclusive can be proved in different ways. The text says in as many words that the Father and Epinoia supplement each other : "the power does not distinguish itself from Epinoia" [55]. And further, "although they (the Father-Nous and

Epinoia) are one, they are experienced as two, since the male-female principle carries the female in itself" [56].

The Apophasis does not appeal to our logical brain-power here but to our deeper intuition. It suggests that originally all was one but that a process of differentiation took place. It is an authentically Hellenic idea that from the primary One dualities proceed that eventually may turn into dualisms. It is equally classical Greek thought that the original entities Nous and Epinoia are intellectual concepts that are related as the brain and its thought. But at the same time the Apophasis tends to hover between Hellenic thought and oriental symbolism since the author elaborates his thinking in terms of sexual imagery.

j. Seeds of dualism

Seeds of dualism are to be found in the developing opposition of male and female. Bousset says that this is typical for Simonianism, the more so because this opposition will link itself with that between light and darkness. He adds that Simonian dualism has a mitigated nature since between the upper and nether world the intermediate air-space is interposed [57].

k. The function of Epinoia

That "Epinoia assumed the Father into herself" must be understood in the sense that she now became the actual creative principle or force. She became "the bearer of the ensuing fate of being (of the universe) the forces of which started with the first reflection (i.e. of the Nous-Father on himself); this (creative process) leads her, in the wake of her own productions, continuously ever deeper into the creation (i.e. into the actual phenomenal world)" [58]. Thus Jonas describes the downward trend that is so typical of Gnostic systems. During this process Epinoia gets further and further away from her lofty origin, loses her self-knowledge, is no longer free, becomes immersed in the world and, finally, enslaved by it; this, Jonas concludes, is what is typically Gnostic in this process [59], and, I may add, it also inaugurates its essential dualism.

Irenaeus identifies Ennoia (Epinoia) with Helena [60], and Simon himself with Nous. She is the first thought of Nous who is the Father. From now on the creative process lies in the hands of a female principle, entity, or being; the universe has no All-Father but an All-Mother. Knowing what the Father wanted (since she is his thought), she descended into the nether regions and created the angels and archangels [61], and they in their turn created the cosmos. We must not overlook the circumstance that the creative process begins only in the nether sphere. The upper sphere is reserved for unchanging and essential concepts; there is a very acute difference between both spheres.

l. The cosmos and mankind

The cosmos, as we know it, is made by the angels, not by any of the higher powers of the upper sphere. At this stage, things definitely took a wrong turn [62]. The offspring of the angels, the created beings, with mankind in the first place, obviously wanted to consider themselves completely independent; out of sheer envy, they did not even acknowledge the creative role of the angels. Men did not even know who the Father was; Ennoia was kept prisoner by the angels so that she was incapable of returning to the Father. She became enclosed in human bodies and migrated without end from one (female) body to another. She is, says Irenaeus whom I still am quoting, like the lost sheep! Finally she landed in a whorehouse and had to take her abode in the body of Helena. This is how Epinoia-Ennoia and Helena came to be identified.

m. A recapitulation

Let us now pause for a moment in order to make things clear to ourselves. The difference between the upper and nether worlds has become more pronounced. The Boundless Power has nothing whatsoever to do with the creation and the existence of the universe, the Father-Nous

99

only in so far that it is his idea to entrust the creative process to Epinoia; it does not appear that he is interested in her sad fate. Her creation of the angels is evidently a blunder from her or the Father's point of view since what they created was something very imperfect, far inferior to the spotless upper world. The result is that the higher principle, Epinoia, gets imprisoned in matter and in this way becomes unrecognizable.

This virtual obliteration puts the higher world at a still greater distance from the nether spheres. There is every reason to dub the opposition between the two regions dualistic; they have grown so far apart that in the nether world nobody knows anything about the Father, let alone about the Boundless Power. The determining factor in the bad world is that it does not 'know' the Father; as Jonas says, here the element of 'agnoia' comes in, of 'unknowing', of ignorance, that has to be countered by 'knowledge' [63].

n. The Redeemer

The angels, the ancient account goes on to say, as governors of this world did their work badly because each one of them wanted to be first. But now the Father took action and descended into the nether world assuming the shape of a man. We must not think here of Jesus Christ of course, but of Simon who is presented as the incarnate Father. "Whoever believes in him and in his Helena need no longer bother about the angels and their misgovernment, for he is free and can do what he likes." We are miles distant here from contemporary biblical Christianity in which Jesus of Nazareth is the Redeemer. In Simon we encounter the first manifestation of the Gnostic Redeemer [64].

o. Simonian antinominianism

This is the typical antinominianism of the Gnostic religion : there is no law for the believers. People are saved by the grace of Simon the Father and not by their just works. This separates the Gnosis decisively from orthodox Christianity in which, although grace is equally necessary, it remains barren without works. Very pointedly Irenaeus says that there can be no good works (in the Simonian system); they can only be called good accidentally -, when they are performed, as I understand it, by the Simonian believer; this is an instance of the inherent subjectivism of such systems. The idea that there are general rules and precepts was invented by the angels who wanted to ensnare mankind, but with the destruction of this world these rules will find their end [65].

p. Simon in opposition to Judaism and Christianity

From the very first Simon showed himself so sharply opposed to both Judaism and Christianity that we are entitled to speak of dualism. He assured his opponents that he himself was the power of the immeasurable and ineffable Light; "neither the lawgiver Moses nor your teacher Jesus does know the Creator of this world" [66]. Here Simon accuses Moses and Jesus alike of 'agnoia'. By the 'Creator of this world' he means Jahve, the Jewish godhead, the principal of the angels who created the world [67]; in other words, it is Jahve who is responsible for the deplorable state of the world. This Jahve indeed went out from the Father but turned against him, pretending to be the supreme godhead himself; he is holding captive the souls that belong to the authentic supreme god [68].

Simon obviously knew quite well what he was doing, for he is reported to have said in a discussion with Peter that he preached 'new and unheard of things'. He adds that the stupid populace would doubtless follow Peter since he preached what they knew already [69]. Jonas considers this utterance authentic; even if such discussions are not rendered literally, the tenor and the tone must have been like this. What Simon announced, says this scholar, was 'the revolt against the world and its God' [70]. With these words Simon's fundamental dualism is very succinctly described.

2. Menander

Simon was the head of a Gnostic community in Samaria; "this was considered by the expanding Christianity as a serious competitor"[71]. Rudolph sees in him an intellectual of sorts with a smattering of Greek education; this also holds for his disciple and successor Menander[72]. Of this man's life precious little is known. He too was a Samaritan, having been born in a place called Kapparetea. His sphere of work was the great Hellenistic city of Antioch. If we may believe Irenaeus, Menander no less than his master was an expert magician[73].

What we know of his doctrine is handed down to us by Irenaeus; it did not really differ from Simon's teaching. He preached the First Power that remains unknown to everyone - once again the idea of the deus absconditus, with the dualism of God and mankind as its consequence. Then there is also the Ennoia who sent out the angels to create the world. It is not expressly said but inferred that the angels made a mess of it. Tertullian adds that our bodies, volatile and defective as they are, are vilified by Menander as being intrinsically evil because they have been created by the angels[74]. Menander was sent to the world by the invisible Powers as Redeemer. He claimed to have control over the angels by means of his witchcraft.

A new element is what he taught about baptism. Through baptism his disciples would receive the resurrection; they would not die but were imperishable and would remain always young and immortal[75]. Menander's baptism promised much more than that of the Christians; it created an élitist set of people essentially different from all others.

What is truly different in Menander is that, whereas Simon professed to be the Boundless Power himself, Menander is no more than an emissary. Since Irenaeus does not speak of 'the Power' but of 'invisible Powers' in the plural, it was not the Boundless One that sent him but some subordinate entities. Leisegang supposes these could be the 'aeons' that in later Gnostic systems play such an important role. This scholar holds that the idea of gnosis is more pregnant here since Menander was in possession of magic knowledge that was capable of holding the angels in awe [76].

3. Saturnilos

Menander who probably died at some time around 80 A.D. was followed by a man called Saturnilos in Greek and Saturninus in Latin. It is not clear whether or not he was the successor of Menander. With him we are leaving Samaria, for he was a Syrian. Once again we are dependent on Irenaeus' report. This is what he tells us.

An unknown Father has created the angels, archangels, forces, and powers. The world itself, with all that it contains, is a special creation of seven angels; man was made by them. These angels were unable to preserve the luminous image of the highest Power, and, instead, created man 'in the image and resemblance'. Here the biblical text of Genesis is contorted since the word 'our' in 'in our image' is omitted; what is meant is that mankind was created in the image of the angels. Dualism is shining through since the highest Power absents itself into unknown spheres. The angels are left to their own (weak) devices, with the consequence that man is no more than a worm.

Then the highest Power pitied man and emitted a spark of life; this spark restores man to life. After death this spark returns to its origin; then the human frame falls apart. This signifies that the human being is not a unity since he is composed of two disparate elements : a very defective and imperfect frame, created by those blundering angels, and a divine spark. These two elements can only cohere for a short time. This a dualistic vision of the human person.

There is yet another dualistic division, this time within mankind. The angels have created two sorts of people, good ones and bad. The bad are kept enthralled by demons; they obviously must be considered hopelessly lost. Purely human activities like marrying and procreating are utterly condemned as the work of the devil. The good will not be automatically saved simply because they are good; they need a Redeemer. What makes them (potentially) good is that they have a spark of (divine) life in them. But does not every human being receive this spark? Perhaps we must interpret this as follows that, if it is true that all people are endowed with this spark, many remain unaware of it and in consequence cannot be helped.

The Powers of the nether sphere hate the Father and want to bring him down. But now the Saviour appears on earth. He is unborn and incorporeal; in consequence, it would be a gross misunderstanding to suppose that he had come in a physical shape. Saturnilus is very close to the docetist doctrine according to which Jesus Christ had only a body in appearance, not a real one. For Christ is the Saviour that is meant here. This is a significant moment in the development of the Gnosis since this is the first time that the person of Jesus of Nazareth is appropriated by a Gnostic prophet and given a place in his own system. Simon and Menander had not done this.

There is a strong vein of anti-Judaism in this system. Jesus the Redeemer has come to ward off attacks on the heavenly Father by overthrowing the Jewish god (= Jahve); this god is only one of the bad angels. For the first time (although Simon suggested it too) we are introduced here to the idea that the Old Testament Jahve is an evil godhead, whereas the heavenly Father is a benevolent one. It is a fair guess that this doctrine of two opposed and warring divinities had an Iranian background. Christ will redeem those who are ready to believe in him, that is those who have the spark of life in them. The majority of the Saturnilians observed a vegetarian diet which attracted many adherents to the sect [77].

When Hippolytus wrote that Saturnilos was teaching the same doctrine as Menander, he was talking rather glibly. For the differences between this system and those of Simon and Menander are obvious. In Saturnilos there no longer is an Ennoia-Epinoia; Helena too has left the stage. Whereas Simon identified himself with the Boundless Power, and Menander is said to be the Redeemer, Saturnilos in contrast proclaims Christ as the Redeemer. Saturnilos' system was more 'personalized' than its Simonian and Menandrian counterparts; in it the opposition is not between rather abstract entities like 'Powers' but more directly between Jahve and Christ.

This kind of polemic against Judaism is new, and equally new is the idea of the divine spark that has fallen down into mankind. The dualism has grown still more pronounced, with the upper and nether spheres, Jahve and Christ, good and bad people, mercilessly pitted against each other, whilst nothing can be more dualistic than the condemnation of sexuality [78]. This is a fair example of how different Gnostic systems can be.

4. Cerinthus

With Saturnilos we have already strayed far away from original Simonianism; Cerinthus, of whom we must speak now, very probably was unacquainted with Simonian doctrine. Cerinthus (or Kerinthos in Greek) was no Samaritan but lived in Asia Minor, in the Roman province of Asia, in or near Ephesus, in the second half of the first century A.D. We know this from a curious story told by Irenaeus. Polycarpus (ca.70-156/157), a famous Christian martyr, who was bishop of Smyrna, related the following anecdote about the Apostle John who, as tradition has it, was the first bishop of Ephesus. The saint wanted to take a bath in the public baths. But once inside he descried Cerinthus and immediately took to his heels without having bathed, crying : "Let us fly lest the bathhouse collapses, since Cerinthus, the enemy of truth, is in it" [79]. Is this not a nice commentary on the often expressed opinion that John was rather close to the Gnosis?

To all intents and purposes Cerinthus was a Jew; he showed himself so deeply interested in Judaism that he cannot have been anything else. In his view the 'Kingdom of Christ' would not be a celestial realm but a terrestrial one - and very earthly at that, since, as Eusebius reports, the pleasures of the body, the belly, and the throat could be enjoyed to the full in this realm. His Jewishness is further accentuated by the fact that he, in contrast to Christian custom, permitted animal sacrifices [80]. He also practised circumcision and observed the Sabbath. The fact that he believed in the restoration of the Temple proves that he was active after 70 A.D.

Perhaps he had once been a Christian, for he was acquainted with the Gospel of Matthew of which, as Epiphanius states, he only used the genealogy. Matthew stresses the Jewish descent of Jesus, and Cerinthus seems to follow the same line. "If Jesus has been circumcised", he wrote, "then he himself (Cerinthus) should be circumcised too" [81].

Cerinthus preached a radical dualism of God and the world. The world, he taught, had not been made by the First God but by a power that was far distant from the origin of the universe and separate from it; it (or he) did not even know this God who is exalted above all. He also preached that Jesus and Christ were two different persons. Jesus was the normal offspring of both Joseph and Mary but all the same an exceptional man surpassing all in wisdom, intelligence, and justice. After his baptism in the river Jordan, the Spirit, sent out by the sublime Prime Principle, descended on him in the shape of a dove. This enabled Jesus to preach the Unknown Father and to perform great things. The Christ lived together with Jesus in a sort of personal union, being almost identical with the Spirit. Both the Spirit and Christ left Jesus when he suffered on the cross, but it was he who rose from the dead. Christ could not share in Jesus' passion because he was purely spiritual [82].

Daniélou feels inclined to connect the doctrine of Cerinthus with that of Jewish (and Christian) Zelots who abounded in Judaism during the first decades of the first century A.D; they were people who expected the speedy coming of the Messiah. Their Messiah, however, would not only be a religious prophet but also, and probably far more, a political figure who would liberate Palestine from the Romans; then a new era of Jewish independence would be ushered in during which the prophecies of the Old Testament would come to fulfilment. We know that for a very long time Jesus' own disciples expected this too of their Master. But because Jesus rejected any connection with Zelotism, many of his initial adherents left him. Perhaps this was the reason why the disappointed Judas betrayed him.

Christian Zelots certainly believed that Jesus was the Messiah. If they were disappointed that Jesus' life on earth had ended without the liberation of Palestine taking place, they put their hope now in the Parousia, the return of Jesus which in their view was to take place very soon; then the pagan power of the Romans would be destroyed once and for all. Daniélou adds that some Cerinthians felt that Messianic times had already begun; they gave expression to this belief by holding banquets with an orgiastic character [83].

The precise difference between Judaism and early Christianity must have been obscure to many people of the decades around 50 A.D. It seems to me that Cerinthus was trying to have the best of two worlds. But he was certainly no orthodox Jew and still less an orthodox Christian.

5. The Gnosis of the Pseudo-Clemenentina

a. On the text

I feel this is the place to make mention of an early Gnostic-dualistic treatise that is equally to be located in the no man's land between Judaism and Christianity. It is to be found in the so-called 'Pseudoclementina', a work that contains a lot of intriguing dualistic material. It consists of two parts, the Homilies and the Recognitions (which I repeatedly quoted in the foregoing sections). They traditionally are ascribed to Clement (not to be confused with the much later Clement of Alexandria), the author of at least one letter to fellow-Christians; he himself in all probability was innocent of the Homilies and Recognitions, hence their title 'Pseudoclementina'. The authentic Clement is usually identified with that Clement I who, after Linus and Anacletus, was Peter's third successor as bishop of Rome. The dates of his time of office are mostly given as 88-96. The Pseudoclementina have been worked over but the original version probably dates from the second century. This means that both the Homilies and the Recognitions may have been compilations from earlier sources. Part of them has a Judeo-

107

Christian background. Once again we are not justified in speaking of orthodoxy. There are passages which portray Christianity as an integral part of Judaism [84].

b. The Spirit of Truth

The book states categorically that the will of God has fallen into oblivion. There were many reasons for this, first of all bad education leading to erroneous ideas. This causes many evils, such as profligacy, unbelief, fornication, and other vices that become so widespread that we may compare the world to a smoke-filled room that, affecting the eyes, leads to blindness; in the same way the inhabitants of this world become incapable of finding God and understanding his intentions [85]. In my opinion, this is equivalent to the doctrine of the deus absconditus or Unknown God.

Those who in spite of the general depravity still love Truth must implore help from the Spirit of Truth that lives in them. They must pray that someone who is outside the smoke-filled house will come and open the door so that the light of the sun may stream into the house and drive out the smoke [86]. One detects several Gnostic and dualistic ideas here : the spark of Truth in some people, their utter helpnessness, the radical opposition of light and dark, i.e. of heaven and earth, and the idea of complete purification.

c. The spiritual Christ

"That man who alone is capable of illuminating the souls of men, so that they with their own eyes discover the road to eternal salvation, that man I call the true prophet" [87]. Without him it will prove impossible to find the right road [88]. This true prophet is not a human being, and not Jesus of Nazareth, but the eternal and spiritual Christ, the ruler of the celestial world and created in the image of God [89]. For the first time he appeared on earth in the person of Adam.

In consequence Adam had to remain sinless; the author puts forward the bold thesis that the report of Adam's fall in Genesis is false. For it would be unthinkable that the first man who came out of the hand of God should not possess the holy spirit of Christ. Therefore, the author continues, it is impossible that somebody whose origin is in impure seed would possess this spirit [90]. There really is no forgiveness for those who believe that Adam sinned [91]. It will be clear that the author is putting forward a doctrine of his own that by no means tallies with Jewish orthodoxy.

d. Two opposed worlds

I must now ask the reader's attention for a passage of the utmost importance. To Adam, the First Man, a companion was given, a female one, the First Woman. She was far inferior to the First Man, just as much as (real, primary) Being differs from (dependent, secondary, participating) being, or the sun from the moon, or the light from the fire. Since she is female she controls the cosmos that is equally female. She is considered to be the first prophetess; she prophecies among all those who are 'of woman born'. Her counterpart is male and proclaims, as the Son of Man, what is important for the world [92].

There are, so much is clear, two separate and opposed worlds, one superior and male, the other, our human world, inferior and female. Jonas would call this an ideology of the male type. There is not, as there is in Simonian Gnosis, a divine role for a supreme woman. In their respective courses these worlds follow binary and opposed paths.

After Adam, mankind chose the wrong course for twenty generations; its principal sin was that it glorified in bloody sacrifices. But God found pleasure in Abraham who, as an astrologer, had always been able to recognize the Creator of the world in the course of the stars. This will be new to the Bible-reader since there is not a word of this in Genesis! It is a telling example of how arbitrarily Gnostics often quoted and interpreted Scripture. The True Prophet, the text goes on, revealed himself to Abraham teaching him about things divine, but after that he retired to his invisible dwelling-place [93]. Later he appeared again, to Moses in Egypt; Moses, however, had to tolerate animal sacrifices since the habit was too deeply ingrained in his people [94]. (Once again, this is sheer fantasy on the part of the author!) And thus the Jewish people continued on its sinful road.

In accordance with a divine ordinance, Moses gave his people the Law, but soon enough this became a source of further corruption. The Law came to contain many lies about the one God who is the maker of heaven and earth and of all that is in it. It was the Evil One who dared to insert these lies into the Law [95]. Moses is exonerated because he is not the author of the Law as it stands [96]. (There is a distinctly anti-Jewish bias in these writings. Judaism must be swept away to make place for a new and superior religion.) The author does not find himself in the position to communicate all that he knows; he will content himself with secretly enlightening the well-intended [97].

At last the time came for the removal of the defects in the Mosaic Law. Now the promised prophet appeared, Christ. He did away with the abuses, abolishing in particular the animal sacrifices and putting baptism with water in their stead. (This is decidedly un-Christian, for what came in the place of animal sacrifices was not baptism but the unbloody sacrifice of Jesus Christ himself in the Eucharist.) Those, the Pseudoclementine author continues, who are baptized in the name of Christ will be saved; all others, he says, will be doomed to perdition [98]. (This is the usual drastic distinction between the good and the bad.)

e. The problem of Evil

God is in the centre of the cosmos radiating his light to all sides. How can one know this light? The writer now grasps the opportunity to haul the Apostle Paul over the coals by the mouth of Peter (the prince of the apostles is used by the author as his spokesman). Peter, referring to Christ's apparition to Paul on the road to Damascus, reproaches him for having become the victim of his imagination. He turns fiercely against the new convert admonishing him to become apprenticed to him, Peter, in order to learn the truth [99]. (Is this the first phase of the anti-Pauline campaign that is still going on?)

God, the author goes on, has decreed that there should be two worlds, the realm of the good and the realm of evil. This does not entail that God created evil; evil has come into the world as a consequence of human freedom of the will. There are many people who voluntarily choose for evil. What God intended to do was to keep the two realms hermetically sealed off from each other. The realm of Evil is the present, created world, that of Good the future, eternal one. On the day of judgment God will abandon the present world to the eternal fire [100].

In my opinion we must certainly not overlook the fact that the world that is destined to disappear is female, while the celestial male world will last in eternity. Here we have the sheerest dualism of the superior and indestructible male element and the inferior female one that will be destroyed in the end. It should not escape our attention that there is no talk here of the Cerinthian two gods, the First Power and the God of the Old Testament. But need I say that the dualism of the two worlds is the most dualistic of all dualisms?

The text now says that, although there are not two gods, there are, nonetheless, two heavens. One is the supreme heaven, the celestial and eternal one which is invisible; the other is the visible vault of heaven. This vault serves as a screen between the upper heaven and the earth so that no unworthy person may cast a glance into the dwelling-place of God . When judgment day arrives and the nether world is destroyed, the screen is no longer needed and will be torn away [101].

The author now finds himself in a nice quandary. As is proper to almost all dualistic systems, the Pseudoclementine ideology has a monistic starting-point. It is the one God who created everything; there is no separate (bad) maker, or Demiurge, of the human world. The author is hitting upon a very old and persistent problem here : how can his idea of a supreme and just God be reconciled with the existence of evil? It is, of course, not his problem alone, but to him it must have seemed all the more perplexing because of the often radical dualism in his system.

Although God is one, there are all the same two opposed and separate courses that are followed, not only in human history but also in the cosmos. The author's solution to this problem is that God created everything in the form of 'syzygies' or pairs of opposites that are constantly battling with each other. "In order to teach people the truth that is present in everything, God, although being one himself, has created all outside himself in two opposed series" [102].

This raises the question whether, if this is true, God is really one. The answer is that the friction between the pairs helps to realize God's plans; in the end all oppositions will be 'aufgehoben', in Hegel's double sense of abrogated and lifted up, i.e. into the eternal realm of peace [103]. This signifies that there is not only a monistic starting-point but no less a monistic final phase. A dualism hedged in between two monisms is very common in such systems.

The Pseudoclementina offer a very curious theory about the origin of evil of which, once again, Peter is made the spokesman. This is probably done to make it acceptable to Christians. Needless to say that there is not the slenderest biblical evidence of what he is propounding. Peter states that God has established two realms and two 'aeons' (main periods). One of these realms is our world that is inferior and volatile and given over to Evil; the future aeon, which is the second world, is eternal and reserved for the good. Each of these two realms has its own king [104]. These kings are the rapid hands of God; they want to hear his will and execute it. They are not alike the other living beings for their glory is equal to that of God; they do not exist outside God and never act against his will.

The author is surely seeking his way on a slippery path! Does he mean to say in this way that God is the creator of evil as well as of the good, perhaps even that evil is a part of God that really belongs to his essence? This once again would raise the question whether God is one or dual. Bousset, who says that the Pseudoclementine author is arguing confusedly here, offers the following solution (if it is one). God did not create evil but only the possibility of evil. The actual and concrete will to do it only comes later. That evil too is a servant of God means that it has to execute the punishments that God orders for the world (since punishments have to be decreed because evil is done, evil punishes itself for its own doings!) [105].

To return to the Pseudoclementina now, after the two kings the four elements were created; these became mixed with each other, outside God to be sure. During the process of mixture things went wrong so that actual evil became a liability in this world. It is not explained who or what was responsible for this failure. Anyhow, soon enough it becomes clear that the king of the future realm is Christ, whereas the devil is the ruler of the present world. They both are God's servants but the author emphasizes that they are not brothers and not sons of God in the same sense. Thus the devil is relegated to a somewhat lower ontological level. After the destruction of this world he will live on in total darkness. Bousset thinks that the king of the present realm has some of the traits of the Old Testament Jahve [106].

We are confronted in this part of the Pseudoclementina with a singular doctrine. Where we would expect the fiercest possible opposition between God, or Christ, and the devil, we find, next to opposedness, two worlds as parallelisms of good and evil, though with different endings. This is something exceptional in this period. A diligent reader may perhaps have been reminded of what I wrote about Zervanism in Vol. V, Ch. I.5b. I myself was struck with a more than superficial resemblance when studying these texts. Now I see that Bousset hit upon the same idea. So if I am wrong, I am erring in good company.

In Zervanism too the good Ormuzd and the bad Ahriman have the same origin, viz. the rather vague divine entity Zervan (= Time). They too are not only opposed but at the same time parallel powers. "There seems to exist an intriguing parallel between this (Iranian) speculation and the original Pseudoclementina" [107]. Bousset is convinced that the author was acquainted with the Iranian system. He (the Pseudoclementine writer) mentions Zoroaster by name, identifying him with the biblical Nimrod who is described as an enemy of God. Zoroaster was the one, he writes, who originated idolatry and caused the corruption of mankind. There follows a lot more about the Iranian prophet. Bousset winds up his long exposition in the following words : "The author of the original Clementina showed an intimate knowledge of the Iranian religion that we rarely find anywhere else" [108].

f. The male-female duality

Pace Bousset, we shall never know whether or not the author of the Pseudoclementina was actually acquainted with Zervanism and was influenced by it. What I want to stress is the resemblance. Zervanite and Pseudoclementine dualism is not exactly the same thing, though. Whereas Iranian dualism is based on the opposition of light and darkness, its Pseudoclementine counterpart is the antagonism of male and female. The author leaves no room for misunderstanding : "What is male is wholly true, what is female is wholly misleading" [109]. Somewhere else it is supposed that there is a male and a female side to God. But seeing that male and female are so utterly contrasted, how can God be one then? Is Pseudoclementine monism as monistic as it seems? Although, as I have often expounded, monism and dualism are shoots of the same trunk, they remain difficult bedfellows, the one always trying to take the place of the other.

Bousset believes that the male-female duality in the last resort goes back to Pythagorean doctrine. He says that, if this is correct, "in this (Pseudoclementine) speculation Greek-Pythagorean and Iranian dualistic ideas were combined ... We have an instance here of how Persian dualism with its oppositions 'light and darkness' entered into a connection with that other opposition of 'male and female', so that the light now appears as identical with the male principle, the patēr, the darkness with the female principle, the mētēr" [110]. The male-female opposition is in itself not alien to Gnostic systems; we already encountered it in Simonian ideology.

6. The Carpocratians

a. The name of the sect

Another Gnostic [111] system that shows a (rather vague) relationship with Judaism and early Christianity is that of the Carpocratians [112]. The story opens with a problem. Speaking of this sect, Origenes calls its adherents 'Harpocratians' with an initial H instead of a C. It is true that he admits in the same breath that he had never met a Carpocratian in his life [113]. Some scholars have inferred from this that Carpocrates never existed. In that case the sect would have as its patron Harpocrates, an Egyptian god who was a manifestation of the god Horus [114]. But if we assume that Origenes who was not personally acquainted with the sect simply was mistaken in the spelling of its name, the problem disappears. In fact, Liboron concludes that "there is no decisive reason to doubt the historical existence of a Gnostic named Carpocrates" [115].

b. Who was the founder?

With this problem out of the way, a second one immediately presents itself. Historical as he may be, perhaps Carpocrates was not the founder of the sect that bears his name, but his son Epiphanes. The authority for this is Clement of Alexandria according to whom Epiphanes was the son of Carpocrates and his wife Alexandria [116]. Some scholars have doubted the historical existence of this Epiphanes too. The name of his mother has been explained as that of the city Alexandria, and he himself as a lunar god. But once again Liboron concludes that "there is no reason to doubt the clear and exact report of Clemens of Alexandria. A Gnostic Epiphanes, the son of Carpocrates, did indeed exist" [117]. But since this young man died at the age of seventeen it is far more doubtful, even improbable, that he should have become the founder of a religious sect. As we shall see, it is nonetheless quite likely that the precocious boy played an important role in the formation of the Carpocratian ideology.

c. Carpocrates

About Carpocrates not much is known. He was born in Alexandria in Egypt and married a woman called Alexandria who came, as Clement stated, from 'Cephalene', probably a group of islands (Ithaca being one of them) in the Ionian Sea. He must have moved to Asia Minor where he was active around 130. He had his son Epiphanes educated in 'the encyclopaedic sciences and the philosophy of Plato'. Young as the boy was, he became the author of a book called 'On Justice' parts of which have been preserved by Clement [118].

d. The supreme godhead

Carpocratian theology is based on the idea of the one supreme godhead who, being 'unborn', has no origin [119]. This prime divinity is 'agnoostos', unknown, unknowable [120], far from the cosmos and mankind, existing in utter seclusion. He is, as Liboron says, the 'Bathos', the mysterious primordial ground of Being; as such he is unfathomable [121]. He has no name; no name can be assigned to him [122]. He is utterly alone since he has no 'paredra', no female godhead acting as his companion, not even Sophia. Liboron supposes that Carpocrates did not give his godhead a name and did not endow him with a female godhead, because he wanted to reach Christian circles [123]. This nameless godhead is the absolute Monad, immeasurably far distant from all other and lower entities, good or bad [124].

e. The negative Powers

This supreme deity emanates 'dunameis' or 'powers' that have no name either except one. There is no proper Demiurge. It is these powers that have made the cosmos [125]. Irenaeus calls them 'angels', a biblical term applied by him to these entities the nature of which he did not really understand [126]. Being far inferior to the unborn Father, they do not share in his pure nature. Filastrius states that they are 'deorsum', downwards, of an inferior nature that is, and do not belong to the upper world. By adding that they are 'prolationes' of God, he not only intends to say that they are emanations of the supreme entity but that they have strayed very far from him [127].

To explain their negative nature, Epiphanius calls them 'fallen angels', he too borrowing a biblical term for want of something better [128]. One of these powers is given a name, that of the devil. "They (the Carpocratians) call one of these angels of the world devil" [129]. But however Christian apologists may name them, so much is indubitably certain that these powers are the adversaries and enemies of the godhead. Their having created the cosmos was an act of hatred against him. One thing remains unexplained, perhaps because we have no complete Carpocratian writings, viz. how the pure First Principle could emanate such vicious powers. Could they have been originally good? But if so, what then made them so bad?

f. The hopeless situation of mankind and Jesus the Redeemer

It will be obvious that the situation of mankind is hopeless. Only some great positive power would be able to help at least a few souls to return to God. This power, in the shape of a human person, is Jesus. He is the son of Joseph which means that he has been born in the usual way. In respect of his origin he does not differ from all other people. But he is far more just than his fellow-beings.

What has been said of his origin only relates to his body, for his soul comes from the unborn Father where it dwelt before it took its abode in the body of Jesus. From the Father he received a special power that enabled him to avoid the evil entities that have made the world [130]. This signifies that the person of Jesus is not a unity : his body and his soul have different, even opposed, origins although they are made to co-exist in one shape [131]. Hippolytus adds something that has a decidedly Platonic ring, viz. that "his (Jesus') soul, that was strong and pure, remembered what it has seen when it dwelled in the company of the Father" [132].

The problem is that Jesus lived in this world as a Jew, and the Carpocratians loathed Judaism. It is true, they say, that Jesus was educated in all the usages and practices of the Jews in conformity with the Law, but he abhorred them. For this reason he received the power to destroy the passions that keep people enchained (i.e. to the Law) in order to chastise them [133]. When Jesus had died, his body was buried in the earth but his soul ascended to heaven. There is no mention of his passion and death on the cross nor of the resurrection. Filastrius adds that Carpocratians believe that only the soul can be saved and that there is no deliverance for the body [134]. This is a distinctly dualistic element.

It seems to me that there are flaws in the reasoning here, perhaps due to the faulty state of the tradition. First, Jesus' soul, when still in the upper world, receives a force enabling him to pass through the region of the inimical angels. Then Jesus, as a human person and a Jew, receives a second force that makes him, so to speak, immune against the Mosaic Law. However, it is stated that he receives this force on account of his resistance to Judaism; it is not explained what enables a person who, after all, is no more than a (Jewish) human being, to begin resisting the Law and keeping away from its pernicious influence. But Gnostic systems are never models of logic.

g. The return to Heaven

All men are composed of body and soul; the soul comes from above and has a recollection of what it has seen there. But carnally and unwittingly as most people live, this memory has nearly completely faded. The proof of this is that they prefer remaining enslaved by Mosaic Law or Christian precepts. But those who take Jesus, that is the Carpocratian Jesus, as their example will be endowed with the same force that was also his. This force will enable them to revivify the celestial memory in their souls and to recall where they came from and where they should return to. They too will be capable of passing unscathed through the sphere of the malevolent demiurges. It is even so that a Carpocratian, if he despises the things of this world (or the demiurges) more than Jesus did, may become superior to him. There also were Carpocratians who deemed themselves more powerful than Peter, Paul, and the other apostles [135].

The possibility remains that the power of some soul or other may not have the strength to throw off the whole load of the Law. It obviously did not fight the demiurges with sufficient vehemence. The consequence is that this soul will not ascend to heaven but will pass into another body as a punishment. Migration of souls is part and parcel of the Carpocratian system. This soul will be freed only when it has paid its whole debt. Carpocratians explain this by a peculiar exegesis of Matth. 5:25 : "You will never get out (of prison) till you have paid the last penny". But whereas in the Gospel text 'prison' is used in a literal sense, they take it to mean the body. For, as Irenaeus writes, "to them the body is a prison" [136]. Once again this is a clearly dualistic element.

The ancient author Theodoretus thought that the Carpocratian conception of metempsychosis was diametrically opposed to that of the Pythagoreans. In the Pythagorean view a soul, while wandering from body to body, must become ever better in the process, till it is finally fit to be released from the wheel of return. But, said Theodoretus, in the Carpocratian system a soul must become worse and worse [137]. To a certain extent this is correct. A person, according to Carpocrates, must indeed wade through mires of sin but not to become ever worse (or eventually better) but to grow in knowledge till, finally, it can leave the cosmos behind it, thus triumphing over the demiurges who enclosed it in a body [138].

h. The 'gnoosis monadikè'

This is what Clement calls the 'gnoosis monadikè' [139], the knowledge that is emanating from the Monad, the unborn First Principle [140]; this knowledge has a liberating power and does not distinguish between what is usually called good and bad, just and unjust [141]. It must be admitted that in the extant texts the word 'gnosis' is not mentioned, but all the same it is evident that this is what is meant. The power of this knowledge is so great that it overrules all human ideas and breaks all bonds, in particular those of Mosaic Law.

j. Epiphanes' 'On Justice'

We must now pass in review the little book 'On Justice' written by Carpocrates' young son Epiphanes; what we possess of it is preserved by Clement of Alexandria in his 'Stromateis' [142]. The first phrase we have runs like this. "God's justice is a kind of community based on equality." A fine example of this is the sun that sheds its light on everything and everybody. God makes no difference between human beings whoever they are; he is equally benevolent to the brute creation. This suggests that Epiphanes brings his Supreme Ruler into far closer contact with the cosmos than his father did. He calls the First Principle Father and Creator [143].

But there is a worm in the bud. For people have given themselves laws - ethical laws are meant - that imply that an action can be unlawful and unpermissible. However, the judgment on what is good or bad is a question of human opinion [144]. Such laws, for instance, presuppose the institution of private property. But private property cuts across the idea of equality and even destroys it since some people possess more than others. The notion of mine and thine has been brought into the world by the laws but in its original state the earth was a communal property in which each had share. As soon as community and equality were abrogated, theft became a reality.

The youthful author applied his ideas in particular to the institution of marriage. Because God has given everything to mankind in common possession, women have also to be thought of as commmunal property. Here we have the usual dualistic distinction between the sexes, for it is another case with the men. Epiphanes wrote - and at this point Clement is quoting him verbally - that "he (God) has made lust strong and irresistible in the male sex so that the human race will continue to exist; no law and no morals nor anything else in the world will be able to extinguish it, for it is the will of God" [145]. And once again quoting more or less literally from 'On Justice' as he says : "Consequently the injunction 'You shall not covet!' must be taken in this sense as though the Lawgiver had said something ridiculous adding something still more ridiculous, namely 'do not covet anything that is your neighbour's'. For he himself who has created lust now seemingly orders to abrogate it, although he does not take it away from any living being. And when he adds 'do not covet the wife of your neighbour', thus forcefully changing common possession into private property, he said something even more ridiculous" [146].

The obvious inference is that, good and evil being indifferent things, 'every thinkable irreligious and godless deed' was allowed. If souls eventually had to migrate to another body, they would pass once again though all the troubles of life. Therefore, it would be better to experience everything during the present life and have done with it. For if one was not really free at the moment of death, he would not ascend to heaven [147]. This is the typical antinomianism of the Carpocratians. In this case it devolves into libertarianism. In order to prove that one is really free, one had to tread conventional moral under foot.

But was this theory put into practice? The gentlehearted Irenaeus doubts it, although he admits that the injunctions mentioned are really to be found in the Carpocratian books [148]. But Clement had no doubts. The adherents of this sect, he says, assemble to share a meal. When they are satisfied, they extinguish the lamps; then they couple themselves with whomsoever they want. Not that they are more reserved in daylight [149]!

k. The adherents

We know very little of the adherents. If Origen, who was born in Alexandria and who kept a school there and later one in Caesarea in Palestine, could say that he never met a Carpocratian in person, the sect cannot have spread very far. When Anicetus was bishop of Rome (155-166), a certain Marcellina arrived there and preached the Carpocratian creed; she is said to have made many Christian converts. Epiphanius who relates this adds that they called themselves Gnostics [150]. They base themselves, he says, on secret teachings of Jesus which they only confide to those who are worthy and true believers [151].

Some of them were marked by a brand on the right ear-lobe. This mark was made with the help of a knife or a needle [152]. Clement of Alexandria supposes this to be a sacramental act, similar to baptism. Could it be, he supposed, that those Carpocratians took John the Baptist at his word when he said : "I baptize you with water ..., but he who comes after me ... will baptize you with the Holy Spirit and with fire" [153]?

They honoured Jesus by venerating a portrait of him, said to be made on the orders of Pontius Pilate; they used to crown it, but next to it they put the images of Pythagoras, Plato, and Aristotle which, says Irenaeus deprecatingly, differs very little from pagan usage [154].

Finally, it is reported that they loved magic, black and white, and love-potions; appearances of spirits and ghosts were the order of the day. They needed all his, the Carpocratians said, to acquire the power to triumph over the rulers and creators of this world, and, in this way, over all the created things in the cosmos [155].

NOTES TO CHAPTER III

1. Wilson 99 : "The Simonian system is certainly the earliest known form of the Gnostic heresy". On the historicity of the person of Simon see the discussion in Lüdemann, Unters. 9-13. Beyschlag, Simon 95, says "dass es einen 'vorchristlichen' gnostischen Simonianismus und damit auch den angeblichen Simon Magus ... wahrscheinlich nie gegeben hat". On the question whether or not Simon was the first Gnostic see Lüdemann, Unters. 20-23.

2. This report situates Simon in the first century A.D. Beyschlag, Simon 218, believes that he (if he was historical) lived in the second century.

3. Acts 8:1-9:25.

4. Just., Ap. 1.26-33.

5. Ir., Ad.Haer. 1.23.2.

6. Pseudoclem. 2.14.4.
7. Pseudoclem. Hom. 2.22.
8. Pseudoclem. Hom. 22.
9. Pseudoclem. Hom. 2.32.
10. Pseudoclem. Hom. 2.35, 3.29 (p. 219/220).
11. Pseudoclem. Actus Vercellenses 4-29, p. 233-245.
12. Hipp., Ref.6.20.
13. Pseudoclem. Hom. 32; Pseudoclem. Martyrium Petri 3.
14. Daniélou, Théol. 84.
15. Nag Hamm. Libr. in Engl. 363.
16. Daniélou, Théol. 85.
17. Quispel, Gnosis als Weltrel. 51.
18. Ir., Adv.haer. 1.23.
19. Quispel, Gnosis als Weltrel. 52.
20. "Although he appears in the Fathers as a heretic, Simon is rather a rival of Christianity and represents clearly an attempt to merge the message of the Church in a farrago of alien thought", Wilson, Gnost.Probl. 101.
21. Quispel, Gnosis als Weltrel. 53-55.
22. According to Lüdemann, Unters. 39, the divinization of Simon is the oldest ascertained part of the system.
23. Quispel, Gnosis als Weltrel. 57-59.
24. Cyrillus, Cat. 6.14.
25. Beyschlag's final conclusion (Simon 219) is that in Simonianism we have, "wenn auch in gnostischer Verzeichnung und unter simonianischer Maske nichts geringeres als den vollen Umriss der frühchristlichen Überlieferung in ihren Hauptpunkten vor Augen". He dubs it 'eine frühchristliche Ketzerei'. While it doubtless is true that there was a certain amount of 'communicatio idiomatum' between Christianity and Simonianism (and other Gnostic systems), Christianity and Gnosis are so radically different that it should be forbidden to speak of a 'Christian Gnosis'.
26. Foerster, Die ersten Gnost. Origini 192.
27. See Vol. III, Ch. I.3e.
28. Eust. comm.ad Hom.Od. I, 154.
29. Ir., Adv.Haer. 1.23.4.
30. As such in August., Civ.Dei 7.28.

31. This must not be taken to mean that Ennoia and Helena were exactly the same beings. Ennoia wandered from female body to female body; she was also in Helena. Lüdemann, Unters. 73 says that "die Richtung im Text (und im Mythos) verläuft ... von der Ennoia zur Helena und nicht umgekehrt".
32. Quispel, Gnosis als Weltrel. 65.
33. Jonas, Gnosis 352.
34. Bousset, Hauptprobl. 83.
35. Jonas, Gnosis 352.
36. Hipp., Ref. 6.9..4.
37. Since we find mention of the Apophasis and of a number of similar Gnostic texts only in the Refutatio, it has been supposed that they are not authentic or even the work of a forger. This opinion has been often combated and is considered untenable by Frickel, Apoph. 11-20. However, Lüdemann, Unters. 29, thinks that Christian authors have smuggled non-authentic elements into Simonianism.
38. As in many cases of this kind, there is not a hundred percent certainty that Simon really was its author. See Frickel, Apoph.meg. in Origini 197-202. On the question whether or not the Apophasis was the first Gnostic document, see Lüdemann, Unters. 24-28. This scholar does not see Simon as its author. Many scholars, among them Widengren, Frickel, Salles-Labadie, and Colpe believe that the historical Simon was the author of the Apophasis, but Beyschlag, Simon 43, although he admits that definite conclusions are impossible, does not think so. On the other hand, this same author, p. 213, holds the quotations in Hipp, as well as the larger part of the report in Ir. 1.23, for the only 'einigermassen gesicherte Quellengrundlage' of Gnostic Simonianism. According to him, pp. 13-18, Ir. is the one reliable witness.
39. One will find a clear exposition of the doctrine of the Apophasis in Frickel, Apoph. 123-128.
40. Hipp., Ref. 6.9.8-10.1.
41. Hipp., Ref. 6.93.
42. Hipp., Ref. 6.9.5-8.
43. Hipp., Ref.6.9.8-10.1.
44. Hipp., Ref.6.17.3.
45. Quispel, Weltrel. 63.
46. Hipp., Ref.6.18.3.
47. Hipp., Ref.6.18.2.
48. Hipp., Ref.6.18.3.
49. Hipp., Ref.6.18.3.
50. Hipp., Ref.6.18.5.

51. Hipp., Ref.6.18.4.
52. Hipp., Ref.6.18.5.
53. Hipp., Ref.6.18.1.
54. Hipp., Ref.6.18.7.
55. Hipp., Ref.6.18.6.
56. Hipp., Ref.6.18.7.
57. Bousset, Hauptprobl. 128.
58. Jonas, Gnosis I, 354.
59. Jonas, Gnosis I, 354/355. Colpe s.v. 'Gnosis II', Reall.f.Ant.u.Christ. XI, 626 : "... so wäre ursprünglich gemeint gewesen, dass Helena vom obersten Gott abgespalten und in die Tiefe gefallen ist und dort von den unteren Mächten festgehalten wird. Damit ist die Selbstzerteilung der göttlichen Einheit eingeleitet, das erste Constitutivum eines gnostischen Mythos".
60. According to Fossum/Quispel, Helena I, Reallex.f.Ant.u.Christ. XIV, 350/351, the figure of Helena was not a part of the Simonian myth from the start. She, these authors seem to say, only became part of it in Ir.' report. However, they also write that the version of Ir. is without parallel in Gnosticism and is doubtless original therefore. They do not deny that Helena was an historical person but she was turned into a myth. This seems to me to contradict what Colpe had to say on the place of Helena in the Simonian system, see note 59.
61. Fossum, The Name of God 233/234 : "That the creation took place by the will and at the command of God ("Ennoia knew what her Father willed", Ir., Ad.haer. 1.23.2) is a very peculiar idea in the history of Gnosticism ... Simon's motive for the arguing of 'many gods' (angels) under God would also seem to be that of freeing God from the blame of the evil in the world".
62. Frickel, Apoph. 127 concludes from the Apophasis that, in this system, the order of the world in some way or other became disturbed. "Man, it seems, can only free himself from this disturbed world order ... by means of Gnosis."
63. Jonas, Gnosis I, 356.
64. Bousset, Hauptprobl. 261.
65. Ir., Ad.haer. 1.23; Tert., De animo 34; Just., Apol. 26.1.3; Epiphan., Pan.haer. 21.
66. Pseudoclem. Recogn. 2.499.2-3.
67. Pseudoclem. Recogn. 2.39.
68. Pseudoclem. Recogn. 2.57.
69. Pseudo-clem.2.37.5-7.
70. Jonas, Gnosis I, 357.

71. Rudolph, Gnosis 315.
72. Rudolph, Gnosis 316.
73. Ir., Adv.Haer. 1.23.5; Just., Apol. 26.4.
74. Tert., De res.carnis 5.
75. Ir., Adv.haer. 1.23.5.
76. Leisegang, Gnosis 107.
77. Ir., Adv.1.24.1-2; Hipp., Ref.7.28; Epiph., Pan.Haer.23.1-2; Tert., De anima 23. My account is based on Irenaeus whom the other ancient authors copy.
78. Leisegang, Gnosis 109/110. Leisegang says that the introduction of the Logos as the image of God signifies 'a Christianization of the original basic idea'; he suggests a resemblance with the Gospel of John. But the ancient texts do not speak of a 'Logos'; they call the 'image of God' 'morphê' and 'poiêma', clearly referring, not to John, but to Gen. 1:26-27. The introduction of Christ does not make the system any more Christian than those of Saturnilus' predecessors. How could this be when we see that Christ is fighting the God whom he in the Gospels persistently calls his Father?
79. Ir., Adv.Haer. 28.4-5; Eus., Hist.Eccl. 4.14.4.
80. Eus., Hist.Eccl. 3.28.4-5.
81. Epiph., Pan.haer. 28.4-5.
82. Ir., Adv.haer. 1.26.1.
83. Daniélou, Théol. 81/82.
84. Douglas Powell s.v. 'Clemens von Rom' in Theol.Realenz. VIII, section 2 Pseudo-Clementines, pp. 118/119.
85. Pseudoclem.Hom. 1.18.1-3.
86. Pseudoclem.Hom. 1.18.5.
87. Pseudoclem.Hom. 1.19.1.
88. Pseudoclem.Hom. 1.19.8.
89. Pseudoclem.Recogn. 1.45.
90. Pseudoclem.Hom. 3.20.1.
91. Pseudoclem.Hom. 3.17.1-4.
92. Pseudoclem.Hom. 3.22.1-3.
93. Pseudoclem.Recogn. 1.31.
94. Pseudoclem.Recogn. 1.36.
95. Pseudoclem.Hom. 2.38.1.
96. Pseudoclem.Hom. 3.47.1-2.
97. Pseudoclem.Hom. 2.39.3-4.

98. Pseudoclem.Recogn. 1.39.
99. Pseudoclem.Hom. 17.14-19.
100. Based on the summary in Neutest.Apocr. 159.
101. Based on the summary in Neutest.Apocr. 160.
102. Pseudoclem.Hom. 2.15.1.
103. Based on the summary in Neutest.Apocr. 160.
104. Pseudoclem.Ho, 20.2.
105. Bousset, Hauptprobl. 137.
106. Bousset, Hauptprobl. 138. The Pseudoclem. author admits that the Bible is, at least partly, God's word, although having become garbled by evil powers.
107. Bousset, Hauptprobl. 142.
108. Bousset, Hauptprobl. 142-150.
109. Pseudoclem.Hom. 3.27.1.
110. Bousset, Hauptprobl. 152-154.
111. Layton, Gnost.Script. 199 says however that "the doctrine of Carpocratians bears no noticeable resemblance to gnostic myth, and so there are no grounds to conclude that the Carpocratians were gnostics in the classic sense of the word".
112. On the Carpocratians there is a book in Latin by a certain Fuldner, De Carpocratianis, Leipzig, 1834, which I did not see. A more recent one is the doctoral thesis of Herbert Liboron, Die Karpokratianische Gnosis (see Bibliography). As far as I know this work that appeared in 1938 has not been replaced by a more recent monograph. There is a chapter on 'Die Karpokratianer' in Leisegang's book on the Gnosis (pp. 257-270). It is to be deplored that Mircea Eliade's Encyclopedia of Religions (1987) does not carry an entry on 'Carpocrates' or 'Carpocratians'. Several older encyclopedias, however, have more or less extensive articles on this subject. Both the articles by G.Bareille in the Dictionnaire de théologie catholique II, Paris, 1923, s.v. 'Carpocrate', pp. 1800-1803, and by G.Krüger in the Realencyclopädie für protestantische Theologie und Kirche, Bd. 10, Leipzig, 1901 3, s.v. 'Karpokrates' have good surveys of the sources and of 18th- and 19th-century secondary publications. Some of the sources are printed in Quellen zur Geschichte der christlichen Gnosis. Herausg. Walther Völker. Tübingen, 1932. Ch. III (pp. 27-37).
113. Orig., Contra Cels. 5.62.
114. Leisegang, Gnosis 257.
115. Liboron, Karp.Gnosis 14.
116. Clem.Al., Strom. 3.2.5.2.
117. Liboron, Karp.Gnosis 16.

118. Clem.Al., Strom. 3.2.5.
119. Ir., Adv.haer. 1.25.1; Hipp., Ref. 7.32. It is true that Epiphanes says that this godhead is the Creator and Father of all that lives, Clem.Al., Strom. 3.2.6. At first sight this is an wholly un-Gnostic idea. But as Liboron points out, the difference is not as great as it appears. Epiphanes too acknowledges "an anti-divine power that has utterly spoiled the cosmos. It is present in the person of the Mosaic Lawgiver", Clem.Al., Strom. 2.2.9, see Liboron, Karp.Gnosis 21, note 2.
120. Epiph., Pan.haer.27.2.1.
121. Liboron, Karp.Gnosis 21.
122. Epiph., Pan.haer. 27.2.1.
123. Liboron, Karp.Gnosis 21.
124. Bareille s.v. 'Carpocrate', in Dict.Théol.Cath. 2, 1800.
125. Ir., Adv.haer. 1.25.2 and 4.
126. Ir., Adv.haer. 1.25.1.
127. Filastrius, Div.her.liber 35.1.
128. Epiph., Pan.haer.27.2.1.
129. Ir., Adv.haer. 1.25.4.
130. Ir., Adv.haer. 1.25.1; Hipp., Ref. 7.32.1.
131. According to Epiph., Pan.haer. 27.3.3, the Carpocratians dubbed themselves Christians. Celsus obviously thought that those Gnostics who acknowledged Jesus were for that reason Christians, Orig., Contra Cels. 5.6.1. But Eusebius, Hist.eccl. 4.22.5 angrily retorts that such Gnostics, citing among others the Carpocratians by name, are only 'pseudo-Christians, pseudoprophets, pseudoapostles'. Liboron, Carp.Gnosis 48, seems somewhat hesitant : "Die Wertung der Gestalt Jesu macht die Karpokratianer ganz gewiss nicht zu Christen, wiewohl sie sich selbst offenbar gerne als solche bezeichnen. Den Charakter einer eigentümlichen Gnosis mit christlichem Einschlag wird man ihnen jedenfalls nicht ganz absprechen dürfen".
132. Hipp., Ref. 7.32.1.
133. Ir., Adv.haer. 1.25.1; Hipp., Ref. 7.32.2.
134. Fil., Div.her.liber 35.4.
135. Ir., Adv.haer. 1.252.; Hipp., Ref., 7.32.3.
136. Ir., Adv.haer, 1.25.4; Hipp., Ref. 7.32.7-8.
137. Theodor., Haer.fab. 1.5.
138. Liboron, Karp.Gnosis 32.
139. Clem.Al., Strom. 3.5.3.

140. Otto Stählin in his translation of the Stromateis, Bibl.d. Kirchenväter, 2. Reihe, Bd. XVII, 260, translates 'monadikē' with 'auf die einzelnen beschränkt' which is wrong.
141. Bareille, Dict.Théol. Cath. 1801.
142. Clem.Al., Strom. 3.6-9.
143. Clem.Al., Strom. 3.7.1.
144. Ir., Adv.haer. 1.25.4.
145. Clem.Al., Strom. 3.8.3.
146. Clem.Al., Strom. 9.1-3.
147. Ir., Adv.haer. 1.25.4.
148. Ir., Adv.haer. 1.25.5.
149. Clem.Al., Strom. 3.10.1.
150. Epiph., Pan.haer. 27.1 and 8.
151. Theod., Haer.fab. 1.5D.
152. Epiph., Pan.haer. 27.5.9.
153. Mt.3:11; Lc.3:16; Clem.Al., Ecl.proph. 25.1.
154. Ir., Adv.haer. 1.25.3.
155. Ir., Adv.haer. 1.25.3.

CHAPTER IV

ANTAGONISTIC, DUALISTIC, AND GNOSTIC-
IZING ELEMENTS IN THE NEW TESTAMENT

In Chapter II of Volume IV of the present series, I argued that the Jewish religion, as presented in the Old Testament, was a homogeneous one, the most uniform and unitary to be found in Antiquity. It was (and still is) utterly undualistic. Still, it proved possible to detect some antagonistic, even dualistic elements within this religious system which were duly described in that chapter. The question now is whether the same may be predicated of the New Testament.

1. On the New Testament in general and its authors

This second and shortest part of the Bible consists of twenty-seven compositions, most of them not very long; one of these, the Third Letter of John, is really no longer than a postcard. The collection comprises four testimonies to the life and teachings of Jesus of Nazareth (the Gospels), the history of the early Church (the Acts of the Apostles), the Letters of Paul, usually including the Letter to the Hebrews, the so-called Catholic Letters (those of Peter, James, John, and Jude), and the Book of Revelation (the Apocalypse). The Roman-Catholic Church, the Orthodox Churches, and the Churches of the Reformation all agree on the authenticity of these twenty-seven documents. It will be understood that the Jewish community does not share in this opinion, since it does not regard Jesus as the Messiah.

The authors of all these books are known by name, with the exception of the Letter to the Hebrews that is traditionally ascribed to Paul but certainly did not flow from his pen. There is some uncertainty among scholars as to whether the Gospel of John, the Letters of John, and the Book of Revelation are written by the same person, and whether this person, especially the author of the Gospel, is the same as John, the disciple of Jesus. I have no reason to take up this issue, with this proviso that I find it strange than anyone can doubt that the disciple and the author of the Gospel are not one and the same person.

The authors of the Gospels and of the Acts present what they have to say as history. Now I know full well that to many modern scholars and to a great deal of the lay public these writings are just as much myth and legend as those of the Gnostics. But this is not the point at issue here. What is really decisive in this context is that in the opinion of the authors of the New Testament they were relating historical occurences, events that actually happened. The authors of the Gospels of John and Matthew evidently were eye-witnesses and have known Jesus personally. The author of the Gospel of John emphatically states that he was present at the crucifixion. "This is vouched by an eye-witness whose evidence is to be trusted. He knows that he speaks the truth so that you too may believe" [1]. This means that the faith of a Christian believer is based not on a myth but on fact.

The author of the Gospel of Mark in all probablity was a convert of Peter and accompanied him on his travels. His book is often supposed to be a faithful rendition of the teachings of the prince of the apostles. There is an old tradition that Mark was the unnamed young man who slipped into the Garden of Gethsemane and saw how Jesus was arrested. The temple-police tried to seize him too but he left the linen cloth, the only garment he was wearing, in their hands and escaped naked [2]. If this supposition is correct, Mark 'signed' his Gospel in this way. If we do not wish to call the approach of Matthew, John, and Mark 'historical', it is, in any case, personal, much more so than that of Gnostic writers.

Luke was not a Jew but a pagan convert to Christianity [3]. Having received an Hellenistic education, he became a doctor [4]. Attached as he was to Paul - and Paul to him [5] -, he accompanied the apostle on many of his travels. Luke did not actually sign his work but in the introductions of both the Gospel that he wrote and the Acts of which he is also the author, he referred to himself in the Hellenistic fashion as 'I' [6]. In the introduction to his Gospel he appears as a modern researcher when he writes that he "has investigated the whole course of events in detail (and) decided to write an orderly narrative ... so as to give you (= the unknown Theophilus for whom the book was destined) authentic knowledge about the matters of which you have been informed" [7].

2. The New Testament as history

All the same, we should not think of New Testament authors, not even of Luke, the best educated of them, as modern historiographers. Nobody in that period, the Hellenistic and Roman authors not excluded, can lay claim to that title. The aim of these early Christian writers was not to write biographies of Jesus as we understand them (neither Mark nor John mention his birth). What these authors did was to use historical material in a literary fashion to a prophetic end. It was this prophetic end that determined their choice of a literary genre as well as their selection of historical events. But it must never be forgotten that the foundation of all this is presented as historical. It is for this reason that Paul wrote : "If Jesus was not raised, then our gospel is null and void and so is your faith" [8]. The apostle confronts his readers with an either-or situation here : either the resurrection was an event that really happened, or there can be no Christian faith.

The framework of the New Testament is decidedly historical . Luke took particular care to situate his story in its historical setting. In the opening chapters he enumerates all the authorities one by one, the Roman governor of Judaea, Pontius Pilate, the Roman vassals in the rest of Palestine, and the High Priests [9]; these are known to us from other sources too. In addition Luke mentions the Roman emperor Augustus as the ruler of the world at the moment of Jesus' birth [10], while Matthew cites Herod as the prince during whose reign Jesus was born [11]. This prince was King of the Jews from 37-4 B.C. [12], the Romans not having assumed direct control of Judaea yet; he is called Herod I the Great. A son of his was Herod Antipas, the 'tetrarch' of Galilee and Peraea from 4 B.C. to 39 A.D. which covers the whole period of Jesus' life [13]. This man was responsible for the cowardly murder of John the Baptist [14]; Jesus referred to him as 'that fox' [15].

Then there are the two genealogies of Jesus in Matthew [16] and in Luke [17], the first one starting with Abraham and going down to Joseph, the husband of Mary, and the second counting from Jesus all the way back to Adam. They certainly are not genealogies in the modern sense of the world, that of Luke counting far too few generations, only seventy-five for a supposed four thousand years, and that of Matthew being too neatly arranged into three series of fourteen generations each - not to mention the fact that the two pedigrees differ from each other. Be this as it may, the authors clearly intend to situate Jesus into the long line of the history of Israel for the purpose of presenting him as an historical person.

Whatever one may think of the prophetic value of the Gospels and the Acts, it will be evident to everyone that they constantly refer to the socio-political history of those days. During Jesus' public life Judaea was ruled directly by the Romans and Galilee indirectly. Romans appear in person every now and then; at the end Pontius Pilate and Jesus confront one another. The sects, groups, and parties that are so much a part of that period in Jewish history are almost omnipresent, the Pharisees and the Sadducees in particular. There cannot be the slightest doubt that the authors want to present Jesus' appearance as having taken place in a strictly historical ambience.

3. The homogeneity of the New Testament

a. Its historicity as an expression of its homogeneity

The historicity of the New Testament is an indication of its homogeneity. This does not mean that the history it has to tell is an 'unbroken' one. On the contrary, it culminated in the drama of the Passion and crucifixion. But its fundamental homogeneity is guaranteed by its basic belief that God himself is guiding the course of history. The New Testament authors suggest and bring this forward constantly, not differring in this from the the writers of the Old Testament. When Matthew begins his genealogy with Abraham, thus presenting the patriarch as Jesus' real ancestor, his intention is to connect him with the history of Israel as God's chosen people. When Luke concludes his genealogical tree with 'son of Adam, son of God', he not only wants to link Jesus' personal life with the history of all mankind but to stress particularly that it all begins with a divine fiat and is always subject to God's will.

b. Its homogeneity expressed as pleroma

This same idea that history is coherent and purposeful is expressed by the term 'fulness (of time)' which is the translation of the Greek 'plèroma', known to theology as 'pleroma'. When Jesus began to preach the gospel, his very first words were : "The time has arrived" [18], literally 'the right moment has become full'. Paul, when writing to the Galatians, used the same expression : "When the fulness of time had arrived, God sent his Son" [19]. This same author expressed the leading idea behind the New Testament when he wrote to the Christians in Ephese : "(God) has made known to us his secret purpose, in accordance with the plan which he determined beforehand in Christ, to be put in effect when the time was ripe (literally : according to the economy of the fulness of the times) : namely that the universe, everything in heaven and earth, might be brought to unity in Christ (literally : be brought under one head in Christ)" [20]. What is proclaimed here is not only the coherence of history but the fundamental unity of the whole cosmos. Nothing could be less dualistic.

c. Its homogeneity expressed by the terms 'Son of God' and 'Son of Man'

This idea of the fundamental unity of all that is is further exemplified by the fact that Jesus is called 'the Son of God' as well as 'the Son of Man'. 'Son of Man' was Jesus' favourite way of indicating himself; this term is exclusively found in his own mouth. Of course, it strongly suggests that Jesus is human and belongs wholly to mankind. However, it also contains a reference to Dan. 7:13-14 : "I saw someone like a Son of Man coming with the clouds of heaven ... Sovereignty and power and glory were given to him, so that all peoples and nations of every language should serve him"[21]. This term 'Son of Man' has a positively Messianic ring and points to a more than simply human nature of Jesus; as such it once again stresses the unity of all that is.

This is not the right place for a discussion on the exact theological meaning of the term 'Son of God'; doubtless it refers to a very special relationship of Jesus with God which he accentuated by calling God his Father. Jesus is bringing everything under one head, horizontally by asserting that he is the Son of Man, and vertically by being called the Son of God. The two lines intersect when Jesus asks his disciples : "Who do people say that the Son of Man is, ... and who do you say that I am?", and Peter answers : "You are the Messiah, the Son of the living God"[22].

4. Dualistic tendencies that are not be found in the New Testament

a. The failing ethical distinction

When people ask me what dualism is, I give this as the shortest possible explanation : it is about unbridgeable oppositions. If they still have some patience left to listen to me, I use Jesus' parable of the tares among the wheat [23]. "A farmer sowed his field with good seed, but while everyone was asleep his enemy came, sowed tares among the wheat, and made off". When the labourers saw the tares sprouting among the grain, they asked their master to let them pull the tares out. "But no," he answered, "in gathering it you might pull out the wheat at the same time." And he instructed them to do nothing at all until the harvest time came; only then could they separate the wheat from the tares.

This parable signifies that in the present condition of the world good and evil are inextricably interwoven, not only in the world around us but in ourselves too. Any attempt to eradicate evil root and branch will lead to wholesale destruction. So we have to bear with the world as it is and our human condition as it is. We have the sanction of God for this (for he is the master, of course). It is God, and not man, who in the end will decide on the fate of the wicked. This means that the most important dualistic distinction, the ethical distinction, that of good and evil, does not figure in the Gospels.

b. 'Two powers in Heaven'?

Another important feature is that there are not 'two powers in Heaven'. God alone is god; there is not a second one, not even one of a somewhat lower order. There is also no 'paredra', no female divinity, as the companion of the sole ruler-god. The Old Testament never tired in explaining that God is unique; in New Testament times this had become such common ground that Jesus could take it for granted.

There is, however, a biblical tradition that there had been a conflict in heaven. The apostle Jude has preserved this. "Remember ... those angels who were not content with the role assigned to them, but abandoned their proper dwelling-place; God is holding them in darkness with everlasting chains, for judgment on the great day" [24]. The author explains the nature of their rebellion by saying that they 'fornicated' with human beings [25].

In all probability this is an allusion to a mysterious passage in Genesis where it is said that 'the sons of God' (angels, that is) took earthly women to wife and had children by them [26]. It is the opinion of some Fathers of the Church that part of the angels became jealous when God had created man 'little less than a god' [27] and rebelled against him. However this may be, the point is that there is no opposition left in heaven, and that God's power remains unimpaired.

Jesus meant as much when he said : "I saw Satan fall, like lightning, from heaven" [28]. He too did not acknowledge an evil power next to God and equivalent to him. I adduce also the remarkable fact that, according to the synoptic authors, the devil did not know who Jesus really was. If he had possessed a power and an insight comparable to that of God himself, he would certainly have known this. Instead, when Jesus was fasting in the desert, the devil put him to a threefold test, not only to get him in his power but still more perhaps to find out who this mysterious man could be. The 'Son of God' perhaps? And if so, what could this then mean exactly? But he did not succeed in his design and had to withdraw empty-handed [29].

Jesus surely was neither obsessed with demonianism, nor with Satanism. He believed in the real existence of the devil and of hell but only rarely alluded to them. What is also totally absent is the old polemics against the idols which was a conspicuous dualistic element in the Old Testament [30]. Very probably Jesus saw no need to continue in this line.

c. Jesus and the Samaritans

Some of the dualistic tendencies that are so typical for the Old Testament are wholly lacking in the Gospels. For instance, there is no trace of the traditional enmity towards the Samaritans [31], at least not in the attitude of Jesus himself. This attitude was not yet generally shared. "Are we not right in saying that you are a Samaritan?", some angry Jews said to Jesus intending to insult him [32]. It is true that Jesus said to the Samaritan woman at the Jacob's well near Sychar that "you Samaritans worship you know not what; we (the Jews) worship what we know" [33]. But the decisive fact is that he spoke with her at all. "What! You, a Jew, ask for a drink from a Samaritan woman?", she exclaimed [34]. Equally amazed Luke reports that the only one of the lepers who came back to Jesus and thanked him, was a Samaritan [35].

Jesus' disciples were not as liberal as he was. When passing through a Samaritan village on their road to Jerusalem, they were forbidden by the villagers to make their night-quarters there. The impetuous 'sons of the thunder', James and John, wanted to call down fire from heaven to consume them. But their Master rebuked these trigger-happy fellows, and they all went on to the next village [36].

If this is not proof enough of a different attitude, at least in Jesus, we have the parable of the Good Samaritan [37]. The story has become so famous that the expression 'a good Samaritan' is now proverbial. A man was robbed somewhere between Jerusalem and Jericho and lay stripped and badly wounded along the road. A (Jewish) priest passed and went on indifferently. A Levite came and could not care less. Then a Samaritan arrived, helped the man, cared for him, brought him to an inn, and paid all the costs from his own pocket. Jesus' argument is all the more telling because the parable in fact is an answer to one lawyer's question "who is my neighbour?". It needs no vivid imagination to see this man standing stupified and with eyebrows raised. What! A Samaritan my neighbour? And he reluctantly answers his own question with a 'the one who showed him kindness'. The word 'Samaritan' does not pass his lips.

d. No hard feelings towards the Romans

Pagans ruled the Holy Land. The Roman citadel in Jerusalem, the Antonia, overlooked the Temple precincts; the guardsmen on its walls could observe every movement on the Temple square. But it has always astonished me that so little enmity to them is shown in the Gospels. Jesus himself seems hardly interested. When some of the Pharisees asked him whether or not it was permitted to pay taxes to the Roman emperor, he, not wanting to be trapped, evasively answered : "Pay to Caesar what belongs to Caesar" [38]. He simply did not wish to become involved in a political dispute, still less to incite the people to rebellion.

Some Romans are shown in a favourable light; they were almost believers, like the centurion at Capernaum whose servant he cured [39], or the officer of the platoon that conducted the crucifixion who exclaimed : "This must have been a son of God" [40]. We could also think of the wife of Pontius Pilate who asked her husband to desist from prosecuting Jesus, because he was 'a just man' [41].

Of course it is true that the Jews desired to be liberated from the pagan yoke; this would be the principal task of the expected Messiah. As long as the population believed that Jesus was indeed the Promised One, they wanted him to take the lead in the war against the Romans, chase the pagans from the Promised Land, and, by becoming King of the Jews, restore the kingdom of Israel. Even his chosen disciples expected as much. The execution of their Master must have been a deeply dispiriting event for his followers. The disciples on the road to Emmaus showed their disappointment to their unkown companion (who was none other than Jesus himself) by saying : "We had been hoping that he was to be the liberator of Israel" [42].

Jesus himself, however, steadfastly refused to have anything to do with whatever kind of liberation movement. He turned down all attempts to make him King of the Jews. "Realizing that they meant to come and seize him to proclaim him king, (he) withdrew again to the hills by himself" [43].

It was only in the last week of his life that he allowed the populace to render him royal homage. That was during his triumphal entry into Jerusalem when the people carpeted the road with their cloaks and accompanied him waving branches cut from the trees. They welcomed him as the 'Son of David' which was a royal title and shouted that "the kingdom of our father David is coming" and that he came 'as king in the name of the Lord'; they even called him 'king of Israel' [44]. Jesus permitted this scene because he must have supposed that by now it should be sufficiently clear that he would only be king on the cross.

In fact, he endlessly reiterated that the kingdom that he really preached was utterly different from an earthly realm. It was to be a kingdom 'not of this world' but existing purely in the spirit and the heart of men. Curiously enough a person who understood this was Pontius Pilate. Jewish leaders accused Jesus before the governor saying : "We found this man subverting our nation ... and claiming to be Messiah, a king", suggesting that he was a rebel against the Emperor [45]. But the governor saw soon enough that this man was not cast in the mould of all those other rebels and would-be kings who had stood before his tribunal. On his question whether Jeus really considered himself a king, the accused answered that he indeed was a king but not of this world. Pilate, strangely enough, did not ridicule him for this answer but seems to have been impressed and even somewhat afraid of this man [46].

e. No antagonism towards the Gentiles

In Jesus' preaching there is nothing to be found of the old Jewish antagonism towards the 'Gentiles', the (pagan) non-Jews [47]. True enough, when Jesus sent out his twelve apostles to preach the Good Tidings, he forbade them to enter Samaritan territory as well as pagan country [48]. Very probably he found that they were not yet ripe enough for such a difficult undertaking. But in the last moments of his life he instructed them to be his witnesses in Jerusalem, in Judaea and Samaria, and 'even in the farthest corners of the earth' [49].

When the first persecution broke out in Jerusalem, some of the apostles found a refuge in Samaria. Philip proclaimed the Messiah there. Hearing of his success, Peter and John went there too. It was then that they had their encounter with Simon the Magician of which I wrote in Chapter III [50]. From a Jewish point of view, this was already a considerable widening of the scope.

To the Canaanite woman (a member of the original population) who asked his help for her possessed daughter, Jesus answered that he "was sent to the lost sheep of Israel, and to them alone". However, when he saw the woman's faith, he restored her daughter to health [51]. This fact, and the circumstance that he found himself at that moment in the region of Tyre and Sidon, prove that he was widening his range of action. It also remarkable that Peter's great confession : "You are the Messiah, the Son of God" [52], occurred near Caesarea Philippi. This town was founded by Herod the Great's son Philippus when tetrarch of Ituraea amd Trachonitis (4 B.C.-A.D. 34). Entirely pagan as this city was, it was named after the Emperor Tiberius. The god Pan and the Canaanite fertility gods were venerated there. That Jesus prompted Peter to his answer right there is at least a suggestion that Jesus did not intend to be a Messiah for Israel alone.

In the course of the years Jesus met with an ever more stubborn resistance to his preaching among leading Jewish circles. He must slowly but certainly have given up the hope that he would be able to win them over. He then began to speak of the rejection of the Jews and of the calling of the heathen. "From east and west, from north and south, people will come and take their places at the banquet in the Kingdom of God" [53]. The simile of the banquet was also used by Jesus in the parable of the unwilling guests. None of those who were originally invited would come; each of them has his own particular pretext. Then the master of the house invited everyone from everywhere, 'the poor, the crippled, and the blind' [54]. The purport is evident : the Jews are rejected, the Good News goes to the Gentiles.

Jesus crowned this in the last moments of his life on earth by ordering his disciples to "go ... to all nations and make them my disciples" [55]. Mark even gives this a universal dimension : "Go to every part of the world and proclaim the Gospel to the whole creation ('kosmos' in his Greek)" [56]. The Acts of the Apostles prove that the disciples acted according to this mandate. Soon enough all of them left Jerusalem and spread over all the Hellenistic world and over Italy. There is an old tradition that Thomas even went as far as India.

It was a decisive moment when Peter made a pagan convert, the very first one, in Joppe (now Jaffa near Tel Aviv); he was one Cornelius, a Roman officer [57]. Back in Jerusalem Peter saw himself severely taken to task by Jewish converts to Christianity because he had violated the Law by eating with the heathen in their house, even unclean food. But the apostle knew how to defend himself [58].

If this was already a heavy blow to the Jewish notion of exclusivity - which, as I argued in Vol. III, amounted to dualism -, the next move was still more destructive. At a later time when Paul and Barnabas arrived in Antioch after travelling through Asia Minor, some Jewish Christians who had come from Judaea, told the ex-pagan converts that they had to be circumcised in order to conform to the Law [59]. The dispute was brought before the Synod of Jerusalem, the first Council ever (A.D. 48); on that occasion the Fathers decided that converts from non-Jewish religion need not keep the Law [60] (I shall have to come back to this conflict). In this way a great obstacle in the path of Christianity was taken away so that soon enough non-Jewish Christians formed the great majority. In his letter to the Christians in Rome, the pagan city par excellence, Paul emphatically declared : "There will be glory and honour and peace for everyone who has done good, the Jew in the first instance, but the Gentile too. There are no human preferences with God" [61].

f. No two sets of human beings in the preaching of Jesus

Neither in the preaching of Jesus nor in that of the apostles is there any trace of a dualist partition of mankind into the good and the bad, into a small group of elect who will be saved, and the enormous 'massa damnata'. To Jesus all people were more or less the same, not really good but certainly not doomed to perdition. Already the Beatitudes are addressed to all mankind without any distinction [62]. Luke, always on the alert for pagans, reports that many came even from Fenicia to hear this.

To the wealthy young man who had called Jesus 'Good Teacher', he retorted : "Why call me good? Nobody is good, except God alone" [63]. Compared to God, no one is morally privileged above another. The heavenly Father, he said, cares for everyone, regardless of moral quality. He "causes the sun to rise on good and bad alike, and sends the rain on the innocent and the wicked" [64]. Not that he had a high idea of his contemporaries! He spoke of 'the adulterous and sinful age' he was living in [65]. "You, bad as you are, know how to give good things to your children" [66]. In the short parable of the master and his servant the moral of the story is : "we are servants and deserve no credit" [67].

Does this imply a wholesale condemnation of mankind as a hopelessly worthless lot? Many other utterances of Jesus prove that he did indeed make distinctions in the moral sphere between people. That God sends the rain on innocent and wicked alike means that there are indeed innocent and wicked. Never was this more evident than in his last great speech a few days before he died. He then said that, at the Last Judgment, the Son of Man would separate mankind into two groups, the sheep and the goats. The sheep are those who have been merciful and charitable during their lifetime, the goats those who have closed their hearts to their fellow-men [68]. What the texts that concern all mankind really have to say is that no one has much to boast of to God; nobody can be his or her own advocate. Everyone is entirely thrown on God's mercy. For this reason the proclamation of the Good News begins with the admonition to repent [69].

g. No negative attitude to women and sexuality in the New Testament

Is the New Testament the source of the discrimination against women of which the Christian Church is so often accused? Jesus himself never spoke a word against the female sex. He was not interested in sexuality; his attitude to women was perfectly relaxed. Neither did the problem get any attention from the authors of the Acts, Revelation, and the Catholic Letters, with one exception that is, however, totally innocuous. Peter admonishes women to submit to their husbands; he is hoping that their (still pagan) husbands might be won for the faith "without one word being said, by observing your chaste and respectful behaviour" [70]. Probably pagan husbands feared that their wives' conversion to Christianity would make them rebel against them. At the same time he exhorts (Christian) husbands to treat their wives with respect; "God's gift of life is something you share together" [71]. This means that men and women are fundamentally equal and that marriage essentially is a communion.

Remains Paul, the black sheep of the feminists. When studying what he has to say on women, marriage, and sexuality, one must not lose sight of two factors that may have influenced his attitude (which is somewhat ambiguous) : he was a bachelor, which was highly exceptional at the time, and he performed a missionary task in a thoroughly pagan environment. More than Jesus and the authors of the New Testament he proves intrigued by these matters, probably because he encountered many pastoral problems of this kind on his way. At least five Pauline letters carry sections on this issue (apart from what is written in the First Letter to Timothy on the situation of widows in the Christian community) [72].

It is evident that Paul prefers celibacy to marriage. "To the unmarried and the widows I say this : it is a good thing if like me they stay as they are (that is : celibate)" [73]. The reason for this counsel is not that he condemns marriage. Not every kind of celibacy is good : "If they (the unmarried) do not have self-control, they should marry. It is better to marry than to burn with desire" [74]. Furthermore, Paul presents this as his own advice rather than a divine commandment [75].

Christians of this period, the apostles not excluded, thought that the return of the Lord was close at hand. Paul was no exception to this : "The time in which we live will not last long" [76]. So why bother about getting married? Another reason for remaining celibate proved more convincing in the history of the Church : unmarried people are more free to please the Lord, whereas married persons are primarily concerned with one another and their affairs. They are pulled in two directions, Paul says [77].

Be this as it may, Paul does not condemn marriage. "If you marry, you are not doing anything wrong, nor does a girl if she marries" [78]. In Corinth, an international harbour, there must have been wide-spread and ostentatious profligacy. In all probability some of the new converts had a loose life behind them. It seems that some Christians tried to counter this with an extreme puritanism, in particular by totally abstaining from sexual intercourse. Paul proves no friend of this; he foresees only misery coming from it. It appears that he had received letters from Corinth with regard to this problem [79]. "You say, 'it is a good thing for a man not to have intercourse with a woman' ". No, says Paul, that is no solution. Let husband and wife stick together; they belong to one another in every respect, physically and sexually too. "Do not deny yourselves to one another" [80]. If a couple wants to abstain, good, but then only for religious reasons and only for a time; married people should not land themselves in difficulties [81]. Neither marriage nor sexuality are deprecated by the apostle.

Paul is often reproached that he preached the submission of women to their husbands, with the tacit implication that he considered them the lesser breed. In effect, Paul nowhere compares man and woman with regard to their human quality. It is true that he wrote that women should be submissive to their husbands [82]. But in the same breath he told the men not to be testy to their wives and love them [83]. They, the men, should love their wives as they love their own bodies, that is as themselves. "In loving his wife a man loves himself" [84]. In the Greek situation this is something brandnew, because this is tantamount to saying that man and woman are equal. "In the Lord's fellowship woman is as essential to man as man to woman. If woman was made out of man, it is through woman that man now comes to be, and God is the source of all" [85].

Paul is also often accused of having been the first to have made the Church into a 'male concern'. This idea stems from a passage in the First Letter to Timothy (if this letter is not by Paul himself, it nevertheless is in the Pauline tradition). There women are told to keep mum in church. "Their role is to learn, listening quietly and with due submission. I do not permit women to teach or to dictate to men; they should keep quiet" [86]. This authoritarian and none too friendly tone is evidence that the author is uneasy or irritated about something. My supposition is that he feared that preaching or teaching by women would be the first and fatal step on the road to a female priesthood. And a female priesthood - Paul and his collaborators were too well acquainted with the pagan world not to know this - would probably mean the contamination of religion with sex. The new converts, they feared, would not be wholly immune to this.

A word must yet be said about submission of women to men in general, as advocated by Paul. First of all, the apostle is not proclaiming an anthropological dogma of the male-female relationship but is speaking of the situation in wedlock, of married women that is. Now everywhere in the ancient world, in Judaism as well as among the pagans, women had to be subject to their husbands. What is new in Paul is that he places this in a religious context. "Wives should be subject as though to the Lord; for the man is the head of the woman, just as Christ is the head of the Church ... Just as the Church is subject to Christ, so must women be subject to their husbands in everything" [87].

Now Paul certainly did not see Christ as the dictator of the Church or as a tyrant, quite the contrary! Therefore he added that "men ought to love their wives in the same way as Christ loved the Church, when he gave himself up on its behalf ... The husband must love his wife as his very self" [88]. I am quite sure that words like these must have sounded revolutionary to ex-pagan husbands! To make it perfectly clear that he did not mean a servile subjection of wife to husband, Paul says, now speaking to all his Christians, male and female alike, married and unmarried : "be subject to one another out of reverence for Christ" [89], that is, they must caringly serve one another.

5. Antagonistic or dualistic attitudes in the New Testament

My tentative conclusion from what is written above must be that the New Testament as a whole, and in particular the Gospels, present a picture that is still more coherent, homogeneous, and uniform than that found in the Old Testament. But, as I argued earlier, there is no system, ideology, philosophy, or complex of thought under the sun that does not contain some contradictory, antagonistic, or even dualistic elements. If this is true, then the New Testament is no exception to this rule.

a. Two sets of people in John

In a foregoing section we saw that Jesus, though he recognized some people as better than others, did not think of two sets of people, the good and the wicked. But John does. In the famous preface to the Gospel that bears his name, he wrote of 'the Light' that came into the world [90] by which he meant the person of Jesus. This 'Light' is opposed to 'the

Darkness' which is, nevertheless, incapable of overcoming it [91]. This indicates a fierce opposition and also a battle between two powers, one of which is divine because it descends from above. The Light is identified with 'the Word' (Logos) that "in the beginning was with God" [92]. However, there are not two powers in Heaven.

The coming of the Word, that is the Light, into the world causes a division among mankind. Some receive the Word readily, becoming thereby 'children of God". Even their human origin is changed through their acceptance of the Word, since they are "born, not of blood nor of the will of man, but of God" [93]. Jesus digressed on this in his nocturnal conversation (related by John) with Nicodemus, a Pharisee, to whom he said that he must "be born again of water and the Spirit", or else one may not enter the Kingdom of God". For "that which is born of the flesh is flesh, and that which is born of the Spirit is Spirit" [94].

This again is a very distinct opposition but not really one between matter and spirit. For the Greek word for 'flesh' is 'sarx'; this is the rendition of the Hebrew 'basar'. With this word the Old Testament not only indicates meat, or matter in general, but our purely human and earthly existence. With 'pneuma' (spirit) John means this same human existence but now suffused by the grace of God.

The opposition I mentioned is worked out further in a passage after the close of the conversation between Jesus and the Pharisee; this obviously represents John's own opinion. "God sent the Son into the world, not to condemn the world, but that the world might be saved through him. He who believes in him is not condemned; he who does not believe is condemned already, because he has not believed in the name of the only Son of God. And this is the judgment, that the Light has come into the world, and men loved darkness rather than light, because their deeds were evil. For everyone who does evil hates the Light, and does not come to the Light, lest his deeds should be exposed. But he who does what is right comes to the Light" [95].

In a later section this distinction also becomes one of life and death. "The Son gives life to whom he will .. He who hears my word (Jesus is speaking) and believes him who sent me (the Father), has eternal life; he does not come into judgment, but has passed from life to death"[96]. To Martha, the sister of Lazarus whom he would raise from the dead in Bethany, Jesus said : "He who believes in me, though he die, yet shall he live, and whoever lives and believes in me shall never die"[97].

Yet another distinction is that between those 'of the world' and those 'not of the world'- the 'world' representing in John that kind of human existence and that part of mankind that turns away from God and is acting and thinking as though he did not exist. This 'world' is characterized by the fact that it rejects its Creator. "He was in the world, and the world was made through him, yet the world knew him not"[98]. In his famous prayer at the end of the Last Supper Jesus said that his disciples were "not of the world, even as I am not of the world". This does not mean that they should live a hermit's life; on the contrary. "As you (the Father) did send me into the world, so I have sent them (his apostles) into the world ... I do not pray that you should take them out of the world but that you should keep them from the evil one"[99]. We do not find here that radical shunning of normal existence that is so typical of esoteric and élitist societies. Early Christianity was not meant to be esoteric.

This same theme of a division of mankind is taken up in the Letters of John. In the First Letter the opposition of Light and Darkness returns. "God is Light and in him is no darkness at all ... He who loves his brother abides in the Light ... but he who hates his brother is in the darkness"[100]. Here too we find two sets of people. "He who does right is righteous ... He who commits sin is of the devil"[101]. Then again there is the opposition of God and the world. "(Some) are of the world, therefore what they say is of the world, and the world listens to them. We are of God. Whoever knows God listens to us, and he who is not of God does not listen to us. By this we know the spirit of truth and the spirit of error"[102].

Perhaps somebody will object that Jesus too separated the good from the wicked. This is certainly true but the difference with John is that, in Jesus' own preaching, this will happen only at the Last Judgment. Only then, at the end of times, "when the Son of Man comes in his glory", judgment will be passed on mankind so that the good, that is the merciful, will be admitted to heaven, whereas the wicked, that is the uncharitable, will be assigned to hell [103]. The distance between the heavenly paradise and hell is absolute. Jesus makes Abraham in heaven say to the miser in hell : "Between us and you a great chasm has been fixed, in order that those who would pass from here to you may not be able to do this, and none may cross from there to us" [104].

b. John as an author with a penchant to dualism

There is some divergence of opinion among biblical scholars on the question of who is the author of these letters and whether he is the same person as the author of the Gospel of John (to say nothing of the Book of Revelation), and again whether this author is identical with John the apostle. Here too there is no need for me to join in this discussion. It has, however, always seemed to me that these different works resemble each other strongly respecting their manner of arguing and in the form of expression chosen by the author(s). This in its turn leads me to the supposition that these possible authors resemble one another so much in character that they seem to be the same kind of person. Or to put it simply, there can only be one person involved. What is relevant to my argument is that this person seems to be endowed with a tendency to dualism.

The apostle John and his brother James were the sons of a probably rather well-to-do shipowner called Zebedee and his wife Salome. It is not impossible that John received some kind of education : his Greek is fairly good, and some knowledge of Hellenistic philosophy transpires through his phrases. Furthermore, the Gospel of John states that John the apostle knew Caiphas the High Priest. This acquaintance with one of the leaders of his people enabled him, during the trial of his master, to enter the court of the High Priest whereas Peter, no more than a common fisherman, had to stand back [105]. Enough to show that John was socially somewhat different from the other disciples, just as the Gospel ascribed to him in no way resembles that of the others.

His was a fierce nature; he and his brother were called by Jesus 'the sons of the thunder' [106]. I have already related that when the inhabitants of a Samaritan village would not extend hospitality to Jesus and his company, James and John wanted Jesus to bid fire come down from heaven and destroy them. For this outburst Jesus rebuked them [107]. In his book on Jesus, Romano Guardini wrote that John in his letters so often spoke of love because he had to convince himself; love did not come easily to him [108].

John who was very young when he joined Jesus, probably still a boy, was doubtless ambitious. The author of the fourth Gospel invariably singles him (or himself) out as 'the disciple whom Jesus loved'. Not one of the other Gospel authors employed this term. At the Last Supper, John lay next to Jesus; when Jesus spoke of the one who would betray him, Peter beckoned to John to ask who of them was meant [109]. Finally, on the cross Jesus confided his mother Mary to John who in this way became Mary's adoptive son to replace Jesus for her [110].

Probably the driving force behind this ambition was Salome, the mother of the brothers. She was one of a small group of women who followed Jesus on his peregrinations, ministering to him and his company [111]. Once she resolutely put her sons before Jesus and asked him to give them the best places in the new kingdom, such as the position of Grand Vizir for the one and Commander-in-Chief for the other. But Jesus refused to enter into this game, and the other apostles took it ill of them, probably because they feared an infringement of their own supposed rights [112].

The Dutch professor Chorus, in his short book on the psychology of the Gospel authors, characterizes John as a man of passion. Such a man lives in a strong tension between reality and ideality. His grip on reality was powerful - see the many realistic details in his Gospel -, but at the same time he was obsessed by an ideal order. Chorus remarks that a complete synthesis between ideality and reality is never feasible; this causes the life of a man of passion to be paradoxical and even tragic

[113]. This is why I said that John was inclined to dualism. If this portrait is correct, then John would be the second person after Plato [114] whose tendency to dualism we can connect with a proclivity to dualism in his personal character. In consequence of this he had also a tendency to harshness. Chorus gives an intriguing example of this. On the occasion of the triumphal entry of Jesus into Jerusalem, Matthew cites the prophet Zechariah : "Look, your king comes to you; triumphant and victorious is he, humble (gentle, meek) and riding on an ass" [115]. John gives the same quotation but leaves out the word 'humble' [116].

c. Two sets of people in Revelation

There evidently are two sets of people in the Book of Revelation; we might even say that they are dualistically opposed. "All the inhabitants of the earth will worship it (the Beast), all whose names have not been written in the book of life of the Lamb" [117]. This same image of a fundamental difference is returning in the image of the one hundred and forty-four thousand who bear the name of the Lamb and that of his Father on their foreheads : "They are without fault" [118]. The number twelve is that of election; twelve times twelve is election par excellence. The number, although doubtless a large quantity of people is meant, also indicates restriction. Opposed to the redeemed stand those who "worship the Beast and receive its mark on their forehead or hand" [119]. They shall "drink the wine of God's anger, poured undiluted into the cup of his wrath" [120].

d. A point against politics

The author's repugnance against the Roman Empire is extremely fierce; he can hardly find enough negative terms to stigmatize it. He never speaks of 'the Empire'; it always is 'the Beast' or 'Babylon'. No other earthly realm is summoned up to destroy and replace it; obviously all kingdoms are equally evil in the judgment of the author. All "the kings of the earth have committed fornication with her (the great harlot of

Babylon) and wallowed in her luxury" [121]. What really is standing over against all earthly kingdoms is the celestial realm of the Lamb (the Son of Man), also called 'the new Jerusalem'.

Underneath all this one senses a polemic against politics as such, in particular against power politics (in which the Roman Empire excelled). This rejection of politics is already to be found in the Old Testament. The prophet Samuel was the protagonist of this when he warned the Israelites against a king. When they, in spite of his admonitions, gave themselves a king though, he exclaimed : "Now you have cast away your God!" [122]. The prophet considered Israel's irrepressible wish to be like other nations as a downright betrayal of Jahve.

In my Volume IV [123] I wrote that the whole subsequent history of Israel is treated in the light of this dualistic opposition between theocracy and 'normal political rule'. The biblical historiographers are obviously not interested in political 'normalcy'; throughout the centuries the prophets stick to the original idea of Jahve's divine rule.

This same antagonism becomes apparent also in the apocalyptic parts of the Book of Daniel. There too the political powers of those days (= the second century B.C.) are pictured as 'Beasts'. The book presents a sequel of four great empires, those of the Babylonians, the Medians, the Persians, and the Macedonians. I stated there that it was the author's obvious intention to pass sentence on these kingdoms as dualistically opposed to God. From his dualistic point of view he condemns earthly kingdoms all and sundry as antagonistic to the reign of God himself. This means a wholesale rejection of political power. I concluded that passage by saying that this anti-political ideology was to have a great career in history [124].

The next instalment of this ideology is in the Book of Revelation. In the Gospels there is no discussion of political power; Jesus proves indifferent to it. In the first historical phase of the Church, as described in the Acts, it was not an issue. Paul counselled quite obedience to the authorities; he is not negative : "They (the authorities) are God's agents working for your good" [125]. Politics clearly presented no problem to him since this is the sole passage in all his letters concerning it. In the so-called 'Catholic letters' (those of Peter, James, John, and Jude) there is only one short reference, viz. in Peter's First Letter where he exhorts his Christians to submit themselves "for the sake of the Lord to every human authority, whether to the emperor as supreme, or to governors as his deputies" [126].

Revelation, however, was composed when the Christians had begun to feel the full blast of the persecution. This had opened the eyes of the author to the undisguised, in his view anti-godlike, nature not only of the Roman Empire but of all earthly kingdoms. He resolutely took his distance from them condemning them lock, stock, and barrel. Christians were now no longer the emperor's obedient subjects but his helpless and innocent victims. But just as in Daniel, the victims won the ultimate victory. The very words of Daniel are quoted again : "They shall reign for ever and ever" [127].

e. Enmity towards the Romans in Revelation

The only New Testament book in which a real enmity towards the Romans is displayed is the Book of Revelation. This enmity often is of such a fierce nature that I do not hesitate in calling this opposition dualistic. It is not directed against individual Romans or against the occupation of the Holy land but against the Roman Empire itself. This is seen as an un-Christian, utterly pagan power; for the Christians it is all or nothing : either they must perish or the Empire. This should not surprise us for Revelation is a rather late book. Irenaeus states that it was written during the reign of the Emperor Domitian (81-96) [128]. This dating would tally with the historical situation which seems to be the background of the book, viz. one in which Christians were persecuted. Domitian was the first emperor to claim divine honours for himself already during his lifetime (former emperors became divinized only after their death). Add to this that in A.D. 71 the destruction of the Temple in Jerusalem, the Jewish cult centre, had taken place, and it will be clear that the author of Revelation must have seen in the Empire a force directed against God himself, even ready to take the place of God.

Ap. 12:3 signals 'a great fiery dragon with seven heads and ten horns'; this monster may be interpreted as Satan, the Antichrist, and the politico-religious imperial power rolled into one [129].

Somewhat further the author reports a vision in which he sees a beast rising out of the sea; this too had seven heads and ten horns. Each of the heads carried 'a blasphemous name' [130]. Here the animal symbolizes the devil, and the heads the kings of this earth, all of them, since the numbers suggest completeness. The 'blasphemous names' refer to the divine titles the Roman emperors used to assume. This is the obvious explanation but perhaps the author has also thought of the claims to divinity of the Egyptian Pharaohs and of the monarchs of the ancient Middle East.

This second Beast is not identical with that first dragon, since "the dragon conferred on it his own power, his throne, and great authority" [131]. The author could not state more clearly what he meant : the Beast is the Empire, and as such an instrument or deputy of Satan. The imperial throne is the seat of the devil. No wonder, then, that the imperial beast "uttered blasphemies against God, reviling his name and his dwelling-place, that is those who dwell in heaven (the angels)" [132].

It is not only Roman officialdom that is denounced here. "The whole world went after the Beast in wondering admiration, and worshipped the dragon because he had conferred his authority on the Beast; they worshipped the Beast also" [133]. In other words, those who admire the Roman Empire are devil-worshippers. Those who refuse to adore it will be persecuted, even killed [134].

f. An eschatological element in the idea of the Kingdom

The very sharp antagonism that we meet in the Gospels is not between Jesus and the Romans. Rather, it was between him and his people at large, whose feverish national expectations he frustrated. The Kingdom of Heaven that Jesus proclaimed was something radically different from the ancient Kingdom of Israel and also of the hoped for new kingdom after the disappearance of the Romans. When the mass of the people realized this, they had seen enough of Jesus.

There is an eschatological leitmotif in this idea of the Kingdom. Before the public appearance of Jesus his relative John the Baptist was already proclaiming the advent of a new kingdom. "Repent, for the Kingdom of Heaven is upon you!" [135]. Soon afterwards, when the Baptist had been arrested, Jesus resumed this message : "The Kingdom of God is upon you. Repent and believe the Gospel (= the good tidings)" [136]. This call for repentance clearly shows that the coming kingdom would be one of a spiritual or moral kind.

The Baptist added that, whereas he was baptizing with water, the "Coming One (= the Messiah) would baptize with Holy Spirit and with fire" [137]. This fire reminds us of 'the eschatological judgment with fire' [138] as it was prophesied, for instance, by Isaiah : "His (God's) tongue is like a devouring fire" [139].

Fire is not only purifying but also destructive, and with this an apocalyptic element is coming into play. John the Baptist, meek and humble though he was, nevertheless uses flaming images. "Every tree that fails to produce good fruit is cut down and thrown onto the fire ...; the chaff he (the Messiah) will burn on a fire that can never be put out" [140]. It is this unquenchable fire in particular that is not only an eschatological but at the same time an apocalyptic element [141].

Jesus used the fire symbol no less than his forerunner. He almost verbally repeated John's words about the barren tree that is thrown on the fire [142]. The eschatological theme returns in Jesus' saying that it is better "to enter into (eternal) life maimed or lame than to keep both eyes and be thrown into the fires of hell" [143]. That there is also a dualistic element is proved by the fact that both John and Jesus spoke of good and poor trees the treatment of which will be entirely opposed.

Paul too, although not an apocalyptic writer, speaks of the Day of Judgment; "that day dawns in fire, and the fire will test the worth of each person's work". Here too a dualistic element is detectable, since the apostle is speaking of two houses, one that will survive the conflagration, and another that will burn down in it. The inhabitant of this house (with which somebody's life is meant) "will escape with his life, though only by passing through the fire" [144]. In this text the fire is at once purifying and destructive. This image finally returns in the Book of Revelation where the Beast (probably the Roman power) and the False Prophet (probably the Anti-Christ) are taken prisoner and "thrown into the lake of fire with its sulphurous flames" [145].

g. Jesus and the Pharisees

A strongly antagonistic element is the running conflict between Jesus and the Pharisees. Constantly at loggerheads, both parties conducted many fierce word battles in which they did not mince their words. The final outcome proved fatal to Jesus. Who were these Pharisees whose very name has become proverbial for 'hypocrite'?

First of all, it must be understood that Pharisees were laymen, not priests. Priests were descendants of Aaron who served the temple and performed the liturgical functions; in particular they were the sacrificers. Pharisees should also not be confused with 'scribes', although scribes and Pharisees are often mentioned in one breath. Scribes were scholars; they acted as writers, copyists, interpreters of sacred texts, teachers of the Law, and were also lawyers and administrators. Pharisees may be best characterized as a religious party. Their original indication in Hebrew was 'perushim' which means 'separate' or 'separatist'; via the Aramaic 'perushaya' and its Greek rendering 'pharisaioi' the term was received into the European languages as 'Pharisees' etc.

From what or whom were the Pharisees 'separated'? They kept themselves rigorously apart from all that was ritually unclean, in particular 'from the pollution of the peoples of the land' [146]; with 'the peoples of the land' the pagans are meant who had immigrated into Palestine during the Babylonian Captivity. This attitude was, of course, of paramount importance in the period of the Roman occupation of the country when it had become almost unavoidable to defile oneself by contact with pagans. During the trial of Jesus his accusers would not enter the praetorium lest they would become unclean with the consequence that they could not eat the Passover meal [147].

But the Pharisees also kept apart from, and looked down upon, the Jewish population in general because the common people were none too strict in keeping the innumerable prescripts. When the chief priests and the Pharisees had sent some members of the temple police to arrest Jesus, they returned with empty hands, because the personality of Jesus had made a deep impression on them. The Pharisees rebuked them : "Are you led astray, you also? Have any of the authorities believed in him? But this crowd, who does not know the Law, are accursed!" [148].

Without unduly defaming the Pharisees, we can say that their guardianship of the Law could easily develop into puritanism. In earlier parts of this series I characterized puritanism as a desire to have things nicer, cleaner, more sublime than they really are. It will be evident that a tension creeps in here, the well-known (often dualistic) opposition between ideal and reality. The Pharisees overrated human capacity to live the good life, even with regard to themselves, which in the event could lead to formalism and hypocrisy. The rank and file of the believers, overburdened as they were, could easily become indifferent or slothful. Pharisees certainly had no mean idea of themselves.

What exactly was the point of discussion between Jesus and the Pharisees? The bone of contention was not that Jesus wanted to dethrone the Pharisees and rob them of their influence. Far from it! He fully acknowledged their authority. "The scribes and the Pharisees sit on Moses' seat; so practice whatever they tell you" [149]. In order to understand exactly what the problem was, I refer to Ellis Rivkin's clear exposition.

"The essential core of Pharisaism", he writes, " was its affirmation of a triad of faith that sharply distinguished it from the priestly system of Judaism from the time of the promulgation of the Pentateuch (ca. 397 B.C.) until the rise of the Pharisees, probably during the Hasmonaean Revolt (= the War of the Maccabees, 166-142 B.C. - F.). This triad of faith proclaimed that 1. the one God and Father so loved the individual that 2. he revealed to his people Israel a twofold law, one written in the five books of Moses (the Torah), and the other transmitted orally from Moses to Joshua to the elders to the prophets to the Pharisees, so that 3. each individual who internalized this twofold law could look forward to eternal life and resurrection for his body". Legislation and conservation of these oral laws was entrusted to the Great Court, consisting of seventy-one teachers of the Law; it is perhaps better known as the 'Sanhedrin' [150].

With important Pharisean tenets Jesus had no quarrel at all. He strongly affirmed the existence of an afterlife and the resurrection of the body; he too saw God as a Father who loved his children. Still less was he averse to the supremacy of Mosaic Law. "Think not that I have come to abolish the Law and the prophets; I have not come to abolish them but to fulfil them" [151]. The problem was in the oral law. Probably the scribes and the Pharisees found that the rules contained in the Torah did not cover every aspect of life because many of them were too vague and too general. Therefore, an extensive system of rules, based on those in the Torah, was elaborated, 613 in number, 248 of them prescripts and 365 interdictions.

It was this additional system, not the Law itself, that was repeatedly and fiercely attacked by Jesus. He ridiculed the extreme minuteness of the Pharisean prescriptions which he obviously considered entirely gratuitous. "You tithe mint and dill and cummin" [152]. Other prescriptions and interdictions in his opinion were harsh and merciless. In one instance he made a clear distinction between the two kinds of law contrasting them with each other : "Moses said : 'Honour your father and mother ... But you (the Pharisees) say : 'If a man tells his father and mother, Anything of mine which might have been used for your benefit is Corban (= set apart for God), he is no longer permitted to do anything for his father or mother. Thus, by your own tradition, handed down among you (Jesus means the oral law here), you make God's word null and void" [153].

Utterances of this sort must have been a source of irritation to the Pharisees. This irritation grew into anger when Jesus attacked their lifestyle accusing them roundly of hypocrisy. These frequent accusations culminated in the ferocious judgment on them that he pronounced in Jerusalem in the last week of his life (he must have known by then that his life was already forfeited). "What they (the Pharisees) preach, they do not practice. They bind heavy burdens on people, hard to bear; but they themselves will not move them with their finger. They do all their deeds to be seen by men ... You neglect the weightier matters (i.e. weighter than your prescriptions) of the Law, justice and mercy and faith ... You outwardly appear righteous to men, but inwardly you are full of hypocrisy and iniquity". He used the strongest of terms : they were hypocrites, blind men, whitewashed tombs but within full of bones and uncleanness, they were serpents and a brood of vipers [154].

There surely was no love lost between the Pharisees and him. But the worst, the really annihilating indictment was this one. "You shut the Kingdom of Heaven against men; for you neither enter yourselves nor allow those who would enter to go in" [155]. What Jesus means here is that the additional load of religious and moral rules was so great that people were tempted to neglect religion entirely and become indifferent.

The idea of Jesus was that one should follow the Pharisees when they proclaimed the Law of Moses but that the oral law should be abolished. In his own circle he already did away with it. He and his disciples did not fast as frequently as the Pharisees [156]; some of his disciples no longer performed the usual ritual washings [157]. The Pharisees accused them of not living according to the tradition of the elders, i.e. according to Pharisaic law [158].

The anger of the Pharisees was raised to a boiling-point by yet another claim of Jesus. He indeed declared Pharisaic law null and void, but not wanting to leave the people without any guidance, he put something else in its place, namely love. In answer to a question by a Pharisee, he said that the first and greatest commandment of the Law was 'to love the Lord your God with all your heart', and the second in importance to 'love your neighbour like yourself'. He then drew the following conclusion : "On these two commandments depend all the Law and the prophets" [159]. Mark that Jesus is referring here not to the Pharisaic tradition but directly to the Torah : the first commandment is to be found in Deuteronomium (6:5), the second in Leviticus (19:18). Jesus brought them forward to serve as the basic attitude for moral behaviour and as the measuring-rod of human acts.

It must have angered the learned Pharisees extremely that this self-made rabbi put himself forward as an authority on the Law, even as an interpreter of the Torah. When the Pharisees accused him of profaning the Sabbath he gave the categorical answer that "the Son of Man (that is, he himself) is lord of the Sabbath" [160].

From the very first there was tension between Jesus and the Pharisees. According to the Gospel authors, the Pharisees and scribes little by little reached the conclusion that Jesus was a dangerous man who had better be out of the way. Since they were human, there was a personal element in their animosity : by drawing such large crowds Jesus undermined their position. But there were other reasons too for their pique. After all, they honestly thought that they were the guardians of Jewish tradition and that it was their duty to keep the people true to the faith. Furthermore, they, together with the priests, found that their policy regarding the Roman presence was eminently suited to prevent a catastrophic clash. The claim that Jesus was the Messiah made them feel uneasy because they feared that he would lead the populace into a rebellion. Soon enough the affair took a dualistic turn : Jesus had to be liquidated.

All four Gospel authors agree that the conflict over the Sabbath brought matters to a head. The Synoptics state that when Jesus had cured a man on the Sabbath day in the synagogue of Kapernaum, the Pharisees started to forge plans against him. Luke only says that "they were filled with fury and discussed what they might do to Jesus" [161]; Matthew and Mark add that "they took counsel against him, how to destroy him" [162]. From the Pharisaic viewpoint this is understandable. Together with circumcision, the observance of the weekly day of prayer and rest was the hallmark of Judaism, marking it off from the surrounding pagan religions. The Pharisees were afraid that Jesus intended to abolish the strict observance of the Sabbath which would result, they thought, in its disappearance.

In a passage that I mentioned already John presents yet another accusation against Jesus. "He not only broke the Sabbath but also called God his Father, making himself equal with God; this was why the Jews all the more sought to kill him" [163]. The claim that a human being was equal with God was utter blasphemy in their eyes.

Jesus himself perfectly realized that the leaders of his people had set their faces against him. Three or four times he told his disciples, much to their confusion, that he would suffer and be put to death in Jerusalem. For the time being he stayed in Galilee and did not journey to Judaea where death awaited him [164]. But on the occasion of the Feast of the Tabernacles he travelled to the Holy City. There he taught in the Temple. It was obviously known in the town that his life was in danger. "Is this not the man whom they seek to kill?" [165]. Already then the Pharisees made an attempt to arrest him but they refrained out of fear for the populace [166]. On yet another occasion Jesus managed to escape from Jerusalem to the rough Jordan valley [167].

The situation became critical when Jesus had raised Lazarus from the dead. It seems that then the actual decision was taken to eliminate him as soon as possible. "From that day on they took counsel how to put him to death .. If any one knew where he was, he should let them (the priests and the Pharisees) know, so that they might arrest him" [168]. Their motivation ran thus : "If we let him go on like this (performing great signs), everyone will believe in him, and the Romans will come and destroy both our holy place and the nation" [169]. Here the political motive, the fear of an anti-Roman revolt, is paramount.

However, the Passover, with that great mass of pilgrims in town, was not the most suitable occasion for capturing Jesus, "lest there should be a tumult among the people" [170]. How glad, therefore, the Jewish leaders were when Judas came and promised to deliver his Master to them in secret [171]. Accordingly, Jesus was arrested under cover of the night in the Garden of Gethsemane. At daybreak he was brought before the Sanhedrin. It proved difficult to find an effective accusation against him. For instance, he had never said that he was the Messiah in as many words. Then the High Priest decided to deliver a frontal attack. "I adjure you by the living God, tell us if you are the Christ (the Messiah), the Son of God?". Jesus answered : "You have said so". This sealed his doom. "He has uttered blasphemy ..., he deserves death"[172].

The problem, however, was that the Sanhedrin did not possess the right of life and death[173]; this was a Roman prerogative. The consequence was that the accused had to be brought before the governor, Pontius Pilate. But this authority proved none too eager to condemn Jesus. First of all, he heartily despised the Jewish leaders whom he doubtless considered stupid fanatics. Then, as an experienced lawyer, he saw right through their fake accusations. And finally, he obviously was somewhat afraid of Jesus. At the same time, however, he also feared the Jewish leaders who threatened to denounce him to the emperor as one who had failed to condemn a 'king of the Jews', a dangerous rebel, that is[174] (his reputation in Rome was none of the best). He therefore allowed them to do with Jesus what they wanted.

A final remark is necessary. I know very well that modern scholars, Jewish as well as Christian, nowadays agree that the Gospel picture of the Pharisees is one-sided. Very probably this picture mirrors the situation of some decades after Jesus' death, when it had become abundantly clear that Judaism and Christianity would go different ways; Christians had been persecuted by Jewish leaders and there had been victims. I shall come back to this. No wonder that the Gospel authors did not have very amiable opinions of Pharisees, priests, and scribes. Nevertheless, even in the Gospels a softer light sometimes shines through the texts.

It is evident that not all Pharisees were opposed to Jesus. One of them, a certain Nicodemus, who also was a member of the Sanhedrin, came to hear Jesus, although he did so under cover of darkness. He called Jesus 'a teacher of God'; Jesus in his turn addressed him as 'teacher of Israel'[175]. Later this same man said to his colleagues that they must not condemn Jesus without a hearing, which cost him a venomous answer from the others[176]. We hear frequently that Jesus was invited to the house of a Pharisee and shared in a meal there. Then there was the Pharisee to whom Jesus said that he was not far from the Kingdom of God [177]. This is all true enough. But what must concern us in the context of this work is not what modern scholars think of the Pharisees but how they are regarded in the Gospels themselves. For this reason I have kept close to the biblical texts.

h. Paul and the Law

The apostle Paul lived in continuous conflict with the Law [178]. In many vehement passages he fulminated against it culminating in his words that it was 'a curse' [179]. This points to an antagonistic, if not downright dualistic stance on his side. How much the problem of the Law occupied him becomes apparent from the fact that the word 'Law' occurrs no less than one hundred and eighteen times in the body of Pauline letters. The main thrust is to be found in those to the Romans and the Galatians with one hundred and three entries between them. That this was a matter of absorbing interest peculiarly to this apostle is proved by the fact that the term 'law' is not once to be met in the Letters of Peter and John.

What made Paul campaign so ferociously against the Law? What exactly did he understand by it? Was he distancing himself only from the Pharisaic tradition or was he in reality aiming at Mosaic Law? A superficial reading of the Letters to the Romans and Galatians suffices to show that what he was aiming his fire at was the Law of the Torah because in these letters the focus of the debate is the question of circumcision. And the commandment of circumcision stems from Genesis where it is ascribed to Abraham. Now, as I mentioned earlier, circumcision, together with the observance of the Sabbath, was one of the two great hallmarks of post-exilian Judaism. Could it be that Paul, as a convert from Judaism, and a former Pharisee at that, was asking himself, probably anxiously, whether or not he was still subject to Mosaic Law?

A more decisive reason for Paul's enmity to the Law is that he was the apostle of the Gentiles in Asia Minor, Greece, Macedonia, and

Rome. As a result of his missionary exertions Christian communities were soon found in the whole eastern part of the Roman Empire. Now the greater part of the converts had been pagans; they were either hardly acquainted with Judaism or not at all and had, of course, never lived according to the Law. Paul realized full well that attempts to pressurize new converts from paganism into following the commandments of the Law would prove to be an insuperable obstacle in the path of Christianity.

In principle the attitude of Paul to the Law did not differ from that of Jesus. He repeated Jesus' words that all commandments of the Law are summed up in this sentence : 'You shall love your neighbour as yourself'" [180]. "He who loves his neighbour has met every requirement of the Law" [181]. He did not hesitate to ascribe a positive value to the Law : "(It) was our custodian until Christ came" [182]; for 'custodian' he used the Greek word 'paidagogos'. The link between positive and negative judgments is made in this phrase : "Through the Law I died to the Law - to live for Christ" [183]. This means, of course, that for him Mosaic Law had had its day, but it is exactly by means of that same Law that the apostle learned to live for God.

The watershed between life before and after the Law is Jesus' crucifixion. "I (Paul) have been crucified with Christ; the life I now live is not my life, but the life Christ lives in me" [184]. The Law had not been annulled in the fullest sense of the word but had rather been fulfilled by having become the Law of Love. Perhaps Hegel's term 'aufheben', in the twofold sense of this German word, is apposite here.

While he was still a Pharisee, the apostle had scrupulously lived according to the Law. "In my practice of the Law I was a Pharisee", he wrote from his Roman prison to the Philippians, "by the Law's standard of righteousness without fault" [185]. But since he knew Christ, he no longer sought "a righteousness of my own based on the Law, (but) the righteousness which comes from faith in Christ, given by God in response to faith" [186]. What did Paul mean by ' a righteneousness of his own'? He meant a 'righteousness that is (a sufficient reason) for salvation worked as it is by deeds'. In Paul's eyes what the Law brought forth or enabled people to perform was 'works', not faith. God is not in our debt when we do good works; these do not justify us. Abraham, for instance, was not justified because of the deeds he performed but on account of his faith [187]. A new type of opposition comes in here that, in a magnified form, was to play a devastating role in the Christian Church, that between faith and works.

With the positing of yet another opposition Paul went an important step further. "The Gentiles", he wrote to the Romans, "who have made no effort after righteousness (i.e. because they knew nothing of the Law and lived according to their lights - F.), nevertheless achieved it, a righteousness based on faith, whereas Israel made great efforts after a law of rightheousness but never attained to it. Why was this? Because their efforts were not based on faith but, mistakenly, on deeds" [188]. The opposition of Law and faith is extended here into one of Jews and (gentile) Christians. This would not have endeared Paul to Law-abiding Jews, in particular not to Pharisees.

Even when Paul gives the Law its due, he sometimes uses very harsh terms to describe it, for instance when comparing the two sons of Abraham, Isaac and Ismael. It is evident that Paul, working out their relationship in a metaphor, lost track and became somewhat confused, but what he means is clear enough. Ismael's mother Hagar was a slave woman, but Isaac's mother Sara was freeborn. Their descendants were respectively the free and the slaves. But these free are not the Jews but the Christians, while the slaves are those still living under the Law, the circumcised.

"If we are in union with Christ Jesus, circumcision makes no difference at all, nor the lack of it" [189]. And even, "those who rely on the Law are under a curse" [190]. "Before this faith (in Jesus Christ) came, we were close prisoners in the custody of the Law ... Scripture has declared the whole world to be prisoners in subjection to sin" [191]. Enough to show how bitterly and tenaciously Paul fought the concepts to which he had once adhered. It is sheer dualism.

j. Tension in the early Church

There can be no doubt that the circumcision question posed a vexing problem to Judaeo-Christians in general (in the first years there were no others). Although the problem did not assume really dramatic forms, we need an explanation here because it shows how Jews and Christians began to drift apart; this will lead us to the next section. When Peter had converted the very first pagan, the Roman officer Cornelius in the city of Caesarea, he baptized this man but evidently did not have him circumcised. What is more, he entered the house of the uncircumcised and ate with them from unclean food, i.e. food forbidden by the Law. Back in Jerusalem, Peter was taken to task by conservative elements called 'the circumcision party', but he succeeded in silencing them [192]. This shows that this was a problem for the entire young Church, not for Paul alone.

This often difficult situation was exacerbated by the action of the so-called 'Judaizers' [193]. These were Christian Jews from the party of the Pharisees, who were of the opinion that all converts, pagans not excepted, had to observe the Law of Moses [194]. They suffered their first defeat on the occasion I mentioned above when they saw to their amazement that the gifts of the Holy Spirit were also granted to pagans [195]. But nothing really definite was decided then so that a few years later the question cropped up again with all the more acrimony.

Paul was resting in Antioch from his first missionary journey through Asia Minor, when some men arrived from Judaea telling the brethren categorically that they would not be saved if they did not let themselves be circumcised according to Mosaic Law [196]. Paul, who saw his life-work threatened, flew into a rage and, supported by Barnabas, the head of the Church in Antioch, entered into a fierce quarrel with the emissaries. Finally, it was decided that Paul, Barnabas, and some others would go to Jerusalem, the 'Rome' of the first decades, and present the question to the apostles and the elders [197]. Perhaps it was somewhat provocative of Paul to take Titus with him because this young man was an uncircumcised gentile Christian [198].

All this led to the Council of Jerusalem (ca. A.D. 45). Paul and Barnabas presented an oral report of their missionary work in Syria and Asia Minor [199]; from Paul's words in Galatians it can be inferred that he told the members that he had not compelled the converted pagans to be circumcised [200]. But the circumscision party protested that circumcision and observance of the Law were necessary [201]. Years later, Paul, still angry, wrote that "false brethren ... slipped in to spy out our freedom which we have in Christ Jesus that they might bring us into bondage" [202]. Once again we meet the opposition, so important in Antiquity, between freedom and slavery.

After much debate and after a long pleading by Peter and an even longer one by James, it was decided that one "should not trouble those of the Gentiles that turn to God" [203] - that is, pagan-Christians need not observe the Law of Moses. On that occasion nothing was said about Judaeo-Christians. However, it was further decided that Paul and Barnabas would occupy themselves with the Gentiles, and James, Peter, and John with the circumcised [204].

It will be evident that this special ruling made the cohabitation of Jewish and Gentile Christians in many places difficult. Paul's starting-point was that both sets of Christians were equal, whereas Judaizers still found that Judaeo-Christians should have pride of place. When Peter came to Antioch in about A.D. 53, "he ate with the Gentiles". But under pressure of Judaizers who had expressly come from Jerusalem - Paul accused James, the leader of the Jerusalem Church of being behind this -, Peter stood back, 'fearing the circumcision party'. If by 'eating' the eucharistic meal is meant, which is not impossible, a particular un-Christian form of discrimination was inaugurated in this way.

All the Jews followed Peter's example; even Barnabas, Paul's old friend, "was carried away by their insincerity". Paul openly rebuked them for this double-dealing, because "they were not straightforward about the truth of the Gospel". "If you", so Paul said to Peter, "though a Jew, live like a Gentile (i.e. do not observe the Law - F.), how can you compel the Gentiles to live like Jews?" [205]. It is not reported what Peter had to say to this; in all probability, he was completely caught off balance. All this proves that relations in the early Church were often poisoned by this tricky problem.

k. The Jews in the judgment of Paul and the Gospels

"In order to come into her own, the Church had to picture Israel as disposed, rejected, or even cursed ... This 'competitive' situation ... has provided the basis for the tragic history of Christian Antisemitism. The development and growth of this hatred can be traced through the books of the New Testament and beyond it to the writings of the Church Fathers and later authors" [206]. I suppose that not only Jews but many, many Christians, including ecclesiastical leaders and theologians, would wholeheartedly endorse this verdict. Especially since and through the Holocaust, Christians have become increasingly conscious of wrong Christian attitudes towards Jews and of vile deeds perpetrated to them by Christians.

This contrition sometimes becomes downright masochism, in particular with regard to 'Auschwitz', that, after all, was instigated by an arch-enemy of Christianity, above all of the Roman-Catholic Church, Adolf Hitler. However, I fully admit that Christians have reason to repent. All the same, I feel that, if we really want to establish a better Jewish-Christian relationship, it will be necessary to proceed carefully and not take recourse to sweeping statements.

For instance, was the cause of Christian antisemitism really that the early Church had to distance itself in a painful way from the Judaism from which it had grown? Couldn't it be that the two drifted apart as the logical and historical consequence of the fact that Judaism and Christianity were fundamentally different religious entities? Furthermore, it seems to me inappropriate and anachronistic to speak of 'antisemitism' at this stage. How could there be antisemitism if the founder of Christianity, all his apostles, all the New Testament authors with the exception of Luke, and all the first believers, were Jews, that is Semites? Mustn't we, if need be, rather speak of 'anti-Judaism'? Let us see how much there is of this in the New Testament, restricting ourselves to this and leaving, for the time being, the Fathers of the Church in peace.

It should never be forgotten how deeply indebted Christianity is to Judaism, its religion and cult. It has adopted the whole of the Old Testament as its own sacred books; countless passages of it are used in Christian ritual, prayer, and meditation. To Christians, just as to Jews, it is 'the Word of God'. The central element of Christian liturgy, has grown straight out of the Jewish Passover meal. Then there is the weekly day of prayer and rest, though no longer the Sabbath or Saturday. Many other elements of the Jewish heritage could be mentioned.

Paul, who is often accused of having effected the definitive breach with Judaism, has authoritatively exhorted his Christians to be humble and grateful because of this indebtedness. He compared the Jewish nation to an olive tree (the olive being the symbol of fruitfulness and health), and a (gentile) Christian to a wild olive. Such Christians, he wrote to the Romans, "have been grafted in among them (= among the branches of the olive tree - F.) and have come to share the same root and sap as the olive". Therefore, "do not make yourself superior to the branches. If you do, remember that you do not sustain the root; the root sustains you"[207]. This means that Christian anti-Judaism and antisemitism are godless and anti-biblical aberrations.

This apostle had also something to say on the 'rejection of Israel'. "I ask, then : Has God rejected his people? Of course not! ... God has not rejected the people he acknowledged of old as his own ... For the gracious gifts of God and his calling are irrevocable"[208]. In the economy of salvation Israel still has an important role to play. "There is a divine secret here, my friends, which I want to share with you, to keep you from thinking yourself wise. This partial hardening has come on Israel only until the Gentiles have been admitted (i.e. to the faith - F.) in full strength; once that has happened, the whole of Israel will be saved"[209].

Paul surely was critical of the Jews because Israel as such had not recognized the Messiah. "You teach others; do you not teach yourselves?"[210]. But it is of the heathen, not of the Jews, that he had really hard things to say [211]. With regard to the Jews he wrote that "there is great grief and unceasing sorrow in my heart". He even went as far as to say : "I would even pray to be an outcast myself, cut off from Christ, if this would help my brothers, my kinsfolk by natural descent" [212]. In my opinion, it is not only unjust but unhistorical to point to Paul as the source of Christian antisemitism. He prided himself on being a Jew. "I was circumcised seven days after I was born; I come from the stock of Israel, from the tribe of Benjamin, Hebrew-speaking as my parents were before me ... (and then, addressing himself to his Jewish opponents) Are they Hebrews? So am I. Are they Israelites? So am I. Are they descended from Abraham? So am I" [213].

The Gospels are of a later date than at least some of the Pauline letters, for example those to the Corinthians. In all probability Mark's Gospel is the oldest of the four, written at some time around A.D. 70. In this Gospel, Samuel Sandmel asserts, "the denigration of Jews, especially the Jewish disciples (the apostles of Jesus are meant - F.), is a leading motif (in Mark) ... The denigration of Jews and their Judaism is related to the main intent but is not that main intent" (this being to be strongly affirmative about Jesus' message) [214]. Now, with the best will in the world, although I have read Mark many, many times in Greek, in Latin, in Dutch, in English, I am unable to detect this denigration.

Of course, the apostles are portrayed in an unfavourable light, on account of their constantly misunderstanding Jesus. But their Jewishness or their Jewish faith are not indicted by this author who was a Jew himself. In effect, he never speaks of 'the Jews' but relates the word battles Jesus fought with Pharisees and scribes. However, the great punitive speech against the Pharisees in Matthew is missing in Mark. I cannot find one word against Judaism. On the contrary, Mark narrates how Jesus cleansed the Temple of all those who were buying and selling and changing money in its courts; he even upset the tables of the money-changers saying that the house of God, the house of prayer, had been turned into a robbers' den [215]. This is a far cry from an attack on Judaism : Jesus is accusing those who had condoned this defilment of what was one of the most holy elements of Judaism.

It is correct to state that "the range of Jewish matters (i.e. in Mark - F.) is so narrow that one could not construct any rounded presentation of Judaism from it" [216]. True, but what Mark intended to present was not a succinct survey of Jewish creed and ritual but the Christian testimony of Jesus. Mirroring as he did the preaching of Peter that was mainly directed to pagans, he saw no reason to be discursive on Judaism.

Matthew, who wrote his Gospel later than Mark, probably around A.D. 85, used the term 'the Jews' once, where he related how, after the resurrection, the chief priests bribed the Roman soldiers to spread the rumour that Jesus' body had been stolen by his disciples. This story, he wrote, "is current among the Jews to this day" [217]. It is this Gospel author who has Jesus say that he had not come to abolish the Law but to fulfil it [218] and quotes him acknowledging the authority of the scribes and Pharisees "who occupy Moses' seat" [219]. There is nothing specifically anti-Jewish in this Gospel.

Still less is there anti-Jewishness in Luke who composed his Gospel around 90. He was a mild man not given to controversy. Although he was not a Jew, the term 'the Jews' does not occur in his book [220].

The Gospel of John was written about 100 [221]; this date is not without importance in our context. Probably Sandmel was correct in writing that "John appears to be contending against three different groupings, the disciples of John the Baptist, the Gnostics (to whom I shall come back later), and the Jews". John occasionally also speaks of Pharisees and scribes but usually Jesus' opponents are 'the Jews", this term occurring about seventy times [222]. It is John's generic term for the foes of Jesus. Harsh words were exchanged between the contending parties. 'The Jews' called Jesus 'a Samaritan and one possessed' [223]; he retorted by saying that "your father is the devil" [224].

John shows Jesus as taking his distance from 'the Jews' and all that they stood for; he makes him even speak of the Law as 'your law' [225]. But does this mean that John had definitively turned against Judaism? Two important utterances seems to contradict this. Jesus said to the Samaritan woman that "it is from the Jews that salvation comes" [226], and, on another occasion when speaking to 'the Jews', that "Scripture (by which he meant the Old Testament - F.) cannot be set aside" [227]. John's overall attitude in all probability reflects the stituation at the turn of the first century A.D. The stream of Jewish converts had almost completely dried up by then, leaving no more than a small trickle. All hopes of winning the Jewish people as such had gone; instead, Christians had met with growing enmity from the side of 'the synagogue' [228].

1. Jewish enmity towards the Christians

Luke's Acts of the Apostles date from some years later than his Gospel. This work doubtless faithfully describes the growing animosity between Jews and Christians. The scene of the first eleven chapters is set in Judaea and centers on the activity of Peter. The beginning is hopeful to a degree : on the very first day of the proclamation of the new message there were three thousand converts, all of them Jews and proselytes, many of them from the Diaspora [229].

For several years to come the young Church was entirely Jewish; there were not yet separate ecclesiastical buildings. To pray one went to the Temple [230]. Preaching there in Solomon's Portico, Peter proclaimed the name of Jesus but exculpated the Jews who delivered Jesus to the Romans saying that they had acted in ignorance [231]. As a result of this speech the number of converts rose to five thousand men. But Peter and John were arrested and taken to account by the Sanhedrin. After deliberation its members resolved to set them free but forbade them to speak and teach in the name of Jesus; this the apostles refused to promise [232].

In spite of the Sanhedrin's opposition, the new community continued to proliferate. Again the apostles were arrested, this time by the Sadducees who were jealous, say the Acts, but they escaped in a miraculous way. The next day they appeared before the Sanhedrin where they were defended by a famous Pharisee, the venerable rabbi Gamaliel. After his intervention the apostles were scourged (the first act of violence against Christians) and set at liberty, with the renewed interdiction to speak of Jesus, which injunction was ignored again [233].

The number of converts among whom there were many Jewish priests grew steadily [234]. Then a deacon, Stephen, was arrested and brought before the Sanhedrin. He held a long speech explaining to the members that Jesus really was the fulfilment of the history of salvation; he ended on a fierce note accusing them of having betrayed 'the Righteous one'. He was condemned to death and stoned [235]. Thus Stephen became the first martyr of the Church; it was the first time that the Jewish-Christian conflict had led to bloodshed.

Later King Herod Agrippa I who since A.D. 41 was the ruler of Judaea and Samaria also lent a hand because "he saw that the Jews approved" this. This is the first instance of a New Testament writer suggesting that the Jewish nation as a whole was inimical to the Christians. James, the brother of John, was killed by the sword, and Peter was locked up in prison but miraculously liberated [236]. This happened about A.D. 44.

From Chapter 13 on Luke is concentrating his relation on the activities of Paul. This apostle and Barnabas were highly successful in Pisidia, a region in Asia Minor; they had nearly the whole town listening to what they had to say. But, Luke writes, 'the Jews' became jealous; they caused a persecution of Paul and his companion, mainly sustained by 'women of standing and the leading men of the town' so that the two had to flee [237]. The same thing happened in Iconium (now Konya) where 'the Jews' sought and received the help of the pagan authorities of the town [238]. In Lycaonia Paul again gained a large following but then Jews arrived from Antioch and Iconium; Paul was stoned but did not die of it [239].

In the course of his second missionary journey which led him to Macedonia and Greece, Paul arrived in Thessalonika (now Saloniki) in about A.D. 51. This town harboured a large Jewish Diaspora community; on three consecutive Sabbath days the apostle preached in the synagogue. He had some success among Jews but more among Greek proselytes. Once again 'the Jews' grew jealous and caused an uproar so that the brethren had to spirit away Paul and Barnabas in the middle of the night. They had a more favourable reception in Beroea but 'the Jews' of Thessalonika came and again the two had to take to their heels [240].

In Corinth, where he stayed for one and a half years (51/52), Paul founded a Christian community. 'The Jews' of the town brought him before the Roman proconsul Gallio accusing him of ungodliness but the Roman did not show himself interested in theological disputes [241].

After his third journey, ending in A.D. 56, Paul was in Jerusalem. 'The Jews' from Asia, viz. from towns where he had founded Christian communities, saw him in the Temple which he visited for a purification rite according to the Law [242], and laid their hands on him. There was a big uproar and Paul only escaped death through the timely arrival of a Roman patrol that brought him into safety.

The commander of the patrol allowed the apostle to address the crowd; in doing so Paul seized the opportunity to relate how he had been converted to Christianity. When he had got to the point when Jesus had told him in a vision to go the Gentiles, the crowd lost its temper and began to scream so vehemently that he had to be brought hastily into the barracks of the Antonia, the Roman fortress in Jerusalem. The next day he appeared before the Sanhedrin. When the High Priest Ananias ordered an attendant to strike him on the mouth, he retorted (not knowing that it was the High Priest) : "God will strike you, you whitewashed wall!". There was very little love lost on either side on that occasion! The gathering came to no conclusion because a quarrel arose between the Pharisean and Sadducean members of it. Becoming afraid that his detainee would be torn to pieces by one or other of the parties, the officer had him transported back to the barracks [243].

Then a party of about forty Jews hatched a plot to kill Paul and obviously got the connivance of the chief priests for this. But a nephew of his gave the thing away to his uncle, and as a consequence the commander had Paul brought to Caesarea under heavy escort [244]. Five days later the apostle was brought to court before Marcus Antonius Felix, since A.D. 52 procurator or governor of Judaea, a very cruel and harsh man. Ananias too had arrived in the mean time accompanied by some elders and an advocate called Tertullus. This man accused Paul of being 'a ringleader of the sect of the Nazarenes and a fomenter of discord among the Jews all over the world'. Paul defended himself eloquently, and Felix, clearly at a loss what to do, took no decision and put Paul under light arrest. He remained in custody for two years; from time to time the procurator spoke with him, hoping to solicit a bribe from him [245].

After two years Porcius Festus became the successor of Felix as governor of Judaea. Once again Paul was brought to court, this time before Festus, and once again the chief priests, who had come down from Jerusalem, brought many grave charges against him. Festus, who was biased in favour of the Jews with whom he hoped to ingratiate himself, asked the accused whether he was willing to stand trial in Jerusalem. But Paul, knowing that his opponents still fostered murderous intentions, refused and, as the Roman citizen he was, appealed to the emperor. Festus, very probably only too glad to be able to wash his hands of this affair, consequently sent him to Rome [246].

Having arrived in Rome after an eventful journey, Paul, although remaining in the custody of a warder, obtained private lodgings where he often had long discussions with local Jewish leaders. Some he converted, others remained unconvinced. Finally, the apostle summed up his efforts in these words - and this at the same time is the conclusion of the Acts - : "This people's minds have become dull ... Therefore, take note that this salvation of God has been sent to the Gentiles; the Gentiles will listen" [247]. This means that after all his attempts Paul finally gave up the Jews as hopeless.

But does this mean that Paul was campaigning against Judaism? Paul himself would not hear of this. "I have committed no offence against the Jewish Law, or against the Temple, or against the emperor"; this is what he told Festus [248]. His offences, in Jewish eyes, were of another kind : he proclaimed that Jesus was the Messiah, and he preached to the heathen, defiling himself by this. It is true that unrest arose wherever he set foot, but it was 'the Jews' who everywhere fomented the uproar.

In the difficult and so often painful relationship of Jews and Christians that certainly will occupy us in later volumes, the first period, that of the decades immediately following the death of Jesus, was characterized not by anti-Judaism, still less by antisemitism, but by the anti-Christian attitude, verging on dualism, of leading Jewish circles. Their ferocious stance becomes somewhat more understandable if we realize, not only that in this period many Jews defected to the new sect, but rather that the Jewish leaders felt the whole venerable Jewish heritage, the Jewish identity, threatened and jeopardized by men like Paul.

On the Christian side too, there is a gradual hardening of standpoints detectable. It is only after the first few years, when Jewish converts still were numerous, that Luke began using the term 'the Jews' as though already pre-empting the final verdict that their conversion had become a hopeless matter.

m. A curse on the 'minim'

One of the most important Jewish prayers is the 'shemoneh esreh', or the 'Amidâh', as Sephardic Jews use to call it. This prayer has to be recited daily in a standing (= amidah) position and facing Jerusalem (in Jerusalem itself the Temple Mount); it consists of nineteen, originally eighteen (= esmoneh esreh) 'benedictions'. Now the twelfth of these benedictions is the so-called 'Birkat ha-Minim', the benediction of the heretics. This can hardly be called a' blessing' since it runs as follows. "May no hope be left to the slanderers, but may wickedness perish as in a moment. May all thine enemies be soon cut off, and do those speedily uproot the haughty and shatter and humble them speedily in our days. Blessed be thou, o Lord, who strikes down our enemies and humbles the haughty" [249]. This sounds more like a curse than a blessing.

Now who are meant by the opprobrious term 'minim' which in a general sense signifies 'sectarians'? This depends on the answer to two other questions. What is the etymology of 'minim', and when was this prayer composed? The etymology is not quite certain. 'Minim' may have been derived from 'Mani', the founder of Manichaean sect, or from

'Ma'aminim Yeshu Notzeri' = believers in Jesus the Nazarene. There is no doubt that at least some of these benedictions were already in use in the Second Temple period, that is in the centuries after the Babylonian Captivity. According to Hirsch, "it is an indubitable fact that the benedictions date from the earlier days of the Pharisaic Synagogue"[250], perhaps the third century B.C.

The Talmud says that the collection was edited by Simeon ha-Pakoli in the academy of Rabbi Gamaliel II at Jabneh in Palestine (A.D. 100); this editing only refers to the definitive codification, not to its origination[251]. The twelfth blessing underwent many changes in the course of time. What I have quoted is the modern version. It is thought that the Birkat ha-Minim was composed by Samuel ha-Katan at the request of Gamaliel II and then intersected into the Amidah.

By the 'minim' or 'heretics' Sadducees, Samaritans, Gnostics, or Judaeo-Christians may be meant. With regard to the twelfth Birkat A.D. 100 seems a rather late date to curse Samaritans and Sadducees since these had been with the Jews for centuries already. Respecting the Gnostics, it seems to me that orthodox Jews of the first century can hardly have regarded these as deviants from the Jewish faith. This leaves us with Judaeo-Christians. Let us note what Ismar Elbogen has to say to this. "(This petition) can be understood only on the grounds of its special introduction into the prayer. (It) was one of the means adopted to separate Christianity from Judaism and to expel the Jewish Christians from the synagogue so as to render it impossible to utilize as places of propaganda the synagogues in which they occasionally prayed. For this reason there was introduced a petition which they could neither listen to nor pronounce themselves. The tension between the Jews and the Jewish Christians had grown so great that complete separation had to be achieved"[252].

n. The Christians seen as sectarians

In conclusion, it should be stated that there was considerable antagonism on both sides ending, at least on the Jewish part, in a complete and definite breach [253]. From the very first beginning the Jewish leaders had their problems with Jesus and later with his adherents. When, soon enough, Gentiles who were not circumcised and did not observe the Mosaic Law, were admitted to the new community, it became fatally clear to the Jewish authorities that the Christians were sectarians, even if they still visited the Temple. This resulted in open enmity and even in acts of violence. The breach was finally sealed by the virtual expulsion of the Judaeo-Christians from the synagogue.

The Jewish stance was of a radical kind and may even be called dualistic since it excluded the Christians from the fields that were most dear to the Jewish heart, those of religion and cult. In these respects Jews no longer wanted to have anything to do with Christians. Although the Christians took their distance from Judaism, knowing full well that they could not be dubbed orthodox Jews, their attitude in the first century A.D. was far less radical. Christians of Jewish origin still adhered to the Temple and to several Jewish customs, while all Christians, Gentiles as much as Judaeo-Christians, based their faith on the Old Testament. And if Christians perpetrated deeds of violence against Jews in a later period, they remained innocent of this in the first century A.D.

6. Gnosticizing tendencies in the New Testament [254]

On the whole, we can agree with Segal when he writes that "the scriptural traditions with which Jesus was associated were not Gnostic" [255]. The mental and spiritual climate in which Christianity originated, that of the Jewish society in Palestine, was not Gnostic; the most suitable term would be 'un-Gnostic'. But the general atmosphere of the surrounding Hellenistic world was 'gnosticizing' to a degree, with its centre in the Samaritan-Syrian region, next-door to the Jewish nation. Furthermore, after only a few years of confinement to Palestine, the new Gnostic faith began to spread, first to Syria, and then all over Asia Minor where, together with the arrival of the Christian creed, several Gnostic sects had begun to flourish. We have already seen that strangely distorted Jewish as well as Christian elements are to be found in Gnostic ideology. Could it also have been possible that, if not downright Gnostic tenets, nonetheless gnosticizing tendencies may be discovered in New Testament writings?

a. The word 'gnosis' in the New Testament

Our first enquiry should be with regard to the use of the word 'gnosis' in the New Testament, along the lines of investigation in Chapter II of how it was deployed by Hellenic-Hellenistic authors [256]. As I said there, the original and colloquial meaning of the word is 'just knowledge, intelligence or understanding'. In this sense it is used by Paul when he says that Christ's love is 'beyond knowledge' [257]; here only plain understanding is meant. This is similar with Peter when he writes that husbands must show understanding (kata gnoosin) towards their wives [258]. But such instances are extremely rare. The verb 'gi(g)nooskein ' too only seldom means 'to know for a fact'.

Most of the time noun and verb denote a special sort of knowledge. Ginooskein soon enough comes to mean 'to detect, to discover, or to recognize'. During the turmoil surrounding Paul on the Temple square, the Roman officer at first "could not get at the truth (gnoonai)" [259]. It means 'to find a sign in a thing by which to know, to recognize in or by something, to recognize as worthy of intimacy and love, to understand somebody's conduct or intentions or what he is aiming at, to know one's character, to perceive one's plans, to read one's mind'. The verb can also be used for carnal knowledge. Mary said to the archangel Gabriel : "How can this be since I do not know a man?" = I am still a virgin [260].

In all these meanings there is already an element of more than pedestrian knowledge. But we reach the level of really superior knowledge when ginooskein comes to indicate knowledge about things divine - which, of course, is fairly common in Scripture. "This is eternal life : to know you, the only true God" [261]; here the knowledge of God is the foundation of a more than ordinary human life. It is also used in a negative sense : "The (pagan) world did not know God", leaning as it did on one special kind of wisdom (sophia) [262].

In its positive meanings the verb can also signify 'knowledge of the nature and the will of God the Father, and of the holy will and affection by which he aims to sanctify and redeem men through Jesus Christ'. Telling instances of the relation between redemption or perfection and knowledge are the following. "Everyone who remains in him (Christ) does not sin; everyone who has not seen him nor does know him is a sinner" [263]; "whoever does not love does not know God, for God is love" [264].

Knowing Christ is also often mentioned - to know his blessings, his consumate kindness towards mankind, and the benefits redounding to us from fellowship with him, and, still more important, his holiness, his divinity, his being the Son of God. An ever higher level of knowledge is "the peculiar knowledge of God the Father claimed by Christ for himself" [265]. "The Father knows me, and I know the Father."

As I said already, the noun gnosis occurs far less frequently. Just like the verb, it almost invariably denotes a special kind of knowledge. In general it means the knowledge and wisdom of God himself [266]. As such it is already embodied in Mosaic Law [267], and still more in the Gospels [268]. Paul considered it his special duty to spread this knowledge and 'to demolish all sophistries against it' [269]. It is an illuminating knowledge giving "the light which is knowledge of the glory of God in the face of Christ Jesus" [270].

Gnosis refers to "the deeper, more perfected and enhanced knowledge of this (Christian) religion, such as belongs to the more advanced". There are, for instance, believers who are able 'to put the deepest knowledge into words', for the benefit of the less gifted [271]. Paul ridicules the Corinthians who think they possess knowledge [272], but he himself boasts of being in its possession [273]. He speaks of 'the knowledge of every hidden truth' [274].

There is, however, no really secret knowledge. During his trial before the Sanhedrin, Jesus testified that he had always spoken openly "for all the world to hear ... I have said nothing in secret" [275]. The apostles went out to bring the message to everyone, Jews and non-Jews alike; to converts the duty fell to do as much on their own initiative. But all the same the New Testament authors were not speaking of a common sort of knowledge, not even of superior human intelligence or of deep psychological insight. What they mean by 'gnosis' is knowledge of higher things, of things divine, of God.

Although in principle offered to all people, it is, nevertheless, not grasped by everybody since many prove incapable of gauging the importance of the message. It is also a kind of knowledge that is connected with salvation or redemption, though it is said nowhere that it actually works redemption. All such characteristics of gnosis (and of ginooskein), as used in the New Testament, make it relate to the significance that 'knowledge' has in Gnostic ideology.

b. Paul and the mysteries

As McL.Wilson explains, "there is much in his (Paul's) thought which could appeal to the Gnostics, and which could be incorporated by them in their systems" [276]. Not only in his letters he used the words ginooskein and gnosis more frequently than the other authors, but he also, like the Gnostics, loved the word 'mystery'; he uses this in twenty-one places. He speaks of God's "secret purpose (mystêrion) ... that is now disclosed to God's people" [277]. Equally, the partial hardening of Israel is a 'divine secret' [278]. There is even a 'mystery of Christ'. The proclamation of Jesus Christ goes according to the revelation of a divine and now disclosed secret (mystêrion) [279]. To the Corinthians the apostle came not with eloquence but only to declare the mystery of God [280] of which he and the other apostles are the stewards [281].

In this context it is doubtless somewhat of a gnosticizing element that not every believer is capable of understanding all the mysteries. This is the case in particular when somebody possesses the gift of glossolaly, that is of speaking in a language that nobody present can understand; it may not be a language at all but a series of ecstatic sounds uttered by a believer. Paul has this to say of it. "If anyone is speaking in tongues, he is talking with God, not with men and women; no one understands him, for he speaks divine mysteries in the Spirit" [282]. This 'speaking in tongues', therefore, is a highly individual thing.

Elsewhere Paul speaks of 'the knowledge of every hidden truth', a text I quoted already; here he words 'gnoosis' and 'mystèrion' are juxtaposed. The apostle is the dispenser of this hidden truth : "We pronounce the wisdom of God as a mystery ...; none of the powers of this world has known this wisdom" [283]. It should not unduly surprise us that the mysteriosophical word 'teleios' crops up here. Normally it means 'perfect' or 'complete' in the New Testament but it may also signify 'initiated'. "Since we have been initiated, we think in this way" [284]; "we instruct everyone in all the ways of wisdom, so as to present each of you as an initiate of the body of Christ" [285].

Outside the Pauline letters the term 'mystery' occurs twice only. When the disciples asked Jesus for the meaning of his parables, he answered : "To you the secret (mystèrion) of the kingdom of God has been given; but for those who are outside everything comes by way of parables" [286]. In the Book of Revelation it is found twice or thrice with no different meaning [287].

c. The Messiah motif

The biblical Messiah motif is far older than the Gnostic ideology and is in itself not a Gnostic idea. But the concept of Jesus Messiah points to an exceptional human being, a more than human, or even a divine being to whom a voice from heaven spoke; it is for this reason that Segal said that this motif is 'mythical in the current anthropological use of the word' [288]. Myth is understood here as something that cannot be explained or presented in ordinary historical or psychological terms. This 'mythical' conception tallies well with the Gnostic predilection for myth, non-historical presentation, and suprahuman beings.

d. The Law given by angels

A curious element is that Mosaic Law was given by angels. Stephen, the first martyr, expressed this idea in his great speech before the Sanhedrin when he stood trial [289]. The Letter to the Hebrews states that "God's word (by which the Law is meant - F.) was spoken by angels" [290]. Passages such as these suggest that there exist intermediate beings, an idea that was dear to the Gnostics too. In one passage the New Testament actually uses the term 'intermediary' [291]. By the same token the use of this word entails that the Law is something of a lesser order, at least inferior to the message of Jesus that came straight from God.

e. The contrast between flesh and spirit

It is a salient characteristic in Paul that he is constantly making such a sharp contrast between 'flesh' and 'spirit'. According to the apostle, a human person consists of 'flesh' (sarx, in Greek) and 'spirit' (pneuma) [292]. That they, although forming a whole, nevertheless are different is expressed by Paul's phrase that he is absent in the body but present in the spirit (with the Colossians to whom he is writing) [293]. Bultmann even saw fit to speak of "a far ranging relationship between Paul and Hellenistic mystics ... The sarx-pneuma concept of Paul shows clearly the character of the metaphysical dualism that was characteristic for the Hellenistic mystery religions. That is, sarx and pneuma are conceived of as natural or substance-like powers" [294].

A sharp contrast is indicated by Jesus' word that has acquired a more or less proverbial character : "The spirit is willing but the flesh is weak" [295]. We find something similar in this text : "Flesh can give birth only to flesh; it is spirit that gives birth to spirit" [296]. Still more radical : "If Christ is in you, then although the body is dead because of sin, yet the Spirit is your life because you have been justified" [297]. Paul knew of unspiritual persons; such a one "refuses what belongs to the Spirit; it is folly to him; he cannot grasp it" [298]. There is, of course, some intimation of there being two sets of people here.

In Gnostic ideology the dualistic distinction of human nature and spirit, of sarx and pneuma, played a most important role. Some of the expressions I quoted are indeed bordering on dualism and as such seem to be gnosticizing. Gnostics sometimes made freely use of them. But in the end there is no dualism in them because in the resurrection body and spirit, sarx and pneuma, will be reunited. Eternal life is not for the pneuma alone. Paul preached the doctrine of resurrection defending it vigorously against sceptics and unbelievers. "If the Spirit of him who raised Jesus from the dead dwells in you, then the God who raised Jesus Christ from the dead will also give new life to your mortal bodies through his indwelling Spirit" [299].

In this context it deserves attention that the New Testament does not advocate an ascetic way of life like so many fiercely dualistic and esoteric societies did and do in order to accentuate the difference between a life of the body and a life of the spirit. Jesus was no ascete like John the Baptist. "John came, neither eating nor drinking ...; the Son of Man came, eating and drinking, and they say : 'Look at him! A glutton and a drinker!'" [300]. It was John, of all persons, who in his Gospel stressed the fundamental unity of the divine and the human, of the celestial and the terrestrial, of the spiritual and the physical, in the person of Jesus of Nazareth. He did this by calling him the Logos, the Word of God that came into the world : "The Word became flesh; he made his home among us" [301]. I might add that Paul did not preach ascetism either.

f. The use of the term 'aeon'

One of the favourite Gnostic terms is 'aeon' ('aioon' in Greek), or age. It is also to be encountered in the New Testament. Originally it means 'period' in a neutral sense. But more often than not it acquires a special, a specific character, for instance that of an indeterminate period. In that case it can come to mean 'perpetuity of time' or 'eternity'. By the same token it sometimes means unspecified ancient times. In other texts, however, the present world period is indicated with it but then in a negative sense. "Jesus Christ ... gave himself for our sins, to rescue us out of the present wicked age" [302].

Here the 'wicked age' is categorised as at once self-sufficient and profoundly un-Christian. Or, to take another example. "Where is your wise man now, your man of learning, your subtle debater of this present age (aioon)? God has made the wisdom (sophia) of this world (kosmos) look foolish!" [303]. Here aeon and cosmos are almost synonyms. 'The god of this present age' is the devil [304]. This is clearly a gnosticizing text and a passably dualistic one too.

In contrast to the present age the future aeon is qualitatively different; one could even say that the distinction has a dualistic character. Two different worlds are postulated in Jesus' saying that nobody arguing against the Holy Spirit will be forgiven, 'either in this age or in the world to come' [305]. Whereas the present aeon is arrogant, full of error, and hostile to the Gospel, the future aeon will an age characterized by the second coming of Christ, followed by the resurrection of the dead. Followers of Christ, although still living in this wicked world, are already partaking of the world to come [306].

g. The use of the term 'archoon'

Another key-word of the Gnosis is 'archoon', or archont. It signifies 'ruler'; in the plural it is used for 'authorities' in a neutral sense. It has quite another colouring when it is used for Christ as the ruler of the universe. This occurs once in the New Testament, in Ap. 1 : 5, where he is called 'the ruler of the kings of the earth'. But the word can also indicate malevolent non-human rulers. For instance, Beelzebul is called 'the archont of devils' [307]. The term assumes a gnosticizing character when the devil is said to be 'the archont of this world', every time in John's Gospel [308]. Paul too doubtless means demons when he speaks of the rulers who govern this present world [309].

Grant draws our attention to an important distinction between Paul and John. Paul once calls Satan 'the god of this age' [310] but not 'of this world'. By making this subtle distinction, says Grant, "his thought remains just outside the domain of the Gnosis. He does not speak of the world being necessarily hostile to God, its creator". With John this is different. For him, Satan has become the archont of this world. Although created by God, the world has come under the sway of the evil one. A strong dualism, at least an ethical dualism, occurs in his treatment of the cosmos ... This dualism, on the verge of becoming metaphysical, is even more strongly expressed in the First Epistle of John. "Everything in this world - the lust of the flesh and the lust of the eyes and the pride of the eyes - is not of the Father but is of the world. And the world is passing away as is its lust; but he who does the will of God remains forever'" [311]. This is Grant's summing up : "The development from Paul's thought to John's is thus away from apocalyptic eschatology and in the direction of Gnosticism. Both remain un-Gnostic in so far as their dualism is temporal and ethical, in short, Jewish. Both come close to gnosis in so far as their dualism is on the verge of becoming physical and metaphysical. John comes closer than Paul does" [312].

7. The anti-Gnostic stance of the New Testament

We should not utilize the term 'gnosticizing' without due caution. For it suggests that New Testament authors, in particular Paul and John, were somehow indebted to Gnostic thought. It might easily have been the other way round; we know how syncretistic and electic Gnostic systems are. There is no doubt that, for instance, a famous Gnostic like Valentinian freely made use of the writings of Paul, especially of the Letters to the Ephesians and the Colossians in which 'Gnostic terms' abound [313].

a. The attitude of Peter and Paul with regard to the Gnosis

When all is said and done, the New Testament as a whole adopts a firmly anti-Gnostic stance. It was Peter, the acknowledged leader of the young Christian community, who set the tone. "It was not on myths, however cleverly concocted, that we relied when we told you about the power of our Lord Jesus Christ and his coming; rather with our own eyes we had witnessed his majesty" [314]. In this passage the apostle categorically states that the Christian doctrine is not a product of mythology or religious fantasy but has an historical foundation. He goes on to warn his flock against false teachers who "will introduce their destructive views ... (but) will gain adherents ... They will trade on your credulity with sheer fabrications" [315]. I have no doubt that Peter is speaking here of the first Gnostic prophets, men like Simon the Magician.

In the beginning of this chapter I mentioned that the author of the First Letter to Timothy spoke scathingly of 'the contradictions of the Gnosis so-called' [316]. "Have nothing to do", its author writes, " with superstitious myths, mere old-wives' tales" [317]. I am convinced that he aimed at the Gnostic myths. Whether or not Paul was its author, this apostle several times categorically stated that he was not operating in the Gnostic line. "Knowledge", he says, "is only partial, and will vanish ... There are three things that will last forever, faith, hope, and love", knowledge not being among them. "I may have knowledge of every hidden thing, but if I have no love, I am nothing" [318]. One could read this as a fundamentally anti-Gnostic statement. And in the Letter to the Ephesians, so often quoted as being germane to the Gnosis, since it proclaims the 'cosmological Christ', it is also stated that the love of Christ is beyond knowledge [319].

b. John and the Gnosis

So far so good, for the two leading men in the young Church were both decidedly anti-Gnostic. But what about that third prominent person, John? Even the most unsophisticated reader of the New Testament can, at its first reading, see that how different John's Gospel is from all other books of the New Testament, At first sight it seems far less historical than the accounts of the Synoptics, and much less practical than the Letters of James and Peter. His emphasis throughout is on symbolism and spirituality. Add to this that, as we saw, there is a fair amount of gnosticizing and Gnostic terms in this Gospel, and it will not surprise us that many have seen a proto- or crypto-Gnostic in John whose writings, in consequence, have been made use of by the Gnostics for their own ends.

So, on the surface of it, this apostle seems to be a deviant among his colleague-authors. It is sometimes supposed that, although John did not really sympathize with the Gnosis, he was well aware of the strong pull it exerted on many aimless people in his days. Therefore, to counter all those Gnostics, Docetes, and Nicolaites [320], by meeting them half-way, he freely made use, it is believed by some, of their terminology and ideas. Be this as it may, there is no denying that in this Gospel there is far more 'Gnostic presence' than in the Synoptics or even in Paul. John, the latest of the Gospel authors, saw himself confronted with a broad front of Gnostic beliefs. Earlier I wrote of his evident dualistic leanings. These enabled him to understand the Gnostics better and to adopt a more profound interest in their dualistic tenets than the others did. But this in itself does not make him a Gnostic [321].

If there is much 'symbolism' in this Gospel, there is at the same time a lot of 'history' in the form of facts reported by an eye-witness. John often marks the dates - the next day, two days later, a week later -, and even the hours - "it was about four in the afternoon" [322]. Assisted by his excellent memory, he was punctilious in this. He was equally exact with regard to locations. "John (the Baptist) was baptizing at Aenon, near Salim" [323]; "Jesus was teaching near the Treasury in the Temple when he said this" [324]. Sixty years after the event he still remembered names. "The servant's name (the one whom Peter cut his ear off) was Malchus" [325]; he knew that the servant-girl who addressed the unlucky Peter in the High Priest's courtyard was a relative of this Malchus [326].

John had a very sharp eye for details, relishing them with gusto, and not only for his symbolic ends. He is the only one to mention that the cut-off ear was the man's right ear. When the dumb-founded Samaritan woman at the Jacob's well went away to the town, she left her jar standing at the well [327]. He relates exactly how much perfume the woman during a supper in Bethany poured over Jesus' feet : a pound [328].

A fascinating example of John's exactitude in description is the episode of his arrival at the open tomb. On Mary of Magdala's report Peter and John went there; John, being much younger, could run faster than Peter and was the first to arrive but did not enter. Then Peter came too and together they went in. "He saw the linen wrappings lying there, and the napkin which had been round his (Jesus') head, not with the wrappings but rolled up in a place by itself" [329]. It is as though he had taken a photo of the interior and was looking at it when describing the scene!

John's delight in graphic descriptions is almost journalistic. One should read his lively record of Jesus' conversation with the Samaritan woman, recording her consternation when he told her to her face, although he had never seen her before, that she had led a loose life, and the astonishment of the disciples who, returning from the town, found him talking with a woman, and a Samaritan at that [330].

Or take that row between the man who was born blind but had been healed by Jesus but was told by the Pharisees that his benefactor was a sinner. "I don't know whether or not he is a sinner. I know only one thing : I was blind and now I can see." And when his interrogators asked him for the umpteenth time how Jesus did this, the guttersnipe brashly retorted : "What? Do you want to become his disciples?", whereupon they used physical force to throw him out [331]. It closely resembles a movie-scene!

What I mean to convey is this. If John's book is spiritual and symbolic, it is also graphic, realistic, and factual. It has, and the author stresses this in an indirect way, a strong historical foundation, linked as it is to times and places and situations. This is a profound difference with the Gnostic approach which is basically mythical. In this light the famous prologue to this Gospel must also be understood. In it John speaks of the 'Logos' that was with God in the beginning, and that even was God. 'Logos' means 'word, communication, or mandate (of God)'; it is something intelligible, or intelligential, having to do with understanding and even with logics. As such it occurs a great many times in the New Testament. "Logos' is the exact counterpart here of 'muthos' a term that is used thrice, and every time in malam partem. I am convinced that when John shows this predilection for the word 'logos', he intends to state that he too is not operating in the Gnostic way.

c. Conclusion

Let me conclude by quoting the words of Wilson at the end of his disquisition on the relationship between the young Church and the early Gnosis. "In the New Testament we have as yet only the first murmurs of the storm which reached its height in the second century, but they are enough to show that the danger had begun to make itself felt. The errors of the Corinthians and the Colossians show how people with their background and outlook might react to the presentation of the new faith by a Paul. The same ideas were widely current, and the very amount of theories shows the grasp which they had on the popular mind. Not the least of the services done by Paul and his fellow-labourers - and by John, I may add - F. - was their exposition of the basic Christian doctrine in the light of contemporary thought, and their resolute rejection of any other Gospel" [332].

NOTES TO CHAPTER IV

1. Jo.19:35-36.
2. Mc.14:51.
3. Col.4:14.
4. Col.4:14.
5. 'Our dear friend Luke', Col.4:14.
6. Lc.1:2; Acts 1:1.
7. Lc.1:3-4.
8. 1Cor.15:14.
9. Lc.3:1-2.
10. Lc.2:1.
11. Mt.2:1; Lc.1:5.
12. It is a well-known fact that the traditional and ineradicable chronology of the Christian era is wrong; it starts a few years too late.

As my teacher of religion in secondary school used to say : "Jesus was born four or five years before the birth of Christ.
13. Mt.14:1; Lc.3:19; Acts 13:1.
14. Mt.14:1-12.
15. Lc.13:32.
16. Mt.1:17.
17. Lc.:23-38.
18. Mt.1:15.
19. Gal.4:4.
20. Eph.1:9-10.
21. This 'Son of Man' is the translation of 'bar nasha' in the Aramaic in which this part of the Book of Daniel is written ('ben adam' in Hebrew).
22. Mt.15:13-16.
23. Mt.13:24-30.
24. Jude 6.
25. Jude 7.
26. Gen.5:1-4. See Vol. IV, Ch. I.11b.
27. Ps.8:5.
28. Lc.10:18.
29. Mt.4:1-11; Mc.1:12-13; Lc.4:1-13.
30. See Vol. IV, Ch. I.9.
31. See Vol. IV, Ch. I.14c.
32. Jo.8:48.
33. Jo.4:22.
34. Jo.4:9.
35. Lc.17:16.
36. Lc.9:52-54.
37. Lc.10:30-37. It should not suprise us that it is Luke who has preserved this parable; as a non-Jew he was not imbued with the inherited hatred of the Samaritans.
38. Mt.22:15-22.
39. Mt.8:5-15; Lk.7:1-10; Jo.4:56-53.
40. Mt. 27:54; Lc.23:47.

41. Mt.27:19. Could she have been 'judaizing' somewhat? For 'just' the Latin text has 'justus' and the Greek 'dikaios' which cannot have been anything else than the translation of the Hebrew 'tsaddiq'. A 'tsaddiq' is somebody who most carefully executes the prescripts of the Law.
42. Lc.24:21.
43. Jo.6:15.
44. Mt.21:6-9; Mc.11:6-10; Lc.19:35-38; Jo.12:12-15.
45. Lc.23:2.
46. Jo.18:33-37 and 19:8.
47. See Vol, Ch. II.15.
48. Mt.10:5.
49. Acts 1:8.
50. Acts 1:1-25.
51. Mt.15:21-28; Mac.7:24-30.
52. Mt.16:16.
53. Lc.13:29.
54. Mt.22:2-10; Lc.14:15-24.
55. Mt.28:19.
56. Mc.16:15.
57. Acts 10.
58. Acts 11:1-18.
59. Acts 15:1-5.
60. Acts 15:6-29.
61. Rom.2:10-11.
62. Mt.5:1-12; Lc.6:17-23.
63. Mc.10:16-17; Lc.18:18-19.
64. Mt.5:45.
65. Mc.8:38.
66. Lc.11:1-13.
67. Lc.7:10.
68. Mt.25:31-46.
69. Mc.1:14.
70. Pt.3:1.
71. Pt.3:7.

72. 1Tim.5:3-16.
73. 1Cor.7:8.
74. 1Cor.7:9.
75. 1Cor.7:25.
76. 1Cor.7:29.
77. 1Cor.7:32-34.
78. 1Cor.7:28.
79. 1Cor.7:1.
80. 1Cor.7:2-5.
81. 1Cor.7:6.
82. Eph.5:21.
83. Eph.5:19.
84. Eph.5:28.
85. 1Cor.11:11-12.
86. 1Tim.2:11-12.
87. Eph.5:22-24.
88. Eph.5:28 and 33.
89. Eph.5:21.
90. Jo.1:9.
91. Jo.1:5.
92. Jo.1:2.
93. Jo.1:12-13.
94. Jo.3:3-6.
95. Jo.5:17-21.
96. Jo.5:21-24.
97. Jo.11:25-26.
98. Jo.1:10.
99. Jo.17:14-16.
100. 1Jo.1:5 and 2:10-11.
101. 1Jo.3:7-8.
102. 1Jo.4:5-6.
103. Mt.25:31-46.
104. Lc.16:26.
105. Jo.18:15-16.

106. Mc.3:17.
107. Lc.9:52-55.
108. Guardini, De Heer. I read this book 45 years ago and am unable to find back the exact page of this quotation.
109. Jo,13:23-24.
110. Jo.19:26-27.
111. Mc.15:40.
112. Mt.20:20-24; Mc.10:35-41.
113. Chorus, Psych. kijk 82/83.
114. See Vol. III, Ch. III.21.
115. Zec.9:9; Mt.21:5.
116. Jo.12:15.
117. Ap.13:8.
118. Ap.14:1-5.
119. This 'charagma' or 'mark' has its origin "in the practice occurring among devotees of a god branding themselves with a mark indicative of their relation to the god ... There is no evidence that an edict of the kind was actually issued in the establishment of the emperor-worship", Beckwith, Apocalypse 641/642.
120. Ap.14:9-10.
121. Ap.18:9.
122. 1Sam.10:19.
123. Vol. IV, Ch. II.13b.
124. Vol. IV, Ch. II.7d.
125. Rom.13:4.
126. 1Pt.2:13.
127. Ap.22:5.
128. Ir., Adv.Haer. 5.30.3.
129. This dragon is known from the Old Testament as the serpent (in Gen.), Leviathan, Rahab, and also as a dragon proper. The numbers seven and ten have no specific meaning but denote fulness : the Empire wants to encompass the whole world.
130. Ap.13:2.
131. Ap.13:2.
132. Ap.13:6.
133. Ap.13:4.
134. Ap.13:8.

135. Mt.3:1.
136. Mc.1:14.
137. Mt.3:11; Mc.1:8; Lc.3:16.
138. Ladd, Jesus and the Kingdom, 103. I am much indebted to this study for these passages.
139. Is.30:27.
140. Mt.3:10 and 12; Lc.3:9 and 17.
141. Ladd, Jesus and the Kingdom 103.
142. Mt.7:19.
143. Mt.18:8-9.
144. 1Cor.3:14-15.
145. Ap.19:20.
146. Ezra 6:21; Neh.10:28.
147. Jo.18:28.
148. Jo.7:44-49.
149. Mt.23:2.
150. The Hebrew name of the Great Court was 'Beit Din ha-Gadol'. 'Sanhedrin' is the Hebrew rendering of the Greek 'synedrion' = assembly, Ellis Rivkin s.v. 'Pharisees' in Enc. of Rel. 11, 270.
151. Mt.5:17.
152. Mt.23:23; Lc.11:42.
153. Mc.7:9-13.
154. Mt.23.
155. Mt.23:13-14.
156. Mt.9:14; Mc.2:18.
157. Mc.7:1-4.
158. Mc.7:5.
159. Mt.22:34-40; Mc.12:28-31; Lc.10:25-27.
160. Mt.19:1-8; Mc.2:23-28; Lc.6:1-5.
161. Lc.6:11.
162. Mt.12:14; Mc.3:6.
163. Jo.5:18.
164. Jo.7:1.
165. Jo.7:25.
166. Jo.7:32 and 44.

167. Jo.10:39-40.
168. Jo.11:53 and 57.
169. Jo.7:48.
170. Mt.26:5; Mc.14:2.
171. Mt.26:14-16; Mc.14:10-11; Lc.22:3-6.
172. Mt.26:57-68, Mc.14:53-65; Lc.22:66-71.
173. Jo.18:31.
174. Jo.19:12.
175. Jo.3:1-10.
176. Jo.:50-52. Nicodemus also helped to bury Jesus in a dignified way, Jo.19:39. Another Jewish authority who was favourable to Jesus was Joseph of Arimathea, also a member of the Sanhedrin; he claimed the dead body of Jesus from Pilate, Mc.15:43. The corpse was deposed in his own tomb, Mt.27-57-60. Luke calls him 'a good and righteous man', Lc.23:50-53.
177. Mc.12:34.
178. Tomson, Paul and the Law, presents a detailed treatment of Paul's handling of Mosaic Law.. In his opening paragraph this author states that (p. 1) scholarship on Paul has been based on three traditional assumptions : 1. the centre of this thought is a polemic against the Law; 2. the Law no longer had a practical meaning for him; 3. ancient Jewish literature is no source for explaining his letters. The first point, he writes, "is the most conspicuous in scholarly literature. In recent years its correctness is increasingly being questioned, but it has also found gallant defenders". Although in my context Paul's conflict with the Law is getting pride of place, I heartily agree with Tomson that this polemic was not the centre of his theology. Paul's attitude to the Law is analyzed at some length by Samuel Sandmel, Judaism and Christian beginnings, New York, 1978, Part IV. Ch. I.
179. Gal.3:13.
180. Rom.13:9-10.
181. Rom.13:8.
182. Gal.3:14.
183. Gal.2:19.
184. Gal.2:20.
185. Phil.3:5-6.
186. Phil.3:9.
187. Rom.4:1-5, referring to Gen.15:6.
188. Rom.9:30-31.

189. Gal.4:21-5:12.
190. Gal.3:10.
191. Gal.3:13 and 21.
192. Acts 10:1-11:18.
193. This term does not occur in the NT but in Gal.2:14 we find 'ioudaizein' which signifies 'to live as Jews do'.
194. Acts 15:5.
195. Acts 10:45 and 11:18.
196. Acts 15:1.
197. Acts 15:2; Gal.2:1.
198. Gal.2:2-3.
199. Acts 15:4 and 12.
200. Gal.2:2-3.
201. Acts 15:5.
202. Gal.2:4.
203. Acts 5:6.
204. Gal.2:10.
205. Gal.2:11-14.
206. Enc.Jew.Rel. s.v. 'Christianity', 88/89.
207. Rom.11:17-18.
208. Rom.11:1,2 and 29.
209. Rom.11:25-26.
210. Rom.2:21.
211. Rom.11:18-32.
212. Rom.9:2-3.
213. Phil.3:5; 2Cor.11:22.
214. Sandmel, Judaism 351.
215. Mc.11:15-17.
216. Sandmel, Judaism 350.
217. Mt.28:12-15.
218. Mt.5:17.
219. Mt.23:2.
220. With the exception of the expression 'King of the Jews' which was used by Pilate and also occurred in the inscription on the cross; as such it is found in Matthew and Mark too.

221. In the Book of Revelation no mention is made of Jews and Judaism.
222. Sandmel, Judaism 390.
223. Jo.8:48.
224. Jo.8:44.
225. Jo.8:17.
226. Jo.4:22.
227. Jo.10:35.
228. Maier, Jüd.Auseinandersetzung 13 thinks that there is "no plausible reason to doubt these (Christian) communications of persecutions and maledictions".
229. Acts 2:41.
230. Acts 3:1.
231. Acts 3:17.
232. Acts 4:1-22.
233. Acts 5:17-42.
234. Acts 6:7.
235. Acts 6:8-8:1.
236. Acts 12:1-19.
237. Acts 13:44-52.
238. Acts 14:17.
239. Acts 14:19-20.
240. Acts 17:1-15.
241. Acts 18:1-7.
242. Acts 21:26.
243. Acts 21:17-23:10.
244. Acts 23:12-34.
245. Acts 24.
246. Acts 25:1-12.
247. Acts 28:16-28.
248. Acts 24:10.
249. Emil G. Hirsch, s.v. 'Shemoneh Esreh', Jew.Enc. XI, 271.
250. Hirsch. s.v. 'Shemoneh Esreh', Jew.Enc. XI, 277.
251. Hirsch s.v. 'Shemoneh Esreh', Jew.Enc. XI, 277.

252. Ismar Elbogen s.v. 'Eighteen benedictions', Univers.Jew.Enc. 4, 24. This view is combated, however, by Maier, Jüd.Auseinandersetzung 136-141 who argues that by 'minim' assimilating and hellenizing Jews were meant, although he does not exclude the possibility that Judaeo-Christians too were included. But hellenizing Jews were there already in the second century B.C.

253. Whether or not there was an express ban on the Christians, with their subsequent exclusion from the synagogue, is a moot point. Maier, Jüd.Auseinandersetzung 131 believes that such a ban did not exist.

254. Interested readers will find much detailed and highly scholarly information in 'The New Testament and the Gnosis", Eds. Logan & Wedderburn (see Bibliography).

255. Segal, Two powers 208.

256. This section is based on the lemmata s.v. 'gnosis' in 1. Griech.-deutsches Wörterbuch NT; 2. Greek-Engl.Lex. NT (see Bibliography).

257. Eph.3:19.

258. 1Pt.3:7.

259. Acts 21:34.

260. Lc.1:34.

261. Jo.17:3.

262. 1Cor.1:21.

263. 1Jo.3:6.

264. 1Jo.4:8.

265. Jo.10:15.

266. Rom.11:33.

267. Rom.2:20.

268. 2Cor.2:14.

269. 2Cor.10:5.

270. 1Cor.4:6.

271. 1Cor.12:8.

272. 2Cor.8:7.

273. 2Cor.11:6.

274. 1Cor.13:2.

275. Jo.18:20.

276. R.McL. Wilson, Gnost.Probl. 77.

277. Col.1:26.

278. Rom.11:25.

279. Rom.16:25.
280. 1Cor.2:1.
281. 1Cor.4:1.
282. 1Cor.14:2.
283. 1Cor.2:7.
284. Phil.3:15.
285. Col.1:28.
286. Mt.13:11; Mc.4:11; Lc.8:10.
287. Especially Ap.10:7, further 17:7 and 17:5.
288. Segal, Two powers 208.
289. Acts 7:53.
290. Hebr.2:2.
291. Gal.3:19.
292. 2Cor.2:7.
293. Col.2:5.
294. Bultmann, Problem der Ethik.
295. Mt.26:41; Mc.14:38.
296. Jo.3:6.
297. Rom.8:10.
298. 1Cor.2:14.
299. Rom.8:11.
300. Mt.11:18-19; Lc.7:33-35.
301. Jo.1:11.
302. Gal.1:4.
303. 1Cor.1:20.
304. 2Cor.4:4.
305. Mt.12:32; idem in Eph.1:21.
306. Lc.20:35.
307. Mt.9:25 and 12:24; Mc.3:22; Lc.11:15.
308. Jo.12:3, 14:30, 16:11.
309. 1Cor.2:6 and 8.
310. 2Cor.4:4.
311. Jo.2:16-17.
312. Grant, Gnost. 176/177.

313. Lyonnet, Saint Paul, in Origini. Pagels in her book on the 'Gnostic Paul' says that Paul is well-known for his anti-Gnostic stand. Nonetheless, Gnostic authors, in particular Valentinian, have made extensive use of his writings. How is this to be explained? What she sets out to do is not to prove that Paul really was a Gnostic, as some earlier scholars, for instance Reitzenstein, have argued. Rather she wants somewhat to correct the prevalent idea of the 'anti-Gnostic Paul'. In her opinion (164) "to read Paul either way - as hyper-Gnostic or hyperorthodox - is to read unhistorically". In so fear as she means to say that Paul's terminology contained elements that proved 'gefundenes Fressen' to Valentinian and other Gnostics, I can remain content with her conclusion.

314. 2Pt.1:16.

315. 2Pt.2:1-3.

316. 1Tim.6:20.

317. 1Tim.4:7.

318. 1Cor.13:1-10.

319. Eph.3:19.

320. In Ap.2:15 the author reproaches the Christians of Pergamum that some of them adhered to the sect of the Nicolaites.

321. Chorus, Psych. 83.

322. Jo.1:39; the moment that John recognized the Messiah remained forever grafted on his memory.

323. Jo.3:23.

324. Jo.8:20.

325. Jo.18:10.

326. Jo.18:26.

327. Jo.4:28.

328. Jo.12:3.

329. Jo.20:1-9.

330. Jo.4:1-30.

331. Jo.9.

332. Wilson, Gnost.Problem 84/85.

CHAPTER V

THE DUALISM OF THE ESSENES

1. On the road to Qumran

Judaea, a small mountainous country in the south of Palestine, lies enclosed between a chalky desert and the Dead Sea to the east, the hot and arid Sinai Desert to the south, the lower hills of Samaria to the north, and the coastal strip of the Mediterranean to the west where the arch-enemies, the Philistines, dwelled. The Judaean mountains are not exceptionally high; their loftiest summit rises to 1012 meters. In winter, the rain clouds rolling in from the west break against the slopes of the central north-south mountain ridge. Its eastern side lies in the 'rain shadow' and is dry and arid. Jerusalem is situated on the central part of the ridge at a height of ca. 765 meters. Because of this altitude and of its exposure to the western sea-winds, the evenings in the Holy City are deliciously cool. Rainfall is abundant; in fact, when I started work on this chapter, there were two exceptionally heavy snowfalls.

This generally rosy picture changes considerably when one leaves the town eastwards to the Dead Sea. The endlessly winding road runs through virtually uninhabited country, a chalky region, yellowish and arid. The road descends unceasingly, twelve hundred meters over barely sixteen miles, which makes an average drop of 8 % per mile. During the trip one passes the sea level and goes further and further downward. For a Dutchman this is by no means unusual but what is exceptional even for him is that he finally finds himself at a depth of four hundred meters below sea level.

2. The site of Qumran

After this fascinating experience we arrive at the northern tip of the Dead Sea, the very symbol of infertility with its salinity of nearly 25 %; happy bathers float about reading their newspapers. The strip between the sea and the rocks on the west is narrow; the ground has a forbearingly barren look and does not seem to invite human settlement. The face of the rocks, rising high into the flaming sky, is imposing. The cliffs are incredibly steep but punctuated with holes, funnels, and fissures. As the Dutch Bible geographer van Deursen once wrote, it looks like a Gothic cathedral in a dilapidated state [1].

3. The discovery

Until the days after World War II nobody took an interest in this abandoned and inhospitable region. Only Palestinian nomads of Arabian stock roamed about there with their flocks of goats. In 1947, Palestine still was a British mandate. Early in that year or in the winter of 1946/1947, three members of the Bedouin Ta'amireh tribe were tending their animals at the foot of the cliffs. What then happened will always remain somewhat unclear. One of their black-haired goats strayed upwards into the rocks and suddenly disappeared. The shepherd-boy, Muhammed ed-Dîb (= the wolf), the youngest of the three, went after it fearing that it had fallen into one of the holes of the cliff-face. Intently he peered into the hole into which he thought his animal had stumbled. Seeing nothing he threw a stone in, and hearing pottery breaking he wriggled himself through the narrow aperture. To his utter astonishment he found himself in a cave some six feet wide and about twenty-four long. Along the wall stood ten great jars of which two were covered with a lid.

An alternative story is that another of those three Bedouins, Dzhuma, who was looking for gold in the caves, found that particular cave with the jars and tossed a stone in. He heard the sound of a breaking jar. He then alerted his comrades, and after three days of deliberation it was decided to inspect the cave jointly. But the young Muhammed could not wait; at daybreak he slipped through the aperture and discovered the jars.

However this may be, the Bedouins opened the jars. Eight of them were entirely empty; of the remaining two, one was filled with red earth, the other yielded three leather rolls, two of which were wrapped in linen.

This strange news went around through the tribe. Amateur Bedouin investigators appeared on the spot. It is rumoured that forty jars were found containing more scrolls. Since the illiterate tribesmen did not know what to do with their find, it is quite possible that some scrolls were hidden away never to turn up again, or perhaps even burned. Anyhow, it seems that the three first discovered scrolls hung for some weeks in a sack on the pole of a Bedouin tent. In this glorious way the story of the world-famous Dead Sea Scrolls began.

4. The scrolls on sale

Hoping that there was money in this venture, our three Bedouins went to Bethlehem in May 1947, bringing with them all that they had found, two complete parchments, parts of five or six others, and fragments of some twenty others. It will never be known how much exactly they had uncovered. In Bethlehem the incomparable treasure was first shown to an Islamite dealer in antiques who did not prove interested. Then two Syrian Christians, members of the Jacobite Church, became involved. Whether the first one to be contacted was Khalil Iskander Shahin, nicknamed 'Kando', or George Isaiah in Jerusalem is unclear. Whoever it was, the two caught fire, made a private excursion to the site, and unearthed some more fragments.

Some days later the two Jacobites informed their bishop, Mar Athanasius Yeshua Samuel, who lived in a monastery in Jerusalem. Although by no means a scholar, the bishop scented something valuable for the library of his monastery. He invited the three Arabs to appear before him. They duly arrived with an unspecified number of scrolls but the porter, who had not been informed of their coming by his superior, turned the raggy and unkempt fellows away. The indignant Bedouins immediately broke off contact with the Jacobite prelate. This happened in July 1947.

What exactly happened after this is once again not clear. One of the Bedouins sold his part of the scrolls to the Islamite sheik of Jerusalem; it was later acquired by Professor Eleazar Sukenik, a Jewish teacher of archaeology at the Hebrew University of Jerusalem. These rolls were in a bad shape, but at last they had fallen into the hands of a competent scholar. Through the intervention of Kando, the better preserved scrolls of the two other men were finally bought by Bishop Athanasius who paid a very moderate sum of money for it. One of the four or five scrolls he had acquired was a document with a length of 7,34 meters containing the whole of the oldest known text of Isaiah.

Since the bishop wanted to ascertain whether a treasure really had come his way, he consulted a Syrian official of the Department of Antiquities; this expert assured him that the documents were totally valueless. Luckily the prelate did not believe him and contacted Professor J. van der Ploeg, a Dutch Dominican priest, who was then staying at the École Biblique et Archéologique of Jerusalem, a foundation of the Dominican Order.

5. The scrolls inspected

Father van der Ploeg subjected the scrolls of the bishop to a first inspection; he saw that the text was in Hebrew, recognized the longest roll as the Prophecy of Isaiah, and concluded that the other documents contained biblical and non-biblical material. He had, however, as yet no idea of their antiquity. Back at the École, he failed to arouse much enthusiasm among his confrères.

In the beginning of September 1947 the bishop, taking his documents with him, travelled to the residence of his patriarch, Ignatius

Ephrem I, at Homs in Syria. As this dignitary too had little acquaintance with matters of this kind, he advised his suffragan to consult a professor of the American Methodist University of Beirouth. But this man was not in town, and the bishop returned home without being any the wiser. After this the bishop was in contact with several other persons; some dismissed the documents entirely, while others supplied information that proved totally false, such as the assertion that the scrolls were of Samaritan origin.

A Jewish doctor made the bishop acquainted with Professor Sukenik who, in November 1947, got the opportunity to inspect the scrolls in the monastery of the library. He was at once convinced that they were incredibly old, much older than all other biblical manuscripts known at that time; he took them to be of the first century A.D. At the same time an Armenian antique dealer notified Sukenik of the fact that there existed still other scrolls of the same provenance, kept somewhere in Bethlehem. Although Palestine was in a chaotic situation because the British were withdrawing leaving Jews and Arabs shooting at each other to their hearts' content, Sukenik succeeded in reaching Bethlehem and brought home a number of scrolls on November 29, 1947.

In spite of Sukenik's urgent requests, Bishop Athanasius refused to sell his scrolls to him. Instead, he sought contact with Dr. John C. Trever of the American School of Oriental Research, the Albright Institute, in Jerusalem; on February 20, 1948, a monk brought a number of scrolls to this institute. Immediately convinced of their exceptional antiquity, Trever photographed them and sent a number of pictures to William F. Albright at the John Hopkins University in the US, one of the greatest experts on Palestinian archaeology. "My heartiest congratulations on the greatest manuscript discovery of modern times! There is no doubt whatever in my mind that the script is more archaic than that of Nash Papyrus (= the oldest known piece of biblical manuscript hitherto - F.) ... I should prefer a date around 100 B.C. ... What an absolutely incredible find!". Thus Professor Albright from whose letter to Trever I am quoting here, was the first to fully recognize the enormous importance of this discovery.

6. The site inspected

The great news was broken to the world by The Times of April 12, 1948, but became swamped by the sensational reports from the Near East where the British mandate over Palestine ended and the State of Israel was proclaimed, followed by a state of war between this brandnew republic and seven Arabian countries. In the course of the fighting the region of Qumran passed into Jordanian hands where it remained till the Six Days' War of June 1967. From then until now it is in Israel occupied territory.

The war ended with the cease-fire of January 7, 1949. Only then it became possible for experts to visit the site of the caves. The scrolls of Bishop Athanasius were no longer in Jerusalem then, for around the time of the armistice he had taken them to New York, where they were deposited in the vault of a bank. By patient investigation work the secretary of the Jerusalem Rockefeller Institute succeeded in tracing Kando in Bethlehem who, after much haggling, sold a number of his fragments to the Jordanian Department of Antiquities. This also occurred in January 1949.

On January 24, 1949, a Belgian captain, Philippe Lippens, a member of the Armistice Commission, succeeded in identifying the cave of the original find. Fourteen days later an expedition went there headed by G.L. Harding of the Jordanian Department of Antiquities, and Father Ronald de Vaux, director of the École Biblique. They were the very first experts to visit the site after the discovery of two years earlier. They were treated to a sorry sight. Treasure hunters, Bedouin and others, had thoroughly searched the surroundings ruining much that might have been of importance. The Ta'amireh Bedouins had been busy in combing out the whole desert spurned on by rumours of generous sums to be paid for documents.

7. The deposits

The result of the scientific expedition was that ten other caves were discovered in which a substantial part of a biblical scroll (the Psalms) was found (in 1956) and, in addittion, some fifteen thousand fragments, many of them in a deplorable state. During the Six Days' War of 1967 the son of Professor Sukenik and the well-known Israeli archeaologist and general, Yigal Yadin, in a slightly dubious operation succeeded in laying hands on yet another scroll that proved to be in the possession of Kando, the so-called 'Temple Scroll'. Important fragments came to light during excavations at Massada, the last Jewish stronghold conquered by the Romans in A.D. 73. In 1965 Yadin, acting for the State of Israel had already purchased the four scrolls of Bishop Athanasius, a wealthy sponsor purveying the required sum of $ 250.000.

As the attentive reader will have remarked, there now exist two distinct deposits of Dead Sea Scrolls, with two different groups of scholars investigating them. One deposit is in the Shrine of the Book, a department of the Israel Museum in West Jerusalem; it is the property of the State of Israel. The other deposit is to be found in the Rockefeller Museum in East Jerusalem and is studied by a number of experts under the direction of the École Biblique. There never has been much communication between both groups of investigators, while the rate of publication has been disappointingly slow [2].

8. What the Scrolls contain

The Scrolls contain three kinds of texts : biblical, non-biblical, and sectarian. Every Bible book is represented in them by some fragments at least, the sole exception being the Book of Esther. The non-biblical texts were already known in Greek and Latin translations, but now we possess important fragments in Hebrew of the Books of Jubilees and Henoch, and of the Testament of Levi. The contents of the biblical texts were known already. Far more disclosing are the sectarian texts, those of the sect that lived at Qumran. These contain commentaries on Bible books, legal tracts concerning Jewish Law and its application, the Manual of Discipline with the rules of the Qumran community, poems and hymns betraying much of the theology of the sect, writings of an eschatological nature with the modern title 'The Scroll of the War of the Sons of the Light against the Sons of Darkness', and finally the Temple Scroll being a description of the Jerusalem Temple and its cult.

With regard to the main theme of this work the biblical material need not concern us, but the remaining documents are of capital importance.

8. The Essenes and the Qumran Community [3]

a. The Essenes mentioned by ancient authors

So far I have studiously avoided the question that will be burning on the reader's lips : who stowed away these scrolls in such an unconventional way? And why did they do this? From the very first the leading experts of both research teams, Professor Sukenik and Father de Vaux, were convinced that the scrolls had something to do with the Essenes, a Jewish sect that had flourished in the last century B.C. and the first of the new era. Up to 1947 these Essenes were only known from literary sources [4]. Around A.D. 50 Philo wrote about them in two of his works [5]. Josephus had rather much to tell of them in three of his books, the longest description occurring in 'The Jewish War', written around A.D. 75-79 [6]. Although he wrote about a generation later than Philo, Josephus' mention of the Essenes in his 'Antiquities' is the earliest in chronological order.

For the period of Jonathan the Maccabee, ca. 160-143 B.C., Josephus distinguishes three 'haireseis' in Judaism, that is three sects or schools of thought, namely the Pharisees, the Sadducees, and the Essenes [7]. He claims to have had personal acquaintance with all three of them : "in order to select the best, I submitted myself to hard training and laborious experiences and passed through the three courses". In the end, however, he did not join the Essenes [8]. In two of his works he gave a description of their sect and of its way of life [9]. A non-Jewish, pagan source is Pliny's 'Natural History' of A.D. 77; a Christian one is Hippolytus' 'Refutatio' of ca. 200 [10].

b. The discovery of the Qumran settlement

This means that modern scholars possessed a more or less accurate idea of who and what the Essenes were. But once the Scrolls were discovered, they desired to know more. Their curiosity was aroused by the fact that the Arabs called some part of the narrow strip between the beach and the cliff-face with the caves 'Chirbeh Qumran' which means 'the ruin of Qumran'. The significance of the word 'Qumran' is unknown. The Chirbeh lies one kilometer west of the sea coast on a stony terrace stretching from north to south parallel to the cliff-face. That ruins of a building could be seen there has been known for at least a century but nobody had bothered to investigate them in this desolate spot.

Under the energetic direction of Father de Vaux six successive excavation campaigns were conducted in the years 1951-1956. What was brought to light was a complex of buildings the central part of which measures 29 x 37 meters; furthermore there is a large tower, a water reservoir, water basins, ovens, a colonnade, workshops, another large hall and a smaller one [11]. Evidently this was a private house but it can best be described as a monastery, the accomodation of a religious community. Many scholars agree that this community was that of the Essenes.

c. The history of the Qumran community

Possibly the first settlers, pious Jews, arrived at this inhospitable spot at some time around 134 B.C. Why they went there is unknown, but it is a fair guess that they felt utterly disappointed by the conventional Jewish way of life, in particular with its religious side. They erected buildings on the terrace where the ruins of an old Israelite fortress stood. Precious little is known of the history of the Essenes in the last century B.C. In 31 B.C., during the reign of Herod I the Great, a heavy earthquake destroyed the main building; probably a fire did the rest. The site was abandoned then and left in ruins. But some thirty years later the Essenes returned, and the buildings were reerected and even extended. Now a second period of community life began. It is supposed by some that John the Baptist passed some time among the brethren.

Although the Essenes of Qumran lived in an isolated spot, they nonetheless became involved in the great insurrection against the Romans that began in A.D. 66. In June 68 a Roman army under the command of Vespasian, working its way southward through the Jordan valley, reached Qumran. It is highly probable that the community fought back when attacked but was soon overwhelmed. The buildings were put on fire. It is a fair guess that the brethren, just before the arrival of the Roman force, hid their most valuable books [12] in jars and stored them away in the caves of the near vicinity. Part of them was probably found by Roman soldiers and torn to pieces [13].

After the last Roman had departed, in A.D. 73, the site remained uninhabited until the years 132-135 when, during the anti-Roman rebellion of Bar Kochba, a Jewish garrison was posted at Qumran. When this had gone too, a deadly silence descended upon Chirbeh Qumran lasting until 1947. Nowadays there is an Israeli settlement at ten minutes distance on foot, the Kibbutz Kalia; if the political situation permits it, busloads of tourist arrive regularly and swarm all over the place. Since I was there myself in August 1962, I cannot object!

d. Who were the Essenes and how to become one

Let it be understood that the Essenes were Jews and were not be found outside Palestine. We should not think of them of having been established only in Qumran [14]. "They settle in large numbers in every town", says Josephus [15]; that there lived Essenes even in Jerusalem is testified by him in many places [16]. One of the eastern gates of the Holy City was called the 'Gate of the Essenes' [17], possibly, as Schürer supposes, "because the house of the Essenes was situated nearby" [18].

The Essenes formed a closed community with all the characteristics of an esoteric association [19]. Admission was only for adults. Philo has it that they preferred candidates already verging on old age since these were "no longer carried under by the tide of the body nor led by the passions, but enjoying the veritable, the only real freedom" [20]. All the same, children - although not their own - could be accepted to be moulded, pliable and docile as they still were, in accordance with Essenian principles [21].

Of course, full membership was not immediately accorded; instead, there was a period of probation. After the first year the candidate had to undergo some ritual ablutions. Then followed one more year of training after which the willing novice had to swear 'tremendous oaths' in order to be enrolled : he promised to practice piety towards the Deity, observe justice towards men, be a lover of truth, forever hate the unjust and fight the battle of the just, and much more in this vein. Of special importance in connection with our theme is that the candidate also swore "to conceal nothing from the members of the sect and to report none of their secrets to others, even though tortured to death" [22]. Only then the candidate became a full member and was admitted to the communal meals [23].

Two things must strike us here. The first is that the community sealed itself off against the outer world by means of the possession of a knowledge of its own. Secondly we find here the usual partitioning into three of esoteric sects which thrive on secrecy : first the great mass of the outsiders, then the group of probationers, finally the select circle of full members. The divisions between the three orders were dualistic : while Essenes kept as much as they could apart from outsiders, the full members kept the junior ones at a fair distance. Not only were the candidates considered inferior, but it was even so that when a full member had but touched a novice, he had to take a bath to purify himself, 'as if after contact with an alien' [24]. Obviously probationers were seen as impure; for this reason they were not allowed to take part in the common meals.

e. The Essenian way of life

The brethren lived in common in communal dwellings [25]; travelling members of the sect - they seem to have been much on the move - were always received hospitably [26]. They were bound to their superiors by strict obedience [27]. One of the most conspicuous traits of Essenian life was communal ownership of property. New members had to yield their possessions to the sect; the idea was that nobody should have more (or less) than another. "All, like brothers, enjoy a single patrimony" [28]. This too made them very different from the mass of the Jewish population.

Most Essenes engaged in agriculture [29] while others were tradesmen [30]. But they were not allowed to occupy themselves with commerce because of the amounts of money involved in it; there was always a risk of personal enrichment. There were no slaves among them because they preached equality of all people, "Nature mother-like having born and reared all men alike and created them genuine brothers" [31].

The working day of the Essenes began with a common prayer after which they went off to their usual occupations. Later they returned, had their first meal together, and went back to their work. At dusk they all gathered again to have their second meal, followed by evening prayers. The meals were taken in silence [32]. There are no indications that the Essenes followed a vegetarian diet [33].

It is important to note that the daily prayers were offered at dawn and dusk, i.e. at sunrise and sunset. The brethren, as we shall see, thought of themselves as luminous people, 'Sons of the Light'; the moments of appearance and disappearance of the solar light were of great significance to them. Contrary to normal Jewish usage with its lunar calendar, Essene chronology was based on the course of the sun with a year of fifty-two weeks, four seasons of thirteen weeks each, and months of thirty days. Perhaps between the seasons additional days were intercalated [34]. This means that the Essene calendar possessed a far greater regularity than the ordinary Jewish one, with the consequence that the religious feasts, like Passover, occurred every year on the same day. The brethren, therefore, celebrated the customary festivals on days when the Jewish population at large was at work. This too set the community apart from the rest [35]. We may even detect some antagonism towards conventional society in it.

f. Essenian misogyny

Although it is possible that women lived in the Qumran settlement, it is virtually certain that the Essene community was an all-male affair. Celibacy must have been the custom [36]; wedlock, however, was not condemned by them in principle [37]. We know that the unmarried state did not exist within the Jewish population, the priestly caste included. In this respect too the Essenes were different. Van der Ploeg supposes that the all-male character and the unmarried state were so much a matter of course in the eyes of the community that express mention of them was superfluous. This author supposes that the so-called 'Community Rule' which was found at Qumran "seems to suppose from beginning to end that it was framed for male persons and was practiced by them" [38].

The attitude of the brethren vis-à-vis the opposite sex bordered on misogyny. "They wish to protect themselves against women's wantonness, being persuaded that none of the female sex can remain faithful to one man" [39]. "A wife is a selfish creature, excessively jealous and an adept at beguiling the morals of her husband and seducing him by her continuous impostures", which verdict is crowned by the final judgment : "she cajoles the sovereign mind" [40]. This is crass dualism in which woman is seen as the demoniacal and destructive seductress. Josephus, however, reports of an Essene group the members of which used to marry since they feared that, if the celibacy rule became general, the human race would soon die out. Their sole aim in taking wives was procreation, for during pregnancy they abstained from sexual intercourse [41].

g. The Essenes and the Temple cult

We have already seen that the Essenians practised several forms of 'apartheid'. The most glaring example of this is that they did not take part in the Temple cult in Jerusalem. In doing so they deliberately stayed outside the main stream of Jewish life that was centred on the Temple. Not for them the joyful song : "We shall proceed to the house of the Lord"! They were, in fact, "barred from the precincts of the Temple that are frequented by all the people" [42]. They did indeed send votive offerings to Jerusalem, but "performed their (own) sacrifices employing a different ritual of purification" [43]. What kind of sacrifices these were Josephus whom I am quoting here does not say but probably not animal sacrifices, since Philo adds that "they have shown themselves in the service of God not by offering sacrifices of animals but by resolving to sanctify their minds" [44].

h. Purity and impurity

The reader will know that for orthodox Jews rules of purity and impurity were, and still are, of paramount importance. For ordinary people daily life was made somewhat laborious by these rules; there were so many persons and objects and occasions to be avoided under the penalty of becoming ritually unclean if one but touched them [45]. With the Essenes, this need of avoidance became quite an obsession [46]. Their strict rules of purity may offer us yet another reason for their not taking part in the official Temple cult, this reason being that the Temple precincts were defiled by ritually unclean priests. It may be supposed that many widowed Jewish priests had remarried or had married a full cousin. Essene purists inferred from Gen. 1:27 ('male and female he created them') that it was forbidden to marry more than once. Lev. 18:13 forbids intercourse with an aunt; the Essenes extended this prohibition to the aunt's offspring. The stern conclusion is : "He who associates with them (the Jewish priests) shall not be held innocent; the more he does the guiltier he is". It will be clear that contact with a Temple priest would make an Essene ritually unclean. However, it should not be inferred from this that the Essenes repudiated the sacrificial cult or the Temple as such. They found the prevailing conditions unsatisfactory but were certainly prepared to resume the cult when circumstances had become more propitious [47].

Another problem with regard to purity was food. Taking food means that one is biologically human, and that one possesses a body with aterial and physical needs not fundamentally different from animal bodies. But the gods do not partake of human food or do not eat at all. The persistent striving of the Essenes after a holiness that would make them 'holier than thou' (that is a holiness that would transcend the ordinary religious observance of Jewish lay people) means that they, in principle, sided with the divine world against the purely human one. There doubtless is dualism in this, as in their entire spiritual make-up. Such people would prefer not to eat at all in order to distance themselves as far as possible from 'the others'. Since this is not possible, the Essenes surrounded their meals with all sorts of cautions.

The Essenes were, of course, not unique in saying grace before meals; it was and still is the custom in many Jewish and Christian households. In all these cases the eating of food is, as it were, sublimated and made different from simply devouring food-stuffs. Specific for the Essenes is that in their refectories it was a priest who said grace. The brethren did not enter the dining room before they had taken a cold bath and draped themselves in white garments that they did not use during their daily work. No non-Essene was admitted. The frugal meal, with allotted portions, was taken in the deepest silence. As Josephus says, "to persons outside, the silence of those within appears like an awful mystery" [48]. This all was done to prevent the habit of eating defiling them.

Use of the toilet too was somewhat problematic. The need to defaecate shows that we are only human. The Essenes took the most strict hygienic precautions of which the habit of bathing after toilet use has a ritual character. According to Josephus, they tried to avoid using the toilet on the Sabbath [49].

One need not be a psychoanalyst in order to conclude that behind this obsession with purity there lurked a deep feeling of guilt. To put it in the words of Dupont-Sommer, there was in this sect a "peculiar strength and depth of the sentiment of being guilty and unclean which explains their anxious need of the water that works purity" [50]. This applies not so much to material filth that can easily be cleaned away but to "the moral imperfection and the uncleanness this causes". Dupont-Sommer very aptly describes the dualistic psychological tension to which the Essenes fell prey. "In these people who, adhering to an ideal of angelic perfection, must observe every day how far they remain from this ideal, there obtained a depressing conviction that they incessantly were the booty of sin, that within them there lived evil, and that, in spite of their exertions, impurity and filth would remain in their innermost selves" [51].

9. Essenian dualism

Having arrived at this point, I feel justified in assuming that by now the reader who before was not well acquainted with the Essenes and with Qumran will have acquired a comprehensive idea of the sect. Therefore, we can now reach for the core of the matter, the sect's dualism. Huppenbauer, who wrote an important book on the dualism of the Qumran texts [52] begins his work with a short disquisition on the term 'dualism' as used in connection with the Qumran texts - no luxury in view of the numerous misunderstandings and misinterpretations to which this terminology is subject [53]. A great scholar like Bousset restricted the meaning of dualism to the battle between God and Satan [54] which, however, gives the idea such a narrow basis that, like Schaedel, we would best speak of 'dialectical polarity' [55]. Huppenbauer prefers the wider definition that is given by the Lexicon für Theologie und Kirche : "(dualism signifies the) solution of problems with the help of two principles standing in a relation of opposedness to each other" [56].

He then makes an interesting distinction between cosmic and cosmological dualism. Cosmic dualism, he says, "occupies itself with <u>the fact</u> (his underlining) of the dichotomy of the cosmos (opposition of light and darkness, above and under). Cosmological dualism, on the contrary, with the help of this dichotomy, at the same time <u>explains</u> (idem) the origin of the world. The assumption of two principles that originally and perpetually exist side by side is a presupposition for cosmological dualism but not unconditionally for cosmic dualism." The opposition of Creator and creature in which he sees a special case of cosmic dualism Huppenbauer dubs 'metaphysical dualism' [57].

Where did the unmistakable and all pervading dualism of the Qumran texts stem from? Could it have been the influence of Zoroaster and his doctrine, as some suppose on the basis of the resemblance of some of these texts to some of the gathas - rather flimsy evidence, as I see it [58]. It is a mental habit of scholars as soon as there is talk of dualism to think of an Iranian origin [59]. It is, however, not necessary, even misleading, to look for a common ancestor of all dualisms, as for instance, an Iranian one.

Another possibility would of course be a marked relationship between Qumran and the Gnosis. Some scholars vigorously assert such a connection, even to the point of seeing in Qumran the origin of the Gnosis; others combat this with equal gusto. Huppenbauer finds himself unable to offer a solution [60]. In my opinion, there is none, which means that Essenian dualism in all probability is authentic, so to speak autochthonous. I do not think that a special ancestor or kinship is needed to explain the existence of Essenian dualism. In the whole Hellenistic world we see, if not dualism, then in any case, a radicalization of viewpoints and standpoints. We find this in a growing measure in Hellenistic philosophy, we find it very markedly in the Gnosis. It is even present in late Judaism and in the New Testament [61]. Radical, antagonizing and dualistic stances formed constitutive parts of the mental make-up in the first century A.D.

a. The dualism of the Community Rule

Let us start with the 'Community Rule' which may be considered the constitution or the handbook of the Essenes; it is also called the 'Manual of Discipline'. It was found in 1947 in Cave I and published in 1951 by M. Burrows [62]. Already in the opening phrase we get an instalment of the fierce dualism that inspires this whole text. Speaking of the new members who are entering the Covenant, the Rule orders the Levites to "recite the iniquities of the children of Israel, all their guilty rebellions and sins during the dominion of Satan ... And the Priests shall bless all the men of the lot of God who walk perfectly in his ways, saying : 'May He bless you with all good and preserve you from all evil! May he lighten your heart with life giving wisdom and grant you eternal knowledge!" [63]. Thus the tone is set : there are two sets of people, those who are under the dominion of Satan, or Belial in the original Hebrew, and 'the men of the lot of God'. The first mentioned are extensively cursed by the Levites : "May He visit you with destruction!" [64].

The determinative text we find in Section III of the Rule, called by Dupont-Sommer 'The Doctrine of the Two Spirits'. According to Huppenbauer, the dualism displayed in this doctrine is anthropological in character since it hinges on the idea of 'spirits' [65]. But shouldn't we rather call it 'ethical' because these spirits are those of truth, justice, and light on one side, and of injustice, falsehood, and darkness on the other?

Before we accord their due treatment to these concepts, we should note two or three things. They are all contained in this one sentence : "From the God of Knowledge comes all that is and shall be" [66]. Not one of the scholars I consulted remarks that the Essenian doctrine has a monistic starting-point, the one and only God; in this, Essenianism does not differ from many another dualistic ideology. It is beyond question that we are perfectly justified to speak of dualism with regard to this sect but not of radical dualism since this term implies the existence from all eternity of two coeval and equivalent beings or principles that are not created by or dependent on a unitary higher being or principle. As I have argued before, the radical type of dualism is rare.

The text of the Rule admirably clarifies its fundamental meaning in this way. "Before ever they (all things) existed, He established their whole design, and when, as ordained for them, they come into being, it is in accord with His glorious design that they accomplished their task without change. The laws of all things are in His hands and He provides them with all their needs" [67].

Von der Osten-Sacken, commenting upon this text, spoke of 'predestination' and 'determinism' [68]. Both concepts, however, are only applicable to human beings, whereas the text speaks of 'all things'. Although I did not look over the shoulders of those who composed the Rule, I feel confident that they did not envision mankind by these words. What they intended to say is, I believe, that God has laid out the fundamental pattern of creation and holds the 'laws of nature' in his hands. This is by no means unbiblical.

God is called 'the God of Knowledge', a term that in the Old Testament occurs only once, in Hannah's (the prophet Samuel's mother) song of praise : "Our God is a God who knows; by him all actions are weighed" [69]. The Hebrew term is 'el de'ot. 'El', the generic word for the godhead, is used throughout the Rule, and not Israel's favourite name bestowed on the people by God himself : Jahve. The Community's God is not so much the Creator, or the Lord of the Covenant, or the God of Abraham, Isaac, and Jacob, but rather the 'God of Knowledge', of 'da'at' (plural : 'de'ot'). This word also occurs also in Gen. 2:9 in the expression 'the tree of knowledge (da'at) of good and evil'; this has a divisive ring, just as in the words that Hannah used : the God who weighs actions. This is also what is intended in the Rule : God knows and judges human actions. Since he, as the fountain-head of essential cosmic unity, is defined as 'God of Knowledge', I deem it possible that there is a gnosticizing element in this.

b. The doctrine of the Two Spirits

God is the creator of two spirits, one of truth and one of falsehood. "Those born of truth spring from a fountain of light, but those born of falsehood spring from a source of darkness" [70]. Here we are confronted with yet another dualistic opposition, that of light and darkness. But does this postulate the existence of two totally different sets of people? Does this mean that moral determinism governs human actions? It does not. "The nature of all the children of men is ruled by these (two spirits), and during their life all the hosts of men have a portion in their divisions and walk in both (their) ways" [71]. So there are not, in principle, two sets of people.

The Spirits themselves, however, are basically opposed. "God has established the Spirits in equal measure until the final age, and has set everlasting division between them. Truth abhors the works of falsehood, and falsehood abhors all the ways of truth. And their struggle is fierce in all their arguments for they do not walk together" [72]. It must be remarked in passing that the two Spirits are abstractions or concepts but not persons; this constitutes an essential difference with Iranian doctrine.

The text does not seem to rule out free choice. "The whole reward for their deeds shall be, for everlasting ages, according to whether each man's portion is great or small" [73]. It is evident that people belong to both classes anthropologically while it is also possible to shift from one division to the other. It may be true that some are born as children of the light and others as children of darkness, but the first mentioned may change allegiance. "The Angel of Darkness leads all the children of righteousness astray ..., for all his allotted spirits seek the overthrow of the sons of light" [74]. What is at stake in the battle of the Spirits is the fate of mankind and at the same time that of every single individual.

Evidently it is not easy to stay out of the reach of the Angel of Darkness, "but the God of Israel and his Angel of Truth will succour all the sons of light", for he loves the Spirit of Light and hates the other [75]. This applies to all people of good will who seriously attempt with God's help to overcome the forces of darkness in themselves. It obviously is far more possible to become a child of the light than a child of darkness. The suggestion implicit in the Rule is that there is only one way of becoming a most pure Son of the Light, and that is, need I say it, to join the Essenes. "He (the Master of the Community) shall admit into the Covenant of Grace all those who have freely devoted themselves to the observance of God's precepts, that they may be joined to the counsel of God and may live perfectly ..., and that they may love all the sons of light ... and hate all the sons of darkness"[76], and "that they may abstain from all evil and hold fast to all good"[77]. "The Master of the Community shall instruct all the sons of light and shall teach them the nature of all the children of men according to the kind of spirit which they possess"[78].

Living in the community and observing its precepts, the Essene "shall be cleansed from all his sins by the spirit of holiness which unites him to God's truth, and his iniquity shall be expiated by the spirit of uprightness and humility"[79]. This participation will be realized only on the condition that the Essenes will stay far away from the wicked world. "They shall separate from the congregation of men of falsehood and shall unite ... under the authority of the Sons of Zadok, the priests who keep the Covenant, and of the multitude of the men of the community who hold fast to the Covenant"[80]. There can be no doubt that with 'congregation of the men of falsehood' the normal Jewish religious community is meant; in this respect, the Essenes practised apartheid.

c. The Sons of Zadok

Who are those 'Sons of Zadok'? Yes, the Essenian priests, of course, but why are they not called 'priests of Aaron'? Zadok was a priest at the time of David; together with Abiathar, another priest, he remained faithful to the king during the rebellion of Absalom[81]. Later, when the revolt had been put down, both Abiathar and Zadok served as priests in Jerusalem[82]. When just before the king's death, his son Solomon was appointed to succeed him, another of his sons, Adonijah, rebelled against the crown-prince. Abiathar chose the side of the pretender, but Zadok stuck to Solomon[83]. As soon as Solomon was king, he ordered Adonijah to be killed and deposed and banished Abiathar[84]. The reward of Zadok who had anointed Solomon[85], was that he became High Priest[86].

The first Book of Chronicles presents the pedigree of Zadok and his descendants, the Zadokites. Four sons of Aaron are mentioned, among them Eleazar, the third son and Ithamar, the fourth son. Zadok is named a direct descendant of Eleazar in the ninth generation[87]. Of the fourth son, Ithamar, a second priestly clan descended of which, however, no pedigree is given [88]. The Ithamarites were obviously considered less important than the Zadokites; they were also less numerous, perhaps in a ratio of 1:2 [89]. What is more, the High Priests right up to the time of the Maccabees seem all of them to have been Zadokites (both priestly classes returned from Babylonia) [90].

The Old Testament in general, and the prophets in particular, had a predilection for Zadokites. Both Eli, with his bad sons Hophni and Phinehas [91], and the rejected Abiathar were Ithamarites. The prophet Ezekiel states three times that alone the descendants of Zadok "may come near to serve the Lord (as High Priests)" [92], adding that "they did not follow the Israelites when they went astray".

These words show why the name 'Sons of Zadok' was so attractive to the Essenes. They too had not 'gone astray' like the rest of Israel. In another document this term is even extended to all the members, where it speaks of "the Priests, the Levites, and the Sons of Zadok who kept charge of my sanctuary when the children of Israel strayed from me (God)", calling these Sons of Zadok 'the elect of Israel' [93]. As Dupont-Sommer says, the term 'Sons of Zadok' has "lost its original meaning of linear descendants of a priest called Zadok" [94].

d. The dualism of the Community Rule

Let us now make a summary of the most important dualistic elements to be found in the Community Rule. First, there is the painful distancing of the Essenes from the rest of Jewry. This is preserved in the idea of the true and false Israel. Then there is the bitter strife between the two Spirits, the good and the evil. Individual man falls apart in two directions and has to fight very hard to let the good Spirit triumph in and over himself; in fact the most feasible thing to do is to join the Essenes whose community is presented as an island of perfection in an ocean of wickedness. In mankind the opposition is that of the just and unjust, of those who fulfil the will of God, and those who do not. In the background arises the cosmic opposition of light and darkness. In consequence, the just are 'Sons of the Light', the others 'Sons of Darkness' [95].

e. The provenance of the Damascus Rule

A document commonly called 'the Damascus Rule', but also 'the Zadokite Fragments', has a provenance different from that of the other Qumran texts since it does not belong to the Dead Sea Scrolls proper. It was known long before, for it has been discovered in the Genizah of Ezra Synagogue in Cairo way back in 1896 and published for the first time in 1910 [96]. Fragments of this document found in the caves of Qumran prove that it belonged to the body of Essenian literature. The Damascus Rule is supposed to have been written around 100 B.C. [97]. I have already mentioned how this document presents us with the reasons why Essenes abstained from taking part in the Temple cult. This introduces us once again to the 'apartheid' theme that so strongly figures in Essenian ideology. In this document too it has a paramount significance.

f. The New Covenant

The text begins by stating that, long ago, Israel was unfaithful to God and in consequence was delivered 'into the hands of King Nabuchodonosor of Babylon'. But three hundred and ninety years after this - in 196 B.C., that is [98] -, God "caused a plant root to spring from Israel and Aaron to inherit his land"; this 'plant root' refers to the Essene movement. Some Israelites were converted from their iniquity but were apparently incapable of discovering a new way of life for themselves [99].

Twenty years later, however (that is around 175 B.C.), God having seen "that they sought him with a whole heart ..., raised for them a Teacher of Righteousness to guide them in the way of his heart" [100]. This is the first time that we meet that important personage, the 'Teacher of Righteousness', the 'moreh zedek'; it is not indicated here who he was. Over against this venerable person stands the figure of the

Scoffer, the 'ish hallatson', "who shed over Israel the waters of lies". Then follows a diatribe against the multitude that "walked in the ways of the Scoffer and agitated against the righteous" [101].

The fate of those who go astray will be horrible : the hand of the Angel of Destruction will be upon them. "They shall have no remnant or survivor. For from the beginning God chose them not; he knew their deeds even before they were created" [102]. "But with the remnant which held fast to the commandments of God, he made his Covenant for ever, revealing to them the hidden things in which all Israel had gone astray" [103]. There are intriguing elements in this text. We are confronted with two possibilities. God either made a totally new Covenant with the Essenes, in this way disregarding the original one with the people of Israel, or this old Covenant now became restricted to the Essenes. The other element is that secret knowledge was communicated to them; this is a gnosticizing element.

g. A new beginning

That there was indeed a totally new beginning is made clear by the following sentence. "For the righteous God has built a sure house in Israel whose like has never existed from former times till now" [104]. Once again the document turns Ezekiel's predilection for the 'Sons of Zadok' to its own advantage by stating that "the Sons of Zadok are the elect of Israel, the men called by name who shall stand at the end of the days" [105]. It is because of this accentuating of the significance of 'Zadok' that this document was also named 'the Zadokite Fragments'. The rest of Israel is given over to Satan (Belial) [106].

The text goes on to say that "the converts went out of the land of Judah to sojourn in the land of Damascus" [107]. It was this term 'land of Damascus' that gave the present document its name of 'Damascus Rule'. The vexing problem, however, is what exactly is meant by 'Damascus'. The Syrian city? This is, of course, possible. The problem then is that, as far as I know, no other indications of an Essenian settlement in Syria, for instance of an archaeological nature, have been discovered. Another possibility is that 'Damascus' is a pseudonym for 'Qumran' [108].

Anyhow, if indeed an Essenian community in Syria is meant, it must have been in close contact with that at Qumran since fragments of the Damascus Rule have been found in the caves there [109]. My personal opinion is that 'Damascus' = Qumran; the Essenes, with their penchant for secrecy and esotericism, were too fond of pseudonyms to take this one at its face value. More important is that the righteous are said to have left the land of Judah. This means that they broke with the notion so dear to the heart of Israel, of Canaan as the Promised Land.

h. The Essenes and political power

The text next takes up a theme that, as we saw, also found favour with Daniel and Revelation's author, that of the abhorrence of political power. "Wrath shall be poured on the princes of Judah [110] ... They are all of them rebels, for they have not turned away from the ways of the traitors but have all wallowed in the ways of whoredom (with this term idolatry is meant - F.) and wicked wealth" [111]. God said of them : "Their wine is the venom of serpents, the cruel poison (or head) of asps" [112].

The document obligingly explains what is meant by 'serpents and asps'. "The serpents are the kings of the peoples and their wine is their ways (= their power politics - F.). And the head of the asps is the chief of the kings of Greece who came to wreak vengeance upon them" [113]. The Hebrew text does not say 'Greece' but 'Jawan' = Ionia by which term Greece is meant. There can be no doubt that 'the head of the asps' is Alexander the Great; the asps themselves are his successors, the Hellenistic rulers. They are no better than the 'serpents' whom Alexander chastised because they too are vipers. The Romans are not mentioned in the Damascus Rule; at the beginning of the first century B.C. they had not yet penetrated into the Palestinian-Syrian region.

j. The Kittim

In one of the Scrolls, 'Habakkuk Commentary', an illusion is made to a political power referred to as 'Kittim', which even may be identical with the political power of the previous text. As its name (attached to it in our days) indicates, this scroll is a commentary on the Old Testament prophecy of Habakkuk, one of the lesser prophets. It has come down to us only in an incomplete state; much of the text is missing. It is a commentary upon a text of Habakkuk (1:6-11) that does not speak of 'Kittim' but of the Chaldaeans or Babylonians whom the prophet describes as swift and violent conquerors. For the Essenian commentator the text is concerned with the "Kittim (who are) quick and valiant in war, causing many to perish. (All the world shall fall) under the dominion of the Kittim" [114]. Now who are these 'Kittim'?

The word is derived from a town on Cyprus called Kition (now Larnaca). At first the term merely indicated citizens of this city, but then it was broadened to 'Cypriots' in general; then it became the name of all those who lived in the Aegean islands. Later it was extended to the Greeks and Macedonians, and finally it comprised the Romans too [115]. In the Books of Maccabees it occurs twice, both times referring to the Macedonians [116]. Anyhow, the few times that the Old Testament uses this term, it refers to a conquering nation of overwhelming strength.

In another of the Dead Sea Scrolls, the so-called 'War Rule', the Kittim are also mentioned, with the addition 'of Assyria' (= Syria) [117]; here the reference is to the Macedonian dynasty of the Seleucids whose original power base was Mesopotamia. There are also 'Kittim of Egypt' who are the Lagid or Ptolemaean rulers of Egypt [118].

So far so good. But the Habakkuk Commentary is only speaking of 'Kittim' without further specifications. Yadin writes that in the scroll all Habakkuk's references to the Chaldaeans apply to the Kittim of its own times [119]. Yes, but what was the time of the Essenian commentator? If we assume that the commentary was composed at a rather late date, then the Kittim are the Romans; in the opposite case they stand for the Seleucids. Since nobody is able to state with sufficient certitude when exactly this text was written, both options have their defenders [120]. Perhaps the commentator himself did not find the actual identification very important.

What is really telling is that the Kittim are portrayed in the most unfavourable manner; they are a dark force of evil. "They do not believe in the laws (of God)" [121]; "all their evil plotting is done with intention and they deal with all the nations in cunning and guile" [122]. They are without pity : "(They) cause many to perish by the sword - youths, grown men, the aged, women and children, and (they) even shall not take pity on the fruit of the womb" [123]. Still worse, they are idolators, for they worship the war god : "They sacrifice to their standards and worship their weapons of war" [124].

It is repeatedly stressed how irresistibly powerful they are. "They shall march across the plain, smiting and plundering all the cities of the earth" [125]; "they inspire all the nations with fear [126], they trample the earth with their horses and beasts [127], they despise the fortresses of the people and laugh at them with derision" [128].

There is an unbridgeable, a dualistic opposition between the realm of power and the world of the faithful. But although the men of violence may seem so overwhelmingly strong, the just need not be afraid. "God will not destroy his people by the hand of the nations". Quite the contrary! "He will execute the judgment of the nations by the hand of his elect [129]; on the Day of Judgment, he will destroy from the earth all the idolatrous and wicked men" [130]. So there can be no doubt with whom the final victory will be.

k. The self-expression of the Teacher of Righteousness

Not only the Damascus Rule, but other documents too make mention of a person, always anonymous, who is called 'the Teacher of Righteousness'. Members of the sect are clearly responsible for most of the many references to him in the Scrolls, But there is a strong possibility that some passages derive from his hand. These are found in the so-called 'Hodayôt', a collection of hymns or psalms that were discovered in the caves.

In these hymns the Teacher presents himself as a privileged person. "I thank you, o Lord, ... for you have shed your Holy Spirit upon me that I may not stumble [131]; you have made me like a strong tower, a high wall, and have established my edifice upon rocks" [132]. "I (thank you, o Lord, for) you have placed me beside a fountain of streams in an arid land and close to a spring of waters in a dry land and beside a watered garden (in a wilderness)" [133]. It is true that we find just the same kind of expressions in the Old Testament psalms and in the Wisdom of Jesus Sirach, but there is also a very personal ring to it. This is so, for instance, when the Teacher speaks of himself in this vein : "I bring into community all the men of my Council" [134]. Here he is revealing himself as a man of authority in the sect.

According to his own testimony, the Teacher of Righteousness is a man of exceptional wisdom and knowledge. He does not owe this wisdom to himself but to God who has revealed it to him, although he hid it from others. "These things (the divine order of creation is meant -F.) I know by the wisdom which comes from you, for you have unstopped my ears to marvellous mysteries" [135]. "You have revealed yourself to me in your power as perfect Light [136], you have given me knowledge through your marvellous mysteries [137], you have enlightened me through your truth, you have granted me knowledge [138], I know your truth" [139]. "I know you, o God, as somebody with insight by the spirit you have given to me ... In the mystery of your wisdom you have opened knowledge (da'at) to me" [140]. It is remarkable indeed how often the term 'knowledge' keeps recurring.

An important feature in the self-expression of the Teacher is that he introduces himself as a teacher. "You have made me a banner (standard) and a discerning interpreter of wonderful mysteries [141], all those who are gathered in your Covenant (= the Essenes) inquire of me" [142] - yet another indication that we are dealing with a man of authority : "Through me you have illumined the face of the congregation and have shown your infinite power" [143]. "(You, o my God) did open a (fountain) in the mouth of your servant; you have engraved by the measuring-rod (your mysteries) upon his tongue (that) out of his understanding (he might) preach to a creature and interpret these things to dust like myself ..., that he might open (the fount) of your truth to a creature whom you uphold by your might" [144].

But this teacher is not a teacher like all others, he is a Teacher of Righteousness, of how to walk straight in the ways of the Lord. "I (will bring forth) a reply of the tongue to recount your righteous deeds" [145]. To him God is just above all. "You (God) are righteous in all your deeds" [146], because "righteousness, I know ..., is not of man : to the Most High God belong all righteous deeds" [147]. Possessing this knowledge, he feels entitled to summon people to follow him in his ways : "O just men, put away iniquity" [148]. Thus he could become "a snare to those who rebel but healing to those of them who repent" [149]. He is "a father to the sons of grace, and as a foster-father to men of marvel" [150].

It soon becomes apparent that the Teacher is surrounded by enemies. He is eloquent as well as circumstantial when relating his sufferings at their hands. I give only a few quotations out of many. "To traitors you have made of me a mockery and a scorn ... I have been a byword for the traitors, the assembly of the wicked has raged against me, they have roared like turbulent seas and their towering waves have spat out mud and slime" [151]. "They, teachers of lies and seers of falsehood, schemed against me a devilish scheme" [152]. "Like (serpents) which creep in the dusk, so do they let fly (their poisonous darts), viper's (venom) against which there is no charm; and this has brought incurable pain, a malignant scourge within the body of your servant" [153]. I could go on quoting in this vein; the poet devotes a lot of space to the conflict with his adversaries. It will be clear that a strong element of dualism has come in here.

l. What others have to say of the Teacher

So much for the self-expression of the Teacher. Let us now see what other Essenian authors have to say of him. The Habakkuk commentary calls him "the Priest (in whose heart) God set (understanding) that he might interpret all the words of his servants, the Prophets, through whom he foretold all that would happen to his people and (his land, or community)" [154]. It will not surprise us that the Teacher proves to be a priest; he could hardly be a man of authority in the Essenian sect if he did not belong to the sacerdotal order. But the term 'priest' refers to his exegetic task rather to the performance of ritual. To the Teacher "God made known all the mysteries of his servants the Prophets" [155]. It is evident that the Teacher is a man with a special charisma.

I pass over short references to him of the same trend in the commentaries on Micah and on Psalm 37. But the Damascus Rule gives some more information. With the destruction of the first Temple a time of punishment for Israel began that did not end with the return of the exiles but lasted 390 years in all. Then a rest of the people sought God and found him again after twenty years. The Lord helped them in their attempts to lead the right life by giving them a Teacher. Now, if we, with G. Jeremias [156], take the dates literally, 168 B.C. would be the year of the appearance of the Teacher. "God raised for them a Teacher of Righteousness to guide them in the way of his heart" [157].

m. What we know of the Teacher

We now know the Teacher of Righteousness well enough to summarize our knowledge of him. I can best do this by using the words of my compatriot van der Ploeg who is a great expert on Qumran. "The Teacher is standing before us as an exceptional personality. He is convinced that God has inspired him, that God has initiated him into the divine mysteries, and that he has revealed to him the hidden sense of the prophetic words. With these 'mysteries' not the, for human beings, incomprehensible mysteries of the godhead are meant that surpass our mental grasp, but those of the divine rule of the world, in particular the decisions God has made concerning the salvation and judgment of mankind; for a very long time God has kept this secret but finally he revealed this to the Teacher ... The Teacher has gathered a group of disciples around him that has grown very numerous to which he has made known the revelations entrusted to him; especially he taught them to keep the Law of Moses strictly. All those who do this while remaining faithful to the Teacher will have nothing to fear from God at the judgement" [158]. What I have written so far on this person shows that he is, in the most literal sense of the word, an exceptional man. He differs fundamentally from his adherents in the sect in the respect that he is the giver, the communicator of the divine secrets that have been revealed only to him, whereas they are the receivers. Concerning the Jewish religious society, to say nothing of the heathen outer world, his position is antagonistic, in more regards than one even dualistic.

I am quite sure that for some time now a question has been burning on the lips of my readers : if this Teacher is an historical person, who then may he be? But alas, to this question there is no answer. Not only the Teacher but almost all other persons in the Scrolls remain nameless and faceless, just as all events remain unspecified. Because of his anonimity, it has sometimes been supposed that a series of successive Teachers is meant, but this guess did not catch fire [159]. Chronologically (there are several theories) he can be localized at some time between 175 and 63 B.C. [160].

n. The Prophet of Lies

Qumran would not be Qumran, and the Essenes not the Essenes, if the Teacher of Righteousness did not have an absolute, a dualistic counterpart. And indeed, there is one, the Man of Lies. At the same time, there is a 'Bad Priest'. The Habakkuk commentary speaks of "those who were unfaithful together with the Man of Lies ('ish ha-kazab'), in that they (did) not (listen to the word received by) the Teacher of Righteousness from the mouth of God" [161]. Thus the Man of Lies is put squarely opposite the Teacher.

Another passage speaks of "the House of Absalom and the members of its council who were silent at the time of the chastisement of the Teacher of Righteousness and gave him no help against the Man of Lies who flouted the law in the midst of their whole (congregation)" [162]. This obviously refers to a specific event. The term 'House of Absalom' must not, of course, be taken literally; it is a cover for some party that persecuted the Teacher. The historical Absalom betrayed his father David; this means that he betrayed a very close relative. I suppose that this suggests a man who was close to the Teacher but nonetheless betrayed him.

The third Habakkuk passage is this. "This concerns the Spouter of Lies who led many astray that he might build his city of vanity with blood and raise a congregation of deceit ... That their labour might be for nothing and that they might be punished with fire who vilified and outraged the elect of God" [163]. This text suggests a rebel who broke away from the sect with a number of its adherents.

A second group of references to an inexorable opponent is to be found in the Damascus Rule. I shall begin with following the useful summary given by Gerd Jeremias [164]. The person in question is designated as 'a Man of Lies' [165], a 'Scoffer' [166], and a 'Preacher of Lies' [167]. His adherents too are scoffers [168]; his is a congregation of traitors [169]. They are a far from peaceful lot since they are called 'warlike people' [170]. And indeed, it is their declared intention "to remove the boundary with which the forefathers had marked down their inheritance" [171].

There is much polemizing against the other party in this document. They were unfaithful and forsook God [172]; thus they became a generation of traitors having departed from God's ways [173]. "They sought smooth things and preferred illusions ... They justified the wicked and condemned the just; they transgressed the Covenant and violated the Precept (= the Law of Moses); they banded together against the life of the righteous pursuing them with the sword" [174]. "The land was ravaged because they preached rebellion against the commandments of God given by the hand of Moses" [175].

But God has set his face against them. "Power, might, and great flaming wrath by the hand of all the Angels of Destruction towards those who depart from the way of the Precept ... God hid his face from the land until they were consumed" [176]. "When the glory of God is made manifest to Israel, all those members who have breached the bound of the Law shall be cut off from the midst of the camp" [177].

The first conclusion G. Jeremias draws goes as follows. "We have before us a strongly formalized polemics from which hardly anything about the specific situation of the opponents can be inferred. But so much, however, is clear that the issue is a religious movement within Judaism that is condemned here. The passionateness of the polemicizing shows that the opposing group presented a serious threat to the (Essenian) community" [178].

This scholar goes on to say that we are unable to connect these opponents with any of the known great schools of thought in Judaism. But "they are a closed religious movement that combines in itself strongly sacerdotal elements; they pollute the Temple (this means that they participate in the Temple cult), they permit polygamy and marriage within forbidden degrees, they combat the community that is behind the Damascus Rule, and say that this is not according to God's will". The upshot can be no other than that the opponents come from Belial, the opposite number of God [179]. Need I say that all this is vintage dualism?

The difference between the Habakkuk Commentary and the Damascus Rule consists in the fact that the Commentary is attacking the leader of the opposing group, the 'Prophet of Lies', whereas the Rule is polemizing against the group as a whole. The Commentary probably dates from about 150 B.C., when the Prophet of Lies was active; the Rule is of a somewhat later date and pictures the situation after the death of this person [180].

Before we now turn to the question whether it will be possible to situate the Prophet of Lies within a more or less precise historical context, we must first ask ourselves a few things about that other negative person, the "Wicked Priest'. The Habakkuk Commentary speaks of a "Wicked Priest who was called by the name of truth when he first arose. But when he ruled over Israel his heart became proud, and he betrayed the precepts for the sake of riches ... He lived in the ways of abominations amidst every unclean defilement" [181]. "He committed iniquity against the Teacher of Righteousness and the men of his council

[182]; he pursued the Teacher of Righteousness to the house of exile that he might confuse him with his venomous fury" [183]. Perhaps he even aimed at the life of the Teacher : "(he rose up against the Teacher) that he might put him to death ...; he laid hands upon him" [184].

But this Wicked One will be, or perhaps has already been, duly punished. "God delivered him into the hands of his enemies ... that he might be humbled by means of a destroying scourge, in bitterness of his soul, because he has done wickedly to the elect" [185]. What transpires is that the Wicked Priest was a powerful High Priest who persecuted the Essenians and perhaps even killed the great Teacher.

The rest is not exactly silence but very disappointing. With their usual predilection for mystery, secrecy, and pseudonimity, the Essenians make it impossible for us to state who the Prophet of Lies and the Wicked Priest are. Are they one and the same person? Their being identical cannot be proved with sufficient certainty. The problem is that the Prophet of Lies headed a religious movement that continued to exist and to harass the Essenian community after his death. Would one think in the first place of a High Priest here? Much depends, of course, on the identity of this group of opponents. The Pharisees perhaps? But G. Jeremias says that the indications in the Qumran texts are so vague that any group in Judaism might be meant by them [186].

He adds that it is impossible to identify the Prophet of Lies with any person that is known to us in late Judaism [187]. It is, however, conceivable that this Prophet of Lies, as an historical person, was a renegade from the Essenian community who left after quarrelling with the Teacher. The vehemence of the attacks on him, and still more the repeated accusation that he is a Liar would support this view. G. Jeremias surmises that the breaking point was reached when part of the first Essenes could not reconcile the Teacher's rejection of the Temple cult with their obedience to the Torah. There obviously was a constant danger that members of the sect would defect to these opponents [188]. If this thesis is correct, then the Prophet of Lies and the Wicked Priest are not identical [189].

And now for the Wicked Priest! There is in scholarly literature an impressive list of possible candidates. With so many conjectures - and none of these conclusive -, I will venture a guess of my own (and more than a guess, I feel). The Wicked Priest was none other than Jonathan the Maccabee. This Jonathan was a member of the Hasmonaean House and a brother of Judas the Maccabee, the great hero of the Jewish War of liberation against the Seleucids. Judas having fallen in 160 B.C., Jonathan assumed the High Command in his place and led his army from victory to victory.

Finally the Syrians got tired of the endless war, with the result that Jonathan was able to return to Jerusalem where he, with the consent of the Syrians, became High Priest. At the Feast of the Tabernacles in 153 B.C. he officiated for the first time bedecked with the sacerdotal vestments. In 150 B.C. the Syrian king entrusted him with military and civil authority over Judaea so that he was now a real priest-king; a few years later some districts in Samaria were added to his realm, the Hasmonaean Kingdom. When a certain Tryphon was trying to oust King Demetrius II of Syria from his throne, he invited Jonathan to come and help him with his powerful army. The Hasmonaean king came to Acre in order to negotiate with Tryphon, but this treacherous man, not really trusting Jonathan, had him assasinated [190].

Now the Wicked Priest is described in the Scrolls as a High Priest and as one who ruled Israel. He was delivered into the hands of his enemies who destroyed him [191]. All this fits Jonathan like a glove [192]. To explain the virulence of the attacks on the Wicked Priest one should consider that although the Hasmonaeans were a priestly family, they very probably were Benjaminites, which meant that they did not descend from Aaron and Zadok. For this reason they could be seen as usurpers of the function of High Priest.

o. The eschatological war against the Kittim

Another scroll, the so-called 'War Rule' [193], describes a war against the 'Kittim' lasting forty years. We shall yet see whether a real war is meant or something apocalyptic or eschatological. One need only read a few lines to discover that what is described is a 'Holy War'. All the standards that will be carried along bear the name of God : the 'Divisions of God, the Assembly of God, the Victory of God', and many others among which one might note in particular 'the War of God' [194].

The idea of a Holy War, which was to have a long career in history, did not originate with the Essenian sect. In fact the 'Wars of Jahveh' by which we understand the conquest of Canaan by the tribes of Israel, should be considered as a first instalment [195]. In principle, all the wars of Israel against infidels were considered holy and the warriors as sanctified. A priest, sometimes even the High Priest, accompanied the soldiers in the field; on many occasions the Ark of the Covenant was carried along with the troops.

The prophet Ezekiel describes a war against Israel in apocalyptic terms [196]. King Gog, ruler of the land of Magog, wil wage war against God's people of Israel; "it shall be in the end of days" [197]. Never again will God hide his face from his people, "for I have poured out my spirit on the house of Israel" [198]. So the idea of a final war that would make the chosen people safe for good and sanctify it for ever was current in Israel.

A similar war with an eschatological character - it will take place 'at the time of the end' - is described in the Book of Daniel [199]; this was written just in the period of the origin of the Essenian sect. It relates a powerful offensive of 'the King of the North' in which several countries, even Egypt, are overrun. But somewhere between Jerusalem and the Mediterranean he will come to a miserable end. The historical Wars of the Maccabees, which occurred in that same period around 160 B.C., are also often described as 'holy wars'. Of the descriptions in Daniel as well as of those in Maccabees we find parallels in the War Scroll [200].

These parallels, I feel, suggest a kind of eschatological war rather than a war based on some Roman or Hellenistic model of warfare [201]. If this is correct, then the 'Kittim', the enemies in this text, are not necessarily the Romans but, in a more general sense, a godless race or nation.

There are, in this Scroll, a lot of prescriptions of a military kind regarding slogans to be put on the banners, and also regarding soldiers and officers, battle formations and battle order. It must be a war of the perfect : "No boy or woman shall enter their camps ..., no man who is lame, or blind, or crippled, or affected with a lasting bodily blemish, or smitten with a bodily impurity ... They shall be freely enlisted for war, perfect in body and spirit and prepared for the Day of Vengeance" [202]. The Essenes' obsessive fear of defilement shines through the following line. "There shall be a space of about two thousand cubits between all their camps and the ... latrine so that no indecent nakedness may be seen in the surroundings of the camp" [203]. Twelve hundred meters is a long distance, even for an Essene, when he is forcefully reminded of the fact that he too is only human [204].

That an ideal rather than a real war is meant is also suggested by the rule that soldiers and officers must have the improbable age of between thirty and forty-five years [205]. This ideal character is stressed still more by the injunction that the army should abstain from fighting during the Sabbatical years [206]; it is obviously taken for granted that the enemy will not make use of this rest [207].

The battle formations will be preceded by seven turbaned priests in white garments and carrying trumpets, followed by seven Levites with rams' horns. These instruments must be blown before, during and after the battle [208]. Before the fighting starts, priests and Levites must pray with the army to implore the help of God against Satan and his host [209]. After the battle and having cleansed themselves 'of the blood of the bodies of the ungodly', the soldiers must again arrange themselves in the initial battle formations and sing together the Psalm of Return [210].

The text continuously dub the enemy, the Kittim, 'the company of Belial, the host of Belial, the army of Belial, the ungodly, the nation of vanity, the angel of malevolence, the angels of destruction', and so on. This enemy is identified with all the mythical and historical enemies of Israel in the past or still posing a threat to the chosen people [211]. First the Semitic peoples are enumerated, Aram Naharaim (= Mesopotamia) [212] and Lud, a region to the north of Mesopotamia [213]. Aram has four 'sons' living beyond (= to the east of) the Euphrates [214], Us, the country where Job came from, Hul (unidentified), Thogar (perhaps the Aramaic Thocharians), and Mash or Massa, the object of many learned speculations [215].

Then the war spreads to the 'sons of Arphakshad' whom we must probably seek in eastern Turkey. Assyria will be conquered and then the march will go eastward through Elam to the Great Desert which means that Persia too wil fall into the hands of the triumphant army. Now the turn comes of the 'sons of Ismael and Keturah', that is of the despised Bedouin in the Arabian Desert, obviously no more than a mopping up operation. Far longer and harder fighting will be necessary to subdue 'the sons of Ham' meaning in this connection Egypt and Ethiopia, while the last ten years of the war will be against the 'sons of Japhet'. His principal son was 'Jawan', who stands for the Ionians, or Greeks [216].

The overall picture will be clear. The first result of the Holy War will be that the ideal frontiers of Israel will be reached so that it will stretch from the Sinai Desert in the south to the Euphrates in the north, with the Arabian Desert covering the eastern flank and the Mediterranean the western one [217]. But these frontiers will be far surpassed because Iran, all Asia Minor, and Egypt are also included. Two things strike us : first that the Romans are not mentioned, and second that this superideal Israel has almost the proportions of the Alexandrian Empire.

Dualistic as this whole picture is, no quarter can be given. "The dominion of the Kittim shall come to an end ... There shall be no escape". No remnant will be left, 'everlasting destruction' will be dealt out, there will be 'terrible carnage' [218]. The triumph of Israel will be total and everlasting; no trace will remain of the enemy. Huppenbauer draws our attention to a curious aspect of this Holy War, exemplified in the word 'flesh' (basar). This is sometimes used in the colloquial sense meaning 'body'; collectively, however, it can indicate 'mankind'. 'Flesh' refers also to the nations (the Gentiles) that Israel will some day rule.

At this point one becomes conscious of a severely critical attitude. "The nations are lacking something that Israel has acquired through election and through redemption." In the Community Rule even the believer, when considering his sinful, only too human state, acknowledges that he too belongs 'to wicked mankind, to the company of ungodly flesh'[219]. But through God's grace he will be purified and join the elect among mankind[220]. "The War Scroll", says Huppenbauer, "transfers this view to the whole world : the nations are only flesh; Israel, on the contrary, is the nation that has been redeemed by God"[221]. The obvious consequence of this attitude is that the Gentiles lose their right to existence. "This shall be a time of salvation for the people of God, an age of dominion for all the members of his company, and of everlasting destruction for the company of Belial"[222]. Nothing could be more dualistic.

p. The Essenes' notion of God

Now that we have done justice to the dualism that appears in the several scrolls, we must turn to some more general subjects. Let us begin with the Essenes' notion of God, since their whole doctrine is centred on him. God is the sole creator; beside him there is nothing[223]. The godless too and the spirits of Light and Darkness[224], including Belial himself[225], are his creatures. He knows all their actions in advance, before they are performed[226]. So there are not two powers in heaven but only one absolute ruler. God is surrounded by a court. 'The Sons of Heaven' stand around him, the 'spirits of knowledge'[227], the Angel of Truth[228], a complete celestial army ready to fight[229].

This, of course, is an extreme monotheism. As such it is very similar to that preached in the Old Testament. But Essenian theology goes further than that. It has its problems with the origin of evil. For if God is holy and pure and without any blemish, how could he be the source of evil? This is impossible! Therefore, there must be an evil power that is different from God. It is at this point, says Huppenbauer, that the Essenes' strict monotheism turns into a dualism. "The postulating an inimical power guarantees that the origin (of evil) can be explained without impairing God's creative majesty" [230]. This is not an absolute and radical dualism but a relative one since this evil power is a creature of God and in consequence dependent on him.

We should not think of this power as an abstraction but rather as a person. The Essenes' favourite name for him is 'Belial'. This name occurs a few times in the Old Testament, mostly meaning an abstraction or collectivity but sometimes also a personification. In other Qumran texts the term may mean 'nothingness' or 'destruction', an abstraction that is, but in the War Scroll it is personified into the figure of the great enemy of the end of times, the resolute opponent of God [231]. He is the real commander-in-chief of the Kittim host and in fact the ruler of everybody who does not obey God. What would please him most is to seduce the children of God [232].

Powerful as Belial is on earth, even though it may seem that the whole world is his domain, in the end he will prove powerless against God. As Huppenbauer writes, "his power is restricted from the first. It is Belial's delusion that he could conduct a successful battle with God". This proves how fundamentally wrong he is [233]. But perhaps his real enemy is not so much God as his chosen people [234].

Belial is not alone. He has his 'goral', his lot or part, that is his company, his court. They are 'the Sons of Darkness'. Belial's 'goral' is contrasted with that of the Sons of the Light. "In his (God's) goral are the sons of justice and the spirits of truth ..., and all the spirits of his (Belial's) lot are the Angels of Destruction" [235]. Belial's goral is constantly pictured in dualistic situations; it is cursed and condemned and damned, and finally utterly defeated by God. "There shall be eternal deliverance for the goral of God but destruction for all the nations of wickedness" [236].

This dualistic opposition of the two gorals is found back in the order of curses and blessings. When the troops are standing ready for battle, priest and Levites must pray like this : "Blessed be the God of Israel for all his holy purpose and for his works of truth! Blessed be all those who (serve) him in righteousness and who know him by faith!

Cursed be Belial for his sinful purpose and may he be execrated for his wicked rule! Cursed be all the spirits of his company for their ungodly purpose and may they be execrated for their service of uncleanness!" [237]

Next to the dualistically opposed pairs God-Belial, the two gorals, and the blessing-curse, there is that of the Light and the Dark. As Von Osten-Sakcen reports, there is no trace of this in the holy-war stories of the Old Testament or in Daniel. But we find the opposition of Light and Darkness in Amos : "Woe unto you who desire the day of the Lord ... It is darkness and not light" [238]. Here the term does not refer to any historical situation but to an eschatological one. In this way it is also used in the Qumran documents. What is new in these texts is the extension of these terms into 'sons of light' and 'sons of darkness', phrases we do not find in the Old Testament [239].

Huppenbauer speaks in this context of 'cosmic dualism' [240]. "Those born of truth spring from a fountain of light, those born of falsehood spring from a source of darkness" [241]. This scholar says that "here a place of the light and a place of the darkness are spatially opposed as two poles, the light above as the celestian world, the darkness beneath as the sheol" [242]. 'Light' is not God himself nor an emanation of him but his domain "in which he is spending blessings and salvation on those who are his" [243].

q. The personal dualism of the Essenes

In a previous section I have already established that in the supernatural sphere there are two spirits, both under God and both dependent on him, that of truth and justice, and that of evil and falsehood. These spirits also dwell in man himself and are battling to possess him. Even the pure and just Essenes are not exempt from this. "The nature of all the children of men is ruled by these (two spirits) ... and (they) walk in (both) their ways" [244]. "The spirits of truth and falsehood struggle in the hearts of men and they walk in both wisdom and folly". But "according to his portion of truth does a man hate falsehood" [245].

Now the Community Rule and the Essenian doctrine allot a sizeable portion of truth and justice to the adherents but during this life they will never be wholly beyond the reach of falsehood. This means that the moral situation of the Essene is dualistic; there will always be two opposed sides to him. Only at the end of times will God destroy the spirit of evil for always. Truth will then celebrate a complete triumph. At the appointed time God will cleanse some of the children of men (i.e. the Essenes) "of all abomination and falsehood" (which implies that not even the pious are wholly pure). Then "there shall be no more lies and all the works of falsehood shall be put to shame" [246].

Because I have described this in foregoing sections, I need not reiterate that there was also a dualistic opposition between the Essenes and ordinary Jewry; in particular they were opposed to the official cult in the Temple and to its priesthood. One is thus justified in drawing the general conclusion that the Essenian sect was profoundly dualistic; its authors were obviously viscerally incapable of positing something without immediately postulating its absolute counterpart. This must have attracted people of a peculiar stamp.

r. Types of dualism

To conclude this chapter, I will now follow Huppenbauer in his disquisition on the several dualisms in the Qumran texts because, as he argues so correctly, we cannot speak of one single dualism in them [247]. While the dualistic theology of the community in its entirety has a strongly ethical flavour, the concretely ethical dualism finds its expression in the need to separate the pure from the impure, and the just from the unjust. This is also found in the opposition of truth and falsehood.

Secondly, there is 'the physical-metaphysical dualism of Creator and creature'; parallel to this runs the dualism of the good spirits with the pious people and the evil spirits with the wicked people. Huppenbauer adds that we must not see this as the usual anthropological dualism but as a theological one based on the idea of redemption. Redemption does not mean that man gets rid of matter and attains his real spiritual self; it rather means that he is lifted up out of his normal earthly existence onto a higher ontological plane, onto the plane of the godhead that is not an interior divinity dwelling in man but the Creator-God of Israel "with whom he has naturally nothing in common". It is, therefore, not the result of a natural process but of grace. Huppenbauer succinctly describes this kind of dualism as 'being flesh' and 'being elected'.

The most important form of dualism in these texts, he says, is cosmic dualism. Here we have the absolute opposition of light and darkness which should not be regarded as physical entities but as ethical concepts. This cosmic dualism should not, however, be confused with a cosmological one since it is not centred on the universe as such but on human actions.

Mythological dualism is rare in the Scrolls. There is some of it in the doctrine of the two spirits and in the God-Belial opposition. But theological dualism is completely lacking since there is no anti-God. Eschatological dualism, however, is rampant. Now is the time of godlessness but in the end God will triumph; then all oppositions and all dualisms will be abolished. Then there will be unity and harmony in everything.

Huppenbauer closes his disquisition with the remark that these dualistic elements serve a psychological end. By accentuating differences, distances, and antagonisms the Essenes aim at magnifying God who is and remains the sovereign ruler over everybody and everything. It also creates room for a different idea of election. No longer is this the Old Testament concept of Israel as the chosen people but that of a restricted number of pious persons destined for the celestial realm of the Light. God has put his chosen into this general climate of discord in order to incite them to choose. They must recognize the antagonisms that are endemic in this world, make a deliberate choice for the good, and so fulfil the will of God. Thus they will be redeemed.

NOTES TO CHAPTER V

1. Van Deursen, Palestina 99/100; this author is quoting Professor van Beek here.

2. Yet another scroll, the copper scroll, is in Amman. This account is based on 1. Van der Ploeg, Vondsten (the account of how this author was the first expert to see the Dead Sea Scrolls is on pp. 20-25), and 2. Baigent & Leigh, Dead Sea Scrolls Deception (this utterly unreliable book nevertheless carries a good description of the discoveries. Very discursive accounts - I shortened my story considerably - are to be found in Allegro, Dead Sea Scrolls, and Trever, Untold Story (for all these works see Bibliography). Some additional information can be gleaned from Lawrence H. Schiffman s.v. 'Dead Sea Scrolls', Enc. of Rel. 4. Yet another authoritative description is that by Yadin, Message, Ch. 1 Discovery, Ch. 2 The Monastery of St. Mark. Finally I mention Vermes, Dead Sea Scrolls, Ch. 1 Discoveries in the Judaean Desert.

3. With respect to the identity of the Qumran community and the Essenes I stick to this verdict of Schürer : "Although a minority of scholars, whilst acknowledging a certain degree of relationship between the two movements, refuse to admit that they are the same, the wide consensus of opinion favours an identification of the people of Qumran with the Essene sect", Hist.Jew.People II, 583.

4. The ancient texts concerning the Essenes have been collected by Adam & Burchard, Antike Berichte (see Bibliography). On these texts and their historical veracity see Vermes, Dead Sea Scrolls, Ch. 5 Identification of the Community.

5. Philo, Hypothetica 11.1-18; Quod omnis homo probus liber sit (Every good man is free) 12.75-13.91.

6. Jos., Jew.War 2.199-61; further in Jew.Ant. 18.18-22 and in Vita 10.

7. Jos., Jew.Ant. 13.171.

8. Jos., Vita 10.

9. The longest is in Jew. War, 2.119-161, the second in Jew.Ant. 18.18-22.

10. Also somewhat erreneously called 'Philosophoumena'. Both Josephus and Hippolytus are supposed to have drawn on an older source that is no longer extant, see Lawrence H. Schiffman s.v. 'Essenes' in Enc. of Rel. 5, 167/168.

11. Van der Ploeg, Vondsten 73-76. Yadin, Message, Ch. 6 The Communal Building of Khirbet Qumran. Dupont-Sommer, Jewish Sect, Ch. 1 The Ruins of the Essene Monastery.

12. See the exhaustive and highly informative Ch. 3, The Qumran Library, in Vermes, Dead Sea Scrolls.
13. Van der Ploeg, Vondsten 81-95.
14. Pliny NH 5.15.73 suggested as much but in this he is certainly wrong.
15. Jos., Jew.War 2.124.
16. Jos., Ant. 13.311-312.
17. Jos., Jew.War 5.745.
18. Schürer, Hist.Jew.People II, 563, note 5. When Philo first states that the Essenes lived in many cities of Judaea and in many villages, Hypoth. 11.1, and next that they avoided the cities "because of the iniquities that have become inveterate among city dwellers", Quod omnis 76, this could mean that, for the reason given, they preferred villages to cities. See also Vermes, Scrolls, Ch. 6 History of the Sect; Milik, Gesch.d.Ess., in Qumran, 1981, 38-120; Rowley, Gesch.d.Qumran Sekte, in Qumran, 1981, 28-57; Schubert, Gemeinde.
19. Dupont-Sommer, Jew.Sect, Ch. V Rules and Rites of the Community of the Covenant; Vermes, Life and Institutions of the Sect.
20. Philo, Hypoth. 11.3.
21. Jos., Jew.War 2.120.
22. Jos., Jew.War 2.139-142. Jos. also mentions Essenes having been cruelly tortured by the Romans during the revolt without in the least giving in, War 2.152-153.
23. Jos., Jew.War 2.138.
24. Jos., Jew.War 2.150.
25. Philo, Hypoth. 11.5; Omnis probus 85.
26. Jos., Jew.War 2.124-126.
27. Jos., Jew.War 2.145.
28. Jos., Jew.War 2.122.
29. Jos., Ant. 18.19.
30. Philo, Hypoth. 11.8-9.
31. Philo, Omnis probus 78-79.
32. Jos., Jew.War 2.128-132.
33. Van der Ploeg, Vondsten 145. The notion that the Essenes were vegetarians goes back on Jerome who ca. 393 in his 'Adversus Jovinianum' 2.14 wrote that Pharisees, Sadducees, and Essenes always abstained from women, wine and meat. Already the slenderest acquaintance with the Jewish history of those days would have shown that this is utterly wrong with regard to Pharisees and

Sadducees. It is sometimes thought that Jerome based himself on Porphyry's De abstinentia 4.11-13 that, in the same terms, refers to Josephus' Antiquities, and his Contra Apionem. Porphyry, however, did not say anything about the Essenes abstaining from meat and wine, neither does Josephus. In his Contra Apionem he does not even mention the sects. Schürer whom I am following here says that Jerome was the first to think of this addition, Hist.Jew.People II, 571, note 60. In fact, deposits of animal bones were found at Qumran, often in jars; these were bones of sheep, goats, lambs, calves, and cows; many of them were scarred. De Vaux thinks that these bones were remnants of meals; it is not probable that they were the refuse of animal sacrifices. No altar was found at the site neither are altars or sanctuaries mentioned in Qumran texts. De Vaux, Archaeology 12-14.

34. This made an annual circle of 364 days, much more accurate than the lunar circle of 354 days but still lacking one day each year and yet another every four years. It is not known whether, or how, the Essenes solved this problem. Schürer. Hist.Jew.People II, 581; van der Ploeg, Vondsten 140/141.

35. Schürer. Hist.Jew.People II, 581.

36. Philo, Hypoth. 11.14; Jos., Jew.War 2.121; Pliny, NH 5.73.

37. Jos., Jew.War 2.120.

38. Van der Ploeg, Vondsten 157.

39. Jos., Jew.War 2.121.

40. Philo, Hypoth. 11.15.

41. Jos., Jew.War 160-161.

42. Jos., Ant. 18.19.

43. Jos., Ant. 18.19.

44. Philo, Omnis homo 75.

45. See Vol. IV, Ch. II.16b.

46. Dupont-Sommer, Schuld u. Rein.riten 61-70.

47. See for this subject Baumgarten, Studies, pp. 57-74 The Essenes and the Temple, in particular his conclusion on pp. 73/74.

48. Jos., Jew.War. 2.129-133.

49. Jos., Jew.War 2.147-148.

50. Dupont-Sommer, Schuld u. Rein.riten 263.

51. Dupont-Sommer, Schuld u. Rein.riten 269.

52. Huppenbauer, Der Mensch zwischen zwei Welten (see Bibliography). This book proved an invaluable guide through the texts, just as that by Von der Osten-Sacken, Gott und Belial (see Bibliography).

53. See the Preface to my Vol. VI.

54. Bousset, Rel.d.Judent. 252-254 and in particular Kap. XVII, Der Dualismus. Die Dämonologie, pp. 331-336.
55. K. Schaedel, Die Söhne des Lichts und das Johannesevangelium. Doctoral thesis of the evangelisch-theologische Fakultät Wien, 1953, 49, quoted by Huppenbauer, Der Mensch 9.
56. Huppenbauer must have been quoting an entry in the first edition. In the second edition, Freiburg 1959, J. Henninger says that dualism (as a term used in the history of religions) "is present everywhere where two supreme beings (or groups of these) are opposed to each other, either in diametrical completion (for instance, heaven and earth, female and male principles), or in enmity (either ethical or purely cosmic, for instance light and darkness, life and death, useful or harmful)". This conception too has a far wider range than that of Bousset.
57. Huppenbauer, Der Mensch 9/10.
58. Huppenbauer, Der Mensch 10 quotes articles by K.G. Kuhn of 1950 and 1952 who spoke of "the place where the preaching of Zarathustra debouched into Judaism". Dupont-Sommer, Jewish Sect, Ch. VII, The Doctrine of the Two Spirits, cited Yasna 30 and 45 to prove this point comparing them with texts from the Manual of Discipline and concluding : "It seems to me beyond question that a text such as this reflects the actual habit of the Gathas on several essential points", 127.
59. See my Vol. IV, Ch. IV.4, and Vol. VI, Preface 3.
60. Huppenbauer, Der Mensch 12/13.
61. See for this subject, Braun, Spätjüd-här.u.früh.christl.Radikalismus (see Bibliography).
62. M. Burrows, The Dead Sea Scrolls of St.Mark's Monastery. Vol.I.II.2. New Haven, 1950/1951. Later in Caves IV and V fragments containing some variants were discovered. There are a number of good translations into German, French, English, and Dutch. I call particular attention, however, to the edition by Lohse (Die Texte aus Qumran, see Bibliography), since this has the Hebrew and German texts on parallel pages, the Hebrew with the Masoretic punctuation, and the edition (without the Hebrew) by Vermes (Dead Sea Scrolls, see Bibliography). I am using the latter translation throughout the rest of this chapter.
63. 1QS1.23-24, 2.1-3.
64. 1QS2.4-9.
65. Huppenbauer, Der Mensch 16.
66. 1QS3.15.
67. 1QS3.15-17.
68. Osten-Sacken, Gott und Belial 125-131.

69. 1Sam. 2:3.
70. 1QS3.17-19.
71. 1QS4.15.
72. 1QS4.16-18.
73. 1QS4.16.
74. 1QS3.21-24.
75. 1QS3.25, 4.1.
76. 1QS1.8-10.
77. 1QS1.4-5.
78. 1QS3.13-14.
79. 1QS3.6-8.
80. 1QS5.1-3.
81. 2Sam.15:24-29 and 35, 17:15 and 19:11.
82. 2Sam.20:25.
83. 1Kings 1:7-8.
84. 1Kings 2:25-27.
85. 1Kings 1:39.
86. 1Kings 1:35.
87. 1Chron.6:1-15.
88. 1Chron.24:1-6.
89. 1Chron.24:4.
90. Ezra 8:2.
91. 1Sam.2:12-17.
92. Ez.40:46, 44:15, 48:11.
93. CD3.21 and 4.1-3.
94. Dupont-Sommer, Jew.Sect 69.
95. Huppenbauer, Mensch 30-32.
96. The editor was Solomon Schechter; His work was reprinted in 1970. A more modern edition is that of Chaim Rabin, The Zadokite Documents, with a translation and notes, Oxford, 1954; the relevant texts are in Part I, Admonition Page four, 20-21 and Page five 8-11. The relevant texts are also printed in a recent book by Davies, The Damascus Covenant (see Bibliography). I should also mention Rowley, The Zadokite Fragments (idem). See Schürer, Jew.His. III,1, 389, and Van der Ploeg, Vondsten 139-140.
97. Vermes, Scrolls 95.

98. "It is very doubtful, however, if we should credit the author with making exact chronological calculations covering this period", Rowley, Fragm. 62.
99. CD1.3-10.
100. CD1.10-11.
101. CD1.14-21.
102. CD 2.5-8.
103. CD3.12-14.
104. CD3.19.
105. CD4.3.
106. CD4.12-13.
107. CD6.5.
108. Yet another possibility has been ingeniously defended by R. North in the Palestine Exploration Quarterly 87 (1955), pp. 34-38 : by 'Damascus' Qumran is meant. He argues that in that period it belonged to Nabataean kingdom which he identifies with 'the land of Damascus'. This theory found little support. Huppenbauer, Mensch 55, note 190.
109. Vermes, Scrolls 66/67.
110. Quoted from Hosea 5:10.
111. CD8.3-5.
112. Quoted from Dt.32:33.
113. CD8.10-12.
114. 1QpHab 2.12-14; the text has been emendated.
115. Dupont-Sommer, Jew. Sect 15.
116. 1Macc.1:1 and 8:5.
117. 1QM1.1-2.
118. Dupont-Sommer, Jew.Sect 15.
119. Yadin, Message 94.
120. See the long and learned discussion in G. Jeremias, Lehrer, 1. Kap. Die Kittim.
121. 1QpHab2.14-15.
122. 1QpHab3.5-6.
123. 1QpHab6.10-12.
124. 1QpHab6.4-5.
125. 1QpHab3.1.
126. 1QpHab3.4.

127. 1QpHab3.10.
128. 1QpHab4.6.
129. 1QpHab5.3-4.
130. 1QpHab13.1-4.
131. 1QH7.6-7.
132. 1QH7.8-9.
133. 1QH7.4-5.
134. 1QH14.18.
135. 1QH1.21.
136. 1QH4.23.
137. 1QH4.27.
138. 1QH7.26-27.
139. 1QH9.9-10.
140. 1QH12.11-13.
141. 1QH2.13.
142. 1QH4.24.
143. 1QH4.27.
144. 1QH18.10-14.
145. 1QH17.17.
146. 1QH4.37.
147. 1QH4.30-31.
148. 1QH1.36.
149. 1QH2.8-9.
150. 1QH7.20-21.
151. 1QH2.11-13.
152. 1QH4.9-10.
153. 1QH5.27-28.
154. 1QpHab2.8-9.
155. 1QpHab7.4-5.
156. G. Jeremias, Lehrer 162.
157. CD1.1-11.
158. Van der Ploeg, Vondsten 70.
159. Van der Ploeg, Vondsten 67.

160. Vermes, Scrolls 58. It has often been argued that the Teacher and Jesus of Nazareth, without being identical, bear a surprising resemblance to one another. Long before the Scrolls were discovered, Ernest Renan proposed the view that Christianity virtually is an Essenianism. Shortly after the publication of the first rolls, Dupont-Sommer, a well-known expert, said as much in his 'Aperçus préliminaires sur les manuscrits de la Mer Morte, L'Orient ancien illustré 4, 1950, 21. In a later essay, Nouveaux aperçus sur les manuscrits de la Mer Morte, L'Orient illustré 5, 1953, 195, he specified this by saying that Christianity is a 'néo-formation essénisante' but not the Essenianism. In consequence, Jesus had to be seen as an 'étonnante réincarnation du Maître de Justice'. This thesis rapidly caught fire once a popularizing press got hold of it. The arguments of Dupont-Sommer were supported by another scholar, J.M. Allegro who did much to popularize it, for instance in Time Magazine of Febr. 6, 1956. Some dub the Teacher 'the first Christ'. Many people obviously found the idea that Christianity is not original but, after all, only an epiphenomenon of another religion. This idea has been amply used in campaigns against the Churches.

The latest instalment of this campaign has been the book by two journalists, Michael Baigent and Richard Leigh, The Dead Sea Scrolls Deception, London (1991) which is hardly more than a vitriolic attack on the Roman-Catholic Church, in particular on Father Ronald de Vaux. They are accused of preventing the complete publication of all the Scrolls because they supposedly contain 'explosive material' that would blow up the Church. It is conveniently forgotten that no rolls or fragments are in the possession of any Roman-Catholic institute. Just as I was working on this chapter it became known that E.J. Brill, publishers at Leiden NL, will publish all the material on seventy microfilms.

Returning now to a possible resemblance between the Teacher and Jesus, I don't think discussion of this point forms part of my task. I refer the interested reader to the balanced and dispassionate treatment of this question by G. Jeremias, Der Lehrer der Gerechtigkeit (see Bibliography), Kap. 9 Der Lehrer der Gerechtigkeit und der historische Jesus. His conclusion is that, while there doubtless exist some resemblances between these two persons, on the other hand the differences are so striking that the thesis of Dupont-Sommer seems totally unjustified.

Yet another thesis of Dupont-Sommer, Les Esséniens, Évidences 59, 1956, 26, is that the Teacher is a Messiah, a divine figure, who will return in glory at the end of times. But the texts themselves contain nothing at all to corroborate this view. This scholar in fact bases himself on one single text : "... until he comes who shall teach righteousness at the end of days" (CD6.22). Dupont-Sommer identified this 'he' with the Teacher as an eschatological figure. This is a rather flimsy base, the more so since the Teacher as such is not mentioned here.

G. Jeremias has devoted a long chapter to this question in his book, Kap. 7 Hat die Gemeinde in dem Lehrer eine eschatologische

Heilsgestalt erblickt? His conclusion is given already at the outset : "An keiner einzigen Stelle hat sich in irgendeiner Weise eine über menschliche Grenzen hinausgehende Funktion des Lehrers gezeigt; nirgendwo fand sich auch nur eine Anspielung auf eine Erwartung, die mit einem wiederkommenden Lehrer verknüpft worden wäre ... Er (der Lehrer) blieb ein schwacher, ängstlicher Mensch, der jedoch in Vertrauen auf Gott die Angriffe seiner Feinde zu ertragen wusste" (p. 268).

161. 1QpHab2.1-3.
162. 1QpHab5.9-12.
163. 1QpHab10.9-13.
164. G. Jeremias, Lehrer 89.
165. CD20.15.
166. CD1.14.
167. CD8.13; 19.25-26.
168. CD20:11.
169. CD1.12; 8.5; 19.17.
170. CD20.14.
171. CD1:16; 5.20.
172. CD1.3.
173. CD1.12-13.
174. CD1.18-21.
175. CD5.21-6.1.
176. CD2.5-9.
177. CD20.25-26.
178. G. Jeremias, Lehrer 95.
179. G. Jeremias, Lehrer 109.
180. G. Jeremias, Lehrer 121.
181. 1QpHab8.8-11.
182. 1QpHab9.9-10.
183. 1QpHab9.4-6.
184. 4QpPS37.4.8.
185. 1QpHab.9.8-12.
186. G. Jeremias, Lehrer 123.
187. G. Jeremias, Lehrer 126.
188. G. Jeremias, Lehrer 126.

189. In Huppenbauer's view the Man of Lies and the Wicked Priest are identical. His beginnings as High Priest were laudable but because of his craving for riches he became unfaithful. The Teacher of Righteousness reproached him for this. They fell out, and the High Priest punished and persecuted the Teacher who fled to the Dead Sea with his adherents. In the opinion of the Essenians the High Priest had now become a Wicked Priest and a Man of Lies as well, Huppenbauer, Der Mensch 50-53.
190. 1Macc.12:39-13-23; Jos., Ant. 13.6.1-6, Jew.War 1.2.1.
191. The Hebrew text of 1QpHab.9.11 says 'be-nega le-kalah' = by a blow, or suffering, leading to destruction which might mean that Jonathan was tortured to death. 1QpHab.12.5 says that God punished the Godless Priest 'le-kalah' = to his destruction.
192. The only other candidate is Menelaus who was High Priest from 172 to 162 B.C. As a Benjaminite he was not a member of the authentic priestly class. He was certainly a greedy man who began his term of office by robbing the temple of its gold vessels, 2Macc.4:32. He was a principal leader of the Hellenizing party in Jerusalem and was supported by the Syrians. Later the Syrians had enough of him and he was put to death. Menelaus is the only High Priest, except Jonathan, who was killed by the heathen. But can it be maintained that he was killed by his enemies? I should say, rather by his friend. Furthermore, unlike the Wicked Priest, Menelaus did not begin his career in an honourable way. G. Jeremias, Lehrer 69-71 argues convincingly that a conflict between Menelaus and the Teacher must have taken place before 170 B.C. which is much too early. This scholar too concludes to the identity of the Wicked Priest and Jonathan, Lehrer 75-76.
193. First published (posthumously) in 1954 by L. Sukenik. The original text is incomplete.
194. 1QM3-4.
195. See Vol. IV, Ch. II.15c-f.
196. Ez.38-39.
197. Ez.38:16.
198. Ez.39:28.
199. Dan.11:40-45.
200. Osten-Sacken, Gott und Belial 62-72.
201. Yadin defends the Roman model.
202. 1QM7.3-5.
203. 1QM7.6-7.
204. Dt.23:3 says that the latrines should be outside the camp but prescribes no distance. Two thousand cubits is the longest distance

a Jew may go a on Sabbath day. In the context of the Scroll this means, therefore, 'as far as possible', van der Ploeg, Rouleau 114.
205. 1QM7.1-2.
206. 1QM7.8.
207. Van der Ploeg, Rouleau 72.
208. 1QM7.9-8.17.
209. 1QM13.
210. 1QM14.
211. 1QM2.10-14.
212. Gen.24:10.
213. Mentioned as such in the apocryphal Book of Jubilees 9:6 and 11; in Gen.10:13, on the contrary, Lud is connected with Egypt.
214. Mentioned as such in gen.10:23.
215. Van der Ploeg, Rouleau 72?73.
216. Gen.10:2-5.
217. Jos.1:4; van der Ploeg, Rouleau 76.
218. 1QM1.5-9.
219. 1QS11.9.
220. 1QS11.14-16.
221. Huppenbauer, Mensch 86/87.
222. 1QM1.5.
223. 1QH10.9.
224. 1QS3.25.
225. 1QM3.11.
226. 1QS3.15.
227. 1QH3.22-23.
228. 1QS3.24.
229. 1QM13.4. This passage is based on Huppenbauer, Mensch 95/96.
230. Huppenbauer, Der Mensch 97/98.
231. Sacken-Osten, Gott u. Belial 73-78.
232. 1QS3.24.
233. Huppenbauer, Mensch 98.
234. Huppenbauer, Mensch 85/86.
235. 1QM13.10-12.

236. 1QM15.1. See for this passage Osten-Sacken, Gott u. Belial 78-80; Huppenbauer, Mensch 84-86.
237. 1QM13.1-6. See Osten-Sacken, Gott u. Belial 108-111.
238. Amos 5:18.
239. Osten-Sacken, Gott u. Belial 80-84.
240. Huppenbauer, Mensch 71, but on p. 28 he qualifies this as 'not a purely cosmic dualism but of moral-religious qualities'.
241. 1QS3.19.
242. Huppenbauer, Mensch 27.
243. Huppenbauer, Mensch 28.
244. 1QS4.15.
245. 1QS4.23-24.
246. 1QS4.18-23.
247. Huppenbauer, Mensch 103-115.

CHAPTER VI

ON THE TALMUD AND EARLY JEWISH MYSTICISM

1. On the Talmud as such

a. The composition of the Talmud

In ancient Jewish literature we can distinguish three main parts. First, there is the Torah by which we understand the Old Testament, and more in particular the so-called 'five books of Moses', the Pentateuch. This is 'the written Torah'. Second, there is the Mishnah, an a elaboration of much that we find in the Old Testament, mainly in the form of prescriptions. 'Mishnah' is a word derived from the Hebrew verb 'shanah' = to repeat, but meaning 'to learn' in Aramaic. Finally, we have the Talmud. Non-biblical and post-biblical literature, especially the Talmud, is called 'the oral Torah', although all this is codified too. Written and Oral Law are closely interrelated. The Oral Law is "the authoritative interpretation of the Written Law ... This view of the Oral Law was a fundamental principle of the rabbis" [1]. Study of the Law, the results of which are to be found in the Halakhah, was the most important task of rabbinic scholarship; "it became the supreme religious study" [2].

Talmud is a Hebrew word signifying 'study' or 'learning'. Actually there exist two Talmuds, the Palestinian (Talmud Yerushalmi) and the Babylonian (Talmud Bavli). The Babylonian Talmud is four times as large as the Palestinian one and is considered the most authoritative. Both collections are written in Aramaic (in its several dialects) but contain a great number of Hebrew quotations [3]. The Talmud has two aspects : the 'Haggadah' (or 'Aggadah'), containing descriptive material, and the 'Halahkah' (= the law), the prescriptions. Both the Haggdah and the Halahkah are in particular concerned with their implications for the situation of Jewry in Babylonia [4].

b. The origin of the Talmud

Since we are speaking of the Torah as the great source of the Talmudic writings, it will be evident that their origin lies back in ancient days, many centuries before the period that is occupying us in this volume. Interpretation of the Torah must have started already at an early date but we find evidence of this only in the period of the Second Temple, that is some time after the Babylonian Captivity. About 400 B.C. "there had begun an oral interpretation of the Pentateuchal texts" [5]. For a long time the historical line is very difficult to follow but in the period after the birth of Christ we get onto more solid ground. This period, the first and second centuries, is the time of the 'Tannaim' or 'teachers'. These Tannaim are a loose group of about 225 Jewish scholars belonging to several, often contending schools or academies in Palestine. The final result of Tannaitic studies and discussions was the publication of the Mishnah, about 200-220, a codification or compilation "in which were summarized all the legal debates and decisions of the tannaim" [6].

The Tannaic Period was followed by the Amoraic Period (ca. 220-470). The Amoraim are 'speakers' or 'interpreters' of the Mishnah working in Palestinian and Babylonian academies. Since the Mishnah had acquired an authority almost equalling that of the Old Testament, its text was regarded as established once and for all. What the Amoraic scholars did was to comment on it without altering or transforming it. The scholarly results of the Palestinian rabbis were finally collected in the Palestinian Talmud [7], that of their Babylonian colleagues in the Babylonian Talmud. The long period of the gestation of the Talmud came to an end in 470. As will be self-evident, we must not conceive of the

Talmud as one consecutive and uniform work but as a collection of dozens and dozens of treatises.

The Babylonian collection, by far the largest one, runs to 5894 folio pages [8]. The authoritative English translation (by a number of scholars), London, 1936-1952, counts thirty-six mostly bulky volumes (plus an Index Volume). However, only a few items in this immense mass of material will be of concern to us. Although the date of the final codification of both Talmud versions lies far beyond the chronological scope of the present volume, the few issues that will occupy us were doubtless studied and debated in the period of our investigation.

2. The Talmud not a dualistic work

Although the Old Testament shows some dualistic elements, it is by no means a dualistic book but rather, regarding its theological stance, a uniform and homogeneous work. The same applies, perhaps even more, as we saw in Chapter IV of this volume, to the New Testament. Neither Judaism nor early Christianity were prone to dualistic tendencies. The great exception was, of course, the sect of the Essenes that for many reasons, and probably not in the last place because of its profoundly dualistic attitudes, kept studiously apart from ordinary Jewish life (which 'apartheid' was a dualism in itself).

If we are justified, as seems reasonable, to extrapolate from Jewish and Judaeo-Christian mental concepts, it is to be expected that the Talmud too will be prone to equally undualistic, in places even anti-dualistic mental attitudes. At the same time, however, since the Bible in both the Old and New Testaments is not wholly free from dualistic tendencies, it is a fair guess that we will find these also in the Talmud.

3. The Jewish-Christian relationship

a. Why Jesus does not occur in the Talmud

Our first question is how the Talmud views the relationship of Judaism with Christianity, and in the first place what is thought of Christianity's founder, Jesus of Nazareth [9]. The name 'Jeshu' indeed occurs in a number of Talmudic texts. A great scholar lik Marcus Friedländer thought that these references were inserted at a late date, perhaps even after the final redaction, and were in fact recoinings of much earlier entries that did not refer to Jesus at all. A modern scholar, Johann Maier, asserts that his own investigation has confirmed the opinion of Friedländer [10]. His conclusion is that Jesus does not figure in the earlier Talmudic versions, at least not in the first and second centuries. Maier infers from this that the rabbis of that period were hardly or not at all interested in Christianity. The real polemics, he says, began only later [11].

The problem, however, is that the Acts of the Apostles relates very fierce collisions between Jews and Christians, mainly Judaeo-Christians. But it is quite conceivable that what official Jewry was fighting was not really the person of Jesus. Jesus of Nazareth, in the eyes of the rabbis, was an historical figure who was duly executed; they did not believe in the resurrection nor did they think that Jesus was the Promised One, the Messiah. The Messiah was still to come. The Jesus whom the apostles were preaching, so they must have thought, was a sham figure and not really dangerous.

No, the man who presented a real danger to Judaism was an ex-Pharisee, Paul of Tarsus, and against him the Jews fought as hard as they could [12]. Ziegler says that "Jewry and its representatives had no reason at all to take action against Jesus himself and did not actually do this. But at the moment that Paul proclaimed the liberation from Mosaic Law, circumcision, and the dietary prescriptions, the fight broke out, to flare up in full blaze as soon as Christian propaganda reached Palestine and tried to convert Jews in their own country" [13]. But this second wave of Christian proselytizing only occurred after 200 and, therefore, falls outside our scope.

b. Once again, who are the minim?

What do we find of the Jewish-Christian controversy in the Talmud? The term 'Christian' itself does not occur in it which does not make matters easier. What is mentioned - and that often - is the 'minim'. As I explained in Chapter IV, 'min' means 'sectarian' or 'heretic'. With this term many deviating groups can be indicated, Samaritans, Sadducees, Gnostics, Judaeo-Christians, and still more, all those tendencies that did not carry favour with the leading circles of Jewish orthodoxy. According to a Sanhedrin text, there existed twenty-four kinds of minim [14] at the time of the destruction of the Temple.

Segal says that "the terms may have changed their meaning over their long history of use" [15]. He maintains that the opinion of Herford that min **always** means 'Christian' is untenable [16]. Occasionally a min could even be a non-Jew, a Roman for instance. However, "it is possible to distinguish historically two semantic phases in the use of the term" [17]. It is Buechler's opinion that until the second century A.D. - he gives the year 135 -, it denoted deviant Jews, and after that, in the later second century and in the third, non-Jewish sectaries, among them Gnostics [18].

If this is correct, first-century Talmudic texts would aim at Judaeo-Christians who then composed the great majority in the early Church. In the Tosefta Shabbat [19] Rabbi Tarfon who lived at the end of the first century of the Christian era, emphatically declared that he would rather burn his son than not burn the books of the Evangelists and the books of the minim if they fell into his hands. He even went so far as to state that if somebody was pursuing him, he would prefer to seek refuge in a temple of idolatry (in a pagan temple, that is) to flying into a house of worship of the minim. There can be no doubt that in this passage the minim are (Judaeo-)Christians [20]. And Rabbi Ishmael added to this that the books of the minim should be blotted out.

c. The Jewish reproach

What exactly did Jewish orthodoxy reproached the Christians for? This both our rabbis make perfectly clear. Rabbi Tarfon in the same passage said that the minim recognize the Divinity but deny him; the difference with (pagan) idolators is that these do not know God. And Rabbi Ishmael accuses the minim of bringing enmity between 'Israel and its Father. In studying the Old Testament as well as rabbinic literature, we must firmly keep in mind that the central tenet of the Jewish creed is that there is only one God. To say that there is no God at all (which was extremely rare in Antiquity) or that that there is more than one godhead would mean denying this all-important dogma. One who does so is a 'kofer', a 'denier' (from 'kafar' = to deny) [21]. The existence of this belief makes the dualistic idea of two worlds, a good one and a bad, each with its own god, impossible for the rabbis.

This is the dogmatic verdict. "He that says that there are two powers in heaven, they (the rabbis) answer him, and say onto him : 'And there is no God with me ...' (Dt.32:39). Thus says the Lord, the King of Israel and his redeemer, the Lord of Hosts, 'I am the first and I am the last, and beside me there is no God' (Is.44:6)" [22]. Which particular group of heretics is actually meant here? Segal believes that Herford was too hasty in applying this text only to Christians. "Samaritans, gnostics and Jewish apocalyptic groups cannot be excluded" [23].

It all depends on the meaning of 'heaven'. If we take this to indicate the supernatural or extra-terrestrial world in general, then indeed Gnostics may be meant. If we take it in its more restricted meaning of the abode of God, then Gnostics are excluded. In that case this passage aims at (Judaeo-)Christians who are somehow supposed to venerate two gods, the Father and the Son. Rabbi Nathan ha-Bavli who settled in Palestine around A.D. 150, by invoking the authority of the Isaiah-text quoted above, intended to give "an answer to the minim who say 'There are two powers', ... so as not to give the peoples of the world an opportunity to say 'There are two powers'" [24]. Here those who are supposed to sustain the doctrine of the two powers are the Gentiles, the 'gojim' in general, but they have obviously taken their cue from the Christians.

Here it must be stated that, as Segal writes, "at its beginnings, Christianity was more 'binatarian' than 'trinatarian', emphasizing only the Son and the Father as God". To orthodox Jews this seemed to imply that there were 'two powers in heaven'. Now this does not necessarily mean that these 'powers' were dualistically opposed; they might be seen as 'complementary instead of opposing deities'[25] (a case of 'ditheism'). What I wish to emphasize here is not that the doctrine attacked as heretical was in itself dualistic but that the attitude of the rabbis vis-à-vis those who professed this doctrine was dualistic - to such a degree that it led to the virtual expulsion of the Judaeo-Christians from the synagogue.

d. No intercourse between Jews and Christians

It is related [26] of a very famous rabbi, Eliezer ben Hyrcanos, also called Eliezer the Great, that he, around A.D. 100, was arrested on account of having intercourse with Judaeo-Christians. He admitted to have found pleasure in a Christian who was teaching 'in the name of Jesus'. Brought before a Jewish court he was acquitted. Afterwards he confessed that he had transgressed the biblical teaching : "Keep your way far from her and do not go near the door of her house"[27] (the woman of deceptive wisdom is meant here). This proves that Jewish authorities looked with displeasure on intercourse between Jews and Christians [28].

4. The Talmud and the Gnostics

It is often difficult to decide to which particular group the term 'minim' is referring in a particular text - Gnostics, Christians, or still others. When the Sages say that the minims' books are manuals of witchcraft, are they aiming at Gnostics or at Christians or at both of them at the same time? But Christians would vehemently deny that they practised magic, whereas some Gnostic sects glorified in it [29]. The rabbinical argument, however, is that God's creational work, in particular the creation of man, clearly makes Gnostic pessimism and cosmic dualism look irrelevant [30].

The idea, Gnostic in origin and equally dualistic, that the world was created by angels was combated by the rabbis [31]. Some uneasiness arose concerning the Genesis text Gen. 1:1 : "In the beginning God created the heaven and the earth". Could this 'and' perhaps signify that there are two different, possibly even opposed worlds, one celestial and the other terrestrial? But one of the greatest Tannaim, Rabbi Akiva (Akiba), authoritatively declared that this 'and' only can mean that both were created at the same time [32]. Concerning the role of the angels the Sages would go no further than making God consult them before the creation of man; as Urbach states, "such statements are conspicuously antithetic to Gnostic doctrine" [33].

According to the point of view of the Old Testament, man is a perfectly integrated unity; we must not think of him as having been composed of two different elements, body and soul [34]. This is a far cry from the following remarkable utterance of Flavius Josephus. "All of us have mortal bodies, composed of perishable matter, but the soul lives for ever, immortal : it is a portion of the Deity housed in our bodies" [35]. This is dualistic anthropology in which Hellenistic and/or Gnostic elements are clearly discernible. But this Hellenized Jewish scholar did not belong to the Sages, although he was born in a priestly family.

However, while the rabbis adhered to the biblical view, their own opinion resulted "from the contemplation of human existence, with all the contradictions that manifest themselves in a man's character and actions" [36]. The Tannaim held that only the first man was created as an integrated whole but that in the origination of all others God and the parents cooperate. The Creator contributes the 'nefesh', the 'breath of life', including the vital parts of man, like his senses, and the parents the rest, bones, skin, sinews, flesh, blood [37]. This is beginning to move in the direction of a different origin of body and soul.

That Josephus was not the only one to entertain a dualistic view of the relationship of body and soul is proved by a speech given by Eleazar, a Zealot priest and a leader in the great anti-Roman revolt. "Death ... gives liberty to the soul and permits it to depart to its own pure abode, there to be free from all calamity; but so long as it is imprisoned in a mortal body and tainted with all its miseries, it (the soul) is, in sober truth, dead, for association with what is mortal ill befits that which is divine" [38]. Stoic and Gnostic influences commingle here to create a dualistic picture of the companionship of body and soul.

Now Eleazar was not a Sage either; such extreme dualistic opinions are not to be expected among the rabbis. But as Urbach, who treated this subject extensively, remarks, dualism is not wholly absent, although "the conception of dualism and the antithesis between flesh and spirit in Rabbinic dicta are less drastic" [39]. The Hellenistic notion of the transmigration of souls was not approved by the Sages, but this notwithstanding, reference is sometimes made to the pre-existence of the soul which, once again, points to a different origin of body and soul.

However, when all is said and done, the Rabbis on the one hand, and the Gnostics and the Hellenistic philosophers on the other, fundamentally disagreed with regard to this subject. Let me wind up this section with Urbach's well-pondered words. "The concepts of the Sages, even when they give expression to the anthropological dualism, and even when they stress the hereafter and the world to come, do not ignore this world. God is the God of history and of all that happens in it, and in the course of history the whole of man - both body and soul - is active. These principles were conducive to the fact that even those Sages who maintained some sort of body-soul dualism, did not draw extremist inferences from it. Fundamentally, Talmudic Judaism retained, despite all influences and deviations, the concept of the unity of body and soul" [40]. If this is correct, which I don't doubt, we may well ask whether this scholar is not applying the term 'dualism' somewhat loosely here.

5. Shades of ethical dualism

A lapsed Jew once asked Rabbi Meir, a Tanna of the second century A.D., what the meaning was of this verse : "God has made the one as well as the other". The Rabbi answered that for every created thing God has also made its counterpart, for instance mountains as well as hills. But, retorted his interlocutor, this is not what your master, Rabbi Akiva (50-135), has taught, since according to this Sage God created the righteous and he created the wicked, he created the Garden of Eden and he created Gehinnom (the nether world, or hell). The interlocutor then quoted Rabbi Akiva : "Everyone has two portions, one in the Garden of Eden and one in Gehinnom. The righteous, being meritorious, takes his own portion and his fellow's portion in the Garden of Eden. The wicked man, being guilty, takes his own portion and his fellow's portion in Gehinnom" [41].

This is a highly intriguing and revealing text. It shows how dualistic conceptions find their origin in totally innocuous notions and oppositions. Rabbi Meir contrasts hills and mountains which for me, as the inhabitant of an entirely flat country, is hardly an opposition at all. But Rabbi Akiva is said to have gone a few radical stages further, towards the opposition of two sets of people, the righteous and the wicked, presupposing the ethical dualism of good and evil. Segal comments here that "we should probably assume that these dualistic ideas were more commonly shared among all sects of Judaism than is evident from orthodox rabbinic texts" [42].

It is an interesting side-commmentary that Rabbi Akiva came only very late to the study of the Torah; in his youth he earned his bread as a shepherd and was wholly unlearned; he could not even read [43]. Could it be that such radical notions were more current among the humbler sections of the people with whom Akiva conversed as a young man than among the scholarly rabbis?

Anyhow, even among these learned men there was a theory of 'man's two impulses, the impulse toward the good, and the impulse toward the evil', but this theory was not thought to be heretical [44]. The Tannaim knew nothing of a realm of Satan to whose dominion the wicked were subjected, contrasted with a realm of God in which the righteous live. "The view shared by the tannaim is all creatures are subject in their lifetime to the rule of the Holy One" [45]. No dualistic theology like in Qumran, therefore.

Nevertheless, "not only the names of the righteous and their deeds are revealed before the omnipresent but also the names and the acts of the wicked" [46]. If it is true that there is no mention of the existence of two opposed realms, there is, at any rate, a strong notion of there being two opposed sets of people - opposed already before they were born. There were even Sages who held that the verse in Genesis "God divided the light from the darkness" referred to the righteous (the 'children of light') and the wicked (the 'children of darkness'). This would mean that the two sets were there from all eternity. Of course, no Tanna ever said that God was the source of evil. Evil is the result of human actions because man is free to choose [47].

The great fear of dualism, in its Gnostic and probably above all in its Essenian colouring that is behind all rabbinic reasoning on this point, obviously induced the Sages to slip into another kind of dualism, that of the two sets of people. But they readily accepted this because in this way they could at the same time exonerate God from the blame of being the origin of evil and deny the possibility of the existence of two separate ethical realms.

6. The formalism of the Halakhah

To many religious minds in Jewry the systematic and scholarly explanation of Mosaic law, as it is codified in the 'halakhah', the legal part of the Talmud, was far too formalistic. It did not satisfy their deeper religious needs. They longed for 'a more profound experience' [48]. In their view the Torah should not be interpreted as a collection of juridical stipulations but as 'the inner secret law of the universe'. They believed that this secret was not be found in articles of law but rather in symbols and signs. Jews with aspirations such as these were, as will be evident, inclined to mysticism and esotericism and exhibited an affinity with Gnostic ideology.

The first century of the Christian era saw a proliferation of theosophic and esoteric currents in Judaism, not only in Palestine but also in Egypt. A pivotal figure in this respect was, of course, Philo, the Jewish philosopher, who lived from ca. 20 B.C. to A.D. 50. Deeply influenced as he was by Hellenistic philosophy - he published all his works in Greek and probably did not even know Hebrew -, he cannot be considered an adherent of Jewish orthodoxy. Since he was born and raised in Alexandria in Egypt, he should be thought of, at least to a large extent, as representative of Aegypto-Hellenistic culture, without, therefore, ceasing to be a Jew. I intend to give him and his ideas an extensive treatment in Chapter I of Volume VIII.

7. Jewish apocalypses

Jewish mysticism developed partly out of apocalyptic literature. The Old Testament contains only one apocalyptic book, or rather a book with apocalyptic sections in it, the Book of Daniel [49]. The only apocalyptic book of the New Testament is the Book of Revelation which I mentioned in Chapter IV of the present volume. As David Flusser states, "the classical period of Jewish apocalypse, a highly developed genre in its own right, is from the second century B.C. to the second century of the Christian era" [50].

This implies that outside the Bible there are a number of Jewish apocalypses, the principal of these being the Book of Enoch. What an apocalyptic author intends to do is 'to reveal', to offer a 'revelation' (from the Greek verb 'apokaluptein' - to reveal). What is revealed is the future, a future that is essentially different from the present situation of the world. Because such a work concerns the future it is by the same token prophetic. The mostly anonymous authors ascribe their vision to prophets of the past, like Baruch or Daniel. The reason behind this attribution is that these writers are convinced that there were no longer prophets; prophecy, however, would return in the final age [51].

Another constitutive mark of this genre is that it is eschatological. This means than an apocalyptic book never is 'historical' in the sense that it presents a coherent and continuous report of events in due temporal order. Rather an apocalyptic presentation cuts itself off from history as it is normally understood, in the Bible too; it even turns against it because this present world is doomed to destruction. Eschatology always means drama : our world will be destroyed, go up in flames for instance; after that there will be re-creation, a new world and a new heaven will appear. This is a clearly dualistic element which is common to all apocalypses.

Apocalyptic authors invariably have a very low idea of their own time : utterly wicked as it is, they contrast it with the impeccable purity of the coming reign. The final victory will go to the good and righteous. The present era, however, is given up as hopeless and incorrigible. Apocalypses often contain much bitter criticism of existing situations in veiled terms.

In the difficult days of the first century A.D., marked above all by defeat at the hands of the Romans and the destruction of the Temple, apocalyptic views became highly popular. Apart from the New Testament Book of Revelation there are strongly apocalyptic tendencies in Essenian literature to which I paid ample attention in Chapter V; the Talmud too presents many apocalyptic views. Flusser recapitulates this as follows. "The apocalyptic historical and cosmic dualism of this world and the next was accepted by all Israel" [52]. It was the anguish caused by the dire conditions of the time that incited the Jews not only to hope for a better world but also to condemn utterly the existing situation and to expect a radical new beginning.

8. Jewish mysticism

a. Asceticism

It will be self-evident that such a mental climate will be a fertile ground for the development of mysticism and esotericism. Esoteric knowledge is to be found in the apocalyptic writings; their authors were knowledgeable about hidden things and 'the hidden secrets of God'.

Esoteric ideas were not so much a religious conviction, let alone a theory, but rather a way of life which led the adherents to adopt asceticism. Ascetic practice was a means for them to take their distance from the abhorred world with its luxury and its consequent neglect of things divine. The Sages, however, did not view this asceticism as a constitutive part of Jewish religious life; they combated it and even abused it [53].

b. What is Jewish mysticism?

When trying to answer the question what exactly (Jewish) mysticism is, we are warned by Gershom Scholem, the great expert on this subject, against making the mistake of thinking that it "is identical with that personal experience which is realized in the state of ecstasy or estatic meditation. (It) is ... much more" [54]. Mysticism gives the notions of "Creation, Revelation and Redemption new and different meanings reflecting the characteristic feature of mystical experience, the direct contact between the individual and God" [55].

The emphasis falls on the individual rather than on the 'people of God'. To the mystic, revelation is not an historical phenomenon that happened once at a given time but an ungoing process, that is to say, for the individual who is privileged to share in it. He sees the divine revelation "as something whose true meaning has yet to unfold itself; the secret is to him the real and decisive one (= meaning)" [56]. A new interpretation was needed therefore. It will be evident that the orthodox and scholarly interpretation by the scribes and the Sages did not appeal to Jewish mystics.

A tendency to mysticism manifested itself among certain Jewish circles in a predilection for speculations on and interpretations of biblical themes, in the occurence of visions, and even in the use of magic. Such speculations centred on the first chapter of Genesis and on the prophecy of Ezekiel.

c. The mystic notion of God

A highly important issue was the notion of God. Jewish mystics felt embarrassed by the distinction between the hidden, unknown God - the deus absconditus - and the God who manifests himself in his creation and in the Bible. As Scholem writes, "the dualism embedded in the two aspects of God ... has deeply precoccupied the Jewish mystics" [57]. This problem would be expatiated upon much later by the authors of the Kabbalah, but it is already discernible in the first stages of Jewish mysticism. Scholem denies that these mystics were dualists; instead, they try to escape from dualism by not conceiving of God "as the absolute Being or absolute Becoming but as the union of both". He admits, however, that "there exists a connection between (this) way of thinking and that of the Gnostics" [58].

In my opinion, the dualistic distinction between a known or knowable and an unknown, unknowable God is unsolvable if one wants to have it both ways. "The mystic strives to assure himself of the living presence of God, the God of the Bible, the God who is good, wise, just and merciful and the embodiment of all positive attributes. But at the same time he is unwilling to renounce the idea of the hidden God who remains eternally unknowable in the depth of His own self" [59]. If this is correct, then Jewish mystics proved unable to overcome their initial theological dualism.

It will not surprise us that the Talmudic Sages were no great admirers of this line of thought. They do not know of a hidden, an unknown, an unknowable God. Of course, their God is Most High and sublime and not to be comprehended by human thinking but, as Schechter wrote, "the fact of God's abiding in a heaven ever so high does not prevent him from being at the same time also on earth ... Thus we may maintain safely that with the Rabbis distance did not imply aloofness or any interruption of God's communion with man". Regarding the relationship of Rabbinic and esoteric theology, he said "that whatever mythologies and theosophies may be derived from the notion of heaven or height, on the one hand, or whatever pantheistic theories may be developed from the conception of the God-fulness of the universe, on the other hand, neither of these opposing theologies was allowed to influence the theology of the Rabbis in any considerable degree" [60]. This is sufficient to explain the fierceness of rabbinic utterances against non-orthodox trends of thought.

d. Angelic mediation

A second point is angelic mediation. Angels are mentioned in a number of Bible books, but beginning with the Book of Daniel angels proliferate. We meet them also in Qumran texts, in Philo, and in esoteric and mystical Jewish writings. Not without reason the Rabbis feared that this would develop into a two-powers doctrine. As Segal states, "there are some cases in which angelic mediation can be seen in a growing dualistic context. Usually, the primary figure (the principal angel, that is) is seen as the opposition to a demonic being like Satan, where he (the angel) pleads the cause of Israel as both heavenly advocate and intercessor" [61].

To this he adds "that traditions similar to the ones which the Rabbis dismissed as 'two powers' heresy in the second century can be seen in sectarian literature of the first century". There is at least incipient dualism in this sectarian literature. "We cannot altogether dismiss the possibility", Segal goes on, "that some apocalyptic groups posited an independent power (independent from God, that is - F.) as early as the first century (A.D.) or that other groups, among them the predecessors of the (Talmudic) Rabbis, would have called them heretics" [62].

e. Merkabah mysticism

The main current of Jewish mysticism in this period bears the name of 'Merkabah mysticism'. The definitive redaction of the most important Merkabah texts took place long after the period under consideration here, perhaps even as late as the centuries after 600. Scholem, however, argues that "large sections of them originated in talmudic times, and that the central ideas ... go back as far as the first and second centuries" [63]. No names of Jewish mystics can be attached to these central ideas. Speculations of an esoteric kind on the first chapters of Genesis and on Ezekiel had been going on already since early Pharaisaic times; there was much discussion the results of which were not made public (as being too dangerous). Now what was the main theme of this mysticism?

It took as its starting-point Ezekiel's vision of God. He saw four celestial creatures who manipulated wheels [64]. We could think of a chariot but the prophet did not use this word here. Instead, he spoke of 'the likeness of a throne (kisse) with somebody seated on it'. "This was the likeness of the glory of the Lord" [65]. In other words, what he saw was the throne of God. The idea of a chariot, instead of a throne, as the seat of God was first expressed in Chron. 28:18, and later by Jesus ben Sirach who said that Ezekiel saw God seated on the chariot of the Cherubs [66]. The word used in these texts is 'merkavah' = chariot; it is from this word that the term 'Merkabah mysticism' is derived (it is sometimes also called 'throne mysticism').

In the view of the mystics the world of the Chariot was a higher world, unattainable for the common believer. One had to ascend to it while leaving the world of every-day experience, and even of common devotion, behind one. The ascent could only be effected with the help of severe ascetic exercises, the recital of ecstatic hymns, and the assuming of a special bodily position (head between the knees). All these extertions are necessary because the God these mystics venerate is not near us but "far removed from the area of man's comprehension, even though his hidden glory may be revealed to man from the Throne" [67].

Scholem is of the opinion that Merkabah mysticism is "in no way heretical ... (because) these texts adhere strictly to monotheistic concepts". Perhaps, but the notion of the deus absconditus at all events implies a dualistic distance between God and humanity. For this reason I feel that this scholar errs when he thinks that "the theology presented ... does not conflict with the biblical concept of God". It does, because the immanence of God in the world is virtually ruled out here. I find it still more baffling when he writes that he is convinced that Merkabah texts show an 'essentially Gnostic character', of which he is convinced, while at the same time he states that they do not conflict with Talmudic orthodoxy. He calls this kind of Gnosis 'rabbinic Gnosis' [68]. In my opinion, Jewish orthodoxy and Gnosis, just like Christianity and Gnosis, are wholly incompatible entities. If we confuse these issues, we are hampering the discussion of them considerably.

f. The Book of Enoch

Since the full development of Jewish mysticism and kabbalism occurred only in a period posterior to that which I am treating, I must restrict myself to what I have stated already. I will now turn to a text we possess, dating, with reasonable certainty, from the first and second centuries A.D. This is the apocryphal Book of Enoch (Henoch) in which a description of the Chariot occurs; this description was an important platform for the development of Merkabah mysticism. The influence of this work on the apocalyptic genre was also very great.

Fragments of this book were found in the caves of Qumran; it must, therefore, date from the first century of our era or even earlier. This is also proved by the fact that it is quoted in the Letter of Jude [69]. It was written by an anonymous author, probably in the Hebrew langguage, but the Qumran fragments are in Aramaic. There has been a Greek translation, only part of which is extant. What we have of it was discovered in Egypt in 1886-1887 [70]. Particularly important is the translation into Ethiopian; from Ethiopia it was brought back to Europe in the eighteenth century [71]; it is known as 1 Enoch. There are several good editions and translations of it [72]. The book derives its name from a passage in Genesis (5:24) where it is said that "Enoch walked with God; then he was no more, for God took him". This was seen as an indication that this Enoch, while still living, had ascended to heaven. For this reason he became a model for the mystics [73].

Since the Ethiopian version, 1 Enoch, in all probability contains the oldest material, we shall focus our attention on this book [74]. It consists of five parts. The third part, the Book of Heavenly Luminaries, or the

Book of Astronomy, comprising Chapters 72-82, is the most ancient, in its original form probably dating from the third century B.C. The learned astronomical discussion, presented in the form of a vision, is of practical importance for the structure of the Jewish calendar (always a tricky problem) [75]. The second oldest part is the Book of Watchers, Chapters 1-36, in its original form dating from about 200 B.C. In it Enoch describes a visionary journey to the farthest edge of the world where he sees seven mountains built of precious stones. The one in the middle supports the throne of God [76].

This part is, in effect, a non-biblical disquisition on the origin of evil. Its dualistic character is already revealed in the opening sentence in which Enoch blesses the righteous but promises the removal of all the ungodly ones [77]. The anonymous author harks back to the story told in Gen. 6:1-4 relating how the children of man had handsome and beautiful daughters, and how the children of heaven, the angels, desired to beget children with them [78]. The children born of this alliance were of gigantic height [79].

This is authentically biblical material. However, the author adds many details, probably drawing on Greek and Near Eastern mythological traditions [80]. The leader of the lustful angels is called Semyaz, for instance; the names of the angelic commanders are also given as well as the place where the heavenly host alights on the earth, the summit of Mount Hermon [81].

In Genesis nothing specific is said about the Giants; they are not stigmatized as the source of evil. In Enoch, on the contrary, they constitute an order different from that of the human race, eating up all the food produce and damaging all nature severely. They also corrupted the people by introducing armour, cosmetics, adultery, magic, and astrology. "And all their conduct (human conduct is meant) became corrupt" [82]. Then three archangels lodged a complaint against the wicked angels before the throne of the Most High accusing them not only of oppressing the earth but also of revealing "eternal secrets which are performed in heaven (and which) man learned" [83].

The Lord now orders the faithful archangels Raphael, Gabriel, and Michael, to make war on the wicked, to "give life to the earth which the angels have corrupted" (the bad angels are called 'Watchers' in this passage), and to destroy the children of adultery. Finally, the deviant angels will be bound and thrown 'into the bottom of fire' [84]. Then a golden age of blessings and happiness will be ushered in in which "all the children of the people will become righteous ... and the earth will be cleansed from all pollution, and from all sin, and from all plague, and from all suffering" [85]. This vision is at once apocalyptic and dualistic.

So far Enoch himself has not been mentioned, but now he makes a rather sudden appearance [86]. When he comes announcing God's judgment to the fallen and humbled Watchers, they ask him to plead their cause before the throne of God [87]. The prophet is prepared to do this and brings a petition to the Most High. He then has a vision in which God orders him to tell the Watchers that his sentence is inexorable [88]. This vision is recounted at some length in Chapters 14-16.

In this section Enoch describes how he was lifted from the earth and transported to the throne-room of God. According to Knibb, this is "the earliest example of such an ascent-vision which was to become such an important element in other pseudepigraphical writings and in later Jewish mystical writings" [89]. For the author of Enoch this presents an apt opportunity to return to the subject that interests him most, the origin of evil. "The giants who were born from body and flesh will be called evil spirits on earth, and on the earth will be their dwelling ... The dwelling of the spirits of heaven is in heaven". The evil spirits will "do wrong and are corrupt ... and cause sorrow ... (They) will rise against the sons of men and against the women because they came out (from them)" [90]. The celestial secrets that the Watchers disclosed to the people are now declared worthless; they only brought sin into the world : "through this mystery the men and the women cause evil to increase on the earth" [91].

This account of the origin of evil is very different from that given in Gen. 3. There the first human beings themselves are sinning, although seduced by the serpent; here, however, the active part is played by the wicked Watchers who are the real cause of sin and evil; the people are hardly more than helpless victims. Heaven and earth are dualistically opposed; in this section there is no talk of hell as the abode of the evil spirits. Furthermore, there is no promise of redemption but only the announcement of final destruction.

Another section is that of the (three) Parables (or 'similitudes'), Chapters 37-71. They are of uncertain date; Knibb believes that they date from the first century A.D., 'from towards the end of the century' [92]. In these Parables there is much talk of 'the Son of Man' (or 'the Chosen One'), based on Dan. 7:13-14 where the prophet in a vision sees 'one like a human being to whom sovereignty and kingly power were given'. The last chapter of the Parables identifies Enoch himself with this Son of Man [93].

What is interesting in our context is that the author of Enoch too adopts that same fierce antipolitical stance that is characteristic of some other Jewish writings of this period, like the Book of Revelation in the New Testament and the Essenian War Scroll. "When the secrets of the Righteous One (= God) are revealed, he shall judge the sinners ...; from that time those who possess the earth will neither be rulers or princes ... At that moment, kings and rulers shall perish, they shall be delivered into the hands of the righteous and holy ones, and from then on nobody shall be able to induce the Lord of the Spirits to show them mercy, for their life is annihilated" [94].

The second Parable is still more outspoken. The Son of Man will "remove the kings and the mighty ones from their comfortable seats and the strong ones from their thrones. He shall loosen the reins of the strong and crush the teeth of the sinners." The reason for their downfall is also stated. "They do not extol and glorify him (God), and neither do they obey him, the source of the kingdom." This means that earthly kings are seen as usurpers of the divine kingship and, therefore, as inherently wicked. "They have become the judges of the stars of heaven ...; all their deeds are oppression ... And their devotion is to the gods which they have fashioned with their own hands. But they deny the name of the Lord of the Spirits" [95]. It is clear that in the eyes of the author of Enoch earthly potentates form a conspiracy against God.

"On the day of judgment all the kings and governors shall see and recognize him (God) - how he sits on his throne of glory ... (Then these) kings, governors, and all the landlords shall (try to) bless him who rules over everything ...(They) shall fall down before him on their faces, and worship him and raise their hopes in the Son of Man." But their late repentance will be of no avail to them. For the Lord "will deliver them to the angels for punishments in order that vengeance shall be executed on them - oppressors of his children and the elect ones" [96]. "Their faces shall be filled with shame before that Son of Man, and from before his face they shall be driven out. And the sword shall abide in their midst, before his face" [97].

We end with the Book of Dreams, in Chapters 83-90 (the last section, the so-called Epistle of Enoch, Chapters 91-107, admonishes the wicked to repent and the righteous to persevere). The Book of Dreams, or Dream Visions, consists of two parts. The first one foretells the Deluge (the biblical Enoch lived before it) when all the sinners will be punished. The second recapitulates the history of the people of Israel but in a daring way since human beings are represented as animals, the patriarchs as oxen, the people as sheep, the Messiah as a white bull with great horns, and so on. The last historic event that can be identified is the War of the Maccabees. In the closing sections the vision becomes truly apocalyptic; this vision bears a certain resemblance to the War Scroll of the Essenes because here too a war of the just against their godless oppressors is described albeit in metaphorical terms.

"The Lord of the sheep came unto them and took in his hand the rod of his wrath and smote the earth; and all the beasts and birds of the heavens (= the oppressors of the faithful) fell down from the midst of those sheep and were swallowed up in the earth, and it was covered upon them. Then I saw that a great sword was given to the sheep; (the following text is somewhat illogical - F.) and the sheep proceeded against the beasts of the field in order to kill them; and all the beasts and birds of heaven fled from before their face." In the final judgment that now follows the godless are condemned. "Another abyss ..., full of fire, was opened in the middle of the ground; and they brought those blinded sheep (= the unfaithful Jews), all of which were judged, found guilty, and cast into this fiery abyss, and they were burned." When the judgment is over, the Messianic realm begins [98].

NOTES TO CHAPTER VI

1. Moshe David Herr s.v. 'Oral law'. Enc.Jud. 12, 1439.
2. Louis Jacobs s.v. 'Halakhah', Enc.Jud. 7, 1156.
3. See Strack/Stemberger, Einleitung, 1. Teil, Kap. VII Sprachen der rabbinischen Literatur, and The Study of Ancient Judaism, Vol. II. Ed. J. Neussner. Nw York, 1981.
4. It am indebted to Prof. N.A. van Uchelen for illuminating me in this difficult and confusing subject.
5. Louis Jacobs s.v. 'Development of Halakhah'. Enc.Jud. 7, 1161.
6. Louis Jacobs s.v. 'Development of Halahkah', Enc.Jud. 7, 1163.
7. Strack/Stemberger. Einleitung 169 says that the final redaction took place at some time around 429, probably in Tiberias.
8. Strack/Stemberger, Einleitung 186 says that it is an encyclopaedia : "everything that was taught in the rabbinical schools and that was seen as fit to be treasured up was incorporated in it : legends ..., anecdotes about rabbis, historical reminiscences, things worth knowing in medicine, biology, mathematics, astronomy, astrology, etc. ..., a national library of Babylonian Jewry".
9. Travers Herford, Christianity 35-96 lists all the passages in the Talmud relating to Jesus.
10. Maier, Jesus 268-273.
11. Maier, Jesus 273-275.
12. Ziegler, Kampf 53.
13. Ziegler, Kampf 73/74.
14. Sanh. 10:6, 29c 57. Segal, Two Powers 7 says 24 is a conventional number. His reference to 10.5 is erroneous.
15. Segal, Two Powers 7, note 7.
16. Herford, Christianity 376.
17. Daniel Sperber s.v. 'min', Enc.Jud. 12.
18. Büchler, Studies 247 and 271.

19. Osefta Shabbat 13.5. The Tosefta is a collection of 'baraitot' ('beraitot' in Aramaic). Baraita (beraita) signifies 'outside' but may somewhat loosely be rendered by 'tradition'. 'Outside' means that these 'traditions' do not form part of the Mishnah.
20. Urbach, The Sages I 26.
21. Urbach, The Sages I 26. An etymologically similar word is the Arab 'kafir' = unbeliever, which is used in Islam. From there it came to denote a tribe in Southern Africa, the Kaffirs. Less specifically it can signify 'boors, stupid people' (Dutch : 'kaffer, a term of abuse which, in primary school, we liberally applied to our classmates).
22. Sifre to Deuteronomy 329, cit. Herford, Christ. 299/300. Hebrew text in Siphre zu Deuteronomy. Eds. H.S.Horovitz/Louis Finkelstein. Corpus Tannaiticum. Abt. 3. Hallachische Midraschim. Teil 3. Band 2. Breslau, 1935-1939. The sifre(i) is "a running exegetical Midrash (commentary) to the Book of Deuteronomy expounding the text chapter by chapter and verse by verse", Daniel Sperber s.v. 'Sifrei', Enc.Jud. 14, 1520. The Sifrei does not form part of the Talmud.
23. Segal, Two Powers 89.
24. Mekhilta (to Exodus), Parasha Hashira (Beshallakh) 4,15,3, cit. Herford, Christ. 300. Translation : Mechiltha. Ein tannaitischer Midrash zu Exodus (deutsch). Herausgeber Jakob Winter und Aug. Wünsche. Leipzig, 1909.
25. Segal, Two Powers 7.
26. Tosefta Shetitat Hullin 2:24.
27. Prov. 5:8.
28. Bergmann, Jüd.Apol. 26/27.
29. See Urbach, sages I, 116.
30. Urbach, The Sages I, 178/179.
31. Urbach, The Sages I, 182/183.
32. Urbach, The sages I, 185.
33. Urbach, The Sages I, 205/206.
34. Urbach, The Sages I, 214.
35. Jos., Jew.Wars 3.8.5.
36. Urbach, Sages I, 217.
37. Urbach, The sages I, 218/219.
38. Jos., Jew.Wars 8.7.
39. Urbach, The Sages I, 224.
40. Urbach, The sages I, 249/250.
41. Haggadah 15a, cit. Segal, Two powers 22.

42. Segal, Two powers 22.
43. Harry Freedman s.v. 'Akiva', Enc.Jud. 2, 488.
44. Segal, Two powers 22.
45. Urbach, Sages I, 273.
46. Urbach, Sages I, 273.
47. Urbach, Sages I, 274/275.
48. See the article 'Kabbalah' (by the Ed.) in Enc.Jud. 10, 439, to which I am indebted for this section.
49. See Vol. IV, Ch. II.7c.
50. David Flusser s.v. 'Apocalypse', Enc.Jud. 3, 179.
51. Flusser s.v. Apocalypse, Enc.Jud. 3, 179, remarks that the Essenian Teacher of Righteousness is an exception to this since he presents himself as a prophet with knowledge of the end of times.
52. Flusser s.v. 'Apocalypse', Enc.Jud. 3, 180.
53. 'Kabbalah', Enc.Jud. 6, 497.
54. Scholem, Major Trends 5.
55. Scholem, Major Trends 9.
56. Scholem, Major Trends 9.
57. Scholem, Major Trends 13.
58. Scholem, Major Trends 13.
59. Scholem, Major Trends 11.
60. Schechter, Some Aspects 29-31.
61. Segal, Two powers 192.
62. Segal, Two powers 201.
63. Scholem, Kabbalah 14/15.
64. Ez. 1:15-21.
65. Ez. 1:26-28.
66. Eccl. 49:11.
67. Scholem, Kabbalah 16.
68. Scholem, Jewish Gnost. 10.
69. Jude 14-15.
70. Apocalypsis Henochi graece. Ed. M. Black. Pseudepigrapha Veteris Testamenti graece. Ed. A.M. Denis and M. de Jong III. Leiden, 1970. Also : The Last Chapters of Enoch in Greek. Ed. Campbell Bonner. Darmstadt, 1968. There are two Slavonic versions of the Greek text, probably dating from the tenth or eleventh centuries A.D. Le Livre des Secrets d'Hénoch. Texte slave et traduction

française par A. Vaillant. Textes publiés par l'Institut d'Études slaves IV, Paris. The Slavonic book is known as 2 Enoch.

71. By the traveller James Bruce.

72. A first translation (into English) appeared in 1821, followed by an edition of the original text in 1838, both by Archbishop Lawrence Bonner.

73. Jehoshua M. Grintz s.v. 'Enoch, Ethiopic Book of', Enc.Jud. 6, 795-797. Mention must also be made of the Hebrew Apocalypse of Enoch, indicated as 3 Enoch. There has been much discussion on the dating of this work. The fact is that 3 Enoch is a composite work in which several traditions come together some of which may be very ancient indeed. The question is when the final redaction took place. Charlesworth's cautious conclusion is that "it is impossible to reach a firm conclusion as to the date of 3 Enoch ... All things considered, then, though 3 Enoch contains some very old traditions and stands in a direct line with developments which had already begun in the Maccabean era, a date for its final redaction in the fifth or sixth century A.D. cannot be far from the truth", The Old Testament Pseudepigrapha I. Apocalyptic Literature and Texts. Ed. James H. Charlesworth. London, 1983, 228/229.

74. Of the several translations I mention that by Charlesworth (see foregoing note), by Siegbert Uhlig, Das äthiopische Henochbuch. Jüdische Schriften aus hellenistisch-römischer Zeit. Band V, Apocalypsen. Gütersloh, 1984, by G. Beer, Das Buch Henoch. Die Apocryphen und Pseudepigraphen des alten Testaments. Zweiter Band, Die Pseudepigraphen des Alten Testaments. Tübingen, 1900, by R.H. Charles, 1 Enoch. The Apocrypha and Pseudepigrapha of the Old Testament in English. Vol. II Pseudepigrapha. Ed. R.H. Charles. Oxford, 1968 (1913 1), and by M.A. Knibb, The Ethiopic Book of Enoch (in consultation with Edward Ullendorf). 2 Vols. Oxford, 1978.

75. Knibb, Book of Enoch 28.

76. 1 Enoch 18.

77. 1 Enoch 1.1.

78. See Vol. IV, Ch. II.11b.

79. 1 Enoch 6-7.

80. Knibb, Enoch 32.

81. 1 Enoch 6.

82. 1 Enoch 7-8.

83. 1 Enoch 9.

84. Jude 6 alludes to this.

85. 1 Enoch 10.

86. Knibb, Enoch 30 supposes that the author took over Ch. 6-11 from a so-called Book of Noah which has got lost.
87. 1 Enoch 12.
88. 1 Enoch 13-14.
89. Knibb, Enoch 40.
90. 1 Enoch 15:8-12.
91. 1 Enoch 16:1-4.
92. Knibb, Enoch 44.
93. 1 Enoch 71:14.
94. 1 Enoch 38:3-6.
95. 1 Enoch 46.
96. 1 Enoch 62.
97. 1 Enoch 63:11.
98. 1 Enoch 90.

BIBLIOGRAPHY

I ORIGINAL SOURCES

A COLLECTIONS

ANTHOLOGIA LYRICA GRAECA I. Ed. Ernestus Diehl. 1936 2 (1922 1).

ANTIKE BERICHTE ÜBER DIE ESSENER. Eds. A. Adam und C. Burchard. 1972 2.

THE GNOSTIC SCRIPTURES. A new translation with annotations and introduction by Bentley Layton. Garden City, NY, 1987.

GNOSTICISM. An Anthology. Ed. Robert M. Grant. London, 1961.

THE NAG HAMMADI LIBRARY IN ENGLISH. Ed. James M. Robinson. Leiden, 1977.

NEUTESTAMENTLICHE APOCRYPHEN. Herausg. Edgar Hennecke. Tübingen, 1924 (zweite, völlig umgearbeitete und vermehrte Auflage) (1904 1).

QUELLEN ZUR GESCHICHTE DER CHRISTLICHEN GNOSIS. Herausg. Walther Völker. Tübingen, 1932.

VORSOKRATIKER, DIE FRAGMENTE DER --. Herausg. Hermann Diels und Walther Kranz. Erster Band. 1974 (1903 1). Erster Band 1974 (1903 1). Zweiter Band. 1972 (1903 1). Cited as DK.

B INDIVIDUAL AUTHORS

ACTUS PETRI
  Neutestamentliche Apocryphen. Herausg. Edgar Hennecke. Tübingen, 1924.

ACTUS VERCELLENSES
  Neutestamentliche Apocryphen. Herausg. Edgar Hennecke. Tübingen, 1924.

AESCHYLUS
Translated by Herbert Weird Smyth. Loeb Classical Library 145 and 146. London/Cambridge (Mass.), 1922 and 1926 1.

ARCHILOCHUS
Fragmenta. Ed. Giovanni Tarditi. Roma, 1968.
Archiloque, Fragments. Eds. François Laserre et André Bonnard. Collection Budé. Paris, 1958.

ARISTOTLE
On the Generation of Animals. Translated by A.L. Peck. Loeb Classical Library 366. London/Cambridge (Mass.), 1937 1.
Metaphysics. Translated by Hugh Tredennick. Loeb Classical Library 271 and 287. London/Cambridge (Mass.), 1933 and 1935 1.
Poetics. Translated by W. Hamilton Fyfe. Loeb Classical Library 199. London/Cambridge (Mass.), 1927 1.
Politics. Translated by H. Rackham. Loeb Classical Library 264. London/Cambridge (Mass.), 1932 1.

AUGUSTINUS
De Civitate Dei. The City of God against the pagans. Translated by George E. McCracken. Loeb Classical Library 411-417. Cambridge (Mass.)/London, 1963-1972.

CALLIMACHUS
Hymns and Epigrams. Translated by A.W. Mair. Loeb Classical Library 129. London/Cambridge (Mass.), 1955 rev. ed. (1921 1).

CLEMENS OF ALEXANDRIA
1. Eclogae propheticae. Herausg. Die griechischen christlichen Schrifsteller der ersten drei Jahrhunderte. Clemens Alexandrinus, 3. Bd. Herausg. Otto Stählin. Leipzig, 1909.
2a. Stromateis. Die griechischen christlichen Schrifsteller der ersten drei Jahrhunderte. Clemens Alexandrinus, 2. Bd. Herausg. Otto Staehlin. Leipzig, 1906.
2b. Des Clemens von Alexandrien Teppiche. Herausg. Otto Staehlin. Bibliothek der Kirchenväter. 2. Reihe, Bd. XVII. Clemens von Alexandreia, Bd. III. München, 1936.

CYRILLUS OF JERUSALEM
Catecheses. Patrologiae graecae Tomus XXXIII. Paris, 1857.

THE DEAD SEA SCROLLS OF THE ST. MARK'S MONASTERY. 2 Vols. Ed. M. Burrows. New Haven, 1950/1951.

THE DEAD SEA SCROLLS IN ENGLISH. Translated by Geza Vermes. Penguin Books. 1975 (1962 1).

DIOGENES LAERTIUS
Lives of eminent philosophers. Translated by R.D. Hicks. Loeb Classical Library 184 and 185. Cambridge (Mass.)/London, 1970-1972 (1925 1).

EPIPHANIUS
Panarion haeresium. Die griechischen christlichen Schriftsteller der ersten drei Jahrhunderte. Epiphanius I. Herausg. Karl Holl. Leipzig, 1915.

EUSEBIUS
Historia ecclesiastica. Die griechischen christlichen Schriftsteller der ersten drei Jahrhunderte. Eusebius II.1. Herausg. Eduard Schwartz. Leipzig, 1903.

EUSTATHIUS
Eustathii Commentarii ad Homeri Odysseam. Tomus I. Leipzig, 1825 (photomechanischer Nachdruck 1960).

EURIPIDES
Translated by A.S. Way. Loeb Classical Library 9-12. London/Cambridge (Mass.), 1912 1.

EZNIK of Kolb
Wider die Irrlehren. Der armenischen Kirchenväter ausgewählte Schriften aus dem armenischen übersetzt. Herausge. Dr. Simon Weber. I. Bd. Bibliothek der Kirchenväter, Bd. 57. München, 1927.

FILASTRIUS
Diversarum hereseon liber. Herausg. Fridericus Marx. Corpus Scriptorum Ecclesiastorum Latinorum. XXXVIII. Prague/Vienna/Leipzig, 1888.

THE GNOSTIC SCRIPTURES - a new translation with annotation and introduction by Bentley Layton. Garden City, NY, 1987.

HERODOTUS
The Histories. Translated by A.D. Godley. Loeb Classical Library 117-120. London/Cambridge (Mass.), 1920-1924 1.

HESIOD
Translated by Hugh G. Evelyn-White. Loeb Classical Library 57. London/Cambridge (Mass.), 1914 1.
Fragmenta Hesiodea. Ed. R. Merkelbach and M.L. West. Oxford, 1967.

HIPPOCRATES
Law
Regimen in acute diseases
The Sacred Disease
Translated by W.H.S. Jones. Loeb Classical Library 148. London-Cambridge (Mass.), 1923 1.

HIPPOLYTUS
Refutatio omnium haeresium. Die griechischen christlichen Schriftsteller der ersten drei Jahrhunderte. Bd. 26. Hippolytus, 3. Bd. Ed. Paul Wendland. Leipzig, 1916.

HOMER
The Iliad. Translated by A.T. Murray. Loeb Classical Library 170 and 171. London/Cambridge (Mass.), 1924 1.
The Odyssey. Translated by A.T. Murray. Loeb Classical Library 104 and 105. London/Cambridge (Mass.), 1919 1.

IRENAEUS LUGDUNENSIS
Adversus haereses. Contre les héresies. Eds. Adelin Rousseau and Louis Doutreleau. Vol. 2 Textes latin et grec et traduction. Paris, 1982.

JEROME
Adversus Jovinianum. Patrologia Tomus XXIII. Paris, 1845.

JOSEPHUS, Flavius
1. Jewish Antiquities. Ed. Ralph Marcus. Loeb Classical Library. London/Cambridge (Mass.), 1957 (1943 1).
2. Vita. The Life. Ed. H.St.J. Thackeray. Loeb Classical Library. London/Cambridge (Mass.), 1956 (1926 1).
3. The Jewish War. Ed. H.St.J. Thackeray. Loeb Classical Library. London/Cambridge (Mass.), 1956 (1927 1).

JUSTINUS MARTYR
Apologia. Die ältesten Apologeten. Herausg. Edgar J. Goodspeed. Göttingen, 1914.

MECHILTHA. Ein tannaitischer Midrash zu Exodus (deutsch). Herausg. Jakob Winter und Aug. Wünsche. Leipzig, 1909.

ORIGENES
Contra Celsum. Die griechischen christlichen Schriftsteller der ersten drei Jahrhunderte. Origenes Werke. 2. Bd. Herausg. Paul Koetschau. Leipzig, 1899.

PARMENIDES
David Gallop, Parmenides of Elea. Fragments. A Text and Translation with an Introduction by --. University of Toronto Press, 1984.

PHILO
1. Hypothetica.
2. Quod omnis homo probus liber sit (Every good man is free).
Ed. F.H. Colson. Loeb Classical Library. London/Cambridge (Mass.), 1954 (1941 1).

PINDAR
  Translated by J.E. Sandys. Loeb Classical Library. London/Cambridge (Mass.), 1915 1.

PLATO
  Epinomis. Ed. Edouard des Places, Platon. Oeuvres complètes. Vol. XII. Paris, 1956.
  Euthydemus. Translated by R.M. Lamb. Loeb Classical Library 165. London/Cambridge (Mass.), 1924 1.
  Letters (Ep.). Translated by R.G. Bury. Loeb Classical Library 234. Cambridge (Mass.)/London. 1975 (1929 1).
  Meno (see under Euthydemus).
  Phaedo. Translated by H.N. Fowler. Loeb Classical Library 36. London/Cambridge (Mass.), 1914 1.
  Phaedrus (see under Phaedo).
  The Republic. Translated by Paul Shorey. Loeb Classical Library 237 and 276. London/Cambridge (Mass.), 1930 and 1935 1.

PLINIUS
  Naturalis historia. Natural history. Ed. H. Rackham. Loeb Classical Library. London/Cambridge (Mass.), 1942 4.

PLUTARCH
  Coriolanus. Translated by B. Perrin. Loeb Classical Library 80. London/Cambridge (Mass.), 1916 1.

PSEUDOCLEMENS
  1. Homilien. Die griechischen christlichen Schriftsteller der ersten drei Jahrhunderte. Die Pseudoclementinen I. Herausg. Bernhard Rehm. Berlin, 1953.
  2a. Recognitiones. Neutestamentliche Apokryphen. Herausg. Edgar Hennecke. Tübingen, 1924.
  2b. Recognitionen in Rufins Übersetzung. Herausg. Bernhard Rehm. Berlin, 1965.

SANHEDRIN. Übersetzung des Talmud Yerushalmi, Bd. IV.4, übersetzt von Gerd A. Wevers. Tübingen, 1981.

SIPHRE ZU DEUTERONONIUM. Eds. H.S. Horovitz/Louis Finkelstein. Corpus Tannaiticum. Abt. 3 Halachische Midraschim. Teil 3, band 2. Breslau, 1935-1939.

SOPHOCLES
  Translated by F. Storr. Loeb Classical Library 20 and 31. Cambridge (Mass.)/London, 1912 and 1913 1.

TERTULLIANUS
  1. De anima. Tertulliani opera pars II. Ed. J.H. Waszink. Corpus Christianorum serie latina. Turnhout, 1954.
  2. De carnis resurrectione. Tertulliani opera pars II. Ed. J.g.Ph. Borleffs. Corpus Christianorum serie latina. Turnhout, 1954.

DIE TEXTE AUS QUMRAN. Herausg. Eduard Lohse. München (1971 2).

THEOCRITUS
The Greek Bucolic Poets. Translated by J.M. Edmonds. Loeb Classical Library. London/Cambridge (Mass.), 1912 1.

THEODORETUS
Haereticarum Tabularum Compendium. Operum Tomus IV. Paris, 1642.

THEOPHRASTUS
De sensibus. STRATTON, George Malcolm, Theophrastus and the Greek physiological pyschology before Aristotle. (Greek text with introduction and translation). Amsterdam, 1964 (reprint of the edition London, 1917).

THUCYDIDES
History of the Peloponnesian War. Translated by C.F. Smith. Loeb Classical Library 108, 09, 110 and 169. London/Cambridge (Mass.), 1919-1923.

VERGILIUS
Aeneis. Translated by H.R. Fairclough. Loeb Classical Library 63. Cambridge (Mass.)/London, 1935.

XENOPHON
Memorabilia. Translated by E.C. Marchant. Loeb Classical Library 168. London/Cambridge (Mass.), 1923 1.

THE ZADOKITE DOCUMENTS. Ed. by Chaim Rabin with a translation and notes. Oxford, 1954.

II SECONDARY WORKS

A WORKS OF REFERENCE

A BIBLIOGRAPHY OF HOMERIC SCHOLARSHIP. Eds. David W. Packard and Tania Meyers. Preliminary Edition 1930-1970. Malibu (Ca.), 1974.

BOISACQ, Emile, Dictionnaire étymologique de la langue grecque étudiée dans ses rapports avec les autres langues indo-européennes. Heidelberg, 1916 (photostatic reprint Heidelberg, 1950).

CHANTRAINE, Pierre, Dictionnaire étymologique de la langue grecque. Histoire des mots. Paris (1968).

CONCORDANCE, A COMPLETE -- TO THE COMEDIES AND FRAGMENTS OF ARISTOPHANES. Ed. Henry Dunbar, revised by Benedette Mazzullo. Hildesheim/New York, 1973 (original edition Oxford, 1883).

A CONCORDANCE TO EURIPIDES. Eds. James T. Allen and Gabriel Italie. London, 1954.
CONCORDANCE TO THE HESIODIC CORPUS. Ed. William W. Minton. Leiden, 1976.

THE ENCYCLOPEDIA OF THE JEWISH RELIGION. Eds. R.J.Zwi Werblowsky and Geoffrey Wigoder. New York/Chicago/San Francisco, 1966.

ENCYCLOPAEDIA JUDAICA. Jersualem, 1971.

THE ENCYCLOPEDIA OF RELIGION. Ed. Mircea Eliade. New York-London, 1987.

A GREEK-ENGLISH LEXICON. Eds. George Henry Liddell and Robert Scott. Oxford, 1966 (new edition revised by Henry Stuart Jones) (1843 1).

A GREEK-ENGLISH LEXICON OF THE NEW TESTAMENT. Ed. Joseph Henry Thayer. Edinburgh (1908, reprint from 1901 4, 1885 1).

GRIECHISCH-DEUTSCHES WÖRTERBUCH ZU DEN SCHRIFTEN DES NEUEN TESTAMENTS UND DER FRÜHCHRISTLICHEN LITERATUR. Herausg. Walter Bauer. 6. völlig neu bearbeitete Auflage. Herausg. Kurt Aland und Barbara Aland. Berlin/New York, 1988.

HERODOTUS. Ed. Reginald Walter Macan. Vol. II. London, 1908. Index II.

HESIOD-KONDORDANZ. Ed. Joseph R. Tebben. A Computer Concordance to Hesiod. Series : Alpha - Omega. Reihe A. Vol. XXXIV. Hildesheim/New York, 1977.

INDEX AESCHYLEUS. Ed. G. Italie. Leiden, 1964 2 (1955 1).

INDEX ANTIPHONTEUS. Ed. Frank Louis van Cleef. Hildesheim, 1964 (reprographischer Nachdruck der Ausgabe Ithaca (NY), 1895).

INDEX ARISTOPHANEUS. Ed. O.J. Todd. Cambridge, 1932.

INDEX ARISTOTELICUS. Aristotelis opera. Vol. V. Herausg. Hermann Bonitz. Berolini, 1870.

INDEX VERBORUM TO ARISTOTLE'S METAPHYSICA. Listes de fréquence. Eds. L. Delatte and others. Hildesheim/Zürich/New York, 1984.

INDEX HIPPOCRATICUS. Herausg. Josef-Hans Kühn und Ulrich Fleischer. Göttingen, 1989.

INDEX HOMERICUS, ed. August Gehring. Leipzig, 1891 (reprographischer Nachdruck, eingeleitet, durchgesehen und erweitert von Ulrich Fleischer. Hildesheim, 1970).

INDEX THUCYDIDEUS. Herausg. M.H.N. von Essen. Berlin, 1887.

THE JEWISH ENCYCLOPEDIA, Vol XI. Ed. G. Hirsch. London/New York, 1905.

JEWISH ENCYCLOPEDIA, THE UNIVERSAL --. Vol. 4. New York, 1948.

LESSICO DI SENOFANE. Ed. Nino Marinore. Roma, 1967 (reprographischer Nachdruck Hildesheim, 1972).

LEUMANN, Manu, Homerische Wörter. Schweizerische Beiträge zur Altertumswissenschaft 3. Basel, 1950.

LEXICO DE LOS HIMNOS DE CALIMACO. Ed. Emilio Fernandez-Galiano. Vol. I. Madrid, 1976.

LEXICON DES FRÜHGRIECHISCHEN EPOS. Begründet von Bruno Snell. 10. Lieferung. Redaktion Eva-Maria Voigt. Göttingen, 1982.

LEXICON HERODOTEUM. Ed. Johannes Schweighaeuser. London, 1830 2 (1824 1).

A LEXICON TO HERODOTUS. Ed. J. Enoch Powell. Cambridge, 1938.

LEXICON HESIODEUM. Ed. M. Hofinger. 4 vols. Leiden, 1975-1978.

LEXICON PINDARICUM. Ed. Johannes Rumpel. Leipzig, 1883.

LEXICON TO PINDAR. Ed. William J. Slater. Berlin, 1969.

LEXICON DER PLATONISCHEN BEGRIFFE. Herausg. Hugo Perls. Bern/München (1974).

LEXICON THEOCRITEUM. Ed. Ioannes Rumpel. Leipzig, 1879.

LEXICON THUCYDIDEUM. Herausg. E.-.A. Beitant, 1843 (photomechanischer Nachdruck Hildesheim, 1961).

LEXICON XENOPHONTEUM. Herausg. Frid.Guil. Sturz. Vol. I. Leipzig, 1801 (reprographischer Nachdruck, Hildesheim, 1964).

LEXIKON FÜR THEOLOGIE UND KIRCHE. Freiburg (1959 2).

LEXIQUE DE LA RHÉTORIQUE D'ARISTOTE. Ed. André Wartelle. Paris, 1982.

MARCOVICH, M., Heraclitus. Greek text with a short commentary. Merida (Venezuela), 1967. See its Index Verborum Heracliti.

A PATRISTIC GREEK LEXICON. Ed. G.W.H. Lampe. Oxford, 1961.
PLATO DICTIONARY. Ed. Morris Stockhammer. New York (1963).

PAULYS REAL-ENCYCLOPÄDIE DER CLASSISCHEN ALTERTUMS-WISSENSCHAFT. Neue Bearbeitung herausgegeben von Georg Wissowa. Stuttgart, 1894-. (Cited as PW).

REALLEXIKON FÜR ANTIKE UND CHRISTENTUM. Stuttgart, 1950-.

SCHMIDT, J.H. Heinrich, Synonymik der griechischen Sprache I. Stuttgart, 1876 (reprographischer Nachdruck Amsterdam, 1967).

VORSOKRATIKER, DIE FRAGMENTE DER --. Herausg. Hermann Diels und Walther Kranz. Dritter Band. Wortindex. 1975 (1910 1). Cited as DK.

A WORD INDEX TO PLATO. Ed. Leonard Brandwood. leeds, 1976.

B MONOGRAPHS

ALLEGRO, J.M., The Dead Sea Scrolls. London, 1956.

ARNOLD, Gottfried, Unpartheyische Kirchen- und Ketzerhistorie; vom Anfang des Neuen Testaments auf das Jahr Christi 1688. Frankfurt am Main, 1700-1715.

ANZ, W., Zur Frage nach dem Ursprung des Gnostizismus. Texte und Untersuchungen zur Geschichte der altchristlichen Literatur, XV.4. Leipzig, 1897.

ARMSTRONG, Arthur Hilary, Gnosis and Greek Philosophy. Gnosis. Festschrift für Hans Jonas. Herausg. Barbara Aland. Göttingen (1978).

AUERBACH, Erich, Mimesis. Dargestellte Wirklichkeit in der abendländischen Literatur. Bern/München, 1977 6 (1946 1).

BAAREN, Th. van, Towards a Definition of Gnosticism. Studies in the History of Religions (Supplements to Numen XII). L'origini del Gnosticismo. Colloquio di Messina, 13-18 Aprile 1966. Ed. Ugo Bianchi. Leiden, 1970.

BAIGNET, Michael, and LEIGH, Richard, The Dead Sea Scrolls Deception. London, 1991.

BAUMGARTEN, Joseph M., Studies in Qumran law. Studies in Judaism in Late Antiquity. Vol. 24. Leiden, 1977.

BECKWITH, Isbon T., The Apocalypse of John. Grand Rapids, 1967.

BENADETE, Seth, Herodotean Inquiries. The Hague, 1969.

BERGMANN, J., Jüdische Apologetik im neutestamentlichen Zeitalter. Berlin, 1908.

BEYSCHLAG, Karlman, Simon Magus und die christliche Gnosis. Wissenschaftliche Untersuchungen zum Neuen Testament 16. Tübingen, 1974.

BIANCHI, Ugo,
1. Perspectives de la recherche sur les origines du Gnosticisme. L'origini del Gnosticismo. Colloquio di Messina 13/16 Aprile 1966. Ed. Ugo Bianchi. Leiden, 1977.
2. A propos de quelques discussions récentes sur la terminologie, la définition et la méthode de l'étude du Gnosticisme. Proceedings of the International Colloquium on Gnosticism. Stockholm, 1970.

BLYTHE, Donald, The Vocabulary of Menander considered in its relation to the koine. Amsterdam, 1969 (reprint of the edition by Princeton University Press, 1913).

BOUSSET, Wilhelm, Die Religion des Judentums im späthellenistischen Zeitalter. Handbuch zum Neuen Testament 24. Tübingen, 1926 (3. verbesserte Auflage, herausgegeben von Hugo Gressmann).

BRAUN, Herbert, Spätjüdisch-häretischer und frühchristlicher Radikalismus. Jesus von Nazareth und die essenische Qumransekte. 2 Bde. Beiträge zur historischen Theologie 24. Tübingen, 1957.

BÜCHLER, Adolf, Studies in Jewish History. London, 1956.

BULTMANN, Rudolph,
1. Das Evangelium des Johannes. Göttingen, 1941 1.
2. Das Problem der Ethik bei Paulus. Exegetika. Herausg. Erich Dinkler. Tübingen, 1967.
3. Das Urchristentum im Rahmen der antiken Religionen. Hamburg, 1962 (1949 1).

BURKERT, Walter, Greek Religion archaic and classical. Oxford, 1984.

CHANTRAINE, Pierre, Morphologie historique du grec. Paris (1961 2) (1945 1).

CHORUS, A., Een psychologische kijk op de vier evangelisten (A psychological view of the four Gospel authors). Haarlem, second impression (without date).

COLPE, Carsten, Gnosis II (Gnostizimus). Reallex.f.Ant.u.Christ. Bd. XI, 538-659. Stuttgart, 1981.

CONZE, Edward, Buddhism und Gnosis. L'origini del Gnosticismo. Colloquio di Messina 13-18 Aprile 1966. Ed. Ugo Bianchi. Leiden, 1970.

CRAHAY, Roland, Élements d'une mythopée gnostique dans la Grèce. L'origini del Gnosticismo. Colloquio di Messina 13-18 Aprile 1966. Ed. Ugo Bianchi. Leiden, 1977.

DANIÉLOU, Jean, Théologie du Judéo-Christianisme. Tournai, 1957.

DAVIES, Philip R., The Damascus Covenant. An Interpretation of the 'Damascus Covenant'. Journal for the Study of the Old Testament. Supplement Series 25. Sheffield, 1983.

DEURSEN, A. van, Palestina. Het land van de Bijbel. Baarn. Fourth impression w.d.

DUPONT-SOMMER, A.,
1. Culpabilité et rites de purification dans la secte juive de Qumran. Semitica 15 (1965). (German edition : Schuld und Reinigungsriten in der jüdischen Sekte von Qumran).
2. The Jewish Sect of Qumran and the Essenes. New Studies on the Dead Sea Scrolls. New York, 1956. (Translation by R.D. Barnett of the original French edition : Nouveaux aperçus sur les manuscrits de la Mer Morte, 1953.)

FOERSTER, W., Die 'ersten Gnostiker' Simon und Menander. L'origini del Gnosticismo. Colloquio di Messina 13-18 Aprile 1966. Ed. Ugo Bianchi. Leiden, 1970.

FOSSUM, J.E.,
1. Helena. In : Gnosis. De derde component van de Europese cultuurtraditie. Ed. G. Quispel. Utrecht, 1988.
2. The Name of God and the Angel of the Lord. The origins of the idea of intermediaries in Gnosticism. Utrecht (1982).

FOSSUM, J.E. and QUISPEL, G., Helena I (simonianisch). Reallex.für Ant.u.Christ. Bd. XIV, 338-355. Stuttgart, 1988.

FRÄNKEL, Hermann, Dichtung und Philosophie. Eine Geschichte der griechischen Epik, Lyrik und Prosa bis zur Mitte des fünften Jahrhunderts. München (Nachdruck 1976 der dritten durchgesehenen Auflage) (1950 1).

FREEMAN, Kathleen, The Life and Work of Solon. With a Translation of his Poems by --. New York, 1976.

FRICKEL, J.H.,
1. Die Apophasis megale, eine Grundschrift der Gnosis? L'origini del Gnosticismo. Colloquio di Messina 13-18 Aprile 1966. Ed. Ugo Bianchi. Leiden, 1970.

2. Die 'Apophasis megale' in Hippolyt's Refutatio (VI.-18) : Eine Paraphrase sur Apophasis Simons. Orientalia Christiana Analecta Bd. 182. Roma, 1968.

GEYER, G.J.A.M., Die Erkenntnistheorie des Aristoteles. Aalen, 1980 (Neudruck der Ausgabe Münster, 1917).

GRANGER, Gilles Gaston, La théorie aristotélicienne de la science. Paris, 1976.

GRANT, R.M., Gnosticism and early Christianity. New York, 1959.

GUARDINI, Romano, De Heer. Utrecht, 1947 (Dutch translation by Gabriel Smit of Der Herr. Würzburg, 1937).

HAARDT, Robert,
1. Bemerkungen zu den Methoden der Ursprungsbestimmung von Gnosis. L'origini del Gnosticismo. Colloquio di Messina 13-18 Aprile 1966. Ed. Ugo Bianchi. Leiden, 1970.
2. Die Gnosis. Wesen und Zeugnisse. Salzburg (1967).

HARNACK, Adolf von, Lehrbuch der Dogmengeschichte I. Die Entstehung des kirchlichen Dogmas. Tübingen, 1931 (5. photomechanisch gedruckte Auflage, 1885 I).

HERFORD, R. Travers, Christianity in Talmud and Midrash. London, 1903.

HILGENFELD, Alfred, Die Ketzergeschichte des Urchristentums urkundlich dargestellt. Leipzig, 1884 (photomechanischer Nachdruck Hildesheim, 1963).

HUART, Pierre, Le vocabulaire de l'analyse psychologique dans l'oeuvre de Thucydide. Paris, 1968.

HUPPENBAUER, Hans Walter, Der Mensch zwischen zwei Welten. Der Dualismus der Texte von Qumran (Höhle I) und der Damaskusfragmente. Ein Beitrag zur Vorgeschichte des Evangeliums. Abhandlungen zur Theologie des Alten und Neuen Testaments 34. Zürich, 1959.

JEREMIAS, Gert, Der Lehrer der Gerechtigkeit. Studien zur Umwelt des Neuen Testaments 2. Göttingen, 1962.

JONAS, Hans, Gnosis und spätantiker Geist. Teil I Die mythologische Gnosis. Göttingen, 1934.

KNIBB, M.A., The Ethiopic Book of Enoch. Outside the Old Testament. Ed. M. de Jonge. Cambridge Commentaries on writings of the Jewish and Christian world 200 B.C. to A.D. 200. Cambridge (1958).

LADD, George Eldon, Jesus and the Kingdom. The Eschatology of Biblical Realism. London, 1966.

LAFRANCE, Yvon, La théorie platonicienne de la doxa. MontréalParis, 1981.

LEISEGANG, Hans, Die Gnosis. Stuttgart, 1955 4 (1924 1).

LESHER, J.H., Perceiving and knowing in the Iliad and Odyssey. Phronesis 26 (1981).

LIBORON, Herbert, Die karpokratianische Gnosis. Untersuchungen zur Geschichte und der Anschauungswelt eines spätgnostischen Systems. Leipzig, 1938.

LÜDEMANN, Gerd, Untersuchungen zur simonianischen Gnosis. Göttinger Theologische Arbeiten Bd. 1. Göttingen, 1975.

LYONNET, Stanislas, St. Paul et le Gnosticisme : la Lettre aux Colossiens. L'origini del Gnosticismo. Colloquio di Messina 14-18 Aprile 1966. Ed. Ugo Bianchi. Leiden, 1970.

MAIER, Johann,
1. Jesus von Nazareth in der Talmudischen Überlieferung. Erträge der Forschung Bd. 82. Darmstadt, 1978.
2. Jüdische Auseinandersetzung mit dem Christentum in der Antike. Erträge der Forschung Bd. 177. Darmstadt, 1982.

MANN, Ulrich, Vorspiel des Heils. Die Uroffenbarung in Hellas. Stuttgart 1962).

MANSFELD, Jaap, Bad World and Demiurge : a 'Gnostic' motif from Parmenides and Empedocles to Lucretius and Philo. Studies in Gnosticism and Hellenistic Religions presented to Gilles Quispel. Eds. R. van den Broek and M.J. Vermaseren. Leiden, 1981.

MILIK, J.T., Die Geschichte der Essener. Herausgeg. von Karl Erich Grözinger and others. Wege der Forschung, Bd. CDX. Darmstadt, 1981. Originally : The Years of Discovery in the Wilderness of Judaea. Studies in Biblical Theology 26. London, 1959.

MURRAY, Gilbert, Five Stages of Greek Religion. Oxford (1930, 1925 1).

THE NEW TESTAMENT AND GNOSIS : Essays in honour of Robert McL. Wilson. Eds. A.H.B. Logan & A.J.M. Wedderburn. Edinburgh (1983).

NOCK, Arthur Darby, Essays on Religion and the Ancient World II. Ed. Zeph Stewart. Oxford, 1972.

L'ORIGINI DEL GNOSTICISMO. Colloquio di Messina, 13-18 Aprile 1966. Ed. Ugo Bianchi. Leiden, 1970.

OSTEN-SACKEN, Peter von der, Gott und Belial. Traditionsgeschichtliche Untersuchungen zum Dualismus in den Texten aus Qumran. Studien zur Umwelt des Neuen Testaments, Bd. 6. Göttingen (1969).
PAGELS, Elaine Hiesey, The Gnostic Paul. Gnostic Exegesis of the Pauline Letters. Philadelphia (1975).

PÉTREMENT, Simone, Le dualisme dans l'histoire de la philosophie et des religions. Introduction à l'étude du dualisme platonicien, du gnosticisme et du manichéisme. Paris, 1946.

PLAMBÖCK, Gerd, Erfassen - Gegenwärtigen - Innesein. Aspekte homerischer Psychologie. Kiel, 1959.

PLOEG, J.P.M. van der,
1. Le Rouleau de la Guerre. Traduit et annoté avec une introduction. Studies on the Texts of the Desert of Judah 2. Leiden, 1959.
2. Vondsten in de woestijn van Juda. Aula-boek 447. Utrecht/Antwerpen (1970, first printed as Prisma-boek 246, 1956). English translation by K. Smyth, Excavations at Qumran. London, 1986.

POWELL, Douglas, Clemens von Rom, Section 2 Die Pseudoclementinen. Theologische Realenzyklopädie. Bd. VIII. Berlin/New York, 1981.

QUISPEL, Gilles,
1. Gnosticism. Enc. of Rel. 5 s.v. New York/London, 1987.
2. Gnosis als Weltreligion. Zürich (1951).

ROWLEY, H.H.,
1. The History of the Qumran Sect. Bulletin of the John Rylands Library Manchester 49 (1966/1967). (German : Die Geschichte der Qumransekte).
2. The Zadokite Fragments and the Dead Sea Scrolls. Oxford, 1952.

RUDOLPH, Kurt
1. Die Gnosis. Wesen und Geschichte einer spätantiken Religion. Göttingen (1980 2, 1977 1).
2. Zum Problem : Mesopotamien (Babylonien) und Gnostizismus. L'origini del Gnosticismo. Colloquio di Messina 13-18 Aprile 1966. Ed. Ugo Bianchi. Leiden, 1970.
3. Randerscheinungen des Judentums und das Problem der Entstehung des Gnostizismus. Gnosis und Gnostizismus. Wege der Forschung, Bd. CCLXII. Darmstadt, 1975.

SANDMEL, Samuel, Judaism and Christian beginnings. New York, 1978.

SCHECHTER, Solomon, Some Aspects of Rabbinic Theology. London, 1909.

SCHNEIDER, Carl, Geistesgeschichte des Antiken Christentums. Bd. 1. München, 1954.

SCHOLEM, Gershom T.,
1. Jewish Gnosticism, Merkabah Mysticism, amd Talmudic Tradition. New York (1965, 2nd improved edition) (1959 1).
2. Kabbalah. Library of Jewish knowledge. Jerusalem (1974).
3. Major Trends in Jewish Mysticism. New York, 1946 (revised edition) (1941 1).

SCHUBERT, Kurt, Die Gemeinde vom Toten Meer. München, 1958.

SCHÜRER, Emile, The History of the Jewish People in the Age of Jesus Christ (175 B.C.-A.D. 135). A new English version revised and edited by Geza Vermes, Fergus Millar and Matthew Black. Vol. II. Edinburgh (1979) (original German edition 1886).

SEGAL, Alan F., Two powers in heaven. Early Rabbinic reports about Christianity and Gnosticism. Leiden, 1977.

SNELL, Bruno, Der Weg zum Denken und zur Wahrheit. Studien zur frühgriechischen Sprache. Reihe : Hypomnemata 57. Göttingen, 1978.

STRACK, Hermann L. and STEMBERGER, Günther, Einleitung in Talmud and Midrash. Siebente völlig neu bearbeitete Auflage. München (1982, 1987 1).

TOMSON, Peter J., Paul and the Jewish law : Halakha in the Letters of the Apostle to the Gentiles. Compendia Rerum Iudaicarum ad Novum Testamentum. Section III : Jewish Traditions in Ancient Christian Literature. Assen/Maastricht, 1990.

THE TOSEFTA. Ed. Saul Liebermann. New York, 1962. Translated from the Hebrew by Jacob Neusner. New York, 1981.

TREVER, J.C., The Untold Story of Qumran. Westwood, NJ, 1965.

URBACH, Ephraim Eliezer, The Sages. Their concepts and beliefs. Vol. I. Jerusalem, 1975. Translated by Israel Abrahams from the Hebrew edition 1971 2 (1969 2).

VAUX, Ronald de, Archaeology and the Dead Sea Scrolls. The Schweich Lectures of the British Academy. London, 1959.

VERMES, Geza, The Dead Sea Scrolls in Perspective. London, 1977.

WIDENGREN, Geo, Les origines du Gnosticisme et l'histoire des religions. L'origini del Gnosticismo. Colloquio di Messina, 13-18 Aprile 1966. Ed. Ugo Bianchi. Leiden, 1970.

WILSON, Robert MacLachlan, The Gnostic Problem. A Study of the Relations between Hellenistic Judaism and the Gnostic Heresy. London, 1958.

YADIN, Yigal, The Message of the Scrolls. London, 1957.

ZELLER, Eduard, Die Philosophie der Griechen in ihrer geschichtlichen Entwicklung. Bd. II.1. 1922 1 (photomechanischer Nachdruck Hildesheim 1963).

ZIEGLER, Ignaz, Der Kampf zwischen Judentum und Christentum in den ersten drei Jahrhunderten. Berlin, 1907.

GENERAL INDEX

Aaron, 155, 221, 235
Abiathar, 221
Abraham, 108, 132, 133, 148, 162, 164, 169
Absalom, 221, 232
Academy of Plato, 11, 13, 14, 75
Achaeans, 38, 40, 47, 63
Achilles, 38, 40, 42, 44, 47, 63
Achsenzeit, 27
Acre, 235
Acts of the Apostles, 86, 89, 130, 131, 132, 140, 142, 171, 172, 174, 259
Adam, 107, 108, 132
Admetus, 63
Adonijah, 221
Aeae, 40
Aegean Sea, islands, 226
Aeon(s), 8, 183-184
Aeschylus, 60-61, 82
Aeson, 60, 62
Agamemnon, 38, 44, 46, 60, 63
Agave, 63
Ahriman, 20, 111
Ahura Mazda, 19
Akiva, Akiba (Rabbi), 263, 264
Albright, William F., 205
Albright Institute see American School of Oriental Research
Alexander the Great, 8, 9, 27, 225
Alexandria (city), 87, 114, 115, 267
Alexandria (wife of Carpocrates), 114, 115
Alexandrian Empire, 238
Allegro, J.M., 244, 251
American Methodist University of Beirouth, 205

American School of Oriental Research, Jerusalem (Albright Institute), 205
Amidah, 175, 176
Amman, 244
Amoraim, Amoraic, 257
Amos, Prophecy of, 241
Ananias (High Priest), 173
Angels, 271
Anicetus, 120
Anacletus, 106
Anaxagoras, 71
Anaximander, 15, 16, 69
Anaximenes, 14, 69
Andromache, 44
Angra Mainyu, 19
Anticleia, 53
Antilochus, 44
Antinomianism, 26, 120
Antinous, 38
Antioch, 140, 165, 166, 172
Antiphon, 71
Antisemitism, 167, 168, 169, 175
Antonia (Roman citadel in Jerusalem), 137, 173
Antonius (father of Simon Magus), 87
Anz, W., 4, 20, 29
Aphrodite, 48, 92
Apocalypse of Enoch (Hebrew = 3 Enoch), 281
Apocalypse of John see Book of Revelation
Apocalypses, Jewish, 21, 28, 261, 267-268
Apophasis megale, 92-93, 95, 97, 123
Apollo, 42

Arabian, Arabs, 202, 204, 205, 206, 209, 279
Arabian desert, 28, 238
Aram Naharaim, 238
Aramaic, 155, 190, 238, 256, 257, 273
Archilochus, 58
Archonts, 8, 184-185
Ares, 48
Argives, 42
Argos (the dog of Odysseus), 48-49
Argos (the town), 46
Aricia, 88
Aristophanes, 68
Aristotle, 14, 15, 48, 74-75, 77, 80, 84, 85, 121
Ark of the Covenant, 236
Armenian, 34, 205
Armstrong, Arthur H., 18, 31
Arnim, H. von, 13, 30
Arnold, Gottfried, 3, 28
Arphaksad, 238
Asceticism, 268-269
Asia (Roman province), 104
Asia Minor, 104, 115, 140, 162, 165, 166, 172, 173, 177, 238
Assyria, 238
Athanasius Yeshua Samuel, 203, 204, 205, 206, 207
Athena, 42, 44, 46, 48, 49, 51, 52, 91
Athenian(s), 9, 65, 66
Atomist(s), 71
Athens, 11
Atomism, 15, 16, 17
Auerbach, Erich, 50
Augustinus, 122
Augustus (Roman emperor), 131

Baaren, Th. van, 28
Babylonia(n), 4, 8, 12, 20, 29, 151, 221, 226, 256, 257
Babylonian Captivity, 21, 155, 176, 257
Baigent, Michael, 244, 251
Bar Kochba, 210
Barbarian(s), 9, 10
Barnabas (companion of Paul), 140, 165, 166, 172
Bareille, G., 126, 127, 128

Baruch, Prophecy of, 267
Baur, Ferdinand-Christian, 4, 29
Beckwith, Isbon T., 193
Bedouin(s), 202, 203, 204, 206, 238
Beelzebul, 184
Belgian, 206
Belial, 218, 233, 237, 239, 240-241
Benadete, Seth, 64, 83
Benjamin (tribe of), 169, 235, 253
Bergmann, J., 279
Beroea, 173
Bethany, 147, 187
Bethlehem, 203, 205, 206
Beyschlag, Karlman, 121, 122
Bianchi, Ugo, 1, 28
Bible, 22, 92, 129, 208
Bleeker, J., 1
Bodewitz, H.W., 78
Boehme, Jakob, 3
Boeotia(n), 59, 60
Boisacq, Emile, 78
Bonner, Lawrence, 281
Bousset, Wilhelm, 4, 5, 97, 110, 111, 112, 123, 124, 126, 215, 247
Brandwood, Leonard, 84
Braun, Herbert, 247
Bremer, J.-M., 77
British, 202, 205, 206
Bruce, James, 281
Buddhism, Budhhist(s), 1, 7, 24-26
Büchler, Adolf, 260, 278
Bultmann, Rudolph, 5, 29, 182, 199
Burkert, Walter, 22, 23, 32
Burrows, M., 217, 247

Caesarea, 87, 120, 139, 165, 173
Caiphas (High Priest), 148
Calchas, 63
Callimachus, 64, 82
Calypso, 43
Canaan(ite), 139, 225, 236
Capernaum, 137
Carneades, 17
Carpocrates, 114-121
Carpocratian(s), 114-121, 126
Catholic Letters, 129, 142, 152
Celibacy, 213
Celsus, 127
Cephalene, 115
Cerinthians, 106

Cerinthus, 104-106
Chaldaeans, 226
Chantraine, Pierre, 33, 77, 78
Charlesworth, James H., 281
China, 27
Chirbeh Qumran, 209, 210
Chorus, A., 149, 150, 193
Christ see Jesus
Christian(s), 3, 4, 6, 19, 29, 87, 88, 89, 90, 101, 104, 105, 106, 109, 110, 115, 116, 120, 123, 125, 127, 130, 133, 140, 141, 142, 143, 145, 152, 161, 163, 164, 165, 167, 168, 170, 171, 171-175, 175-176, 176-177, 177, 178, 179, 185, 186, 189, 197, 198, 200, 203, 215, 259, 261, 262, 267
Christianity, 3, 4, 5, 6, 22, 26, 27, 28, 88, 89, 90, 99, 100, 101, 106, 107, 114, 122, 130, 140, 141, 147, 161, 163, 167, 168, 173, 176, 177, 251, 258, 259, 262, 273
Chronicles, Book of, 221
Chrysippus, 18
Chrysothemis, 62
Churches of the Reformation, 129
Circumcision, 105, 259
Claudius (emperor), 87
Clement of Alexandria, 12, 106, 114, 115, 118, 119, 120, 121, 126, 127, 128
Clement, bishop of Rome, 106
Clytemnestra, 61
Coelesyria, 27
Colossians, 189
Colpe, Carsten, 123
Comedy, Greek, 17
Commentary on Micah (Essenian), 230
Commentary on Psalm 37 (Essenian), 230
Community Rule, 208, 213, 217-219, 222-223, 239, 242
Conze, Edward, 25, 26, 32
Copper Scroll, 244
Corinth, Corinthians, 60, 140, 173, 189
Cornelius (first pagan convert), 140, 165
Corpus Hippocraticum, 67

Council (or Synod) of Jerusalem, 141, 166
Creon, 61, 62
Creusa, 62
Critias, 71
Croesus, 65
Cyprus, Cypriots, 226
Cyrillus of Jerusalem, 90, 122
Cyrus I, 65

Damascus, 109, 224, 249
Damascus Rule, 223, 224, 225, 227, 232, 233
Danaäns, 44
Daniel, 22
Daniel, Book of, 21-22, 151, 152,, 271 190, 225, 236, 267, 276
Daniélou, Jean, 1, 89, 105, 106, 122, 125
Danube, 65
Darius I, 65
David (king), 221, 232
Davies, Philip R., 248
Dead Sea, 201, 202
Dead Sea Scrolls, Chapter V passim
Delatte, L., 84
Delphic maxim, 57-58, 60, 69
Delphi, 62
Delphi, oracle of, 12
Demeter, cult of, 22
Demetrius II (king of Syria), 235
Demiurge, 8, 18
Democracy, 9
Democritus, 71
Demonianism, 136
Descartes, René, 35, 42
Detienne, Marcel, 24, 32
Deursen, A. van, 202, 244
Deus absconditus, 94, 107
Diaspora, 171, 172
Diehl, Ernestus, 81
Diels, H., 71
Dio Crysostom, 85
Diomedes, 43, 47, 48, 52
Dionysus, Dionysiac, Dionysian, 12, 23-24, 63
Ditheism, 262
Divine Man, 7
Docetism, Doocetes, docetist, 103, 187

Dominican (Order), 204
Dositheus, 89
Dualism, dualistic, 5, 7, 8, 9-10, 11, 16, 19, 20, 22, 23, 25, 26, 36, 73, 74, 76, 88, 89, 92, 93, 94, 95, 97, 98, 99, 100, 101, 102, 104, 105, 106, 107, 109, 110, 112, 117, 118, 119, 129, 133, 134-145, 145-177, 211, 213, 215, 216, 216-243, 255, 258, 261, 262, 263, 264, 264-266, 268, 270, 271
Dukas, Paul, 87
Dupont-Sommer, A., 215, 216, 218, 222, 244, 245, 246, 247, 248, 249, 251
Dutch, 34, 78, 201, 202, 204, 247, 279
Dzhuma, 202

Ecclesiastes, Book of, 21
École Biblique et Archéologique de Jérusalem, 204, 206, 207
Eleazar, 221
Elam, 238
Eleazar (Zealot priest), 263, 264
Electra, 61, 62
Eleusis, mysteries of, 10, 12, 22
Eli, 222
Eliezer ben Hurcanos (the Great), 262
Elpenor, 40
Empedocles, 12, 93
Egypt(ian), 9, 28, 63, 91, 92, 109, 114, 115, 226, 236, 238, 267, 273
Elbogen, Ismar, 176, 198
Emmaus, 138
English, 1, 34, 247, 258
Enoch (biblical person), 277
Enoch, Book of, 207, 267, 273-278, 281
Ephesus, 104, 133
Epicurus, Epicurean(s), Epicureanism, 11, 13, 15, 16, 17, 18, 76-77
Epinomis, 76, 85
Epiphanes, 114, 115, 119, 127
Epiphanius, 105, 116, 120, 124, 125, 127, 128
Esoteric, 33, 55, 59, 62, 65
Essenes, Essenian, 27, 89, 208-216, 258, 266, 268, 276, 280
Esther, Book of, 207

Ethiopia(n), 238, 273
Eucharist, 109
Eudoxus, 75
Eumaeus, 40, 49
Eumedes, 64
Euphrates, 10, 238
Euripides, 62, 82, 90
Europe(an), 26, 155, 273
Eurycleia, 49, 50, 51
Eurymachus, 48
Eusebius of Caesarea, 77, 104, 125
Eusthatius, bishop of Saloniki, 91, 122
Existentialism, 10
Ezekiel, Prophecy of, 224, 236, 269, 272
Eznik of Kolb, 31
Ezra Synagogue, Cairo, 223

Fathers of the Church, 2, 135, 167, 168
Felix, Marcus Antonius, 173, 174
Fenicia, 141
Filastrius, 115, 117, 127
Flusser, David, 267, 268, 280
Foerster, W., 122
Fossum, Jarl E., 124
Fränkel, Hermann, 16, 31
Freedman, Harry, 280
Freeman, Kathleen, 81
French, 1, 34, 247
Frickel, J.H., 123, 124
Friedländer, Marcus, 259
Fritz, Kurt von, 38, 43, 45, 79
Fuldner, 126

Gabriel, 178, 275
Galilee, 132, 160
Gallio, 173
Gallop, David, 84
Gamaliel I, 171
Gamaliel II, 176
Garden of Eden, 265
Gehinnom, 265
Gehring, August, 37
Genesis, Book of, 102, 108, 162, 266, 269, 272, 273
Gentiles, 139-141, 162, 164, 165, 166, 168, 173, 174, 177, 238, 239, 261

German, 1, 3, 4, 26, 34, 247
Germany, 6
Gethsemane, Garden of, 130, 160
Geyer, J.A.M., 84
gignooskein (verb), 8, Ch. II passim, 178-180
Gitta, 87
gnosis (Greek noun), 3, 7, 8, 25, Ch. II passim, 178-180
Gnosis, Ch. I passim, 36, 54, 55, 68, Ch. III passim, 185, 186, 187, 189, 217, 273
Gnostic(s), 2, 3, 4, 6, 7, 8, 10, 11, 12, 13, 14, 15, 17, 18, 19, 36, 37, 54, 55, 59, 68, 73, 76, 77, Ch. III passim, 130, 170, 176, 177, 178, 183 180, 181, 182, 185, 186, 187, 188, 189, 200, 260, 261, 262-264, 266, 273
Gnosticism see Gnosis
Gnosticizing, 9, 21, 27, 31, 72-74, 177-185, 185, 224
Goethe, Johann Wolfgang, 87
Götterburleske, 17
Gog and Magog, 236
Gospel of John, 5, 125, 129, 130, 145, 148, 149, 170-171, 184, 187, 188
Gospel of Luke, 80, 131, 132, 170
Gospel of Mark, 130, 169, 170, 196
Gospel of Matthew, 105, 130, 132, 169, 170, 196
Gospels, 129, 130, 132, 136, 145, 153, 169, 179
Granger, G.G., 74, 84
Grant, Robert M., 2, 28, 184, 185, 199
Great Vehicle see Mahayana Buddhism
Greece, 26, 27, 162, 172
Greek(s), 4, 5, 7, 8, 9, 10, 14, 15, 17, 18, 19, 26, 31, 33, 34, 36, 38, 44, 46, 48, 55, 56, 59, 68, 70, 76, 77, 80, 81, 87, 91, 93, 97, 101, 102, 104, 112, 146, 155, 172, 178, 191, 207, 225, 226, 238, 267, 273, 274
Grintz, Jehoshua M., 281
Guardini, Romano, 149, 193

Haardt, Robert, 29, 30
Habakkuk, Prophecy of, 226
Habakkuk Commentary, 226, 228, 231, 232, 233
Hades, 16, 40, 52, 54, 55
Haggadah, 257
Halahkah, 256, 257, 266-267
Hannah (mother of Samuel), 219
Harding, G.L., 206
Harnack, Adolf von, 4, 29
Harpocrates, 114
Hasmonaean House, 235
Hasmonaean Kingdom, 235
Hasmonaean Revolt, 156
Hebrew(s), 52, 146, 155, 169, 190, 191, 194, 204, 207, 207, 218, 225, 247, 253, 256, 257, 267, 273
Hebrew University of Jerusalem, 204
Hector, 39, 42
Hegel, Georg Friedrich, 90, 110, 163
Helena (of Troy), 63, 87, 90, 91
Helena (consort of Simon Magus), 87, 90-92, 93, 98, 99, 103, 123, 124
Hellenes, Hellenic see Greek(s)
Hellenism, Hellenistic, 2, 6, 7, 8, 9, 10, 17, 27, 28, 64, 67, 77, 91, 101, 130, 131, 140, 177, 178, 182, 217, 225, 236, 263, 264, 267
Hellenization, 4, 10
Henninger, J., 247
Henoch, Book of see Enoch, Book of
Hera, 40, 43
Heracles, 56, 63
Heraclitus, 11, 12, 69-70, 77
Herford, R. Travers, 260, 261, 278
Hermon, Mount, 274
Herod I the Great, 131, 132, 139, 209
Herod Agrippa I, 172
Herod Antipas, 132
Herodotus, 64-65
Herr, Moshe David, 278
Hesiod, 56-57, 58, 70, 81
High Priests (Jewish), 131
Hinayana Buddhism, 24-25, 26, 32
Hippocrates, 67

Hippolytus of Rome, 4, 29, 92, 94, 96, 103, 116, 122, 123, 124, 125, 127, 209, 244
Hirsch, Emil G., 176, 197
Histiaeus, 65
Hitler, Adolf, 167
Hittite, 34
Holocaust, 167
Homer, 17, 36-56, 58, 68, 77, 91
Homeric epics, 22, 36-56
Homs, 205
Hophni, 222
Huart, Pierre, 65, 66, 83
Hul, 238
Huppenbauer, Hans Walter, 216, 217, 218, 239, 240, 242, 243, 246, 247, 248, 249, 252, 254, 255

Iconium (Konya), 172
Idaeus, 38
Ignatius Ephrem I, 204-205
Impurity see Purity
India(n), 7, 9, 26, 27, 140
Indo-European languages, 34
Indo-Iranian languages, 34
Indus, 9, 10, 26
Ion, 62, 63
Ionia(n)(s), 225, 238
Ionian Sea, 115
Iphicles, 56
Iphigeneia, 63
Iphitus, 52
Iran(ian), 4, 5, 6, 7, 8, 19-20, 29, 89, 92, 111, 112, 217, 238
Irenaeus of Lyons, 3, 87, 89, 98, 100, 101, 102, 104, 115, 118, 120, 121, 122, 124, 125, 127, 128, 152
Isaac, 164
Isaiah, George, 203
Isaiah (prophet), 154
Isaiah, Prophecy of, 204, 261
Ishmael (Rabbi), 260, 261
Isis, 92
Islam, 279
Islamite, 203, 204
Ismael, 164
Israel (people), 27, 140, 151, 156, 161, 163, 168, 169, 180, 223, 224, 225, 233, 236, 237, 238, 239, 243, 261, 268
Israel (state), 206, 207

Israel Museum, 207
Israeli, 207
Ister see Danube
Italy, Italian, 1, 87, 88, 140
Ithaca, 48, 115
Ithamar, 221, 222
Ithamarites, 222
Ituraea, 139

Jabneh, 176
Jacobite Church, Jacobite(s), 203, 204
Jacobs, Louis, 278
Jaffa see Joppe
Jahve, 93, 100, 103, 104, 111
James (apostle), 137, 148, 149, 172
James (first head of the Church in Jerusalem), 166
Jason, 60
Jaspers, Karl, 27, 32
Jeremias, Gerd, 230, 232, 233, 234, 249, 250, 251, 252, 253
Jericho, 137
Jerome, 245, 246
Jerusalem, 87, 136, 137, 139, 140, 158, 160, 165, 174, 175, 201, 203, 204, 205, 206, 207, 214, 221, 236, 253
Jesus of Nazareth, Jesus Christ, 88, 90, 99, 100, 103, 104, 105, 106, 107, 109, 116, 117, 121, 125, 127, 129, 130, 131, 132, 133, 134, 135, 136, 136, 138, 139, 140, 141, 142, 143, 145, 146, 147, 148, 149, 153, 154, 155, 156, 157, 158, 159, 160, 161, 162, 163, 165, 169, 170, 171, 172, 174, 177, 178, 179, 181, 182, 183, 184, 187, 188, 190, 195, 251, 259
Jesus (ben) Sirach, Book of the Wisdom of, 21, 228, 272
Jew(s), Jewish, Jewry, 20-22, 89, 92, 100, 103, 104, 105, 106, 108, 109, 117, 129, 130, 132, 136, 137, 138, 139, 140, 152, 159, 160, 161, 164, 166-171, 171-175, 175-176, 176-177, 177, 179, 185, 194, 197, 198, 205, 207, 208, 209, 210, 211, 212, 214, 215, 221, 242, 245, 254, 257, 258, 259, 260, 261, 262, 266,

267, 268, 269, 270, 271, 273, 274, 276, 278
Joachim da Fiore, 90
Job, 238
Job, Book of, 21
Jocaste, 62, 63
John (apostle), 104, 130, 131, 137, 139, 145-155, 160, 166, 171, 185, 186-189, 189, 200
John the Baptist, 87, 89, 121, 132, 154, 170, 183, 209
John Hopkins University, 205
Jonas, Hans, 1, 6, 8, 10, 20, 30, 92, 97, 98, 99, 100, 108, 123, 124
Jonathan the Maccabee, 208, 235, 253
Joppe, 140
Jordan (river), 105, 210
Jordanian, 206
Jordanian Department of Antiquities, 206
Joseph (husband of Mary), 105, 116, 132
Joseph of Arimathea, 195
Josephus, Flavius, 208, 210, 214, 215, 244, 245, 246, 253, 254, 263, 279
Joshua, 157
Jubilees, Book of, 207, 254
Judaea, 131, 132, 139, 140, 160, 165, 171, 172, 173, 201, 235, 245
Judaeo-Christians, 165-167, 176, 198, 259, 260, 261, 262
Judaism, 5, 21, 22, 27, 89, 90, 93, 100, 103, 104, 105, 106, 107, 109, 112, 117, 145, 156, 161, 162, 167, 168, 169, 170, 175, 176, 197, 208, 217, 233, 234, 258, 259, 264, 265, 267
Judaistic, 7
Judaizers, judaizing, 165, 191
Judas Iskarioth (apostle), 105, 160
Judas the Maccabee, 235
Jude (apostle), 273, 281
Justin the Martyr, 87, 121, 124, 125

Kabbalah, 270
Kaffirs, 279
Kando, 203, 204, 206, 207
Kapparetea, 101

Kerinthos see Cerinthus
Khalil Iskander Shahin see Kando
Kibbutz Kalia, 210
Kition, 226
Kittim, 226-227, 235, 237, 238, 240
Knibb, Michael A., 275, 276, 281, 282
Krüger, G., 126
Kuhn, K.G., 247

Ladd, George Eldon, 194
Lafrance, Yvon, 84
Lagid dynasty, 226
Larnaca, 226
Latin, 102, 191, 207
Law of Moses, 109, 117, 119, 155, 156, 157, 158, 159, 162-164, 165, 166, 170, 173, 174, 176, 179, 182, 191, 195, 208, 231, 232, 233, 259, 266
Lazarus, 160
Leigh, Richard, 244, 251
Leisegang, Hans, 5, 6, 29, 101, 125, 126
Lesher, J.H., 45, 79
Lesser Vehicle see Hinayana Buddhism
Letter to the Colossians, 182, 185
Letter to the Corinthians, First, 169, 180
Letter to the Corinthians, Second, 169, 179
Letter to the Ephesians, 185, 186
Letter to the Galatians, 133, 162, 166
Letter to the Hebrews, 129, 130
Letter of John, First, 147
Letter of John, Third, 129, 130
Letters of John, 130, 169, 185
Letters of Paul, 129, 181
Letter of Peter, First, 152
Letter to the Romans, 162, 163, 168
Letter to Timothy, First, 143, 186
Leumann, Manu, 79
Levi, Testament of, 207
Leviathan, 193
Levite(s), 137, 218, 222, 237, 240
Libertarianism, 120

Liboron, Herbert, 114, 115, 126, 127
Libya, 65
Liddell-Jones Greek-English Lexicon, 33
Linus, 106
Lippens, Philippe, 206
Lohse, Eduard, 247
Lud, 238
Lüdemann, Gerd, 121, 122, 123
Luke (biblical author), 130, 131, 133, 136, 141, 167, 175, 189, 190
Lycaonia, 172
Lyonnet, Stanislas, 200

Maccabees, 221, 277
Maccabees, Book of, 226
Macedonia(n)(s), 9, 151, 162, 172, 226
Mader, Ludwig, 45-46
Mahayana Buddhism, 24-26, 27, 32
Maier, Johann, 197, 198, 259, 278
Malchus, 187
Mani, 90, 175
Manichaean, 175
Manual of Discipline see Community Rule
Mann, Ulrich, 8, 30
Mansfeld, Jaap, 19, 31
Marcovich, M., 83, 84
Mark (Gospel author), 130, 131, 158
Martha (sister of Lazarus), 147
Mary (mother of Jesus), 105, 132, 149, 178
Mary of Magdala, 188
Mash, Massa, 238
Masoretic, 247
Massada, 207
Matthew (apostle), 130, 131, 133, 150
Media(n)(s), 151
Mediterranean Sea, 28, 201, 236, 238
Medon, 47
Meir, 264-265
Melissus, 71
Menander (playwright), 68
Menander (successor of Simon Magus), 90, 101-102, 102, 103

Menelaus (Jewish High Priest), 253
Menelaus (Homeric hero), 42, 63, 91
Mentes, 48
Merkabah mysticism, 271-273, 273
Mesopotamia(n), 20, 28, 29, 226
Messiah, 105, 106, 129, 138, 139, 140, 159, 160, 161, 168, 174, 181, 200, 238, 251, 259, 277
Messina, Congress of, 1, 6, 7
Meyers, Tania, 79-80
Michael, 275
Middle Academy, 15, 17
Milete, 65
Minerva see Athena
Minim, 175-176, 260, 261
Mishnah, 256, 257, 279
Misogyny, 213
Monism, monistic, 94, 110, 218
Monotheism, 239
Mosaic Law see Law of Moses
Moses, 100, 109, 157, 256
Mosheim, Johann Lorenz von, 3, 29
Muhammad ed-Dib, 202, 203
Murray, A.T., 44, 78, 79
Murray, Gilbert, 14, 30
Muses, 37
Mysticism (Jewish), 266, 267, 269-278

Nabataean Kingdom, 249
Nabuchodonosor, 223
Nag Hammadi, 89
Nash Papyrus, 205
Nathan ha-Bavli, 261
Nazism, 6
Near East, 206
Nekyia, 55
Neoptolemus, 61
Nereus, 56
Nestle, Wilhelm, 17
Nestor, 38, 43, 44, 45
New Academy, 17
New Testament, 3, 5, Ch. IV passim, 217, 258, 267, 268, 276
New York, 206
Nicias, 66
Nicodemus, 146, 161, 195
Nicolaites, 187, 200

Nimrod, 111
Noah, Book of, 282
Nock, Arthur Darby, 5, 29, 30
North, R., 248

Oceanus, 60
Odysseus, 37, 39, 40, 41, 42, 43, 44, 46, 47, 49, 50, 51, 52, 53, 54, 55, 63
Oedipus, 60, 61, 62
Old Testament, 52, 103, 105, 111, 129, 133, 135, 151, 168, 171, 177, 193, 219, 222, 226, 228, 239, 240, 241, 243, 256, 257, 263
Olympian gods, 16, 17
Olympian religion, 22-23, 27
Orestes, 61
Origenes, 114, 120, 126, 127
Ormuzd (Ormizd), 20, 111
Orphicism, 2
Orphic(s), Orphism, 2, 10, 22-24, 27
Orphic poem, 23
Orthodox Church, 129
Osten-Sacken, Peter von der, 219, 241, 246, 247, 253, 254, 255
Overbeck, Franz, 29

Packard, David W., 79
Pagels, Elaine H., 200
Palestine, Palestinian, 10, 27, 86, 105, 106, 120, 131, 155, 176, 177, 201, 202, 205, 206, 210, 225, 256, 257, 259, 260, 261, 267
Pan, 139
Pandora search system, 77
Paraclete, 90
Paris (Trojan prince), 91
Parmenides, 12-13, 14, 16, 17, 70, 71, 75
Parousia, 106
Parthia(n)(s), 10
Patroclus, 42
Paul (apostle), 3, 33, 109, 118, 130, 131, 133, 140, 141, 142-145, 151, 154, 162-164, 165, 166, 168, 169, 172-175, 178, 179, 180-181, 182-183, 184, 185, 186, 187, 189, 195, 200, 259
Pellas, 60

Penelope, 39, 40, 41, 48, 49, 50, 51, 55
Pentateuch, Pentateuchal, 156, 256, 257
Pentheus, 63
Peraea, 132
Pergamum, 200
Pericles, 66
Peripatetics, 14
Perls, Hugo, 84
Perses, 57
Persia(n)(s), 151
Peter (apostle), 87, 88, 100, 106, 109, 110, 118, 130, 139, 140, 142, 148, 149, 165, 166, 171, 172, 178, 185, 186, 187, 188
Pétrement, Simone, 5, 29
Phaeacians, 40
Phaedra, 62
Pharaohs, 153
Pharisees, 132, 137, 146, 155-162, 162, 164, 165, 169, 170, 171, 173, 188, 208, 234, 245, 259, 272
Pherecydes, 12
Pherecles, 41
Philip (apostle), 86, 139
Philippus (son of Herod the Great), 139
Philistines, 201
Philo Alexandrinus, Judaeus, 208, 211, 214, 244, 245, 246, 267, 271
Philoctetes, 61
Philoloas, 72
Phinehas, 222
Phoenicia(n), 12, 27, 92
Pindar, 59-60, 81
Pisidia, 172
Plambōck, G., 78
Plataeans, 66
Plato, 11, 12, 13, 14, 15, 16, 17, 30, 36, 54, 55, 72-74, 74, 75, 80, 84, 115, 121, 150
Platonic, Platonism, Platonists, 5, 8, 31, 91, 116
Pliny, 209, 245
Ploeg, J. van der, 204, 211, 230, 244, 245, 246, 248, 250, 254
Plutarch, 70, 84
Polycarpus, 104
Polydamas, 39

Pontius Pilate, 121, 131, 132, 138, 139, 161, 195, 196
Porcius Festus, 174
Porphyry, 246
Poseidon, 43, 47, 60
Powell, Douglas, 125
Powell, Enoch, 83
Pregnostic(s), 2
Presocratic(s), 10, 12, 17, 69-72, 83, 93
Priamus, 42
Proclus, 77
Prometheus, 57, 60, 61
Prophet of Lies, 231-235, 253
Proselytes, 171, 172
Protestant, 26
Proto-Gnosis, Protognostic(s), 2, 22, 27, 186
Proverbs, Book of, 21
Psalms, Book of, 207
Pseudoclementine books, 87, 106-113, 122, 124, 125, 126
Ptolemaean(s), 226
Purity, 211, 214-216, 237
Pythagoras, 13, 69, 72, 112, 121
Pythagorean(s), 10, 12, 22, 31, 69, 72, 76, 118

Quispel, Gilles, 3, 6, 28, 29, 89, 90, 91, 94, 122, 123
Qumran, 5, 7, 27, 201-210, 225, 246, 266, 273

Rabin, Chaim, 248
Rahab, 193
Rahel (mother of Simon Magus), 87
Raphael (archangel), 275
Reitzenstein, Richard, 5, 29, 200
Renan, Ernest, 251
Revelation, Book of, 129, 130, 142, 148, 151, 152, 155, 181, 197, 225, 267, 276
Rivkin, Ellis, 156, 194
Rockefeller Institute, Jerusalem, 206
Roman(s), 2, 9, 10, 19, 104, 105, 106, 131, 132, 137-139, 152-153, 153, 154, 159, 160, 161, 165, 173, 178, 207, 210, 225, 226, 236, 237, 238, 245, 253, 260, 264, 268

Roman-Catholic, 81
Roman-Catholic Church, 129, 163, 167, 251
Roman Empire, 150, 151, 152, 155, 163, 193
Roman Forum, 88
Rome, 87, 88, 120, 141, 163, 174
Rowley, H.H., 245, 248, 249
Rudolph, Kurt, 1, 6, 21, 28, 29, 30, 31, 32, 101, 125
Ruler cult, Hellenistic, 28

Sabbath, observance of, 104, 159, 168, 215, 254
Sabbatical years, 237
Sadducees, 132, 171, 173, 176, 208, 245, 246, 260
Salles-Labadie, J.M.A., 123
Salome (mother of the apostle John), 148, 149
Samaria, Samaritan(s), 10, 27, 86, 87, 89, 101, 102, 104, 136-137, 139, 149, 170, 172, 176, 177, 187, 188, 190, 201, 235, 260, 261
Samaritanism, 5, 27
Samuel, 151
Samuel ha-Katan, 176
Sandmel, Samuel, 169, 170, 195, 196, 197
Sanhedrin, 157, 160, 161, 171, 172, 173, 179, 194, 195, 260
Sanskrit, 34, 78
Sara, 164
Satan(ism), 136, 265, 271
Saturnilians, 103
Saturnilos, 102-104, 104, 125
Saturninus see Saturnilos
Sceptics, Scepticism, 15, 17, 77
Schaedel, K., 216, 247
Schechter, Solomon, 280
Schiffman, Lawrence H., 244
Schmidt, Heinrich, 34, 35, 78
Schmidt, Isaac Jacob, 26, 32
Schneider, Carl, 5, 29
Scholem, Gershom, 269, 270, 271, 272, 280
School of the Garden, 11
Schürer, Emile, 210, 244, 245, 246, 248
Segal, Alan F., 177, 198, 199, 260, 261, 262, 265, 271, 278, 280

Seleucid Empire, 9
Seleucid(s), 226, 227, 235
Semitic, 238
Semyaz (fallen angel in Enoch), 274
Shaman, 88
Shrine of the Book, Jerusalem, 207
Sidon, 139
Simeon ha-Pakoli, 176
Simon Magus, 86-100, 103, 121, 122, 123, 139, 186
Simonianism, 90, 92, 97, 100, 104, 108, 112, 121, 122, 123
Simonians, 91
Simony, 86
Sinai Desert, 201, 238
Sinai (Mount), 90
Sisyphus, 57
Six Days' War 1967, 206, 207
Smyrna, 104
Snell, Bruno, 37, 46, 57, 58, 78, 81
Socrates, 66, 67, 68, 73
Solomon (king), 221
Solon, 58-59, 81
Sophist(s), 71
Sophocles, 61-62, 62, 82
Sparta, 91
Sperber, Daniel, 278, 279
Speusippus, 13, 75
Stählin, Otto, 128
Stein, Gertrude, 75
Stephen (deacon in Jerusalem), 172, 182
Stoa, Stoic, 11, 15, 16, 17, 18, 76, 91, 264
Stockhammer, Morris, 84
Stratton, George Malcolm, 84
Sukenik, Eleazar, 204, 205, 207, 208, 253
Sybil, 12
Sychar, 136
Syncretism, Syncretistic, 7, 28
Syracusa(n), 65, 66
Syria(n), 9, 10, 27-28, 86, 92, 102, 166, 177, 203, 204, 205, 225, 226, 235, 253

Ta'amireh, 202, 206
Tabernacles, Feast of the, 235

Talmud, Talmudic, 176, Chapter VI passim
Tanna(im), Tannaitic, 257, 263, 264, 265, 266
Taoism, 1
Taphians, 48
Tarfon (Rabbi), 260
Teacher of Righteousness, 223, 226-231, 231, 232, 233, 234, 251, 253, 280
Telemachus, 38, 39, 43, 44, 47, 48, 49, 55
Temple of Jerusalem (and its cult), 105, 137, 152, 160, 169, 173, 177, 178, 208, 213-214, 214, 223, 233, 234, 242, 257, 260, 268
Temple Scroll, 207, 208
Tertullian, 101, 125
Tertul, 261lus (advocate), 173
Thales, 69, 77
Thebans, 66
Themis, 60
Theocritus, 64, 82
Theodoretus, 118, 127, 128
Theophilus, 131
Theory of Forms, 13, 75
Theory of Numbers, 12, 13
Theosophy, 3
Thessalonika (Saloniki), 172, 173
Theseus, 63
Thetis, 38
Thocharians, Thogar, 238
Thomas (apostle), 140
Thucydides, 17, 65-66, 83
Tiberius, 139
Times, The, 206
Timothy, Letter to, 3
Tiresias, 62, 64
Titans, Titanic, 23-24
Titus (disciple of Paul), 165
Tomson, Peter J., 195
Torah, 157, 158, 159, 234, 256, 257, 265, 266
Tosefta, 279
Trachonitis, 139
Tragedians, Greek, 60-64, 68
Tragedy, Greek, 17
Trever, John C., 205, 244
Trojans, 38, 42, 44, 47, 48, 91
Troy, 87, 91
Tryphon, 235

Turkey, 238
Typhoeus, 57
Tyre, 87, 139

Uchelen, N.A. van, 278
Unknown God, 7, 21
Urbach, Ephraim Eliezer, 263, 264, 279, 280
Us, 238

Valentinian (Gnostic), 185, 200
Vaux, Ronald de, 206, 208, 209, 246, 251
Vegetarianism, vegetarian(s), 12, 24, 103, 212
Vermes, Geza, 244, 245, 247, 249, 251
Vespasian, 210

Wars of Jahveh, 236
War of the Maccabees, 156, 235, 236
War Scroll or Rule, 208, 226, 235, 236, 239, 240, 276, 277
Wartelle, André, 84
Wicked Priest, 233-235, 253
Widengren, Geo, 1, 7, 20, 29, 31, 123
Wilson, Robert McL., 6, 29, 121, 122, 180, 189, 198, 200
Wisdom (as a person of the Old Testament), 21
Wisdom of Solomon, 21

Xenocrates, 11, 13, 15, 16, 17, 76
Xenophanes, 17, 55, 69
Xenophon, 66-67, 68

Yadin, Yigal, 207, 226, 244, 249, 253

Zadok, 221, 222, 235
Zadok, Sons of, 219, 222, 224
Zadokite fragments see Damascus Rule
Zadokites, 221, 222
Zebedee (father of the apostle John), 148
Zekariah (prophet), 150
Zeller, Eduard, 13, 30
Zelots, Zelotism, 105, 106

Zervan, 19-20
Zervanism, Zervanites, 19-20, 111, 112
Zeus, 23, 24, 38, 41, 44, 47, 48, 57, 60, 63, 91
Ziegler, Ignaz, 259, 278
Zoroaster, Zoroastrianism, 12, 19-20, 111, 217